The Struggle for Socialism in the "American Century"

James P. Cannon

WRITINGS AND SPEECHES, 1945-47

The Struggle for Socialism in the "American Century"

PATHFINDER PRESS NEW YORK

Edited by Les Evans

Library of Congress Catalog Card Number 75-20719
ISBN: 0-87348-550-5 (cloth); 0-87348-551-3 (paper)
Manufactured in the United States of America

First Edition, 1977

Pathfinder Press
410 West Street
New York, N.Y. 10014

COVER PHOTO: New York City, looking north toward the financial district from the tip of Manhattan island, 1946.

CONTENTS

James P. Cannon

About the Author

James Patrick Cannon was born in Rosedale, Kansas, on February 11, 1890, into a working class Irish family. Won to socialist ideas by his father, he joined the Socialist Party in 1908 and the Industrial Workers of the World in 1911 when he was twenty-one. In the IWW Cannon worked with Vincent St. John, "Big Bill' Haywood, and Frank Little as a strike organizer and journalist. As a leader of the Socialist Party left wing after the Russian revolution, he joined the Communist Party in September 1919 and was elected to its Central Committee in 1920. One of the key leaders of the CP in its first decade, he served on the Presidium of the Communist International in Moscow (1922-23) and headed the International Labor Defense (1925-28). Won over to Trotsky's Left Opposition at the Sixth World Congress of the Comintern in Moscow in 1928, he was expelled from the CP later that year for Trotskyism. With Max Shachtman and Martin Abern he was a founding leader of the Communist League of America, the first American Trotskyist organization, and served as editor of its newspaper, *The Militant.*

Cannon was a founder of the Socialist Workers Party in January 1938 and a participant in the founding conference of the Fourth International held in France later that year, where he was elected to the International Executive Committee. Convicted with seventeen other leaders of the SWP and of the Minneapolis Teamsters union in 1941 for opposing the war policy of the American government, Cannon served thirteen months of a sixteen-month sentence at Sandstone penitentiary in 1944-45. Cannon was the national secretary of the SWP until 1953. Thereafter he was the party's national chairman, and later national chairman emeritus until his death on August 21, 1974.

James P. Cannon's more than sixty years of active struggle in the cause of socialism are recorded in his many books. Published in his lifetime were *Socialism on Trial* (1942), *The Struggle for a Proletarian Party* (1943), *The History of American Trotskyism* (1944), *America's Road to Socialism* (1953), *Notebook of an Agitator* (1958), *The First Ten Years of American Communism* (1962), *Letters from Prison* (1968), *Speeches for Socialism* (1971), and *Speeches to the Party* (1973). This volume is one of a posthumous series of his writings and speeches.

INTRODUCTION

This volume of James P. Cannon's writings and speeches covers a tumultuous period in American history and in the life of the Socialist Workers Party. It begins with Cannon's release from Sandstone penitentiary in Minnesota in January 1945, where he had served thirteen months for his and his party's opposition to World War II. The war that he and seventeen other leaders of the SWP and of the Minneapolis Teamsters union had gone to prison to oppose was still raging when he returned to civilian life. Hitler still ruled in Berlin over a collapsing empire that would soon be divided and dismembered by the pincers of the Russian advance in the east and the Anglo-American drive in the west. What would the world look like at the end of five years of imperialist slaughter?

A new world relationship of forces was taking shape. Germany, Japan, and Italy would cease for years to come to be significant imperialist powers. Europe and the Soviet Union were in ruins. The colonial empires of France and Britain were shaken to the core. The character of the postwar world would be dominated by the role of the United States.

American imperialism was the unchallenged victor of World War II. With the exception of the greatly weakened Soviet Union and the territories occupied by its troops, the riches of the planet lay open for the taking. But the Yankee giant could not survive on plunder alone. It also had to have order. What kind of order it could achieve, how extensive, and how long lasting—that was the essence of postwar politics for every political tendency from the capitalist right to the revolutionary Marxist left.

The rulers of the United States were not country bumpkins, but they were provincials in the business of world politics. They naively imagined that some combination of business know-how, American technology, and brute force could subvert the laws of history, abolish the class struggle, and place the nations of the world on American rations. Their dream was not so grandiose as Hitler's—or rather, their rhetoric was more restrained. Hitler talked of a thousand years of the Third Reich. The propagandists of American imperialism contented themselves with prophesying a hundred years of empire. Their slogan in the postwar years was the "American Century." This watchword was coined by publishing magnate Henry R. Luce in a 1941 editorial in *Life* magazine.

In this widely reprinted tract Luce declared that the time had come "to accept wholeheartedly our duty and our opportunity as the most powerful and vital nation in the world and in consequence exert upon the world the full impact of our influence, for such purposes as we see fit and by such means as we see fit. . . . It now becomes our time to be the powerhouse from which the ideals spread throughout the world."

That was the program of American finance capital after World War II. Discounting the "ideals," the powerhouse was there, and the willingness to use "such means as we see fit." While in prison in 1944, Cannon and the other leaders of the SWP watched the course of the war and political developments closely. After his release in January 1945 he was prohibited by the terms of his parole from writing or speaking publicly for a number of months—the first group of selections in this volume are all private letters, or speeches at internal party meetings. His parole expired on April 30. The following day he gave his first public address, on May Day in New York City. (Published here for the first time, under the title "The End of the War in Europe.") Cannon made three basic points. On the meaning of the war itself:

"Now what have they at the end of this long and terrible war? What have they got to show for all their promises? What can they show, the masters of the world, but ruined cities, mounds of corpses, and millions of starving people? That is the auspices under which American imperialism enters its day of glory as the master of the world. . . . That is the credential they bring before mankind as warrant of their right to rule the world for one hundred years. But they have not convinced us of it. We didn't believe them in the first place, and far fewer people can believe them now."

On the new relationship of American imperialism to the rest of world capitalism:

"Since 1914, and ten times more since this present war, American imperialism, in expanding its power and its controls over the whole earth, in becoming the exploiter of the world thereby extends its economic base away from the sure foundation of the forty-eight states united on one continent. . . . And every weakness in the economy of world capitalism at any point runs a tremor throughout the foundations of American imperialism because its foundations are on that economy too. Every revolutionary disturbance—and there have been many and will be ten and one hundred times more, one after another in all parts of this agonizing world—will shake the stability of this deceptive Moloch of American capitalism which appears on the surface to be so sure and so powerful."

And finally, on the immediate prospects in the United States:

"I believe that it is reasonable for us to assume that the workers, and the returning soldiers, and the young generation who have been so cruelly deceived and betrayed by all those to whom they looked for intellectual guidance in this dark period are going to revolt against all those people. . . . I think we can count on the development of the class struggle in the United States, in the situation which I have outlined here, on a colossal scale and see it even as near at hand."

Much of this book is concerned with the defense of these basic ideas within the Socialist Workers Party and within the Fourth International, the World Party of Socialist Revolution, founded by Leon Trotsky in 1938. As can be seen from the above, Cannon's analysis contained both a long-term and a short-term assessment. In the long term, American capitalism would be unable to stabilize its rule on a world scale. The shock of new revolutionary upsurges would shake its home foundations and lead ultimately to socialist revolution in the key bastion of world capitalism. In a word, socialism remained the realistic goal for our epoch, and to win it required a revolutionary, proletarian combat party based on the program of Marxism and the organizational principles of Lenin. In the short term, Cannon was convinced that the U.S. military victory alone would not guarantee any extended period of stability or prosperity either in Europe or America, much less in the colonial nations.

The counterthesis, expounded in the SWP by two of its prominent leaders, Felix Morrow and Albert Goldman, themselves just released from Sandstone prison, began from different premises. At root it consisted of awe at the global power of U.S. capitalism and a loss of faith in the capacity of the Soviet working class to put an end to the terrible crimes of Stalinism. Stalinophobia—abhorrence at Stalinism to the point of seeing it as the principal evil force in the world—led them to a tacit bloc with "democratic" imperialism against Stalinism and the reduction of the aims in the struggle against capitalism to a series of timid reforms. This spirit of pessimism and defeat did not, of course, originate with Goldman and Morrow. It was the outlook of reformist labor leaders and once-radical intellectuals throughout the United States and much of Europe.

This postwar dispute over perspectives was not confined to the SWP, but involved the whole of the world Trotskyist movement. It was the first major internal struggle in the Fourth International since the assassination of Leon Trotsky in 1940, and confronted its leadership with a crucial test. In Europe the sections of the International were at the very beginning of the process of rebuilding after the decimation of the war years. The European contingent of the International's leadership had yet to establish its authority in the newly reconstructed sections.

Goldman and Morrow, while in a relatively small minority in the SWP, found considerable support for their unhappy prognosis elsewhere: among the emigré leaders of the Fourth International who staffed its International Secretariat in New York during the war. This included such people as Jean van Heijenoort, who had long served as Trotsky's secretary. A large minority of the French section of the Fourth International, led by Yvan Craipeau, sided with Goldman and Morrow. This group won a majority of the section in 1946 and held it into 1947. The small exile group that spoke for the German section adopted essentially similar positions, as did, on many questions, the majority of the British section led by Jock Haston and Ted Grant. Between 1946 and 1950 virtually all of these people broke from the Trotskyist movement.

On the side of Cannon and the SWP majority were ranged the French majority (after April 1946, a minority), led by Pierre Frank and Marcel Bleibtreu; the Belgian and Italian sections, led respectively by Ernest Mandel and Livio Maitan; a minority in the British section, headed by Gerry Healy; and the European Secretariat, created at an underground conference in France in 1944, whose secretary was Michel Pablo.

Before examining more closely the conflicting positions,

something must be said about the historical context in which they were fought out. Viewed in the broadest sweep, two opposing historical tides moved the postwar world. On one side, the end of the carnage of the war opened the sluice gates of working class radicalism that had been channeled in support of the Western imperialist democracies by the threat of Hitlerite fascism. In 1945 and 1946 this great power surged forward in implicit or explicit challenge to the capitalist victors of World War II. But it did so with inadequate—or openly treacherous—leadership. On the other side, pressing on the workers' movement and seeking to engulf and drown it, was the backwash of capitalist reaction. By 1947, for a complex of reasons, none of which were preordained in 1945, this latter current, represented by the American capitalist class, emerged triumphant, at least in Europe and North America. This paved the way for the stabilization of an American empire that would wield global power for decades.

As Cannon predicted, the American triumph never succeeded in restoring the kind of stability that existed before World War I, or even in the 1920s. The explosion of the colonial revolution remained beyond its power to suppress or contain. In addition, the war and the immediate postwar period saw a tremendous expansion of the territories in which capitalism had been overthrown and replaced by the nationalized, planned economies of workers' states—in Eastern Europe and North Korea, and later in China and North Vietnam. But these were deformed workers' states, dominated by Stalinist parties which are narrowly nationalistic in their outlook, ready to adopt a live-and-let-live attitude toward capitalist oppression outside their own immediate borders.

In essence, then, American capitalism's victory in the war made it overwhelmingly predominant in a world capitalist system that had been seriously weakened as a whole. This fundamental assessment of the postwar relationship of forces proved to be completely accurate. More immediately, the SWP and the Fourth International had to propose tasks and tactics to meet the period of turmoil at the war's end. These depended on two principal factors: the level of militancy and combativity of the working class, and the size and authority among the masses of the revolutionary party. This equation proved to be different in Europe and America.

In Europe at the beginning of the war the Stalinist and Social Democratic parties had commanded mass followings, while the

Trotskyists were still an isolated and numerically tiny movement. On the continent, the Social Democracy was largely shattered by the fascist occupations and was rebuilt only when the war was over. The Stalinists, however, retained their grip on the mass movement in France, Italy, and Greece. More accurately, after being deeply discredited by their neutrality toward fascism during the Stalin-Hitler pact between 1939 and 1941, they regained an authority they did not deserve after the Nazi invasion of the Soviet Union in June 1941. The heroic resistance of the Russian masses to Hitler, in spite of the tyrannical and incompetent Stalin bureaucracy, inspired the workers of Western Europe and led them into the underground resistance movements led by the Communist parties.

With the end of hostilities, in Europe in May 1945 and in Japan in August, a huge political vacuum appeared over a large part of the globe. In big sections of the world the only effective power was the armed resistance movements or the Russian army. This was the case throughout Eastern Europe; in France, Italy, and Greece, where despite the Allied occupation the real force on the scene was the Stalinist-led resistance movement; in North China, North Korea, and in Vietnam. A revolutionary orientation by Moscow and the parties that looked to it would have brought down capitalist rule in all of these places, and, by extension, in the colonial domains of Africa and Asia formerly held by the French, German, Italian, and Dutch imperialists. All the objective material conditions were assembled for such an outcome, including the anticapitalist consciousness of the working masses.

But such a step ran counter to the basic drives of the reactionary, narrowly nationalistic bureaucratic caste whose spokesman Stalin was. Instead of the revolutionary overturn of capitalism, Stalin committed himself in the Allied conferences at Yalta, Teheran, and Potsdam to a division of the world by spheres of influence, guaranteeing the defense of capitalist property relations.

The Communist parties of France and Italy supported and even joined postwar capitalist governments and helped to disarm the resistance movements. With Stalin's aid, the completely discredited ruling classes of France and Italy were able to remount the saddle. This was one necessary precondition—though not the only one—for the quarter century of post-World War II relative capitalist stability and prosperity in the advanced industrial countries.

Even with Stalin's complicity and his betrayal of the European working class it took a few years for the Stalinists to dragoon the workers they led into acceptance of the restoration of indigenous capitalist rule and for the Social Democracy to revive its organizations. And even then, capitalist control over the workers' movement through its indirect agents could not be secure as long as Europe hovered on the brink of starvation and its economic plant lay in ruins.

While not so promising for revolutionary victory as the immediate months after the end of the war, the potential for mass revolutionary action remained in Europe until the economic revival that was finally solidified through the Marshall Plan after 1947 and the economic boom that accompanied the Korean War. Although the European working classes were deeply radicalized, the small and persecuted Trotskyist movement was unable to grow in time to win a mass hearing and was thus unable to influence the course of events.

The situation in the United States was different from that in Europe in a number of respects. The war was not fought on American soil. At the war's end the American capitalist class emerged with its productive plant intact. The government of the United States was not shattered as were those of continental Europe.

The radicalization of the 1930s had not yet run its course; it would be brought to a definitive end only in 1947. But while it flared up in the postwar labor strike wave and other struggles, the interruption of the war had sapped much of its dynamism. Most important in this respect was the integration of the leadership of the militant industrial unions of the CIO into the state apparatus in wartime. The tradition of radical trade unionism remained, as did a significant ferment among Blacks, evidenced in the March on Washington movement and the Harlem rebellion during the war, and the politicizing effect of the drawing into industry of masses of women workers in wartime. In addition there was an unprecedented ferment among American GIs in Europe and Asia, who resisted the attempts by Washington to use them against the colonial revolution after the defeat of Germany and Japan.

The war years, however, had eroded much of the more deeply

radical attitudes of distrust of capitalism that marked the depression period. A combination of significant wage concessions in 1946, repression against the socialist and communist left, and the propaganda of the anticommunist witch-hunt finally succeeded in reestablishing a climate of acceptance of the capitalist status quo and distrust of radical change.

Immediately after the war, however, the SWP was in a relatively favorable position to intervene in the mass struggles that took place, particularly the labor upsurge. The Communist Party, its principal rival in the workers' movement, was still much larger—it had grown to perhaps 100,000 members—but it did not wield a hold on the working class comparable to that of the French and Italian CPs. It had been deeply compromised by its advocacy of the "no-strike pledge" after the German invasion of the Soviet Union. It had vehemently opposed the fight for Black rights during the war, on patriotic grounds. It had joined with the government in hounding working class militants who insisted on defending the rights of labor in wartime. For example, it had publicly applauded the conviction of the Trotskyists under the Smith Act in the 1941 Minneapolis "sedition" trial.

The SWP, in contrast, though much smaller, had extended its influence in the working class during the war by its consistent defense of workers' rights and its championing of the Black movement. The SWP had entered the war years under difficult circumstances. In 1939, a large minority of the party, led by Max Shachtman and James Burnham, capitulated to the pressure of government propaganda and renounced the party's position of defense of the Soviet Union from imperialist attack. In April 1940 this group split from the SWP to found the rival Workers Party, taking with them some 40 percent of the party's membership. This reduced the SWP to about 500 members.

With the American entry into the war and the indictment of the SWP leadership, most avenues of growth were temporarily closed off. The workers accepted the necessity of the war; not, perhaps, as enthusiastically as in World War I, but without serious dissent from the policies of Roosevelt. But by the beginning of 1945 when Cannon and the others were released from prison, a change had taken place. With the end of the war in sight, workers, Blacks, and soldiers were less ready to make sacrifices needlessly and were more openly resentful of the war profiteering of big business.

The week after Cannon's May Day speech, Germany surrendered to the Allies. In the month after that, two million workers lost their jobs and joined the ranks of the unemployed. A wave of postwar inflation threatened to impoverish millions more who still had work.

The wartime labor shortage had spurred large-scale Black emigration to northern cities, where Blacks were the most militant sector of the oppressed. In 1941, A. Philip Randolph led in the creation of nationwide committees around the call for a Black March on Washington to end discrimination in defense industry. The SWP was highly active in these committees and began to recruit Black members. The NAACP grew from a membership of 85,000 in 1940 to some 530,000 in 1946. And in August 1943, in the aftermath of anti-Black riots in Detroit in which twenty-six Blacks were killed, the first of the modern ghetto rebellions took place, in Harlem. Angry Blacks were an important contingent in the membership of the major industrial unions in the postwar strike wave that broke out after the surrender of Japan in August 1945.

On September 17, 1945, the Oil Workers union called a strike of its 43,000 members in twenty states. On September 21, 200,000 coal miners went on strike. In November, New England textile workers and midwestern truck drivers went out. And these actions were only the beginning.

On November 21, the United Auto Workers struck General Motors. It was the first time the union had ever succeeded in completely shutting GM down, as 225,000 workers walked out coast-to-coast. This proved to be a drawn-out and bitter strike. It lasted through a long, cold winter of mass picketing, concluding when GM gave in to large wage demands in mid-March 1946. In the same period, 800,000 steelworkers staged a twenty-six day strike in January and February 1946 that blanketed the entire basic steel industry.

Art Preis, in his book *Labor's Giant Step: Twenty Years of the CIO* (Pathfinder Press, 1972), contrasts the scope of the postwar strike wave with the strikes of the 1930s:

"The tremendous advance of the class struggle during the postwar period can be seen by a comparison of the strike statistics for 1937 and 1945-46. In 1937, the epic year of the CIO's rise, there were 4,740 strikes involving 1,861,000 strikers, for a total loss of 28,425,000 man-days of work. In 1945 the number of strikes was 4,750 with 3,470,000 on strike, almost double the 1937 figure, and a loss of 38,000,000 man-days. In 1946 the number of strikes reached 4,985 with 4,600,000 strikers and 116,000,000 man-days lost."

The strike wave was paralleled by a virtual revolt among American troops stationed in Europe and Asia. With the end of the war, Washington sought to use the vast U.S. military machine to restabilize the former colonial world—in particular, to aid Chiang Kai-shek in the Chinese civil war and to ferry French troops to Indochina and Dutch troops to Indonesia.

On Christmas Day, 1945, some 4,000 U.S. soldiers in Manila staged a demonstration demanding to be brought home. In Guam, 3,500 troops conducted a hunger strike to protest the American government's delay in demobilization. In Paris on January 8, 1946, thousands of GIs marched down the Champs-Élysées demanding "Get Us Home!" It was this rebellion by the GIs that prevented a U.S. intervention in China in the late 1940s comparable to what it would later do in Vietnam in the 1960s.

The Trotskyists of the SWP plunged into the ferment. The party had gone through a long preparation for such work and was able as a consequence to realize rapid and important gains. Through the split with the petty-bourgeois Shachtmanite faction in 1940 and the policy of conscious proletarianization of the party afterward, the SWP was overwhelmingly working class in composition at the end of the war. Its average member was a trade unionist. The party had functioning national fractions in auto, steel, maritime, rubber, railroad, longshore, packinghouse, shipyard, and a number of other basic industries. In the two years between its November 1944 convention and the November 1946 convention the SWP more than doubled in size, recruiting 1,000 new members, mostly industrial workers. From less than 650 members in 1942 it grew to some 1,500 members in 1946.

Much of the recruitment to the party came from among the most oppressed sectors of the working class. Whereas before the war, Black membership in the party nationally numbered only in tens, by the time of the 1946 convention there were more than a hundred Black members in New York City alone, and a large percentage of the membership of the party branches in such cities as Detroit, Newark, and Philadelphia was composed of Black workers. Much of the party's contact with militant Blacks came through the trade union movement, but many joined through its work in the NAACP and through its campaigns in defense of Black prisoners faced with the death penalty in frame-up cases in various states. In 1946 the party waged a major campaign against the Ku Klux Klan in Fontana, California, where white racists had burned to death an entire Black family.

It was with the aim of assimilating and training the wave of new working class and Black members that Cannon proposed to the party leadership the drafting of the "Theses on the American Revolution," adopted by the Twelfth National Convention of the party in November 1946. This resolution summarizes many of the fundamental ideas of the SWP on American perspectives. It summarizes the party's view of the new role of American imperialism in the postwar world as well as Trotsky's writings on the relationship between the coming American socialist revolution and the struggle for world socialism.

The "American Theses" develop these basic positions: (1) The American victory in World War II made U.S. imperialism the principal bastion of world capitalism, and as a consequence the American socialist revolution would be the most decisive single event in the world victory of socialism. (2) American imperialism, by expanding qualitatively its economic base from the territory of the Western Hemisphere to the whole of the world market, would be subject to the shocks of foreign revolutions, in the colonial nations and in Europe, in a far more direct way than in the past. (3) With all its wealth and power, American capitalism is not immune to the laws of class struggle. (4) The economic contradictions of world capitalism outlined by Marx and Lenin operate on the U.S. economy and would in the future precipitate a profound economic and social crisis that would propel the working class onto the road of anticapitalist revolution. And (5), to ensure victory in that impending class conflict required the construction of a disciplined, homogeneous revolutionary combat party, proletarian in program and composition, that aspired to organize and lead the working class in the successful fight for power.

These ideas were true in 1946 and they remain true today. They are the bedrock on which the revolutionary Marxist party is built in the United States. Goldman and Morrow rejected the ideas codified in the "American Theses." Although they began from much further to the left, having been members and leaders of the revolutionary party, Goldman and Morrow's evolution in the 1940s was in many respects typical of a whole generation of the radical intellectuals of the 1930s.

Albert Goldman had a long, if erratic, history in the American communist and socialist movements. He had become a lawyer in the late 1920s, joined the Communist Party in Chicago, and was a prominent labor attorney. Cannon convinced him to join the Trotskyist movement in 1933. Goldman was deeply individualistic, given to self-doubt, and prone to sudden political leaps. In 1934 he bolted the Communist League of America with a few of his close associates and joined the Socialist Party of Norman Thomas. When the Trotskyists entered the SP in 1936 as a left-wing faction, they reestablished contact with Goldman and he became a front-rank leader of the SWP from the time of its founding in 1938. He served as Leon Trotsky's American counsel and as the chief defense lawyer in the Minneapolis case, in which he was also a defendant.

In 1943 Goldman began to voice doubts about Leninist organizational methods. He became consumed with a fear of Stalinism that led him to see "Stalinist germs" in the democratic self-discipline of a revolutionary workers' party. Until he went to prison, Goldman voiced no disagreements with the broader program of Marxism. But that experience—and the disbarment which followed automatically from a felony conviction, preventing him from practicing law—had a deep effect on him. After the war he adopted a broad range of political disagreements along lines formulated by Morrow.

Goldman's political career after 1945 was one of steady retreat from Marxism into pessimistic acquiescence in the capitalist status quo. In May 1946 he left Morrow in the SWP and went over to Shachtman's Workers Party with a small group of followers. Two years later he joined the SP. By 1950 he had even broken with the SP and renounced Marxism, supporting the American government in the Korean War. In 1952, at a hearing in Chicago of the Atomic Energy Commission, which had denied a security clearance to one of his relatives because of Goldman's radical past, he testified that he collaborated regularly with the FBI in identifying members of the Communist Party he had known when he was in the CP.

Felix Morrow was one of the group of young Jewish intellectuals gathered together by Elliot Cohen at the end of the 1920s around the *Menorah Journal.* Others of this circle included Herbert Solow, Lionel Trilling, Clifton Fadiman, and George Novack. A number of people from this group became active in labor defense work in the orbit of the CP, and Morrow joined the CP in 1931. At the end of 1933, he and Novack were won to Trotskyism and joined the Communist League of America. (Solow became a close sympathizer at that time, and joined the Trotskyists with the formation of the Workers Party of the U.S. in 1934.)

In the Trotskyist movement Morrow was an able and energetic journalist. He worked on the *Northwest Organizer,* the newspaper of the Minneapolis Teamsters, in 1937-38 and, after Shachtman's split from the SWP in 1940, edited *The Militant* and the party's theoretical magazine, *Fourth International.* His 1938 book, *Revolution and Counterrevolution in Spain,* reprinted by Pathfinder Press in 1974, is well worth reading today.

Morrow from the beginning, however, maintained a major reservation about Marxism: he rejected its philosophical method, dialectical materialism. He had studied philosophy under John Dewey at Columbia University, was a close friend of Sidney Hook, and did not succeed in shaking off his pragmatic training. This led him to judge world events as World War II developed by the simplistic method of projecting existing trends into the distant future. By 1943 he became convinced that both American capitalism and Russian Stalinism were unshakable, and he placed in question and finally abandoned the possibility of socialist revolution.

His perspectives in the postwar world differed fundamentally from those of Cannon and the SWP majority. This emerged most strongly on the "Russian question" and then spilled over into the main areas of strategy and tactics.

Morrow's line of reasoning is worth exploring because it so typified the radical American intelligentsia who capitulated to the capitalist status quo at the beginning of World War II and who moved far to the right in the era of McCarthyism and the anticommunist witch-hunt of the late 1940s and 1950s. Morrow joined in this retreat some years later than most of the others, but once on that road he followed it undeviatingly to its logical end. After his expulsion from the SWP in November 1946 he broke definitively with Marxism and became a supporter of the cold war.

The scientific class analysis of Marxism approaches society from the standpoint of its historical evolution. The impasse of modern society lies in the survival of private ownership of what are essentially social means of production, and the artificial division of the world economy into antiquated nation-states, each armed to the teeth. While different tactics must be devised to meet specific concrete situations, governments must be judged by their place in this broad historical framework. The Soviet Union, despite the monstrous Stalinist bureaucracy that exists there, is an economy wrenched free of expansionist private property and the rule of a capitalist class. This gives to Stalinism an historically episodic character—a poisonous byproduct of the degeneration of a socialist revolution and of its regime that developed in a backward country while capitalism still ruled in the major industrial nations. The solution to the problem of Stalinism is twofold: the organization of the working class in the lands it controls to overthrow it in an antibureaucratic revolution; and the victory of the socialist revolution in the imperialist heartland of the United States, Europe, and Japan. Until the workers overthrow Stalinism, of course, Marxists should defend the economic gains represented by the planned economies of the existing workers' states from the threat of imperialist attack.

Morrow began from a different premise. Reacting to the overwhelming pressures of his imperialist environment, he came to see only the prevailing power of the governments of the world and to disbelieve in the capacity of the working class as a serious contender for power anywhere. Without a class analysis he was left with the pragmatic method of choosing the "lesser evil." He observed that Stalin's Russia was more repressive than "democratic" America (leaving out, of course, the oppression that American imperialism meted out to its national minorities and to peoples under its domination outside its own borders).

Trotsky never denied that at a given moment Stalinism is more repressive than a particular bourgeois democracy. On the contrary, in the Transitional Program, the founding programmatic document of the Fourth International, he explicitly compared the bureaucracy's methods of rule to those of the fascists, saying that "Stalin's *political* apparatus does not differ save in more unbridled savagery." But Trotsky did not stop with these kinds of comparisons. He probed the causes of Stalinist reaction and the agency by which it could be defeated. In the world relationship of social forces, Stalinism is ultimately an indirect representative of imperialism in the workers' movement. It can be beneficially destroyed only by the workers themselves, as part of their generalized fight against capitalism.

The logic of Morrow's course was to give "critical" support to American imperialism against the Soviet Union. He took that step fully and explicitly only after he left the SWP. But his direction was evident to his opponents in the SWP from the time he returned to the faction fight from prison at the beginning of 1945.

As early as 1943, when nothing had yet been settled in Europe, he began to insist that it was hopeless to expect socialist revolutions after the war.

In some ways it is difficult to reconstruct Morrow's full positions and direction from the documents of the 1943-46 dispute. Cannon remarks on this a number of times in this book. While Morrow and Goldman adopted a tone of increasing hostility toward the party leadership, and openly challenged Leninist organizational methods, their political differences emerged only in stages, and then often by implication and emphasis.

Morrow claimed that the SWP and the European leadership of the Fourth International were insufficiently critical of the reactionary role of the Soviet army in Eastern Europe; that they had an apocalyptic vision of revolutionary possibilities in Western Europe; and that they underestimated the importance of democratic demands in countries such as France and Italy at the end of the war. Above all, he insisted that they ignored the "national question" in Europe. By this he meant that the German and later Soviet occupations had reduced the countries affected to the status of oppressed peoples, and that the struggle for socialism should be deferred to the struggle for national independence regardless of its leadership.

The majority replied that Morrow had become Stalinophobic and tacitly abandoned the position of defense of the Soviet Union; that he had an unfounded confidence in capitalism's ability to survive and prosper; that he was retreating from a transitional program aimed at socialist revolution and settling on a minimum program of piecemeal reform; and that, in the guise of opposition to Hitlerism and to the anti-working class conduct of Stalinism, he was adapting to a class-collaborationist alliance with the capitalist class of long-standing imperialist countries such as France.

Until well into 1946 the majority's case against Morrow was based largely on inferences rather than written positions by the minority, and on things Morrow said verbally and did not commit to writing.

On European perspectives Morrow insisted on placing the central emphasis of the Trotskyist intervention on democratic demands, the unqualified slogan "For a Republic" (against monarchies in Belgium, Italy, and Greece), and on building national resistance movements to Allied or Soviet occupation. The majority stressed the integration of democratic demands and struggles into a broader program of transitional demands aimed at preparing the working class for the struggle for state power.

Morrow's conception of the weight to be given to democratic demands revealed a sharp divergence from the concepts of the Transitional Program, although initially this appeared as striking inconsistencies in documents that continued to restate many of the strategic fundamentals of Marxism. For example, while insisting that he still favored propaganda for workers' control of industry, factory councils, and other slogans taken from the Transitional Program, he was able to write in July 1945 on the tasks of the French Trotskyists:

"Do not be afraid of making *Vérité* appear entirely as an organ fighting for nothing more than real democracy. That is fighting for a great deal today!" ("European Perspectives and Policy," *Fourth International,* March 1946.)

His full views were stated only at the very end of the fight, at the November 1946 SWP convention. In a document entitled "'The National Question' in Europe" (November 10, 1946) he wrote:

"If the triumph of the socialist revolution can alone provide a stable historical basis for the flowering of national and democratic liberties, it is, in the final analysis, at the close of an historic period. Meanwhile, in the course of the transitional period, the socialist movement should support these [nationalist] struggles without pretending to confuse them with the proletarian struggle for socialism nor submit them ultimatistically to it."

And that is written about imperialist Europe in 1946!

Not all of Morrow's criticisms were rejected. Despite the sharp tone adopted by Goldman and Morrow, Cannon and the majority leadership sought to listen closely to their objections. Where the minority perceived flaws or weaknesses in the majority positions, these were discussed and, where appropriate, corrections were made. An example is Morrow's insistence at the November 1943 plenum of the SWP National Committee that more stress be placed on democratic demands in the anticapitalist struggles in Europe. This was discussed over the following year, and at the November 1944 convention a number of Morrow's amendments to the party's documents on Europe were adopted. Again, in May

1946 at an NC plenum Morrow raised the demand that the party call for the withdrawal of Soviet as well as Allied troops from the occupied countries of Europe. This was initially rejected but later that year was reconsidered and adopted, though not with the motivation that Morrow gave to it.

But while agreement could be reached on some of the disputed questions, others proved irreconcilable. For the United States as well as for Europe, Morrow proposed an implicit retreat to a minimum program of reforms. This can be seen in the debate over the response of the working class to the postwar wave of inflation. Cannon and the party majority proposed the slogan outlined in the Transitional Program: "For a Sliding Scale of Hours and Wages." (The sliding scale of hours, popularized under the slogan "Thirty Hours' Work for Forty Hours' Pay," was aimed mainly at eliminating unemployment.) The sliding scale of wages later became known in the trade union movement as the "escalator clause." In a union contract it provided for automatic increases in pay as the cost of living rose. This placed the onus for inflation directly on the employers and demonstrated that capitalist profits and not wage increases were the cause of inflation.

Morrow rejected the use of this slogan, proposing instead to adopt the slogan of Walter Reuther and the United Auto Workers leadership: "Wage Raises Without Price Increases." While initially directed to General Motors, Reuther publicized this slogan mainly in connection with a call for the continuation of government wartime price controls. There are several problems with the Reuther slogan. It does not specify any definite relationship between the size of wage increases and the level of prices. This robs it of its value as a guide in the fight to keep wages abreast of price rises. But on the price side as well it does not specify by what means price rises are to be prevented. In practice the UAW called on the government to do this. But capitalist governments have been historically both unable and unwilling to seriously regulate prices.

The Trotskyist movement, in the Transitional Program, proposes consumer price control committees, broader than just the union movement, which could organize boycotts or demonstrations aimed at particular producers or retailers. This concept is lost in the vague Reuther slogan, which becomes more a pious wish or an appeal to the goodwill of the employers than a program for action.

One area in which deep differences with Goldman and Morrow surfaced early was on the character of the revolutionary party. This arose in 1945 through their proposal for reunification with Shachtman's WP. Cannon correctly viewed this as a reconciliation on their part with the Stalinophobic petty-bourgeois opposition that had split to the right from the SWP in 1940. It involved not only adaptation to Shachtman's program, but a conception of the party as a loose federation of warring factions and "free-thinking" individuals and not as a disciplined instrument of the working class struggle for state power.

It became clear from mid-1945 that Goldman and Morrow were not waiting to persuade the SWP majority of their organizational concepts but were acting on them in practice. They openly admitted that they were meeting regularly with the Shachtmanite leadership, coordinating tactics with them behind the backs of the members of the SWP. It was for these disloyal acts that Morrow was expelled from the SWP at its November 1946 convention.

Goldman and Morrow came to a parting of the ways in May 1946. At that point, Goldman, who had counted on provoking his own expulsion by the "Cannonites," became exasperated with the party's patience and went over to the WP with a group of his followers in Chicago. Morrow's pretense to Marxist orthodoxy then began to unravel rapidly. In a speech on the international situation to a plenum of the National Committee in May he declared that "all the reasons we gave for defending the Soviet Union have disappeared" (SWP *Internal Bulletin,* vol. VIII, no. 8, July 1946).

In a document he submitted to the November party convention he came out in support of massive Jewish emigration to Palestine. The party majority had throughout the war campaigned for the right of Jewish emigration to the United States to escape from the holocaust of Nazism. The Roosevelt and Truman administrations refused to grant this demand and excluded hundreds of thousands of European Jews who then perished under the fascists. But the party was opposed to Jewish emigration to Arab Palestine, where such an influx could only be at the expense of the Palestinian people. Such a Jewish state could only be sustained by imperialist aid and become a beachhead for imperialist opposition to the colonial revolution in the Middle East. Morrow argued for the establishment of a Jewish state—although he was critical of the official Zionist leadership—by ignoring the rights of the Palestinians. He presented the question as though the only thing involved was the fight between the Jewish emigrants and the British colonial authorities who then still ruled Palestine. In his document "Bolshevik Politics Versus Neo-Economism" (November 1946) he compared the SWP leadership to Pontius Pilate for refusing to go along with him on this.

In the same document he proposed that the party abandon the Leninist practice of using election campaigns to explain its socialist program to the masses, saying instead that "The party should put into an election platform only such demands as it can seriously hope to fight for if it should be elected to the office for which it is running."

At the convention Morrow declared his commitment to Marxism and the fight for socialism. But his break with Marxism after he left the SWP was even more precipitous than Goldman's. Despite Morrow's close collaboration with Shachtman during the fight in the SWP, he did not even join the Workers Party on his way to the right as Goldman had done. He became an anticommunist during the cold war.

To place in perspective the amount of space in this collection devoted to this internal fight it is necessary to know Cannon's role in the SWP in the division of labor in the party leadership after the eighteen Minneapolis defendants returned to activity from prison. Cannon in 1945 was fifty-five years old. A younger generation of party leaders had come to the fore during the war years. This expansion of the leading team permitted Cannon to delegate important areas of work, such as day-to-day party administration, the direction of trade union activity and work among Blacks, and the task of aiding politically in the rebuilding of the Fourth International.

Cannon, as the party's national secretary, took overall responsibility for the course followed by the party, but did not write or speak extensively on every aspect of its work. He functioned as the *political* leader of the party, helping to develop political positions and timely interventions on major world and national events. In addition, he took special responsibility on major questions of inner-party relations and disputes—which are always at root the question of the character of the party. This last included both the political struggle with Goldman and Morrow and the SWP's relations with Shachtman's Workers Party.

There is an epilogue to the SWP-WP unity discussions of 1945-

46. Cannon insistently rejected the likelihood of fruitful unification with the Shachtmanites throughout the period while Goldman and Morrow were in the SWP, although he was willing to discuss the matter with Shachtman on several occasions. This attitude changed at the beginning of 1947. At that time Michel Pablo, representing the International Secretariat of the Fourth International, visited the United States and met with the leaders of both parties. Pablo was anxious to promote a fusion. He concluded an agreement with Shachtman for the WP to accept the discipline of the Fourth International (this was of course a purely moral commitment, as reactionary legislation prevented either the SWP or WP from maintaining membership in the FI), and to join the SWP as a minority.

It is clear from the ensuing events that the leaders of each party had a very different impression of the exact terms Pablo had proposed. Cannon later described the whole affair as a "comical misunderstanding." In any case, the SWP leadership, on the assurance that Shachtman did not intend to rejoin the SWP simply as a raiding operation or with the intention of immediately renewing the old faction fight—that is, that he would loyally accept majority rule—agreed to the unification. Cannon proposed to the SWP membership to go through with it.

These apparently solid agreements were followed almost immediately by a new spate of sharp attacks on the SWP in the Shachtmanite press. In this same period the Truman Doctrine of "containing communism" was announced, followed shortly by the Marshall Plan to rearm and rebuild Europe. This produced a further shift to the right by the Shachtmanites which, by the summer of 1947, put a definitive end to the prospect of unity.

The Workers Party then drifted further and further rightward, finally dissolving itself in 1958 to join the Socialist Party. There Shachtman and those close to him constituted the SP's far right wing, going so far as to support the American government's war in Vietnam in the 1960s and 1970s, and serving as advisers to such reactionary labor bureaucrats as Albert Shanker and George Meany.

What interest do the unity negotiations with the WP have today? In a certain sense, it was a nonevent—after two years of discussion the unification never took place. But that would be too narrow a view. The revolutionary party will be built in many ways; not only through the recruitment of individuals but by fusions with entire groups converging with the party's line but with remaining political differences with the party majority. Such fusions can be a step forward for the party, through the resulting expansion of its membership; but they can also be destructive if there are not sufficient political grounds for unification and genuine agreement on organizational norms. The party can also be built through splits—and the final closing of the door on reunification with the Shachtmanites constituted, in effect, a second stage of the split with them. When political differences in the revolutionary party deepen and harden to the point that a hostile internal grouping takes shape that can no longer accept the party's program and loyally participate in its work, it is the responsibility of the party leadership to protect the integrity of the party.

Knowing when and on what basis to unify or to split is an art of leadership, an art of which Cannon was a master. These decisions cannot be made simply by the comparison of programs on paper unless the divergences are so obviously great as to be incompatible in a single organization. They involve the political direction in which people are moving, shifts in their practice, and the possibility for loyal collaboration. At the root is the question Cannon asks many times in the course of this book: What kind of party are we trying to build? His answers are a rich education in Bolshevik leadership.

There remains one issue in the 1945-46 dispute in the SWP that should be touched on, and that is the counterposed economic prognoses of the party majority and the Goldman-Morrow faction. Morrow argued that the European revolution had been definitively sidetracked by mid-1945, and that American capitalism had entered an extended period of stability and boom. Cannon and the party majority, at least through the end of 1946, held that socialist revolution was still a possibility in Europe in the near future; and that the conjunctural postwar American economic upturn was the result of essentially artificial factors such as war spending and the expansion of public debt. They predicted that the American economy would collapse in a new depression in a few years' time.

Conjunctural predictions, as any Marxist knows, have a conditional character and are not always borne out in the complex of actual events. The depression that Cannon predicted in the late 1940s did not materialize until the world recession of 1969 and the American depression of 1974-75. But that does not exhaust the question. It is useful to examine the arguments on both sides, as part of the necessary assessment of the reasons for the postwar stabilization of capitalism in America and Europe (this never extended to the colonial world).

Reading Morrow's documents, for example, reveals that his prediction was based more on faith than on serious economic analysis. In a resolution submitted to the 1946 party convention, "Against the Political Committee's 'Theses on the American Revolution' and 'Tasks of the SWP in the Present Political Situation,'" he grounds his entire prognosis on two fundamental assumptions:

1. "Far from inflation being inevitable under declining capitalism, including the United States, as the Political Committee's resolution on wages and prices asserted, it was a temporary phenomenon in a victor country whose productive machinery remained not only unimpaired but expanding. . . . The *long-term* effect of the decline in prices will be to expand both the home market and export trade for a period of years" (emphasis in original).

But the expansion of American capitalism, which finally came not in the 1940s but only in the 1950s and 1960s, was not at all based on capitalism's ability to control inflation and lower prices. It flowed from entirely different causes, and inflation remains today an endemic feature of American capitalism.

2. On the availability of markets for American goods, "An even greater vacuum exists abroad, not only in consumer goods but in available fields for capital investment, thanks to the destruction of the German and Japanese empires, the weakening of British imperialism, the low level of stabilization of the French and Dutch economies, *and the utter inability of Stalinist totalitarianism to expand production in the USSR*" (emphasis added).

Morrow is wrong, writing in 1946, on the absorbing capacity of the shattered economies of the imperialist countries, and dead wrong on the inability of the Soviet planned economy to restore industrial production without American aid. On the basis of arguments such as these, Morrow can prove only that he believes in the "American Century." Morrow's underlying motivations, his nonrevolutionary perspective, were more important here than his rationalizations. This is verified by his conduct when some of his conjunctural predictions were confirmed. He did not then seek to devise new tactics that would help revolutionists to orient to an unfavorable situation. He turned his back on the revolutionary movement altogether and repudiated Marxism.

Cannon also started from a general perspective; in his case the commitment to socialist revolution and the construction of a Leninist party. But his perspective was neither changed nor shaken by the developments that disproved some of his conjunctural predictions. He was able to accept the reality of the postwar stabilization of capitalism and the postponement of revolutionary possibilities, and to change tactics accordingly.

At the same time, while Cannon's predictions were too categorical, they were founded on economic realities and not on wishful thinking. In retrospect, telescoping events, it may appear that the long postwar boom was settled by the American military victory in World War II and was a foregone conclusion by mid-1945. In fact, while this laid the preconditions for the boom and established its objective material basis, there were further requirements to insure its realization that had not been met in 1945 or even 1946. Three central political-economic factors were necessary before the military victory could bear fruit:

1. The European revolution had to be staved off and an iron grip reestablished on the European working class. The Stalinist parties, especially in France and Italy, contributed mightily to this effort, but as long as the economy remained in a shambles the possibility remained of spontaneous explosions that would outflank the Stalinists to the left.

2. The American labor movement had to be housebroken. While the postwar labor upsurge was restricted to wage demands and occurred within the framework of the consolidation of bureaucracies in the unions of the CIO, it still posed a serious threat to American economic stability. One indication was widespread agitation for the formation of a labor party. This was not resolved in favor of the ruling class until the passage of the Taft-Hartley Act in June 1947, giving the government unprecedented powers to intervene in the internal life of the trade unions and to halt strikes. The anticommunist witch-hunt that began in full force in the same period had as one of its principal aims to forestall the unseating of any of the conservative union bureaucracies by a leadership willing to struggle against the enforcement of the government's new law.

3. Europe and Japan had to be rebuilt or they would not be able to provide a serious market for American exports. Further, if economic stability were not achieved, the door would be left open for new revolutionary cataclysms whose effects could plunge the American economy into a crisis. Limited U.S. investments would not be sufficient to accomplish that and would be endangered

unless a massive program of aid was undertaken at the same time. The American government following World War I had made no move to participate in European reconstruction, even demanding reparations from conquered Germany. Had it followed a similar policy after World War II the results would have been economic and political disaster for world capitalism.

But the decision to underwrite the European recovery was not made quickly or easily by American imperialism. The decisive turn on this score came only in June 1947 with the announcement of the Marshall Plan, which poured tens of billions of dollars into Europe and Japan. This massive "aid" laid the basis for the resurrection of industrial production, the creation of paying markets, and a gigantic field for American investment. Even with this step, the European boom did not succeed in taking off until the additional spur of the Korean War beginning in 1950. From that point on, American investments spiraled to the point that by the late 1960s the "Gross National Product" of American-owned corporate subsidiaries abroad was the third highest in the world, ranking behind only the domestic production of the United States and the Soviet Union.

Thus as late as mid-1947, and perhaps as late as 1950, the possibilities of the kind of deep economic crisis Cannon predicted were very real. By the time of the Korean War a new series of economic factors came into play that fueled the long-term boom that was to come. These included the markets generated by the rebuilding of Europe and Japan; the so-called Keynesian revolution, based on a permanent massive arms budget, heavy deficit spending, and large-scale public debt; the development of new industries and introduction of new technologies, such as the mass expansion of automobile sales among working class consumers, automation, the electronics and computer industries, and other innovations, that proved to be big growth sectors in the postwar period.

In addition, the Allied regimes at the end of the war were able to maintain and benefit from the historic lowering of the real wages of European workers under Nazi rule. In effect this lowered the value of labor-power and increased the share of national income appropriated by the capitalist class—including American investors.

Finally, the U.S. victory opened up to American exploitation the raw materials of a host of colonial and semicolonial countries previously dominated by its imperialist rivals. Not the least prize in this field, though it did not assume its full importance for some years to come, was Middle Eastern oil, taken from Washington's British ally.

It was the exhaustion of all but the last of these sources of growth and the intensification of interimperialist rivalry in the late 1960s that finally brought the postwar boom to an end. In recent years we have seen the maturing of all of the classical conditions for a long-term capitalist downturn.

In 1947 the reactionary anticommunist offensive of the government began to take hold in the trade unions and in other areas of American life. This presented the party with sharply restricted opportunities compared with the immediate postwar period. As the tide began to turn against the labor upsurge of 1945-46, the SWP found itself swimming against the stream instead of with it. The party leadership sought to prepare the members for the difficult period ahead.

In the unions the party had been locked in battle against both the conservative officialdom and the Stalinists, who were themselves union bureaucrats in a number of major industrial organizations. As the Social Democratic and Democratic Party union officials began to line up behind the government in the mounting anticommunist campaign, it became necessary to sharply distinguish the revolutionary criticism of Stalinism made by the SWP from the attacks of the red-baiters.

Cannon first confronted this question in an exchange of opinion with Ruth Fischer, an exiled former leader of the German Communist Party who had been briefly associated with the Trotskyist movement. In 1947 she was close to the Workers Party. She had proposed an indiscriminate "united front" against Stalinism. In reply, Cannon wrote his *American Stalinism and Anti-Stalinism*, one of his finest expositions on the character of Stalinism, on revolutionary tactics in the trade unions, and on how revolutionists respond to government reaction. There he wrote:

"We Trotskyists, as everybody knows, are also against Stalinism and have fought it unceasingly and consistently for a very long time. But we have no place in the present 'all-inclusive' united front against American Stalinism. The reason for this is that we are anticapitalist. Consequently, we can find no point of agreement with the campaign conducted by the political representatives of American capitalism in Washington, with the support of its agents in the labor movement and its lackeys in the literary and academic world. We fight Stalinism from a different standpoint.

"We fight Stalinism not because it is another name for communism, but precisely because of its betrayal of communism and of the interests of the workers in the class struggle. Our exposition of the question is made from a communist point of view, and our appeal is directed not to the exploiters of labor and their various reactionary agencies of oppression and deception, but to the workers, who have a vital interest in the struggle against the capitalist exploiters as well as against perfidious Stalinism."

This clear class line served to orient the SWP in the years of the cold war and witch-hunt that were to come, and to preserve its character as a proletarian party committed to the communist future.

* * *

Only six of the fifty-five items in this volume are currently in print in other forms. The rest are either published here for the first time or long out of print. They are taken from a variety of sources (the introductory note preceding each item indicates its origin). First are articles and speeches published at the time in *The Militant* and in *Fourth International* magazine or in the SWP's internal bulletins. Other materials are taken from the files of the Socialist Workers Party national office, such as letters to the National Committee or to the branches of the party, transcripts of discussions included in the minutes of the party's Political Committee, etc. A large part of the collection is taken from Cannon's private papers, which are at the Library of Social History in New York.

This volume includes the majority but by no means all of Cannon's writings that have been preserved for the years 1945-47. Left out are letters of a routine or repetitious character, some of his public speeches of less general interest than those presented here, and further material on the dispute with Goldman and Morrow and on the unity negotiations with the Workers Party.

A number of the items in the book have been abridged, particularly the previously unpublished stenographic transcripts of internal party speeches. The source notes indicate in each case which these are. The transcripts were taken down in shorthand by a stenographer, invariably with omissions and gaps. Lapses in the original typescript are indicated by ellipses (. . .). To distinguish our abridgements from those in the original we have used ellipses in square brackets [. . .].

There were two considerations in deciding what to excerpt and what to print in full: keeping this volume to reasonable size, and eliminating unnecessary repetition. The internal party speeches were given weeks and months apart. In the case of ongoing developments such as the debate with the SWP minority or the negotiations with the WP, Cannon would remind his audience of the previous stages of the discussion. Since the speeches appear here together in this volume, the deletions have primarily removed repetitious summations of this kind, but left intact all new material in each speech.

As in other volumes of this series we have not altered the practice of the writer and stenographers, under threat of governmental persecution, of using pseudonyms in internal party gatherings and correspondence. Where we have been able to identify the persons referred to, their real names have been added in brackets in the text the first time the name is used or where there might be confusion with another person with a similar name. As an aid to the reader there is, in addition to extensive notes, a glossary of names, including pseudonyms, organizations, and periodicals.

Les Evans
May 1977

A MESSAGE ON GETTING OUT OF PRISON[1]

February 2, 1945

This message was sent to a meeting of 800 persons at the Hotel Diplomat in New York held to celebrate the release of the last twelve of the eighteen political prisoners in the Minneapolis labor case. The text is from The Militant, *February 10, 1945.*

I deeply regret that I cannot be with you tonight. I caught cold on the train, and in view of the fact that I intend to go back to work shortly, the doctor thinks it best that I do not go out for a few days. It is only a small matter—nothing serious. In every other respect I am in good shape, and eager to return to my work, as are all the other men of Sandstone, Danbury, and Alderson. Alderson is where our Senator[2] put in her hard and bitter thirteen months among the poor lost convict women who are cast out and abandoned and have no one to help them. Grace worried about them and tried to befriend them. Our hearts ached for our Senator there all alone with such a "hard way to go," as the convicts say. But she stood up and played her part and set us an example. We are proud of our Senator. All the rest of us did the best we could and we hope you approve of the way we conducted ourselves.

If I were to be present at the meeting, the thing I would like most to say would be how deeply, how profoundly, I thank you for your solidarity, your kindness, your friendship. I would like to say that I want to put on record in public my heartfelt gratitude to Roger Baldwin. He is not of our political and philosophic faith, but he is a principled fighter for what he believes in. Roger Baldwin believes in the rights of man. If I were present tonight and were permitted by time limitations to say only one sentence, to raise one slogan, I would say: "Long live the Rights of Man!" I *always* believed in this, but now I understand it better.

I would also thank the distinguished chairman of the Civil Rights Defense Committee [James T. Farrell] and its efficient and hard-working secretaries and all the others who worked with them. But we really do not have to say how we appreciate them. There cannot possibly be any doubts of that.

A LETTER TO NATALIA SEDOVA[3]

March 6, 1945

This letter to Trotsky's widow, who continued to live in Mexico City, has not been previously published. The copy in Cannon's files is marked "confidential."

Dear Comrade Natalia,

I have not been feeling well since my return and only today returned to work for the first time. That alone accounts for the delay in answering your letter of January 6. I previously sent you a formal acknowledgement of this letter so that you would know I had received it and intended to reply. Meantime, I discussed matters with my esteemed colleagues and we have come to agreement on all questions.

1. I think there is some justice in your criticism of the inadequate treatment of the change of line on the question of the USSR at the convention.[4] You are wrong, however, to attribute this to design on the part of the leadership. As I view the matter, the convention occurred at a time when the discussion of this decisive question had not yet fully unfolded even in the leading circles, and had only begun in the membership through the medium of the internal bulletin. From this I conclude not to condemn the convention, but rather to say that the convention resolution has to be taken as a step toward a more thoroughgoing reconsideration of the new situation on the basis of our fundamental program.

We have discussed this matter with Stein [Morris Lewit] and others who carried the party on their shoulders during our absence, and find agreement on this point of view. We have agreed upon the following procedure:

(a) *The Militant* shall carry an editorial statement sharply calling attention to those paragraphs of the convention resolution dealing with the question of the USSR and Stalinism, and elaborating on the reasons for them. Simultaneously, the quotation which appears next to the picture of L. D. [Trotsky] on the editorial page is to be replaced by another one corresponding more to the new situation.[5]

(b) The internal bulletin is to remain open for further discussion and clarification of the question.

(c) The next number of the magazine is to devote its main emphasis and pose sharply the question: "Whither the USSR?" The statement of the Spanish group, "The Defense of the Soviet Union and the Tactic of the Revolutionaries," is to be printed in this number of the magazine, together with an extensive statement on the new situation by the editorial board.

(d) The question is to be placed on the agenda of the projected plenum of the NC and a special resolution adopted.

I believe that by proceeding along these lines we will succeed in completely dispelling any impression that the change of slogans is to be passed over lightly. At the same time, we can hope to bring about a salutary ideological reorientation, not only of our own party membership, but of all the other parties as well, who attentively follow the material presented in our magazine.

2. Your impression that the convention cut across, or was designed to cut across, the discussion on any of the important political questions, is incorrect. The convention, in fact, decided, on the basis of a motion originally sponsored by me and my friends in Sandstone, to permit a continuation of the discussion on the political resolution in the internal bulletin after the convention. Since our return, the minority presented a request that the internal bulletin be opened up for a discussion and review of all questions in dispute. This proposition was accepted by the majority. They can also have another convention if they want it.

In addition to that, an edition of the international bulletin containing, I believe, all, or most, of the critical articles submitted by you and the Spanish group, is now at the printers, if it is not already off the press.[6] It is being put out in printed rather than in mimeographed form to facilitate easier international distribution.

We are unconditionally in favor of opening up an international discussion on the broadest scale, and the SWP will clearly state its position on all questions in this discussion.

3. The convention, which was due under the constitutional rule, was projected long before the disputes broke out in sharp form. There was a strong sentiment of the membership to hold a convention, as we had had no national gathering for two years. The only question in everybody's mind was as to the feasibility of holding a convention in the absence of the eighteen. We, on our part, took the position that the convention, like every other phase of party work, should be carried through regardless of our absence; this would demonstrate that the party is not dependent on any single leader or even on a whole group of leaders. We thought that party morale and self-confidence would be strengthened by such a demonstration, and this estimate of the question proved to be completely correct. None of the absent leaders objected to the holding of a convention, and preparations proceeded on a broad scale, with a free and absolutely unrestricted discussion.

The unexpected proposal to postpone the convention at the last minute, after delegates had already been elected in many branches and all preparations had been made for the affair, was manifestly inept and untimely.[7] A living, functioning party organization cannot be juggled around this way.

To further elucidate the original motivation for the holding of the convention I quote here from a memorandum which was sent out to all the party leaders by Stein early in the summer:

> For some time now we have felt the need of a national gathering. We have been weighing in our minds the character of such a gathering, whether it should take the form of an active workers' conference or a convention. We are all of the opinion that a convention would be preferable. It will be two years in October since the last convention, and we have no constitutional provision for a postponement of a convention. If we are to hold a national gathering in the face of the difficulties of transportation and accommodation of delegates, then a convention would be the preferable medium.
>
> A large section of the membership has been new and has not had the experience of a convention. They have not seen in practice how the organization operates and arrives at decisions. A convention would be a great educational medium for the new people. The membership has put in a period of hard work in the recent campaigns and many have expressed the desire to meet for an exchange of experiences in the past campaigns and to plan new ones. There is in addition the need of a political discussion of the events that have transpired on the world arena, and as they would necessarily have to be summarized in resolutions.

> The only reason we have not raised the convention question earlier is because we hesitated to undertake it in the absence of the eighteen, and to go through with it without their participation. But it appears to us that just as we have demonstrated in all the phases of the party activity that the party must carry on and even step up its tempo despite the imprisonment, it would have a good effect to demonstrate it also in this case where the internal political life of the organization is concerned. Our plans are for a convention to be held toward the latter part of October, immediately after the release of the short-termers.
>
> The political discussion would take place around the last plenum resolution, supplemented by a resolution that would bring it up to date, plus a resolution on America and other problems that anyone may wish to raise. We would also present to the convention a program of action and the proposals on education, launching a campaign for the realization of this program.
>
> We would like to have your opinion on this proposal as soon as possible, and whether the document Felix [Morrow] wrote last December, or any other document that you may have in mind, should be published in the preconvention discussion, if it is finally decided to hold such a convention.

In writing this letter to you, I asked Stein if he wanted to add anything more on this point and he sent me the following note:

> It would be worthwhile to point out here that the preconvention discussion, as well as the discussion at the convention, is determined not merely by us, but also by the character of the opposition and the type of issues they raise. The fact is that no one in the opposition raised the Russian question for discussion before the convention. Roland's document was presented several days prior to the convention when all the delegates were on their way to the convention; and his document, too, discusses primarily the organization question in relation to the Russian question.[8] The fact that an opposition arose against our plenum resolution, and that Morrison [Goldman] raised all the organization questions he did, played a large part in determining the character of the discussion.

4. I note that you object to the nonelection of Roland to the National Committee. The convention had a different opinion and there is nothing that can be done about it now. The decisions of the convention must be respected, not only in the letter, but in the spirit too. The minutes of the nominating commission, consisting of 21 delegates, show that 19 votes were cast against Roland, none for him, and two abstentions. The convention minority (5

delegates) were not willing to take the responsibility of sponsoring him—he was not even nominated on the floor of the convention—and the rest of the delegates (55) were adamant against him. I don't think this had anything to do with his suddenly discovered "political differences"—which nobody had ever heard about before—but was rather a judgment on his conduct. Our party members insist on leaders standing up in front where they can see them. This sentiment of our militant rank and file has my hearty endorsement.

In the SWP system the slate of nominees for the NC is not presented by the leadership, but by a *nominating commission* consisting exclusively of convention delegates. In this commission each district of the party is given proportional representation. The leaders do not interfere with the work of the commission. When the commission finally presents its slate, the floor is then opened for other nominations, and full discussion, before the elections take place. For an elucidation of our system, see the letter of Martin: "Comments on the Selection of the National Committee" (*Internal Bulletin* vol. VI, no. 13).[9]

As to the necessity of "creating favorable conditions in order for Roland to continue his work"—you don't need to worry about that. It is the traditional method of our party to make use of the services of everyone who is capable of doing any kind of work whatever, regardless of any disputes which may be going on at the same time. The minority was given representation in the National Committee proportionately greater than its strength in the party—almost double. One of the three places on the party Secretariat—the body which exercises immediate control over organization matters, finances, etc.—is assigned to a member of the minority. They have full representation on the editorial boards of both publications. As far as I know, they have made no complaints except those which invariably arise from the ineluctable fact that it is not comfortable to be in the minority. The majority hasn't the slightest intention of persecuting anybody or depriving anybody of the free possibility of contributing to the party work, according to his ability.

5. I have noted carefully your remarks about routinism. But I believe you exaggerate the extent of it in the SWP; and I cannot follow you when you imply an identification with Stalinism. Routinism is an inherent tendency of every organization and leading staff which has broken out of the circle existence and is busy with many tasks. That is the conservative side of

organization which, if it is not subjected to constant criticism and correction, can lead in the end to the negation of the very purposes which the organization originally proclaimed.

L. D. wrote very illuminatingly about this question in his criticisms of the German Social Democracy before the First World War. It was he also who explained, for the first time to my knowledge, that organization itself, with its unavoidable routine, contains a conservative element. The thing is to understand it, to put routine to use, to subordinate it and control it, but by no means to break up the organization and start all over again. Without organization there can be no party; and we have to remind ourselves continually that the central problem of our epoch is precisely the problem of building the revolutionary party.

Along with the tendency to lapse into routine, there goes also the other tendency of all committees and executives who are busy with a thousand tasks—the tendency to resent criticism to one degree or another. I personally have never seen a committee of high or low degree, national or local, which did not at first show manifestations of this tendency. Yet, without free criticism on a national and also on an international scale it is hardly possible to correct the unavoidable errors which arise in the complex and complicated situation of our epoch, and find the right road.

It is my firm opinion that one of the most important qualities of leadership is precisely the ability to examine criticism objectively, including even that criticism which may be inspired by malice and bad will, and to extract any grain of merit it may contain. But nobody is born with this gift. This capacity—the capacity to listen attentively to the voice of criticism and not to fear it—is one of those qualities which must be *learned*. I believe that I am one of those who learned it, partly through experience—blows over the head—and partly through the patient instruction of L. D. Trotsky. I wrote on this question to my hard-working colleagues several times from prison, calling attention to some tendencies to fall into routine which I had been able to see more clearly from a distance, and warning them not to take a resentful attitude toward criticism.

In the next stage of the discussion I intend to write on this question also, and in connection with it I will quote some correspondence between me and L. D. which I believe will be very helpful for the education of the comrades.

I very well remember one time in particular when I was

occupied with a thousand petty tasks—in organizing the definitive split with the Socialist Party and preparing our own convention[10]—that some of the most important political letters addressed to me by L. D. remained unanswered for days; and eventually, before I realized what was happening, for weeks. I only awakened to the seriousness of my routinist error when I received a letter from L. D., polite and friendly as always in tone, but very sharp in its critical content, as regarded my dereliction. I learned a great deal from that single experience. My answer to him—which I will quote in the discussion—will show that I understood the essence of the matter after he had called it to my attention.

I am absolutely confident that the leading staff of our party will overcome and will subordinate any routinist tendencies and clear the road for the free exchange of criticism, nationally and internationally, and thereby facilitate the correction of all errors openly and honestly.

6. You say that Stalinism is not a superstition, but a reality. I know that. But American imperialism is still less a superstition and still more a reality. I do not permit myself to forget this. Indeed, I cannot forget it because I have seen too many members and sympathizers of our movement succumb to its pressure during these past sixteen years of our struggle against it. Time after time I have seen people begin by muttering about the danger of Stalinism in our party; then go over from that to the denunciation of our organization methods as "Stalinist"; and finally wind up in the camp of American imperialism, thereby reconciling themselves to "cooperation" with its Stalinist satellite.

The latest, but by no means the only example, is Burnham. In the Winter 1945 issue of *Partisan Review,* which has just appeared, this doughty fighter against "the danger of Stalinism in the SWP" contributes an article entitled "Lenin's Heir." It is a paean to Stalin. Here are a few salient quotations: "Stalin proves himself a 'great man' in the grand style." "The Moscow Trials have stood the test of action."[11] "The truth—so weighty with consequence for our age—becomes more plausible: that under Stalin, the Communist revolution has been, not betrayed, but fulfilled." "If anyone betrayed Bolshevism it was not Stalin but Trotsky." "Stalin is Lenin's heir. Stalin is communism."

I could extend this letter to the length of a thick pamphlet citing instances with documentary proofs of a more or less similar evolution of scores of people who began with a "struggle against germs of Stalinism in the SWP." These facts are well known to our party membership, and that is the reason they react so violently to this kind of talk. It is better in my opinion to leave Stalinism out of it. It is far better to put the matter more correctly and to say: Every party organization has a conservative side inherent in the nature of organization itself. Routinism and the stifling of criticism can create the danger of strengthening the conservative side of organization until it devours the party. Therefore, let us be alert, let us constantly check ourselves and examine our work to see to it that we do not lapse into habits of routine. Let us keep the way clear for the voice of criticism from any source. And, at the same time, let us go on with our work of building the party with confidence that we will succeed.

7. There is one more matter which disturbed us greatly at Sandstone. That was the apparent straining of relations between you and our acting leading staff in New York over the disposition of critical articles submitted by G. [Grandizo Munis] and the Spanish group. This issue seemed to us absolutely incomprehensible, as it is our disposition to welcome rather than to resent the critical intervention of international comrades. We are only one part of the international movement. It is only by cooperation, and the free exchange of opinion with the others, that we will be able to solve our complicated problems on an international scale. L. D. taught us that *international collaboration* is the essence of internationalism.

When Rose [Karsner] wrote to me about this matter, I answered her under date of October 17: "We are disturbed by Natalia's complaints about Grandizo. She should be given full satisfaction in this matter without delay. I had previously made a note to ask him to write more for the magazine."

We couldn't see the slightest reason why any or all the critical articles should not be published, either in the magazine or in the internal bulletin. Stein answered me right away that the whole thing was a misunderstanding; that he and the group in New York had no disposition whatever to refuse publication to the articles; that the next issue of the magazine was to contain two contributions from the Spanish group and that correspondence was in process about a third article—concerning the national question, I believe, although I have never seen it to this day—as to what disposition should be made of it.

Since my return to New York I have gone into this matter very thoroughly with both Stein and E. R. Frank [Bert Cochran]. They both insist that there was no basis whatsoever for the assumption that they wanted in any way to deprecate, still less to suppress, any contribution of the Spanish group. I am convinced that this is their real attitude and that in the future every possible source of complaint on this score will be eliminated; that such differences and disputes as may arise between us on political and theoretical grounds will be strictly confined to their proper sphere, and properly discussed without the exacerbating intrusion of secondary questions.

8. It appears to me that Morrison maintains his solidarity with us on all the main questions of the program. For example, the amendments which he presented to our Fifteenth Anniversary Plenum shortly before our imprisonment all seemed to me to be of a secondary character. Some of them were good and were accepted by the majority, and he voted for the resolution in its final form. But at the plenum he began a most irrational attack on our "organizational methods," and has since developed his position into a very wide divergence.[12]

In this question Morrison is repeating Burnham point for point and almost word for word. (See "The War and Bureaucratic Conservatism," the organizational program of the petty-bourgeois opposition, which is included as an appendix to my book, *The Struggle for a Proletarian Party.*) We completely refuted the Burnham thesis in my counterdocument, "The Struggle for a Proletarian Party." One might add that we did not confine our refutation to the literary form. We have exemplified our methods consistently in a sixteen-year uninterrupted struggle to build the party. It will be very difficult for anyone to convince us that we have been wrong all the time and that the fruits of our work have little or no value. The position of Morrison is false to the roots. Our method of building the party is the correct method, and we are going to stick to it.

I know that L. D. Trotsky had a high regard for the SWP and was always friendly to its leadership. To be sure, he made more than one criticism, but his criticism was always designed to help—and did help—never to undermine and discredit. In simple truth, during the last years of his third exile, the SWP was Trotsky's own adopted party. He exercised an almost direct supervision and leadership of its most important political activity; and we always went together hand in hand with him on the international field. For example, the Transitional Program which he wrote for the founding world congress of the Fourth International, was first submitted by him to the plenum of the SWP and was adopted and presented to the world congress, at his request, as the proposal of the SWP.[13]

9. I believe that many of the disputes and conflicts arise over the circumstance that the SWP is rapidly undergoing a transformation. The party is completely breaking out of the circle stage of existence; expanding its activities on all fronts, and recruiting hundreds of new workers who have never had any previous political experience. Some comrades do not seem to be able to understand what is happening before their eyes and cannot adjust themselves to the new situation. We on the other hand, who are completely alien to the circle spirit, swim in this new environment of an expanding workers' movement like fish in the water. Our thoughts and discussions at Sandstone were devoted primarily to the problems of the American revolution and the building of the American party. We think that we, for our part, can best serve the international movement by building a strong bastion on the soil of the most powerful imperialism.

The problem of building a revolutionary party in the U.S. is quite different from that in the older European countries. The American workers in the mass have no political tradition. They are only now beginning to awaken to the idea of political independence. They have never had a mass labor or socialist party of their own. We must recruit and build a revolutionary vanguard party out of this unschooled mass of militant workers who are without previous political experience. It appears to me that the European comrades, almost without exception, overlook the peculiar nature of our unique problem. In the course of the ensuing discussion I shall endeavor to elucidate our conception of the American problem, and I hope to add something to its clarification.

10. Some misunderstanding apparently arose over my contribution to the discussion on the Russian question, which appeared in *Internal Bulletin,* vol. VI, no. 9. If I am not mistaken, you are under the impression that my article was inspired by your second letter. No, that is incorrect. When I wrote my article we had before us only your first letter. While your formulations were not very clear to us, you seemed, at least by implication, to put a cross over the Russian revolution.[14] We did not agree with this interpretation of the situation at all. My letter was not intended to express agreement, but disagreement. This circumstance dictated the form of my article. Shortly afterwards, your second

letter, in which you formulated your position much more clearly and precisely, made an entirely different impression, and it seemed to us that we were much closer to agreement on the main question. I have carefully noted the further development of your position in your third letter and the critical remarks of G. directed against my article. In the course of the discussion I intend to write more on the question.

There is no doubt that my thinking on the Russian question lagged behind the development of the onrushing events. The article which I wrote from Sandstone represented the beginning of a reorientation inspired in part by your letter, but mainly by the radical change in the military situation. As I view the situation now, my letter from Sandstone represents not fully developed thoughts, but rather half-thoughts on the question. In the next period, and in the course of the discussion, I hope to carry them through to the end and bring them up to date.

11. Our weekly paper is going through a process of transition conformable to the great expansion of our influence in the labor movement and the addition of *tens of thousands* of new readers, most of whom have had no previous political affiliation or experience. For example, in opening the new subscription campaign, our comrades, mobilized from coast to coast for a "Red Sunday," secured *1,526* new paid subscribers *in a single day.* This is more than the total paid circulation our paper attained in the first five years of its existence.

It is obvious that we are at the beginning of a qualitative change in the situation of the party vis-à-vis the awakening militant workers of America. The problem is to adapt the paper to the understanding of these new thousands of politically unschooled readers, without sacrificing its political character and destroying its interest for the most educated party members. The problem of combining these functions is not an easy one to solve and requires a period of experimentation and criticism. We discussed this problem many times at Sandstone. Our ideas on the question, submitted as a contribution to the discussion, appear in the letter entitled, "On the Party Press," by Martin, in the *Party Builder,* vol. I, no. 4.[15] If you have the opportunity to read this article we would be glad to hear your comments on it.

* * *

Morris Stein just communicated some news which seems to me to make a most agreeable postscript to this letter. He just received word that Comrade Orlando, the woman leader of our group in Italy, took a little time out from the struggle to give birth to a baby girl—and has named her "Natalia." I greet the new baby's first cry of life as the battle cry of the living revolution.

Fraternally,
J. P. Cannon

Natalia Sedova

Grace Carlson

ON THE MEMORY OF CARLO TRESCA

March 27, 1945

This unpublished letter to Margaret de Silver, widow of the murdered Italian-American anarchist leader Carlo Tresca, recalls Cannon's long friendship with Tresca and their close collaboration in labor defense and civil liberties cases.

Dear Margaret,

I hope you will forgive me for the unseemly delay in acknowledging your letter. I haven't been feeling well since I came home and only today have started to work again, beginning with neglected correspondence.

I was very glad to meet you on the street that day and also to hear from you, as always.

In Sandstone we followed with keen interest the report of the anniversary meeting, warmly applauding your valiant fight against the official indifference and neglect, a fight which, viewed properly on the positive side, is a part of the general fight for human value, and for truth and justice.[16] Soldiers of this great cause are not too many these days. For that reason each individual soldier must be appreciated all the more highly.

In catching up on my neglected reading of our press since I returned, I noticed that the comrade who accompanied me from my home to Sandstone gave a brief description of my workroom: "The walls border on austerity—only two pictures in the entire room, one of Trotsky, the other of Carlo Tresca." I had never noticed this before and looked at the walls to check the accuracy of the description. That's the way it is, all right. And I think I will let it stay that way.

Keep pitching. I am still hoping to get squared away sometime to write up my recollections and appreciation of Carlo and to help keep his memory green for younger generations and show them the inspiring figure of an honest man, a good fighter for causes greater than self. God knows the betrayed youth of America need a few examples of this kind.

Fraternally,
[James P. Cannon]

THE NEW OPPOSITION BLOC IN THE SWP

April 4, 1945

This previously unpublished letter to Murry Weiss in Los Angeles is Cannon's first assessment of the factional activities of Albert Goldman and Felix Morrow after the Minneapolis prisoners returned to party work.

Dear Murry:

I have not yet heard from you and some others in response to the letters previously sent to you. It is quite important that you acknowledge the receipt of this material and let us know your opinions. We want to be sure that we are in agreement with each other and able to work together unitedly in the critically important next period of the development of the party.

We have had a number of discussions here in an effort to arrive at a precise analysis of the nature of the problem posed by the emergence of the new opposition bloc. You know it is our longtime practice to make sure what we are doing and where we are going before we start any kind of an action. This method always takes time and involves delay, but in return it safeguards us against wandering off in the wrong direction and having to retrace our steps afterward.

We have been following our old method in dealing with the present problem, and as a result, I believe that we now have a much clearer appreciation of the problem and of the course we must follow. We are all in complete agreement here. It remains to communicate our opinions to the comrades in the field and invite their suggestions and criticisms in preparation for a more thorough consideration of the whole question when we meet at the forthcoming plenum.

As I wrote before, the factional situation in the Political Committee, and also in the New York local, has been greatly accentuated since our return. I understand the same thing is true of Chicago. There are three main factors at the bottom of the new developments:

(a) The common experiences at Sandstone, which united the Minneapolis worker group—to which I have always belonged fundamentally—more closely together in personal solidarity and mutual respect and confidence, had a directly opposite result in the case of Morrison [Goldman] and Morrow. All political and personal relations between us and Morrison, which didn't amount to much from the first day, were completely discontinued as far back as last June, and between us and Morrow about 90 percent. I will not take time to recount this whole disgraceful story here. Rather, I will confine myself to the statement that no part of the fault, not even one-tenth of one percent of the fault, lies on our side. Our conduct under these conditions was 100 percent correct in every respect. All the fault is on the other side. That's the only basis upon which we will ever discuss it with anybody.

We left Sandstone with the conviction that personal relations with Morrison had been disrupted and broken off forever without any possibility of repair, and that political relations henceforth can only be of the most formal, businesslike character. We have conducted ourselves since our return from this standpoint. Morrison, on his part, who associated and fraternized with such scum of the prison as Bioff and Browne, the trade union racketeers, while openly manifesting his contempt and hostility to all of us, including the Bolshevik trade union militants of Minneapolis, also carried over the Sandstone attitude into the New York Political Committee situation. Naturally, these personal relations, or more correctly, this lack of such relations, did not facilitate harmonious collaboration in the work of the Political Committee after our return.

(b) The leaders of the opposition bloc maintain that their position was misrepresented at the convention and in the reports of the convention which appeared in the December number of the magazine. They claim that they really support the convention resolution, that it incorporates most of their ideas in the form of amendments, and that the majority exaggerated the differences and put them in a false light for factional reasons.

(c) In the heated atmosphere which has characterized every meeting of the Political Committee, they have launched on a frenzied campaign of grievance-mongering, construing every administrative action, every organizational decision, and every oversight or minor technical error of the editors as further evidence in support of their thesis that the leadership has suffered a degeneration along the lines of Stalinism.

(d) This attitude has been carried over into the New York branches where, in line with their theory that the party needs more "discussion," they take the floor at every meeting with one insignificant criticism of the party leadership or another, without first going through the formality of discussing the matter in the Political Committee. They have openly organized a membership caucus, invite the youngest and most inexperienced members of the party, and give them tendentious reports of the proceedings of the Political Committee and denigrate and defame its individual members.

(e) So far we have left the initiative entirely to them, confining ourselves to answering their criticisms when presented in the branches, and refraining from any membership caucus organization. Naturally, this situation could not last for a long time. The rank-and-file supporters of the party leadership, seeing the opposition bloc operating in caucus formation in the branches, and aware that they were holding outside factional meetings, began to clamor for the organization of a countercaucus.

On this background we held a meeting of the majority members of the Political Committee last Sunday in order to consider the situation once again and chart our course. The natural impulse in such a situation is to organize a countercaucus and proceed to a ruthless factional fight all up and down the line. In view of the attitude taken by the opposition bloc there did not seem to be any alternative. We could not confine ourselves to expostulations in the Political Committee while they are disrupting and demoralizing the rank and file in the branches.

Nevertheless, we have had to recognize two negative factors in such a perspective. First, is the circumstance that up till now the political differences have been only intimated and implied, by no means fully developed in such a form as to make it clear to the objective observer that two fundamentally conflicting political lines are involved. The second negative factor is the danger that the international movement would not understand a sharp factional fight, apparently heading toward a split, without a sufficiently plausible political basis; and there have been certain indications that the weaker and more inexperienced elements in the international movement—and some with axes to grind—would tend to support the opposition as a persecuted and misrepresented minority.

With this in mind, we felt obliged to come to an agreement amongst ourselves on an analysis of the opposition bloc, as it has developed up to this point, before proceeding any further with the organization of the struggle against them, and to regulate the tempo of the struggle on the basis of this objective analysis.

In one of your letters written during the party discussion you gave a synopsis of the analysis you had made in your speeches at the preconvention membership meetings in Los Angeles. If I remember correctly, you said that in the organizational sphere a Souvarinist conception of the party, the assumption that Bolshevism naturally evolves into Stalinism, was already manifest in Morrison's articles. On the other hand, contrary to some of the hasty judgments expressed by other comrades, you maintained that the political differences, so far as they have been developed in written form up till now, were by no means fundamental, at least not obviously so; and that we would have to await the further development of the two positions in order to say definitely whether it is a question of two conflicting political lines or not.

This opinion, as stated in your preconvention letters, coincides entirely with our own view of the situation. In the field of party organization the tendency of Morrison is a genuine Menshevik tendency, with a bloodline going straight back to Martov in 1903. Recently, since my return, I had an opportunity to read for the first time Lenin's classic work on organization, entitled *One Step Forward, Two Steps Back.* This book, recently published for the first time in England (it has never been published in this country) became available to us in a very limited number of copies only a short time ago.[17] *One Step Forward* is Lenin's exposition of the circumstances and causes of the original split with the Mensheviks at the Second Party Congress in 1903.

Our dispute is a repetition of the original debate. The ideas, the arguments—yes, even the state of mind and the "moral" judgments—of Morrison and Company repeat Martov in 1903 almost word for word. The same can be said for our position on the organization question, for our arguments and our conception of what is important and what is unimportant, with only this slight difference—we repeat what Lenin said forty-one years ago. It is astonishing to see how every serious fight on the "organization question" follows so closely and almost so literally the pattern set by the great prototype of 1903, the party congress where both Menshevism and Bolshevism first began to take definite shape.

The opposition bloc is unmistakably conciliationist toward the petty-bourgeois Workers Party, supersensitive to the criticisms and opinions of the petty-bourgeois intellectuals on the fringes of the radical movement, and contemptuous of the public opinion of the proletarian cadres of the party. Conciliationism, as you know, is a common trait of all forms and varieties of Menshevism in all their stages of evolution.

I believe there can be no difference of opinion amongst us that we must fight them on this ground to a finish without any compromise whatsoever. So much for the organizational question.

When we come to the political differences, however, the situation is by no means so clear. Here their line, insofar as they have one different from ours, is not clearly stated but only *implied*; it is intimated in nuances, emphasis, and approach, but nowhere have they yet ventured to challenge us directly on programmatic questions. And they even heatedly maintain that we exaggerate the differences when we attribute to them a different opinion than ours on the strategical perspectives of the European revolution. For that reason, an all-out fight, culminating in a split, toward which their frenzied course has appeared to be directly leading them, might be very difficult to explain on political grounds to the radical worker public, and especially to the international movement. Such a factional fight and split, in which the organizational question is the dominating factor, might very well serve to confuse rather than to clarify matters outside the party; and even, to a certain extent, inside our own ranks.

There are many instructive examples to warn us against the excessive overhead costs of such a split. The first and best example is the original Bolshevik-Menshevik split itself in 1903. There has been a rather widespread impression that "Lenin split on the organization question" and that this is the way to build a Bolshevik party. A study of *One Step Forward* shows that this impression is completely erroneous. Lenin did not want that split. He offered numerous concessions to avoid it and offered other compromises afterward in an effort to heal it. The split of 1903 was decidedly premature, an "anticipatory" split, as Trotsky I think once described it.

The fundamental political divergences between Bolshevism

and Menshevism developed only later, gradually, over a long period of years, and did not become finally and irrevocably definitive until 1917. During the intervening period Lenin was plagued with the continual necessity of explaining and justifying the split, and of contending with a conciliatory faction in his own ranks. He had to go through unity negotiations, and at one time, a formal unification in a single party with the Mensheviks. (See *Left Sickness* [*"Left-Wing" Communism—An Infantile Disorder* (1920)].) Trotsky in his *History* [*The History of the Russian Revolution*] and elsewhere has related how the Bolsheviks and Mensheviks had common organizations in Russia even after the February revolution [in 1917] prior to Lenin's return.

Most of the half a dozen or so splits which took place in the early Communist movement in America were without adequate political foundation. As a result, they were not sufficiently comprehensible either to the sympathetic radical workers outside the party or to the bulk of the party members themselves, and were followed in each case by unity maneuvers and negotiations, formal unifications and new splits. A great deal of time and precious energy was wasted in the unnecessary splits of the early Communist movement in America, and a great many potentially revolutionary workers fell by the wayside in discouragement as a result.

A classic example, a split over organizational questions enormously accentuated by personal antagonisms—*a split which did not take place*—is the long internal struggle of the pioneer period of our own American Trotskyist movement (1930-33).[18] The account of this important chapter in our history remains to be written. Let it suffice for the present to say that Trotsky refused to sanction the split on the ground that it could not be explained in political terms to the radical worker public. He said: The confusion would hamper the efforts of both sides to attract new elements; the prestige of the movement as a whole would be lowered; members of both factions taking part in the split would fall aside from the movement in discouragement. He insisted that the two factions make a truce and agree to work together, plunge the party into mass work, and await further developments to see whether the implied political differences would develop in full form and to such an extent as to necessitate a split. This truce under the immediate intervention of Trotsky and the International Secretariat was made in 1933.

To be sure, the definitive split did eventually take place—in

1940. But that was seven years later, over principled differences and political disputes of such depth and scope as to be clear to everybody. Meantime the party did some good work despite internal friction. Following the truce and the developments of mass work new alignments took place and the eventual split, which came in 1940, after the political differences were fully matured and explainable to all, had a salutary effect on the further development of the party, as we all know.

The split in the English movement was not explicable on political grounds. It did untold damage to the movement and left it in a weakened position even today, after the unification finally brought about by the intervention and pressure of the international movement.[19]

I believe these examples are enough to show that splits, like unifications, are operations of the utmost seriousness and must be approached with all the necessary attentiveness and objectivity. I do not at all mean to imply that in waging a ruthless faction fight against the opposition bloc, we would thereby desire or advocate a split. Just the contrary. I mean only to recognize that a split is the objective logic of such a struggle. Anyone who does not understand that a ruthless factional struggle in a heated atmosphere, with the party divided into caucus formations, contains the danger and even the probability of a split, only shows that he has not made a serious study of the history of the political movement and has not learned anything from it.

We considered all these questions in a thoroughgoing discussion which took place among the majority NC members. Of course, we know very well that it doesn't depend entirely on us. We can't prevent people from splitting if they are bent on splitting any more than Lenin could in 1903. But we can at least make the attempt. And in case of failure, we can show clearly, by the record, where the responsibility lies.

We came to the conclusion that we should make an attempt to put the factional struggle under control, regulate its tempo, and, if possible, prevent a premature, abnormal, and unprofitable development. We decided to take the initiative to propose a truce to the opposition members of the National Committee with the object of ameliorating the heated factional atmosphere; of creating a situation more normal and more suitable for collaboration in the daily work of the party; while awaiting the further development of events to make clear to the factions themselves, and to the radical worker public and the international movement, whether the present unripened political differences will develop into deepgoing divergences or toward agreement.

We decided to make any reasonable concessions that might be necessary to liquidate current grievances on concrete organizational questions in order to clear the road for a more objective literary discussion of the political shadings and the basic differences of conception as to how to build the party. This proposal was formally made to the minority in written form by Stein, on behalf of the majority, as follows:

New York
April 2, 1945

Comrades Goldman, Morrow and Shoenfeld

Dear Comrades:

The internal situation in the party has sharpened considerably since the convention despite the fact that there are no apparent fundamental political differences between the majority and the minority.

I am authorized by the majority of the PC to invite you to meet with its representatives for the purpose of discussing ways and means of ameliorating the situation.

Please consider this proposal and let me know of the best time for such a meeting.

Fraternally yours,
M. Stein

The minority expressed their readiness to accept the proposal. Thereupon the majority designated a committee of three to confer with them in working out the details of the truce. You will be promptly informed of the results of the negotiations.

In the meantime, here is one additional item of information. We had heard from various sources that Morrison was meeting with Shachtman. We decided to raise the question in the PC. Here I quote the relevant extracts of the PC minutes of April 2 covering this point:

Question by Stein: I have heard rumors that you have been meeting with Shachtman.

Answer by Morrison: I have met and conversed with Shachtman several times. He was a friend of mine when he was in the party and he still is a friend of mine. Time and events have dissipated the coldness that entered into our relationship after the faction fight of 1939-40. In addition to being a friend I consider him as devoted to the proletarian revolution and therefore as a comrade who is not in the same party because of a serious mistake that he made. I hope that he will correct himself and rejoin our party.

We discussed no question which in my opinion required any report to the PC.

Question by Martin: I would like to inquire if affairs of the SWP were in any way the subject of your discussions with Shachtman.

Answer by Morrison: I would say no is a 99 percent correct answer. Naturally in any discussion a remark here or there is made, but we consciously steered clear of anything in the SWP except that he made his remarks as to what he knows and what he wrote in the *NI* [*New International*].

You can write your own comment.

Yours fraternally,
J. P. Cannon

ON THE INTERNAL SITUATION

April 16, 1945

The following statement was adopted by the Political Committee of the SWP and was published in the May 1945 Fourth International.

All members of the Political Committee, representing both the majority and minority point of view as developed at the Eleventh Party Convention, have jointly discussed the party situation and have unanimously agreed upon the following statement to the party membership:

1. There are no clearly defined differences at the present time on programmatic questions.

2. There is no disagreement on the analysis of the situation in the United States and the problems and tasks of the party as outlined in the convention resolution.

3. The differences on the convention resolution dealing with "The European Revolution and the Tasks of the Revolutionary Party" are not fundamental in character. The differences, insofar as they have found definite expression thus far, are rather secondary in character and relate primarily to questions of interpretation and emphasis. It remains to be seen whether, in the course of events and further discussion, the present differences will be reconciled in agreement or developed into principled divergences.

4. There are no concrete organizational questions in dispute at the present time.

5. There appear to be differences, or tendencies toward differences, on the organization question in general; on the conception of the party, its attitude toward other parties, its

methods of functioning, and the methods of building it. It remains yet to be seen, however, whether these differences can be reconciled in the course of common work and free discussion, or will be deepened, become more definitive, and require explicit elucidation in conflicting resolutions on the question.

6. In view of the large area of general agreement, and the limited and as yet rather undeveloped nature of the disagreements, the PC members of both tendencies—majority and minority—are unanimously of the opinion:

(a) It is possible and obligatory to collaborate harmoniously and constructively on the basis of the convention decisions to carry on the work of the party and build up the party.

(b) There is no basis for sharp factional struggle or for the existence of factional formations in the party ranks.

7. An educational discussion of the existing differences is to be continued and regulated by the NC as authorized by the convention.

THE TRUCE WITH THE MINORITY

April 17, 1945

This letter to J. Andrews (Jules Geller) in Akron, Ohio, contains Cannon's motivation for the PC statement "On the Internal Situation" of April 16. It has not previously been published.

Dear Comrade:

At last night's meeting of the Political Committee we adopted the attached statement on the internal situation by unanimous agreement. This was the final outcome of the discussions we initiated on the subject, as related in my letter to Murry.

In some respects this statement represents a unique development in internal party struggles; I cannot remember any exact precedent for it. And it is very important that we try to understand just what has happened in the light of our agreed-upon aims. I have seen "peace agreements" in the old Communist Party days, signed by factions professing complete agreement on all resolutions, become the starting point for new outbreaks of intensified factional warfare. There have also been occasions when really serious differences have been suppressed, compromised, laid aside by agreement in the interests of "harmony." This document is something else again.

We drafted the statement and, with some very minor amendments, it was accepted by the minority. On our part, it represents an attempt to put the situation precisely and frankly as we see it. The political differences are not concealed, but are defined, rather, as unripened. From this the statement draws the conclusion that a sharp and definitive factional struggle over unripened differences would not be justifiable. We do not undertake to predict what the further evolution of the differences will be; that question is left open. Instead, a period of educational discussion, while awaiting further development of the two positions, is provided for.

Many comrades think as you do, that the criticisms and amendments brought forward by the minority indicate a different "line" from ours, at least by implication. That, as you will remember, is the way we characterized their position as far back as the Fifteenth Anniversary Plenum more than a year ago. But as long as they confine themselves to criticisms and amendments and do not counterpose a conflicting resolution to our resolution, a split would be rather difficult to explain to the radical worker public and to the International, and even to a section of our own membership. From this we draw the conclusion, not to declare a unanimous agreement on everything, and not to stop the discussion on such points as are actually at issue, but rather to limit the discussion to such points as are clearly in dispute at the present time.

It is not sufficient for us to be convinced that the present differences will lead to more profound conflicts in the future. The party members cannot be educated by factional struggle over what is in our minds. Generally speaking, they can learn and take positions intelligently only on the basis of clearly demonstrable political differences. We must wait patiently until we see what further developments disclose. In the long run this course will involve far less overhead charges than a heated factional struggle in which the issues and differences might appear to be exaggerated, with the ever-present danger that such a struggle would lead to a premature split.

The two points of the statement which deal with the organization question also state the issue precisely as we understand it at the present time. In accepting the statement the minority acknowledges that there are no concrete organizational disputes at present. I don't know whether they realize it or not, but in the essence of the matter, this is a big retreat on their part from their previous rather hasty designation of the party regime as "Stalinist" to one degree or another. In a Stalinist regime, or any kind of bureaucratic administration for that matter, the organizational abuses and grievances are always painfully "concrete."

The statement frankly declares that there are differences, or tendencies toward differences, on the organization question in general, and in its most fundamental aspects—the conception of the party, its attitude toward other parties, its methods of functioning, and the methods of building it. It would be very difficult to state the "organization question" more comprehensively than that. But here again, as of today, the opposition has confined itself to rather hazy criticisms and objections to concrete actions, without venturing to lay a counterresolution on the table.

These two sections of the statement put no obligations upon us whatsoever. We stand on our clearly defined conceptions as they have been expounded in party resolutions and documents, and exemplified in the whole tradition of our movement. We defend these conceptions any time they are attacked, either directly or by implication. The opposition, on the other hand, is obliged, it seems to us, either to reconcile themselves to our "organization methods," or to pile up their criticisms until quantity takes qualitative form in a counterresolution. Sooner or later they will have to do one thing or the other. We can well afford to wait till they make up their minds or become finally convinced one way or another by the further experiences.

The point in the resolution which declares there is no basis for the existence of factional formations in the party ranks at the present time has obvious advantages from the point of view of the party and all those who base themselves on its fundamental interests. Caucus organizations consume a vast amount of time and energy which are unavoidably diverted from the constructive work of the party, at least to a considerable extent. On the other hand, closed caucus organizations, maintained on anything approaching a permanent basis, constitute a standing threat to the unity of the party. This is not a law, of course; there is nothing "inevitable" about it. But the history of the political movement shows that closed permanent factional organizations have oftener led to splits than to eventual reconciliation and the strengthening of party unity.

Having stated as precisely as we could just what the present differences consist of and to what extent they are limited, the statement then goes on to declare that sharp factional struggle is unjustified in the present situation, but provides for an "educational discussion of the existing differences" under the regulation of the NC. Precisely what does this mean? It is neither a "peace agreement," in the sense usually employed in relation to factions which have reconciled their differences, nor a declaration of all-out factional warfare. It is something in between.

We are inclined to regard it as a "truce," which will facilitate collaboration in the constructive work of the party, while clarifying such disputes as clearly exist to serve educational purposes, and awaiting further developments. This is the sense in which we intend to apply it.

We cannot predict what the outcome of the experiment will be. In any case, we believe the party membership will appreciate the effort that has been made by the majority to normalize the internal situation and facilitate concentration on the constructive work of the party, without in any way suppressing, compromising, or glossing over such differences as clearly exist.

Yours fraternally,
J. P. Cannon

PS: Comrade Stein and I have agreed on a certain division of labor for the time being. Since he is fully occupied in the office, I am undertaking to handle the correspondence with you and other comrades on internal questions. Anything you want to write about the internal situation can be addressed to either one of us, as we work together hand in hand. But all such material should be written in separate letters from others dealing with routine organization matters. The latter must be placed in the official file and must sometimes be brought before the Secretariat and the PC. Please make careful note of this in future correspondence.

JPC

THE END OF THE WAR IN EUROPE[20]

May 1, 1945

This May Day speech, given at Webster Hall in New York to an audience of 500, was Cannon's first public address after his release from prison. The other major speaker was Albert Goldman. The text is taken from an unpublished and uncorrected stenographic transcript, slightly abridged.

As our esteemed chairman reminded you, we have been away for a while. It seems, to me at least, like a long time since I have made a speech, and naturally I am a little nervous in getting started. But I hope to overcome that as I go along because all I really intend to do is to continue what I was saying when I was so rudely interrupted.

In essence, it is what we have been saying throughout our entire conscious lives; and what our predecessors, the great pioneers of socialism, have been saying since 1848.

We are approaching the one-hundredth anniversary of the *Communist Manifesto,* the first great document which proclaimed the coming downfall of capitalism and the inevitable victory of the proletariat. Today, ninety-seven years later, it remains our program and our banner. Nothing is clearer in the world today than this: that the failure of the workers to carry out the historic mission imposed upon them by the decline of capitalism does not and cannot bring any relief or prosperity for them but only a continuation of enslavement and devastating wars which in the present period of the death agony of capitalism grow ever more monstrous in devouring mankind.

It is a great satisfaction, I must tell you, to be here with you tonight and to be able to say a few words. But it is a still greater satisfaction just to be present at the meeting on this day of all the days in the year that is most dedicated to the future and to the hopes of a better world. After all, the speeches always have been the least important part of May Day celebrations. The important thing, the inspiring thing, is simply that people come together wherever they may be, in small groups or large, in one country or another, at liberty or at work, in shops or in concentration camps, in jails. [. . .]

As the present war in Europe draws to its agonizing close and with the end of the present war in the Orient not very far away, the victors are meeting in San Francisco to prepare the next war.[21] Even before they have been able to arrange the formal declaration of the finish of the five-and-a-half-year war that has cost tens of millions of human lives, they are meeting, and over the meeting of the victors is the shadow of the next war, which they don't even any longer promise to avoid. They only express hopes that it will not come too soon. The battlefields of Europe and the Orient, the ruined cities, the devastations, the hunger, and the dead, counterposed to the opulent setting of the conference in the San Francisco Opera House seems to me to symbolize the whole present reality. [. . .]

Who are the victors in this terrible devastating war? Who won freedom? The victors, you must understand and never fail to make it clear—the victors in the first place are the Wall Street money sharks. They are the only ones who have won the war, they and their satellite imperialism in Great Britain, which in the course of the war has yielded three-fourths of its position to the Wall Street Moloch and the Stalinist satellites of Moscow.

U.S. imperialism emerges from this war as the master of the world, and it seems to those who cannot see clearly that it is all-powerful. Some of the statesmen at Washington and their representatives in Frisco, and their generals and admirals on the battlefields and the high seas, deceive themselves in the effulgence of these great victories that have been produced as a result of the terrific preponderance of the American economy. They deceive themselves.

I do not think that America is all-powerful. Let us not make that mistake. The modern Rome, the master of the world, whose light-minded statesmen dream and even talk of dominating and exploiting and policing the world for one hundred years, has a cancer at its heart. But today they are the victors.

Now, who are the vanquished in the war as it stands today, up to the present moment? The war and its consequences are by no means concluded. After the formal ending of the hostilities comes the aftermath, and the victors and the vanquished may change places then. But the vanquished as of this moment are only incidentally the rivals of American imperialism—the German imperialists, and the Italian imperialists, and the Japanese. They are only the incidental victims. They will have to sacrifice a great deal. They have to sacrifice some of their apparently all-powerful fascist politicians who have come to such an ignominious end. But fundamentally the vanquished are the people of Europe and of Asia, and, although they don't know it yet, the people of the United States of America.

Out of the imperialist war that lasted nearly six years, the people of the whole world are the victims. And they are the victims not of a mistake of this or that statesman or general and not of this or that bad will of some maniac in power. They are fundamentally the victims of the capitalist system, which is in its death agony, and which is incapable of maintaining peace or prosperity in the world and cannot but continue to plunge the world into one holocaust after another until the masters of the future take control of society and institute a rational system.

I spoke of the present stage of the war because it's not ended yet. After today comes tomorrow, and you may say that we are now facing a new stage in the development of the worldwide struggle which has to settle eventually once and for all whether the world shall be reorganized on a rational basis which will insure human solidarity and peace and further development of mankind or whether it shall plunge from one continual series of devastating wars into the abyss.

Let's take stock at this turning point with the formal ending of hostilities in Europe and the obvious impending end of the war with Japan in the East. And let us look back a minute and see what was thought and what was said by the different people and the different parties when this mad business began. You know what the imperialists said, that the war would be conducted to ensure four freedoms in the world. Democracy, peace, prosperity—that is what the masters of society promised to the people would be the outcome of this crusade with arms in hand.

And the labor lieutenants of American capitalism repeated it after them. Word for word they repeated it after them, became their agents to harness the labor movement to the war program imposed upon the workers in the labor movement. The no-strike pledge tied it in with the government, bound it hand and foot, and justified everything on the ground that there would be an equality of sacrifice between the workers and the imperialists, and that after the war everything would be all right.

What did we say, what did we do? I believe it's very important for every worker who is trying to find his way in the new situation to examine the records of the different parties during this last period. We said from the very beginning: It isn't a war for democracy against fascism; it isn't a war for justice and freedom. That is not true. It is a war of imperialist rivals; it is a war for profits to be coined out of the blood of the people of Europe and Asia, and eventually for the enslavement and degradation of the workers here at home.

That was what the SWP and the Fourth International said from the very first day. And that is the way we conducted ourselves in the one place in this country where we, through our party and our affiliated comrades, were in a position to determine the policy of a trade union, in Minneapolis. At the same time the whole labor bureaucracy of the United States, national, district, and local, capitulated to the imperialist war machine, and became the allies and agents of it in the labor movement.

One group of trade unionists stood up against the war, against the deception, against the betrayal, and our party with them—that was the real meaning of Minneapolis and the meaning of the Minneapolis trial. [. . .] It seemed like an appropriate symbol, as though there was some external power compelling the thing to display dramatically the real essence of the persecution, that we were sentenced to prison on December 8, the very day they were passing the declaration of war in Congress. The very time that they were gearing the war machine for action, eighteen representatives of our party were sentenced to prison in Minneapolis.

That was a magnificently truthful symbol of the fact that the imperialists recognized in our party the authentic voice of opposition to the imperialist war and they thought and sought to silence the voice of our party. But as you know, they didn't succeed in that. They failed most remarkably, and from now on our voice will be heard louder than ever. It will be louder because more people are joining us and adding their voices with those who held true to the cause in the dark days we just passed through.

Now what have they at the end of this long and terrible war?

What have they got to show for all their promises? What can they show, the masters of the world, but ruined cities, mounds of corpses, and millions of starving people? That is the auspices under which American imperialism enters its day of glory as the master of the world. Look what we are standing on. Blood and mud and death and destruction and starvation and oppression and despair, which they are the chief architects of. That is the credential they bring before mankind as warrant of their right to rule the world for one hundred years.

But they have not convinced us of it. We didn't believe them in the first place, and far fewer people can believe them now. I can say that, despite the efforts they made by one means and another to change our minds and improve our morals. They never convinced us of anything. Our truth is stronger than ever today and we are more convinced of it than ever today. We say that a social system which yields such a ghastly harvest as this is not fit to live and cannot long endure, because the people of the world in order to provide the means for their mere existence will be compelled to do away with such a social system.

Imperialist America appears to be all-powerful. That is a dream and a tremendous illusion. The greatest days of American imperialism, as far as stability and strength are concerned, are already behind it. American capitalism grew under the most favorable auspices imaginable for any country of a capitalist order. It began after the American revolution without being cluttered up with all the remnants. It began with a great, almost unlimited continent with incalculable resources of every kind—agricultural, mineral, all conceivable abounding resources over a tremendous territory at its disposal. It began after capitalism in Europe had already reached the point of accumulating surpluses which could be invested in the United States. And American capitalism received a forced growth in its early days through the enormous investment of European capitalism to such an extent that even in 1914 the United States was still a debtor nation, indebted to Europe. [. . .]

Now, in that period, especially from the end of the Civil War up till 1914, American capitalism, confined within the forty-eight states, expanding and developing within its own territory without entanglements in the economy of Europe, and with an almost unlimited domestic market of its own, was expanding at a more rapid rate than any other country. That was the heyday of American capitalism. That was the day when it was so strong and so rich and so secure that it was almost impossible to develop a really serious labor movement in the United States. Opportunities—in comparison, of course, with capitalist Europe—were so great that the labor movement suffered a continual drain. Generation after generation of people found it possible to make their way into a better financial and social position.

The conditions of the American workers, relative to the European, were in the main so good that it was impossible to produce that revolutionary discontent that alone can generate a militant labor movement. The workers did not develop even the class psychology up till the First World War. And the traditional idea of the American worker that at least his children would be able to escape from wage slavery, although it never had by far as great a justification as the illusion, nevertheless had a certain plausibility because of the prosperity in the United States. It robbed the working class movement of its spirit, its will. In Europe, the great majority, almost the entire working class, supported its own parties. The American working class, even to this very day, hasn't developed to a class-conscious position, or launched a party of its own. [. . .]

Since 1914, and ten times more since this present war, American imperialism in expanding its power and its controls over the whole earth, in becoming the exploiter of the world, thereby extends its economic base away from the sure foundation of the forty-eight states united on one continent. [. . .] And every weakness in the economy of world capitalism at any point runs a tremor throughout the foundations of American imperialism because its foundations are on that economy too. Every revolutionary disturbance—and there have been many and will be ten and one hundred times more, one after another in all parts of this agonizing world—will shake the stability of this deceptive Moloch of American capitalism which appears on the surface to be so sure and so powerful. [. . .]

In addition to all that, the modern imperialist master of the world faces its proletarian nemesis at home. One would think sometimes that the capitalists would curse Marx for this terrible thing called the contradictions of the capitalist system. But Marx didn't make it; he only explained it. That the greater they developed their industrial plant in America, the more they developed their productive capacity [. . .] the greater they increased the size of the proletariat in America. The more they condemned that proletariat to permanent existence as a propertyless class, the greater strength it acquired by being massed together in ever-greater concentrations in industry, and the greater power it consequently developed, and the ever-greater certainty that here in the very heart of American imperialism is arising what Marx and Engels called its gravediggers.

The European revolutions—we have seen the beginning of them in Italy. We have seen the starved and beaten and devastated people of Greece show what the revolutionary impulses of the masses are.[22] We saw what the workers of Milan have done in the past week. After more than twenty years of fascist degradation, imprisonment, concentration camps, violence, and death, they rose up as the only power in the country and hung Mussolini by his heels from the side of a gas station. This is a perfect illustration of the real relation between the power of the workers, organized and moving, and the simulacrum of power of the political agents of a dead capitalist system who are in power only because the workers are not organized and moving.

And we don't doubt that the people of Europe will not reconcile themselves to the prospect of starving themselves to death for the sake of the democratic victory in this war. We do not doubt that the example of the Italian workers in the south, and now in the north, will spread through Europe in one place after another and one time after another. Through defeats and setbacks they will learn better and coordinate their forces more firmly together and proceed with the revolution.

The European revolution—I tell you that the capitalist class believes in its danger more than some wiseacres on the fringes of the movement believe in it, the ruling class believes in it and fears it. This European revolution casts a great ominous shadow over the Belshazzar's feast at Frisco. But that is only one shadow. The other is the one that is going to be cast over it tomorrow by the awakening workers of the United States of America, and the returning soldiers of America who are going to be coming back by the millions and asking: What do we get out of it? Where is our victory? Where is our peace?

And are they going to receive their share of the victory? Does anybody believe that this country's rulers are planning and preparing and that they can guarantee, even if they wanted to, the 60 million jobs, and peace now, and an automobile to drive, and a safe and secure existence in which one can raise a family and look forward with confidence to the future? Well, you had better read the newspapers, and particularly the financial pages, and see what the policy of big business is. The policy of big business is a union-busting campaign just as they began after the last war.

They celebrated victory with three cheers for democracy in 1918, and then they began a great open-shop drive and anti-red campaign to smash the labor movement of the United States. That is already indicated as the policy, and the necessary policy, of the masters of American industry who have delayed their equality of sacrifice until after the war.

You see, when they talked about a policy of equality of sacrifice, the labor leaders told the workers in the unions, that means you sacrifice half and they sacrifice half. They put that formulation over on the workers for a long time. But the bosses didn't mean that at all. They meant—to the workers—you sacrifice half now, and after the war will come the other half. No one can have the slightest doubt that American industry, which has expanded to such a great stage of development, cannot continue to operate on such a scale when the production of war machines and munitions is greatly reduced or eliminated.

What will the factories work at? Certainly not to supply markets which have been dried up and further devastated by the terrible destruction of the war. Certainly not the machines to send to devastated Europe, because Europe cannot pay. And they don't want to give them away to the victims of our victory.

No, the whole reality that anyone looking at the obvious economic facts knows, and every financial writer in the country is fully aware of, and every industrialist for that matter, and everybody except Murray and Hillman and Green knows, is that there must be a tremendous reduction in the productive activity of American industry. With that will be a tremendous unemployment of the workers, along with wage cuts, which always accompany a depression and competition among the workers. And then, for good measure, in order to show the workers how much they appreciate the sacrifices they have made so far in agreeing to the wage freeze [. . .] prices will really begin to spiral upward in the inevitable inflation which must ensue from this tremendous debt of 250 to 300 billion dollars.

And then there will be reactionary legislation against progressive tendencies in the [. . .] labor movement and then persecution of militant labor leaders and organizations.

We said and repeated many times that the persecution of the

Socialist Workers Party was only the beginning, the first experimental step, and that is one reason perhaps why it was not more violent. There will be others on a wholesale scale. Look at the case of De Lorenzo the other day.[23] At the moment the war is approaching an end, a man past the draft age, with several children, who was a trade union official and who would have been rated as exempt on three grounds—age, family, and indispensability— [. . .] suddenly becomes a member of the U.S. army, under the draft. Now that is a symbol of the will of the dominant powers in Washington to revenge themselves on every tendency in the labor movement. Not only communists, such as we are, but every progressive and militant and honest element in the leadership of the trade unions must expect persecution. And the rank and file of the American labor movement, resisting the attempt to destroy their unions, will have to get used to the specter of fascist gangs, recruited from the scum of society and financed by big business to break up the workers' organizations.

That is what the American imperialists have got cooked up as the fruits of victory for the American proletariat. But [. . .] I believe one can safely say without the slightest fear of exaggeration that the workers and soldiers in the great mass have no faith any longer in the rosy promises which were made to them and which were never intended to be and never could be fulfilled. The workers wherever they have had a chance have broken through the chains, the no-strike pledge, to defend their unions. [. . .]

What does the great mass of the soldiers really think? There is no doubt that they were against Hitler. There is no doubt about it. In the great mass they were convinced that the thing had to be fought through. They were deceived and betrayed, but not completely deceived because they didn't believe in the promises of benefits for themselves. We were told by people returning from [the war] that in the Orient the most popular slogan of the soldiers was, "The Golden Gate in '48; the Breadline in '49." That is what they are expecting to have to come back to, and that is their way of saying that they have no faith whatever in all the promises that have been made to them.

I believe that it is reasonable for us to assume that the workers, and the returning soldiers, and the young generation who have been so cruelly deceived and betrayed by all those to whom they looked for intellectual guidance in the dark period are going to revolt against all those people, all those ideological influences, and all those parties [. . .] and look around to see if there aren't some people, some party that stood up courageously and honestly and told them the truth. I believe that the time is not far off when [we will see] a great movement in that direction and I do not see anywhere they can look except toward the Socialist Workers Party.

I think we can count on the development of the class struggle in the United States, in the situation which I have outlined here, on a colossal scale and see it even as near at hand. And in this struggle which the workers cannot avoid there will be forced upon them, there will come an awakening of the workers' class consciousness and a beginning of an understanding for the first time of their position in society as a class and the necessity of acting as a class. They will have to break with this traditional leadership which is cowardly and corrupt and tied to the machine of the master. [. . .]

And they will be compelled by all the logic of the struggle to look toward independence in politics, an independent labor party, and toward revolutionary advances on every front in a situation in which the revolutionary party which we represent will get its hearing and will acquire the commanding influence over the great masses of workers.

Now, we see that perspective not as a wish and not as an imaginary one, but we see it as flowing from the whole logic of the necessary development and that is why we face the future with confidence, and that is why we say that revolution is on the agenda in the United States of America as in all the other places of the world. This is the revolutionary epoch and we, as the heralds of the revolution, have every right to confidence in the future. Power will decide it. The two greatest powers in the world today face each other on the continent of North America, in the United States of America which, as Trotsky once expressed it, is the foundry where the fate of mankind will be forged. Two powers face each other: one, the power of American imperialism, the present master of the world, and the other is a still greater, although not yet conscious power, the American proletariat, whose power is greater than that of American imperialism and greater than that of any force in the world, once it becomes conscious of its own social position and potentiality. [. . .]

We know that the [workers of the world] will have setbacks and defeats. But just as the imperialists of the United States have been and are the greatest prop and support of capitalism in

Europe and on a world scale, so the United States proletariat, that other American power, that class which has not known defeat, which is young and confident and full of unbounded energy and initiative, the American working class, with its unlimited powers and courage and hope, will come to the aid of the foreign proletariat and merge its struggle with them. And they will attack this monster of American imperialism in its inner citadel. [. . .] That is the best way we can signify our devotion to the world-conquering idea of internationalism on this May Day. [. . .]

The crime of the Stalinists today is fundamentally that instead of coordinating themselves with the progressive movement of the workers to free themselves, they act as agents of imperialism in the labor movement of the world. The crime of Stalinism is the crime of betraying the proletariat to world imperialism. And that is why it is necessary to understand that against Stalinism we have got to counterpose another and different kind of leadership for the struggle against the rotten leadership and the power of the outlived social system of capitalism.

All the defeats of socialism, all of them, have been due solely to the lack of leadership. The task upon which the future of humanity depends is to create the leadership for the revolutionary struggle. That means, in one word, to create the revolutionary party. The workers, by their social position in society, by their numbers, are the greatest power in society. All the workers need and all they have ever needed since 1914 is to believe in themselves, to understand their power, and an honest party to lead them. And from that we must say the task of all tasks is to build the party in America and on a world scale and thus the whole problem of our epoch, of all the hopes and prospects of humanity, becomes concentrated in a single formula.

To the robber League of Nations which they set up after the last world war, Lenin and Trotsky counterposed the Third International, the Comintern. To this new robber League of Nations which they are contriving at San Francisco now, we, the modern communists, the heirs of Lenin and Trotsky, counterpose the Fourth International. And to the imperialist rulers here at home in America we counterpose the Socialist Workers Party.

We are confident that the European workers and the colonial people will do their part in this grandiose world struggle against the brigands of United States imperialism. [. . .] We must undertake to do our part here at home. We mustn't ask the workers of Europe and the colonies to make it for us. Let us do our share, and in view of the more favorable position in which we have been situated, let us do a little more than our share.

Whatever happens abroad in the immediate future, whatever defeats and setbacks the revolutionary workers may encounter in their struggle against such tremendous difficulties, we intend to fight it out in the United States. This struggle, the issue of our whole epoch, the issue of fascism or communism, will never be settled in the world until it is settled here in America. And here it depends on the party.

Alone as individuals we are nothing. But with the party and through the party we are everything. And therefore join the party, build the party, and write on the banner of the party once again what Marx and Engels wrote in the first *Communist Manifesto* ninety-seven years ago. [. . .] They said the downfall of the bourgeoisie and the victory of the proletariat are equally inevitable. In the face of the present-day triumph of imperialism, we repeat those words: the downfall of capitalism and the victory of the proletariat are inevitable. Equally so, and in spite of everything we stand by that conviction and we are ready to live and die by it. And today, just as our great masters and leaders of ninety-seven years ago, we say let us advise the workers of America and of the whole world to inscribe on their fighting banner the old slogan: "You have nothing but your chains to lose, and a world to gain. Workers of the world unite!"

WRITING FOR THE PARTY PRESS

May 1945

This previously unpublished letter was to Theodore Kovalesky, who at the time wrote a weekly column for The Militant *called "Diary of a Steel Worker."*

Dear Comrade Kovalesky:

The letter you wrote to the editors about your future work was considered, and I was requested to answer it.

The plan you project of devoting more time to writing, and of broadening its scope, is right in line with our idea of what the paper needs most in the next period.

In this connection I call your attention to the article of Martin on the press in the last number of the *Party Builder*.[24] These ideas were incorporated in the discussion and conclusions of the recent session of the "Militant Institute," which is reported in this week's paper and will be elaborated in the forthcoming number of the *Party Builder*. When you notice that we contemplate republication of old socialist novels, you can see how eagerly we would grasp, and how much we would appreciate, original fiction from one of our own people.

I don't think you should worry about artificially orienting yourself toward "the profundities of precision politics." Different people have different natural inclinations and talents. It takes a combination of all of them to make a party which really represents the workers, knows how to appeal to them from all sides in their various stages of political development, and thereby knows how to lead them. Similarly, it takes a great many different kinds of writing to make a really popular political paper and one which is at the same time politically clear and strong.

The unique value of your writing, as I see it, derives from the fact that you supply a quality of propaganda, and a most important one, which is too frequently lacking in the "highly politicalized" writing. Both these qualities, and one might say, all nuances in between, are necessary to make up the rounded and balanced eight-page *Militant* which we envisage.

I think you should let your own writing impulses have their way. Just write what you feel like writing and let the "technical problems"—publication, etc.—take care of themselves; more precisely, let the party worry about them. I think you have an open field in the eight-page *Militant* for anything you write, including your novel in serial form. Possible later publication in book form must be thought of in connection with our perspective of an expanding movement. If we are right in this perspective—and all signs seem to bear it out—then it implies also an expansion of the capacities of our own publishing house.

At the same time, a substantial growth of our party in membership and influence will make any kind of a book, fictional or otherwise, which appeals to our members and sympathizers, a more attractive business proposition to commercial publishers. Once they see in our movement a potential "market" for certain types of books, some of the publishing houses which are interested in making money—and I believe this includes a considerable section of these people—will be inclined to cater to this market. This was the case in the heyday of the Socialist Party. All the old socialist novels were published by commercial houses who relied for their main sale on the people influenced by the ideas of socialism. The same thing held true with the development of the Communist Party into a rather formidable movement. Not a small number of books published in the last ten years or so have counted on the favorable reception they were calculated to receive from the CP and its sympathizers.

If we are looking in the right direction with regard to the perspectives of our movement—when we look forward and not backward—then a great many problems which seem insuperable at the present moment, with the given relation of forces, will almost automatically solve themselves.

We all (the Minneapolis group) read your column at Sandstone and we all appreciated it. This was a rather severe test for you as a new contributor. We are all workers who know from our own experiences and evolution, and our experience in the mass movement, what kind of writing appeals to the rebel worker who is just awakening to political consciousness. We are also, more or less, "precision politicians" who have a sharp eye for the political line in any piece of writing. On both counts we thought your pieces were OK.

Yours fraternally,
James P. Cannon

PS: I was greatly interested in your statement that you had spent two and a half years in the Workers Party. As I understood it, you had been there only a short time. I intend to devote a good deal of attention to this question in connection with the struggle we are going to open up against the debilitating tendencies of conciliationism with the Shachtmanites which have begun to be articulated in our ranks. I would be very interested to know just how you happened to get into the WP, what were the factors which estranged you from it, and what induced you to join the SWP. Also what conclusions you draw from that experience.

Laura Gray

ON BLOCS IN THE TRADE UNIONS[25]

May 12, 1945

These remarks were made in the discussion following the report on union activity at a plenum of the SWP National Committee held in New York City, May 12-14, 1945. The text is from a previously unpublished and uncorrected stenogram.

I have grown accustomed the last year or two to the habit that Comrade Goldman has learned to indulge. Whenever he begins to speak, either in the plenum, or the Political Committee, or in a discussion, I almost feel that he begins by flattering my intelligence with some such remark as he made here in the beginning of his speech—that this proposal of his is so simple, so ABCish, he wouldn't have to explain it to anybody if they weren't so stupid that they can't think for themselves. Now I don't resent that so much personally because I have gotten accustomed to it. But I resent that grandfather approach to the leaders of the party. And I venture the prediction that if Goldman learns nothing else in the course of the discussion which will unfold and deepen, he will learn better than that.

I am going to speak only on the one question of bloc with the Shachtmanites, although there are many other parts of the trade union question that I have a deep interest in and perhaps I can speak later on that.

Now, Comrade Goldman says this proposal of his, that we shall make a formal approach to the Shachtmanite party with a proposal for a bloc all up and down in the trade union field, that is so simple, he says, and so ABCish, that we shouldn't even have to discuss it. The whole history of Bolshevism proves it, etc. If it is so simple, why did Goldman wait five years to propose it to us?

We have been confronting each other in the trade union movement and everywhere else as opponent parties for five years, and almost on the fifth anniversary of the split, he reminds himself that he has been tail-ending for almost five years on this very simple question.

Now, it is not so simple. Under certain conditions, it would be correct, according to the experiences of our history, and under other conditions it would not be correct. The motivation for such a proposal must be primarily political. And that is demonstrated by the fact that in the five years of our struggle with the Shachtmanites, Goldman never even thought of proposing to us a trade union bloc with them on a formal basis, until he conceived the idea that we should make a political unity with them in one party. So that shows that the motivation is political primarily. If you eliminate the political consideration and say it is a simple ABC question from a trade union tactical point of view, then we must say that Goldman has been a long time in discovering it.

Now we are approaching the trade union movement from this point of view: that we want to develop the militancy of the workers in struggle against the bureaucracy and all opportunist and petty-bourgeois tendencies in the labor movement, and to build our party in the process. That is a simple ABC statement of Bolshevik aims in the trade unions.

He is quite right when he says that we cannot present ultimatums to the workers. "Here we are—come to us or suffer the consequences." That is correct. The thing is to find a road to the workers, who are going to make the revolutionary trade union movement and whose best cadres will become the cadres of our party. Find a road to those potentially revolutionary workers of the future. And the rival political parties and groups and cliques haven't got these workers, with the exception of the Stalinists, and they can't help us much in getting them.

We have had an extensive experience with all kinds and all methods of blocs with other tendencies, groups, and parties. I often wonder what Goldman means when he talks about the history of Bolshevism that is supposed to teach us everything. I know the history of our movement in the United States, which I consider an integral and one of the richest parts of the history of Bolshevism, and I draw a good many conclusions from the experiences of our history which go back to 1919. That is quite a while—twenty-six years.

We made just such a bloc as he proposes with the Shachtmanites on a national scale with another political group once, so we are not scared of the proposition as in itself undebatable. We made a bloc with the AWP [American Workers Party] prior to the fusion. And it encompassed not only trade union work. It began really in a defense organization. Not just a casual participation, but a formal agreement with the Musteites that they, together with us and some other people, would set up a committee for the defense of a comrade named Bellussi, who was to be deported, and that we should try to build this into a permanent defense organization, the Non-Partisan Labor Defense. It was a real bloc, real collaboration in defense work.[26]

We formed a propaganda bloc with them whereby we held joint public meetings on issues of the day. For example, in Paterson, New Jersey, we held a joint meeting after the strike of the textile workers on the lessons of the Paterson strike in which Muste and I both spoke, under the joint auspices of the AWP and the CLA. And by prior agreement, we said virtually the same thing, taking different sides of the same subject. We had an agreement with them for cooperation, a real bloc, in unemployed work and in trade union activity wherever we had common fractions. That bloc had this distinguishing feature to it: that it was a bloc between friendly parties who were looking toward unification into a single organization. And I believe that from the profitable results of that experience, if we ever in the future reach the point of friendliness and a tendency toward coalescence with another political party, we will put such a proposal on the table of the National Committee and it will not be rejected. The essence of that bloc was cooperation. The element of rivalry between competing organizations was reduced almost to zero. That was the consideration.

Now we had other blocs in our Bolshevik history, episodic blocs on single, concrete issues, with rival parties and other political groups. We had some in the past; we have some now; and will have in the future. We had a bloc with the Lovestoneites as far back as 1933. We had a tacit bloc, although not a formal one, with the Lovestoneites for quite a while in the UAW against the Stalinists when they were a part of the Martin movement.[27] We had a bloc with the Lovestoneites against the Stalinists on numerous occasions and we had a bloc with the Stalinists against a gang of fakers in the New York food-workers' union as late as 1940. We had a bloc with Lundeberg and the syndicalists and IWW elements in the maritime unions against the Stalinists.

Just recently we made a decision in the Political Committee to send some people into a general anti-Stalinist bloc in the UAW in New York, which consists of some Shachtmanites and other anti-Stalinists and some UAW officials who, as far as I know, don't have any strong political ideology but want to keep their jobs. As a matter of course we said, "Sure, go and join that bloc and see what we can get out of it. See what the situation is. We don't have to stay there." The essence of these blocs is that they were episodic agreements in single concrete actions or a series of concrete actions. They were not designed to lead to political unity, and the element of political rivalry between us and the other political groups was not in the least moderated.

From the different kind of blocs referred to in our experience I think you can conclude that as far as our understanding of the question has gone, that the nature of the bloc, not the bloc itself, is determined in each case primarily by political considerations. The bloc with the Musteites was one sort of bloc; these others I have mentioned here, a different kind; and the reason they were different is because the considerations of a political nature were different in the other cases.

Now Comrade Goldman's motion proposes to proceed to a bloc on the order of the first one I mentioned—the bloc with the Musteites—all up and down the line, a formal agreement between the National Committees of the two parties. And he proposes that we proceed to this action in the trade union movement before the political premises of such a bloc—that is, the aim and trend toward unification of the parties—has been established or has been accepted by our party. Now that, I think, is not quite a correct method for Bolsheviks who are thinking, thinking, thinking, all the time.

One could say that represents an attempt to maneuver the party into a political direction which it has not yet decided to take, by implication. And I don't think that is the correct way for us to organize a trade union action, and I don't think it is the right way to educate the party. If I were in his position I would put the emphasis on a political resolution, to move toward unification with the Shactmanites, and argue that out in the party first, and then tell them all the practical conclusions that would flow from it. But I don't think I would try to induce the party to adopt the practical conclusions before they have adopted the political premise, and, above all, say it is an ABC question.

First it is necessary, in my opinion, in order to accept Comrade

Goldman's motion, I think it is first necessary to convince the party that it must change its attitude toward the WP as a venomous enemy of the SWP. Until that is accepted—and I don't mean to predict that it will be accepted—the proposal of Comrade Goldman, which presupposes in my opinion a change in attitude, is somewhat out of order. The discussion takes place upside down in a practical conference called to discuss trade union work, when it should take place in the political realm before the party as a whole. It is not in the first instance a trade union question. In the first instance it is a political and a politically motivated proposition.

Now, if we maintain our present attitude toward the WP, not to mention their present attitude toward us, we still have the problem of the Shachtmanites in concrete local cases—that is true. Do we make a bloc with them in a given local union where they have members and we have members, or do we reject it, "putting on the robes of priestly purity"? Well, I haven't kept track of what has been done in the recent period locally. I am waiting with great interest to hear the reports more adequately. But I assume that our comrades who, if they have not graduated from the higher grades, have at least a firm grasp on the ABCs—I assume that they make a bloc or reject a bloc with the Shachtmanites in each case in accordance with the circumstances. That they would consider the National Committee, if it sent out blanket instructions, "Don't talk to the Shactmanites in the trade unions" . . . that would be wrong.

And if the National Committee did that, they would probably be criticized by the right-thinking members of the party. Or if they sent down an instruction that in every case the comrades should make a bloc with the Shachtmanites in their trade union work, I believe that would be equally wrong. I am pretty sure that what you have been doing in your practical work, with the full agreement of the committee, is that you have determined your course toward them in each case according to the circumstances. One of the circumstances is the people themselves; what kind of people are they? Are they useful to you or not? Another circumstance is the relation of forces; have they got enough people to make a dent in the situation so that you can't operate without them? Then you would be very foolish not to penetrate into any movement in which they have influence. The whole situation as it exists concretely in each case, I believe, will determine your tactics.

You see, what is most terrifying about this motion of Goldman's is that it is an all up-and-down bloc and it is permanent. I wouldn't be so much afraid of the party making an error and ordering it to go into a general bloc with the Shachtmanites, but I wouldn't want to have a rider on it saying that you can never get out of that bloc, because that would be a bad state. I imagine that in your local work you have had the experience in more than one case of trying a bloc with the Shachtmanites, then trying to get loose from it, then trying another arrangement, and adapting your situation as best you could. But if we make a bloc on a national scale it wouldn't help you very much.

In my opinion we don't have—I am speaking now of the present relations between us and the Shachtmanites and our present mutual regard for each other's party—we don't have and cannot have a uniform, inflexible rule. We have to decide each case separately, and here I believe the reports of the comrades at the plenum on past experiences in concrete cases will be very illuminating for the further discussion of the question. I will not anticipate what the reports of these experiences with these hell-roaring Shachtmanites have been, but I think that we old-timers can anticipate most of them because we know the Shachtmanites. And in looking forward to possible future relations with them in the trade union movement we should be clear on two points, and I hope that this will not be seriously disputed. The first point is the character of the Shachtman organization as a typical petty-bourgeois intellectualist tendency in the labor movement. The second point is the history of this group on the trade union question and in trade union work.

Now we have those things to sort of guide us in estimating future possibilities and I don't at all discard changes here and there in individual members or groups of the Shachtmanites. I am not one of those who believes I am the only one able to learn. But it is a question of the tendency as a whole that I am speaking of. When we talk about history, remember that eleven—almost twelve—years of the history of Bolshevism in America were spent in legal cohabitation between us and the hard central core of the Shachtman group. Eleven years in one organization, and then for five years we have been watching them as opponents outside of our party, and occasionally we have been running into them here and there for these five years. So we certainly ought to know them. If we don't know them by now, then we are almost as stupid as Goldman takes us to be. And because we know them, we know how to deal with them.

Now I am confining myself to the trade union side of the discussion. I hope to have a few words to say on the other, more fundamental, aspects of the question in the course of the party discussion. But here it is the trade union question. In the first eleven years of our dealings with the Shachtmanites—I mean those leaders of the WP who evolved and crystallized as a more or less common tendency, petty-bourgeois and intellectualist in character—we only had two conflicts with them on the trade union question that I recall. I think Stein can bear me out. Well, you might conclude from that, only two conflicts in eleven years; how did that happen? It happened this way, that in the first five years we didn't have any conflicts because Shachtman-Carter-Abern-Glotzer kept their hands off the trade union policy of the party.

In 1933, in the heat of the faction fight, losing themselves for a moment in the intensity of the faction fight, and taking hold of issues that they should never have touched, they decided to challenge us on the trade union question. And there, in that very first demonstration of independence, you may say, they revealed the whole concept they have of the trade union movement, of their irresponsible and intellectualist approach. It is a very interesting story, but time does not permit me to go into detail. I will telescope it as much as possible. In 1933, after we had been bottled up in New York for five years, the situation in the labor movement opened up a little and a progressive labor conference was organized in Gillespie, Illinois, under the sponsorship of the Progressive Miners, in which we had a party member.

This was at that time a quite promising movement, independent of the UMW. As so often happens with progressive unions which get either expelled or split away from a parent body, they began to develop dual-union tendencies and they issued a call for a new federation of labor.[28] We were of the opinion that this was a big mistake, that both they and the other friendly groups they might enlist would only further intensify their isolation from the AFL, which was the most important union in that day. We strongly counseled against it and I wrote Allard to that effect. He wrote back that if I would come out there he could arrange for me to speak at this conference and he would like for me to do so because the. . . .

Naturally, Glotzer couldn't go and, to make a long story short, I did get down there and got a chance to speak before the trade union conference consisting exclusively of trade union delegates, and I was represented merely as a "trade unionist from New York," representing some progressive trade unionists in New York. I made a speech. In general we considered it a political success. Allard was satisfied. And just the very fact that a representative of the isolated Trotskyists had a chance to speak to a few hundred trade unionists in convention, for the first time in the five years since our expulsion, was a great source of satisfaction to us. Well, they made a big case of me, that I had practically betrayed the banner of the CLA because I had spoken before this group as a trade unionist and not as the national secretary of the CLA. I "hid the face of the party." . . . until Trotsky intervened very vigorously with a letter he wrote which became our guide for trade union tactics in many respects thereafter, about the necessity of penetrating into the mass movement by such means as we can and not standing on political formalities.[29]

After that we had no more conflicts with Shachtman, Burnham, Abern, or Glotzer or Carter—for the simple reason that after that single experience they left the trade union question severely alone. That, so to speak, was our department. Everything that we proposed was accepted by them, and I might also say that almost everything that was done in that field was done by us. Up until the auto crisis of 1939.[30] I don't know if I ought to mention that or not in the presence of so many auto workers, but here again this group permitted itself to undertake to lay down the line, not only politically, but of procedure and practical application of it in the unions, and you know what the result of that auto crisis was. Most of you who were in the party at that time remember it well, and those who weren't should study George Clarke's article called "The Auto Crisis," which unfortunately up to this present time has not been printed as part of the permanent record of our fight with the petty-bourgeois opposition before the split. They showed there, as they showed in the previous dispute with us and in all their independent work since, that complete lack of realism, that complete lack of feel of a bona fide workers' organization and how to deal with it.

I believe that we can profit by a study of past experiences with the attempts to form permanent blocs of rival political parties and groups. I want some examples from history on that. You can't find it in our history since 1919. Such things existed only once—that was with the AWP in the period precedent to the fusion. That is the only time I know. Every attempt, every attempt to form a working permanent basis of cooperation of rival political parties since 1919 has met with complete failure in every case. In defense work it was tried; in the Trade Union Educational League it was attempted. Nothing ever came out of it. Nothing ever came of it because the partisan attitude of the rival parties in every case was too strong to enable a long-lasting permanent cooperation in any field of work—only isolated episodic instances and they have not been too frequent in the history of our movement.

What is the cause of it? Because we never understood the ABC of the united front? Not at all. We understood quite a bit about the united front. [. . .] And we don't understand it at all as a snuggling up to political enemies. That is not the united front. That is illegitimate cohabitation that disregards the conflict of temperaments. Every once in a while one runs across a recurrence of this pious hope that somewhere, sometime, there could be a getting-together for some kind of action in which no party would seek advantage. Do you know where I saw that last? I saw it in the testimony of the four comrades who were censured for forming a clarification bloc with the Shachtmanites.[31] But the thing that hit me in the eye when I read that testimony of the trial committee was the statement of one of our comrades, who since left the party I believe, and I think she did right—that they [did not see the need to win an advantage for one party or the other.] But the Shachtmanites were trying to get party advantage out of it. Well, that always happens.

It is a peculiar thing, the theory that you shouldn't seek party advantage at the expense of your opponent. That is a Menshevik concept, but they never live up to it. Because they are always too narrow. The revolutionists take into consideration [how] the revolutionary party will gain; whereas the Menshevik parties and groups of all types think first and primarily of themselves, and they are always the most narrow. But we don't ever repeat that hypocritical formula about not seeking party advantage. We are seeking party advantage all the time, and when I say party—in order to make myself perfectly clear—I mean the Socialist Workers Party.

We aim to build the Socialist Workers Party in struggle against other parties. Against other parties who are our rivals in the labor movement. And only to the extent that we build our party and gain the upper hand over the others, only to that extent—and here is where you come back to the trade union question—can you really build a left wing in the labor movement with a stable direction. Without the leadership of the Trotskyist party you cannot count on a revolutionary left wing. The party must be the core of it and the party must lead it, not in partnership with opponents but. . . .

Our fundamental method in the unions is to get new workers into motion. That is our fundamental method and aim: to get new, awakening workers who are in revolt against the status quo on various practical questions of the day, and to develop these militants around the SWP fractions. That is what we are working in the trade union movement for. And as for the rival political groups—and I don't mean only the Shachtmanites; I mean the Stalinists and the Social Democrats and the trade union bureaucrats and the Oehlerites who you will always have under one name or another up to the moment of the revolution—I want the party to understand that these opponent political and ideological currents, whether formally organized into parties or in loose groups or as individuals bound together by a common ideology, as the labor fakers are, they are not our helper. And they are not going to help us revolutionize the trade union movement. They are rivals and obstacles in the way of our objective. And our tactics toward them have to be decided first of all from that fundamental consideration. I wouldn't give two cents for the future of this party if it adopted any different attitude toward rival political currents. Nothing will happen to you except that you will be [knocked down] and kicked aside.

And our attitude toward all other groups—I don't care what you call them—has to be decided in each case concretely. [. . .] Our relations toward these rival political parties is to maneuver and struggle against them. On that basis I don't see any possible ground for our party to accept the motion of Goldman for a formal permanent nationwide bloc with the Shachtmanites on the trade union question because I don't think they are our political brothers. They are our political opponents. And if one thinks they are practically the same thing as Trotskyists, only a little cheaper, and that we should be in the same party, well, let us discuss that. In no case can we adopt this.

STOP THE ATTACKS ON NIGERIAN WORKERS![32]

July 17, 1945

The following telegram was sent to the British colonial secretary in London with a copy to the British governor in Nigeria. The text is from Cannon's files.

The Socialist Workers Party has received word of arrests of Nigerian Trades Union Congress leaders, suppression of Nigerian newspapers, and threat of banishment of Azikiwe, newspaper editor. We protest this trampling of civil liberties in these dictatorial actions against Nigerian strikers and their supporters. We are mobilizing American labor public opinion to demand democratic rights for Nigerian labor.

James P. Cannon
National Secretary
Socialist Workers Party
116 University Place
New York

ON "UNITY WITH THE SHACHTMANITES"

July 25, 1945

The following speech was made to a New York membership meeting of the SWP. The text is taken from SWP Internal Bulletin, *vol. VII, no. 7, August 1945.*

1. The Evolution of Goldman's Policy

For the past year and a half we have been witnessing an attempt on the part of Comrade Goldman to bring about a fundamental change in party policy by the step-at-a-time method. Without clearly stating his objective at any time—and perhaps without even formulating it in his own mind—he had been trying to lead the party to a complete reversal of an established position by "stages." At the Fifteenth Anniversary Plenum, a year and a half ago, Goldman gave his first faint indication of a conciliatory attitude toward the Shachtmanites, and began to express doubts about the Bolshevik system of organization and its alleged tendency to degenerate into Stalinism. The plenum, taken by surprise by such an untimely reminiscence of the past, showed no sympathy for this strange and alien note in our discussion.

About a year ago, at the time of the famous "censure of the four," we noted that Goldman's violent objections contained a political undercurrent of the same type. We know that various comrades objected to the censure. Some thought it was too severe an action in view of the fact that rank-and-file comrades were involved. Others were of the opinion that the action was tactically inadvisable. We all recognized that differences of opinion on these points were quite legitimate. But Goldman's contribution to the discussion bore an entirely different character. He tried to justify indiscriminate fraternization and even collaboration with Shachtmanites, without the approval of the party and behind the back of the party, as a perfectly normal procedure. The party leadership correctly rejected and condemned Goldman's argumentation as a manifestation of conciliationism toward the petty-bourgeois opposition. The [November 1944] convention endorsed this point of view.

The minority at the convention, I am told, violently objected to this imputation. But later developments have shown how correct it was.

At the May plenum of the National Committee Goldman took a further step along the same path—again on a small "tactical" proposal. He proposed that we approach the Workers Party for the construction of a permanent national bloc for trade union work. As you know, the plenum rejected this proposal on the ground that it presupposed a change in our political attitude toward the Shachtmanites, a change which the party had not yet authorized. The plenum refused to adopt the tactical implications of a line before debating and settling the question of the line itself.

A few weeks ago we had another small tactical proposal from Goldman. This was his motion that we enter into an election agreement with the Shachtmanites in New York by agreeing to withdraw one of our candidates in exchange for a withdrawal of one of theirs, or something of that sort. As you know, the Political Committee rejected this proposal too. We rejected all "nibbles" at the question of changing our attitude toward the Shachtmanites as long as we had no proposal to change it fundamentally. The attempts to introduce a fundamental change of line in any question in stages by small tactical steps is the classic method of opportunism. Bolsheviks first discuss and decide *the fundamental line* in every important question and *then* discuss its tactical application.

2. Two Concrete New Developments

We now have two concrete new developments.

The first is a motion by Goldman and Morrow that we approach the Shachtmanites with an offer to readmit them into the party on the 1939-40 terms and that the Political Committee appoint a committee to begin negotiations with them on this basis.[33] Parenthetically, I might remark that the proposal for the Political Committee to appoint a committee to begin negotiations for the carrying out of a line not yet authorized by the party shows a conception of party organization functioning that is somewhat strange to us. The party convention condemned "conciliationism" with the Workers Party. The PC has a full right to propose a change of this attitude but has no right to introduce such a change and take practical steps to implement it on its own authority. These "fine" points of organization procedure, these "formalities" which are such an essential part of our conception of party organization, don't weigh very much in Comrade Goldman's mind.

The Political Committee procedure was a quite different and far more correct one. Its decision was to refer the matter to the next plenum of the National Committee and in the meantime to indicate what its recommendations would be for the consideration of the plenum. I have been appointed by the Political Committee to explain its point of view here to you tonight.

The discussion in the Political Committee on this motion brought out some developments of the political activities of Comrades Goldman and Morrow which are pertinent to the question under discussion and will be of interest to you.

Prior to the last plenum we heard numerous rumors of repeated conferences of Goldman with Shachtman. When questioned about it in the Political Committee prior to the plenum, he blandly informed us that he had had numerous meetings with Shachtman and had discussed the question of unity, etc., with him. Needless to say, these meetings with leaders of an opponent party had taken place without the prior knowledge or authorization of the Political Committee. When the latest proposal was under consideration in the Political Committee meeting of July 12 we again made inquiries as to whether other meetings with the leaders of the Shachtmanites had taken place in the meantime. Here are some extracts from the minutes of the Political Committee of July 12:

Question by *Stein* of *Goldman*: Did you have any negotiations with the WP or any of its members on this?

Answer by *Goldman*: I had no negotiations with anybody.

Question by *Stein*: Did you have any talks with them on their attitude to this?

Answer by *Goldman*: I had many talks with them.

Question by *Stein*: What was their attitude? Whom did you talk with?

Answer by *Goldman*: They refused to commit themselves. Shachtman, Carter, Gates [Albert Glotzer], Johnson [C. L. R. James], Erber—that is all I can remember.

Question by *Stein*: You say they refused to commit themselves?

Answer by *Goldman:* They refused to commit themselves.

Question by *Stein*: Would you like to give us a report of the talks you had, exactly what transpired?

Answer by *Goldman*: With all of them I urged them to reenter the party and all of them said that they do not think that with Cannon and the Cannonites in the party that they should. However, if there is any move on our part, they will have to consider it, discuss it, and take some attitude. They admit that their attitude to Cannon should not be an objection to unity, and therefore they are willing to discuss the question. That is the essence, but they will not commit themselves.

Question by *Stein*: I would like to ask Morrow the same questions: whether he had any discussions with members of the Workers Party along these lines?

Answer by *Morrow*: I have run into a few of their rank-and-filers. Those are the only ones I have asked how they feel about coming back. I would say the general sentiment is rather negative among those I talked to.

Question by *Stein*: Whom did you talk to?

Answer by *Morrow*: I will be hanged if I can even remember their old party names. Some of the younger people who left. Most of them were in the Yipsels.

Question by *Cannon*: You had no talks with any of the leaders of the Workers Party?

Answer by *Morrow*: Sure, I had talks.

Question by *Cannon*: Give us a list of their names.

Answer by *Morrow*: Surely; Coolidge [E. R. McKinney], Gates [Glotzer], Shachtman.

The second new development is the announcement of the minority that they have formed a closed faction to conduct "an organized struggle" in the party. Thus the "truce" is broken and in its place we have a declaration of war. Worst of all, the caucus meeting to organize the faction was held at the same hour that the New York party local had called a mobilization of party members to gather signatures on the nominating petitions of our candidates in the New York election, and in conflict with this party mobilization. Thus the new faction is tainted at its very origin by an antiparty action.

What are the "war aims" of the announced faction? They are clearly set forth in the "call" which they have circulated as a sort of factional manifesto. The war aims of the faction as set forth in this "call" are: (1) Unity with the Shachtmanites and (2) fight the "Stalinist" regime in the Socialist Workers Party. Say what you will about this platform, no one can say it is a new one. We have heard it before. It is the old familiar pattern. Throughout our history every opportunist political tendency has invariably coupled its political proposals with an indictment of the party regime and organizational methods, which have invariably been characterized as "Stalinist."

3. The Documented Record of the Struggle

Both of these questions and the struggles around them have a history and fortunately for the younger members of the party it is a *written history—written* and *documented* in the published books which record all stages of the historic struggle of 1939-40 against the petty-bourgeois opposition led at that time by Burnham, Shachtman, and Abern—namely, *In Defense of Marxism* and *The Struggle for a Proletarian Party*. The documents of the 1939-40 fight are a part of the rich political capital of the party.

These documents recapitulate the whole forty-year struggle between Bolshevism and Menshevism. These documents must be studied by all the young members of the party who did not have the opportunity to participate in this struggle and who wish to prepare themselves properly for an understanding of the fundamental issues in the present discussion. The attitude of a party member toward the history of his own party is one of the surest signs of his seriousness, or his lack of it. We learn from our own experiences as well as from the experiences of others, and the lessons of these experiences must not be forgotten. They must be incorporated into the flesh and blood of the party so that old errors will not be repeated and gains achieved in struggle not light-mindedly thrown away.

In order to discuss properly the motion for "unity with the Shachtmanites," we must first go back and establish what the fight and split was about in the first place. If we were right, we must maintain our position. If we were wrong, the errors must be pointed out concretely and then corrected. Up to the present we have heard no open statement by the minority, no frank and explicit contention, that we were wrong and Burnham-Shachtman right. But, as we have seen, the policy of the minority is unfolding in "stages." Perhaps this will be the next stage. But even before they have openly avowed their solidarity with the Burnham-Shachtman conception of party organization, we can already see that it is implicitly contained in their recent speeches and proposals. That is the essence of the matter; and that is what makes this meeting of such great and decisive importance for the future of the party.

For the first time since the split of 1940, our *line* in the historical fight is challenged. We intend to discuss this question thoroughly and to the end because we firmly believe that the concept of the party is fundamentally decisive for the building of the party. I intend to make many speeches on this subject in the course of the discussion. Tonight, however, there is only time for a brief synopsis which can serve as an introduction for more elaborate remarks later.

As you know, the struggle of 1939-40 culminated in a split. The printed record—"the books"—show what the issues were and who was responsible for the split. We characterized the faction of Burnham, Shachtman, and Abern as a "petty-bourgeois opposition," not only on the Russian question as Goldman would represent it, nor on any single point of difference. We characterized their whole systematic line of conduct and political methods as well as organizational conceptions and practices, and their basic composition, as petty-bourgeois. Here is the way Comrade Trotsky described this faction, which later split and formed the Workers Party:

> It is necessary to call things by their right names. Now that the positions of both factions in the struggle have become determined with complete clearness, it must be said that the minority of the National Committee is leading a typical petty-bourgeois tendency. Like any petty-bourgeois group inside the socialist movement, the present opposition is characterized by the following features: a disdainful attitude toward theory and an inclination toward eclecticism; disrespect for the tradition of their own organization; anxiety for personal "independence" at the expense of anxiety for objective truth; nervousness instead of consistency; readiness to jump from one position to another; lack of understanding of revolutionary centralism and hostility toward it; and finally, inclination to substitute clique ties and personal relationships for party discipline.[34]

Trotsky accused Shachtman not of a political error here and there but of an "outright theoretical betrayal." He denounced the idea of a split "as a despicable betrayal of the Fourth International." He characterized the first number of the *New International*—the magazine which they stole from the party—as a "petty-bourgeois counterfeit of Marxism."[35] The documented record of the struggle shows that we left no ambiguity whatsoever in our analysis of the basic character of the opposition faction which later became the Workers Party. We were right on the political questions in dispute at that time—and they were wrong. We were right on the "organization question"—in reality the *conception* of the party—and they were wrong. If our minority now disagrees with this appraisal, let them point out their disagreements concretely. Then we will discuss the questions again. If they can convince the party that we have been incorrect in our estimation of the struggle up till now, the estimation can be changed. But they will not succeed in changing it by indirect implication, without presenting the issues frankly.

The record shows that we tried to prevent the split by every kind of means, that we offered the most extraordinary concessions to keep them in the party. In spite of that, they rejected the decisions of the party convention. They rejected the subsequent conditions of the Emergency Conference of the Fourth International.[36] They repudiated national and international discipline. They defied the public opinion of the entire Fourth International, all the sections of which, as far as I know, supported the majority. They split the party, formed a rival party, and declared war on our party. That is how the record stood in the spring of 1940.

This documented record of the fight must be studied line by line by every member who wishes to prepare himself seriously for an understanding of the present discussion. It was in the struggle against the petty-bourgeois opposition and the victory over it that our party became a party.

4. The Development of Our Party Since the Split

The split was a very deep one, costing us no less than 40 percent of the party membership. In spite of that, the split caused no demoralization in our ranks and brought no "catastrophe" to our movement, as they had confidently predicted. We went forward from the first day. We gained in struggle against them as party against party, as we had previously defeated them in the struggle as faction against faction. Our great work of proletarianization *transformed* the party from a discussion group into a genuine workers' organization.

Our younger cadre of proletarian leaders who had been somewhat overshadowed and kept in the background by the intellectuals and fast talkers in the old party came forward and developed in the new party. In the year 1944 when all the older and more experienced leaders were out of action, this younger cadre showed its caliber! The year 1944 was the richest year of accomplishment in the entire history of our movement. (Except 1945, which will be richer yet.) We have another reserve cadre of precious talents among the comrades who have been drafted into the military forces. If the whole present leading staff were put out of action and these absent comrades would return, they could construct a whole Political Committee, if necessary an organizing bureau and an editorial board. And the party would have every right to put confidence in their capacity to lead the party firmly and worthily.

We have been recruiting new members steadily and at an ever-accelerating pace since the split. Our numerical preponderance over the splitters increases from month to month.

The Militant, which Trotsky once criticized very sharply for its intellectualism, has become a real workers' paper; not only a brilliantly written paper *for* the workers, as Trotsky described the old *Militant,* but also a paper *of* the workers. The popularity of our paper is attested by the astonishing successes of our great subscription campaigns. A year ago the National Committee rather hesitatingly asked the membership to get 3,000 new subscribers, wondering at the same time if the goal had not been set too high. The membership responded with a total of about 7,500 new subscriptions. Again this year, a goal of 10,000 new subscribers was set by the party leadership and you responded with more than 22,000. Fund campaigns, with goals undreamed of in the old days, have been oversubscribed in every case.

How is all this to be explained? Does this give a picture of a party that is demoralized, stagnating, or going backward because of the absence from our ranks of the old petty-bourgeois opposition? All the facts speak most eloquently to the contrary. The steadily mounting successes of our party can only be explained by its homogeneity, by the revolutionary morale of the party membership, by their confidence in the party and in the leadership, by their ardent party patriotism. These sterling qualities cannot be manufactured at will. They can only be the reflection of the nature of the party itself.

The old party was paralyzed by its predominantly petty-bourgeois composition. This was the basic cause which threatened it with destruction, plunged it into the terrible crisis of 1939-40. Trotsky warned us time and again that there was no salvation for the Socialist Workers Party except along the line of proletarianization. He said in one of his articles:

"The class composition of the party must correspond to its class program. The American section of the Fourth International will either become proletarian or it will cease to exist."[37]

Look at the composition now! The basic proletarian cadres of our party are concentrated in large and flourishing fractions in auto, maritime, shipyard, steel, and other basic industries. This is the proletarian core of the party. In the 1939-40 factional fight Burnham and Shachtman found an automatic source of strength and support in the bad social composition of the party. The petty-bourgeois elements, especially in New York where they were predominant, responded to the opposition faction almost by reflex action. By the same token it is clear that the source of the pitiful weakness of the present opposition, as far as numerical support is concerned, is to be found in the predominant proletarian composition of the present party.

5. The Development of the Petty-Bourgeois Opposition Since the Split

How has the petty-bourgeois opposition, which split from the party in 1940 and formed a rival party, developed since the split? And what is their present attitude toward the Socialist Workers Party? We don't need to send a committee to meet them in order to find the answer to these questions, as Goldman has proposed. We have more reliable information as to their membership strength than they give to Goldman. Our information is more reliable and comes from our qualified representatives in the field, who observe them closely and know almost precisely what their strength amounts to. As to their policy in general and their attitude toward us in particular, we don't need to inquire about that either. It is clearly revealed in their press for anyone who is interested to read.

They deepened the theoretical and political differences of 1940 and developed new ones. The anti-Marxian theory of a new "bureaucratic class" displacing socialism as the historic successor to capitalism—a theory which was kept in Burnham's briefcase during the old faction fight—has now been adopted as the official policy of the Workers Party. To be sure, this wonderful "theory" of this remarkable new "class" is so far restricted to "one country." But that can't last long. The Shachtmanites, like all other opportunists, develop their policy in "stages."

They condemned our military policy as a sort of social patriotism in the spirit of pacifist abstentionism. They have adopted the liquidationists' "Three Theses" on the national question in Europe, which all Marxists in the Fourth International have condemned as a revision of Marxism.[38] They have revised the program of the Fourth International on China and on India.[39] They have differed with us in almost every case in the concrete application of our labor party policy. Even on the comparatively simple question of trade union work, and the methods of conducting it under conditions of war and virtual illegality in the unions, their methods have had very little in common with ours.

Now unity, like every other practical political question, must be discussed concretely, not hypothetically. And one of the most important prerequisites for a serious consideration of unity between two political groupings is their attitude toward each other. These attitudes do not fall from the sky. There are political and social reasons for them as a rule. These factors always prevail over personal feelings. The entire history of the movement is convincing proof of this. Goldman has given us some information as to the present attitude of the Workers Party toward us after a separation of five years, although we didn't really need it.

In the very same meeting of the Political Committee where he made his motion to appoint a committee to begin negotiations with the Workers Party he reported what he had learned in his numerous conversations and conferences with the leaders of the Workers Party which I have previously quoted. They didn't think that with "Cannon and the Cannonites" in the party, they should reenter the party. Since the policy of "Cannon and the Cannonites" has been supported by about 95 percent of our party, this would seem to be a rather serious obstacle to any practical consideration of unity at the present time. That at least is the way the Shachtmanites understand it. Their slogan is not "Unity with the Socialist Workers Party!" but "Leave the Socialist

Workers Party and Join the Workers Party!" This is the slogan they have carried in their paper in the past; and only recently Comrade Dan Leeds in Chicago reported to the party that Shachtman had invited him and his friends to act according to this slogan.

By this I do not mean to say that the Shachtmanites are opposed to unity in general or to unity with anybody. Far from it. They want unity all right, but not with us. In the very recent period they have been assiduously seeking unity with the organization of the Socialist Party Yipsels, who have been nestling very snugly in Norman Thomas's Socialist Party throughout the war, and whose leaders are consciously Souvarinist, consciously anti-Bolshevik. We for our part would consider unity with such people an indecent betrayal of principle. Those who reject Bolshevism have nothing in common with us. But Shachtman offers to accommodate the anti-Bolshevik Yipsels as readily as he accommodated himself in the old fight to the bloc with the anti-Bolshevik Burnham against Trotsky and the majority of our party.

Just listen to this: In *Labor Action* of April 2, 1945, appears an open letter from the Workers Party to the convention of the Yipsels. The letter begins by saying, "The Workers Party sends you and your convention warm fraternal greetings." That, I must say, is a quite proper and cordial salutation to the convention of a friendly organization with which one is seeking unity. Perhaps a similar greeting was sent to the recent convention of our party, but if so it got lost in the mails and was not received by the convention. The letter takes note of the Souvarinist idiosyncrasies of the Yipsel organization and dresses them up euphemistically, as follows:

> We know that many of you have significant differences with the Workers Party, particularly on questions relating to historical estimations, more particularly on the question of historic Bolshevism or Trotskyism and of aspects of the Russian Revolution.

Now isn't that put daintily? Can you imagine a fancier literary formulation, a more delicate way of brushing the Souvarinist Yipsels with a feather so as not to hurt their feelings? After all you see, it is only a question of "historical estimations." Historical estimations! Estimations of what? Of historic Bolshevism and aspects of the Russian revolution! That is to say, of the fundamental principles and conceptions and estimations upon which our movement is founded. There are "differences" on these questions, says Shachtman. In that case a principled Trotskyist would state frankly what the differences are and demand a discussion of them and a prior agreement on the questions as a condition for unity. That is the way, for example, we proceeded with the American Workers Party, before the unity which was executed in 1934. That is the way Lenin and Trotsky taught us to proceed in each and every case.

But Shachtman, in a hurry for unity, takes a far more accommodating view of the matter. "To us," says the open letter—referring to the differences on questions relating to "historical estimation"—"this is the least disturbing aspect of the problem of our relations." And on that basis they say to the convention of the Yipsels:

> We propose to you:
>
> Join ranks with the Workers Party!
>
> Let us be more concrete. We propose to you:
>
> That the YPSL shall fuse with the Workers Party and operate as its youth organization.

After hearing this, let no one accuse the Shachtmanites of being opposed to "unity" at all times and under all conditions and with all organizations. But they are discriminating in their search for unity. Like every other political grouping they seek unity with those whom they feel to be closest to them and reject the idea of unity with others. Their attitude is clearly shown by a juxtaposition of their comradely unity offer to the Souvarinist, anti-Bolshevik Yipsels and the attitude they displayed toward our party at about the same time.

Just two weeks before they sent their touching offer of fraternal unity to the Social Democratic Yipsels, they put on record once again their irreconcilable hostility to our party. *Labor Action* of March 19, 1945, contains the following editorial statement: "The Workers Party has very serious and fundamental disagreements with the Socialist Workers Party. . . . Nor do we agree with many practices of that party nor its concepts of what a revolutionary socialist party should be." Should we, perhaps, send a committee to inquire if this was a typographical error in their paper? If they have "fundamental disagreements" with us on political questions, and if they don't agree with our "concept of what a revolutionary socialist party should be"—on what basis should we propose to unite with them? On the basis of "fundamental disagreements"? That was never our concept of the basis for unity.

One of the strongest distinctive features of international Trotskyism has been its accurate analysis and exposure of Stalinism as the betrayer of communism, its unremitting struggle against the Souvarinist, Social Democratic, and bourgeois-liberal campaign to identify the two, and to lump Stalinism and Trotskyism together as simply variant expressions of the same fundamental doctrine, i.e., communism or Bolshevism. The press of the Workers Party yields more and more to this monstrous misrepresentation. They use the words "Stalinism" and "communism" interchangeably. In almost any issue of *Labor Action,* reporting struggles in one trade union or another, they identify the Stalinists as "Communists" and thereby contribute as much as they can to the confusion and miseducation of the workers who read their press.

Take this same issue of *Labor Action,* dated March 19. There is an account of an internal fight in what they call "the Communist-Stalinist-infested and controlled United Farm Equipment & Metal Workers of America." This Social Democratic expression, "Communist-Stalinist," is not an isolated error of the writer. It represents a political line which is repeated over and over again in the article. The article refers to "the Communists at the Tractor works." It goes on to say, "the Communists have resorted to the most desperate measures." It continues, "the Communist thugs have beaten up McCormick workers." It refers to a former president of the local who "was defeated by the Communists in the last election." It goes on to condemn the "moves on the part of the Communists" and refers again to the "physical beatings meted out by the Communists."

What is the political *tendency* shown here? Is that a tendency toward political reconciliation with us who wage an irreconcilable struggle against the Stalinists *in the name of communism*? Or is it a tendency toward capitulation to the reactionary dogma that Stalinism and communism are the same thing, that Stalin is "Lenin's heir," as Burnham explained in his latest article in *Partisan Review.*

During the past year, while our minority was softening its attitude toward the Shachtmanites and snuggling up to them, the press of the Workers Party enormously sharpened its attacks on our party. While Goldman has been explaining to us his sudden discovery that the Workers Party is a "revolutionary Marxist-Leninist organization," the latter has shown no disposition to return the compliment to our "bureaucratic jungle."[40] Quite the contrary. In the *New International,* March 1945, Shachtman explains: "The future of the SWP as a revolutionary organization is, at best, a dubious one. We recognized that five years ago. What has happened since has only made this fact plainer and caused many others to realize it." (The "others" whom he refers to are Goldman, Morrow, and Company.)

Again in the *New International* of April 1945, Shachtman explains that unity with us is impossible because of "the sterile, bureaucratic regime which the Cannonites have imposed upon and continue to maintain in the SWP, a regime which the new minority in the SWP rightly describes as Stalinist in its trend." The "regime" they are talking about is the regime which was specifically endorsed by more than 90 percent of the party delegates at our recent party convention.

In this same article which reviews the split of 1940 and the subsequent developments, Shachtman defends the position of the petty-bourgeois opposition on every point; justifies their action in splitting; justifies even their demand for the right of the opposition to have its own independent public organ.

In the face of this record I think we are entitled to say that those who want to be "unity brokers" should address their sermons to the Shachtmanites, and not make fun of our party by addressing them to us.

6. The Basis for Unity

When we Trotskyists make unity with another group we do it only on a rigidly principled basis and no other. We never refused such a unity and never will. On the contrary, the record of the past shows that we have always sought and taken advantage of every opportunity to find a principled basis of unity with other groups which were moving, however confusedly, in our direction. But we never wasted our time, and I hope we never will waste our time, in futile "negotiations" for unity with political groups moving in an opposite direction. For us, the program is decisive; and by program we mean the whole program and not 50 percent of it and 50 percent of its opposite.

We are urged "to eliminate the confusion caused by two parties." That is a good idea. But one must undertake to carry it out realistically. That means either (1) to eliminate the differences which account for the existence of the two parties, or (2) to explain them clearly. The worst method of all is to transfer the confusion inside our party. That would only make the confusion more confounded and paralyze our party activity in the process.

It is vain to hope that we can eliminate rival parties and groups in a labor movement surrounded by capitalism and subject to all its direct and indirect pressures which are transmitted into the labor movement through various political groups, parties, and tendencies. Lenin couldn't do it and neither could Trotsky. Lenin only struggled to make his own party dominant and to keep its own line clear and free from opportunist political dilution and organizational diffusion. There will always be minority groups and parties, up to and even after the workers' conquest of power under the leadership of a single revolutionary party. And that will always create a certain amount of confusion. But it is better to have the confusion outside the party than inside. At least that was Lenin's idea; and the historical test demonstrated that it was a very good idea. The worst confusion of all would be caused by transforming our own party into a federation of factions. That is a program for confusion combined with paralysis.

7. Two Conceptions of a Party

Our conceptions of the revolutionary party are explicitly set down in official resolutions and other documents adopted by the party and printed in the book devoted to *The Struggle for a Proletarian Party*. We have discussed and decided this question many times in the past and have always firmly rejected the concept of the party as a federation of factions, which became popularized in this country under the name of the "all-inclusive party." We had some experience with this theory of organization during our sojourn in the "all-inclusive party" of Norman Thomas and Company. At the conclusion of that experience we had a debate with Burnham and Carter, just prior to the convention where the present Socialist Workers Party was formally constituted, nearly eight years ago. The convention resolution set forth the position of the party on this point, as follows:

> Experience has proved conclusively that this "all-inclusiveness" paralyzes the party in general and the revolutionary left wing in particular, suppressing and bureaucratically hounding the latter

while giving free rein to the right wing to commit the greatest crimes in the name of socialism and the party. The S.W.P. seeks to be inclusive only in this sense: that it accepts into its ranks those who accept its program and denies admission to those who reject its program.[41]

When the petty-bourgeois opposition of 1939-40 revived the agitation for "all-inclusiveness," the party responded by reaffirming this resolution at the convention of April 1940. This same convention which steered a firm course toward proletarianization and away from the sterile atmosphere of the discussion circle, to which our minority wants to drag us back, spoke out in advance against it:

> To attract and to hold workers in the ranks of the party, it is necessary that the internal life of the party be drastically transformed. The party must be cleansed of the discussion club atmosphere, of an irresponsible attitude toward assignments, of a cynical and smart-aleck disrespect for the party.[42]

Trotsky, who fought longer and harder than anyone for genuine party democracy, against a real and not an imaginary Stalinist bureaucratism, never gave any support to the idea of the party as a federation of permanent factions. His great criticism of the program in 1928, while dealing his heaviest blows at the bureaucratic monolithism introduced by the Stalinists, nevertheless declared: "A fighting party can never be the sum of factions that pull in opposite directions."[43]

It appears more and more that our minority is adopting the discredited organizational conceptions advocated by the petty-bourgeois opposition of 1939-40 and applied in practice in the Workers Party since the split. They have not openly espoused "The War and Bureaucratic Conservatism," that bible of Menshevism on the organizational question compiled by Burnham, Shachtman, and Abern, but they adopt its basic ideas one by one and attempt to pass them off on the party in the name of "the spirit of Bolshevism." Are they trying to make fun of us? Do they think we have forgotten everything we fought about in the old fight? We don't seem to talk on the same plane. We don't seem to want the same thing. The kind of a party they are dreaming of would never be a workers' party, but only a new and deteriorated version of the discussion club from which we emerged through the struggle and split with the petty-bourgeois opposition of 1939-40. Nobody can drag us back to that.

8. The Dangers of Factionalism

The latest action of our minority is a step on a dangerous path. The call for the formation of a faction—a party within the party—is a declaration of war that is bound to sharpen the atmosphere, all the more so because it is an ill-considered and unjustified decision. I hope they will reconsider this decision and return to the truce which they signed a bare three months ago.

As you know, the Bolshevik party does not prohibit factions. Sometimes they are unavoidable when great principled differences are involved, especially if the party leadership infringes upon the democratic rights of a minority and deprives them of normal means of ideological struggle. There is nothing of that kind in our party, as you know. Serious, responsible, and loyal comrades will always think ten or a hundred times before resorting to closed faction organizations because they know that, even in the best case, faction organizations are a standing menace to the unity of the party. The history of our movement shows conclusively that the formation of separate factions has led more often to splits than to ultimate reconciliation and the dissolution of the factions again in one party. We must learn from the experiences of the past in this question as in all other questions.

It would be difficult to think of a flimsier justification than that which the minority has offered for their hasty and light-minded decision. A bare three months ago they joined with us in a declaration to the party. This declaration stated that in view of the undeveloped nature of the differences, there was no basis for sharp factional struggle or for the existence of factional formations in the party ranks. But now they allege that someone insulted Comrade Goldman in a discussion within the confines of the Political Committee, so they announce the formation of a faction to avenge the insult.[44] That is subjective politics of the most infantile kind. To be sure, insults do not contribute to the normalization of the party atmosphere, but Goldman should be the last one to make complaints on this score. He should be the last one to complain about the party "atmosphere." All he has to do is to change his own attitude and tone and the "atmosphere" will change automatically.

It would be far better for the minority to take a more grown-up, more responsible, and more loyal attitude toward the party. Better go back to the terms of the truce while there is yet time. Better agree once again, in the language of the truce, "to collaborate harmoniously and constructively on the basis of the convention decisions to carry on the work of the party and build up the party." If they insist on their reckless decision to organize a closed faction, it will raise the question of the necessity of a more serious, a more thorough, and searching inquiry into the reasons. The party will have to probe more deeply into the theoretical and political reasons which are implied but not clearly stated, into the social compulsions which drive them on such a reckless course.

It is an axiom in our movement, and in the last great fight Comrade Trotsky emphasized it once again, that "every serious factional fight in a workers' party is a reflection of the class struggle." The existence of one closed faction inevitably calls forth the organization of a counterfaction. That is the law of factional struggle. If two factions are formed, if they become closed and hardened and intensify their struggle, the party cannot content itself with the examination of the mere superficially stated differences. The party will have to probe deeper and establish the fundamental causes, the hidden reasons which lie at the bottom of the factional frenzy but are not openly and frankly avowed. The party will have to establish the social basis of each faction and make a decision as to which is the petty-bourgeois and which is the proletarian tendency in the unbridled factional fight which "reflects the class struggle."

9. Untimely Talk About "Unity"

The proposal for "unity with the Shachtmanites" is not a concrete and realistic proposition for our party at the present time. The attitude of the Shachtmanites—an attitude which springs from political considerations—rules it out. And the formula of the minority is especially inept, untimely, and unrealistic. "The conditions of 1940" were a formula based on concrete conditions existing at that time. Among these conditions were the facts that the petty-bourgeois opposition had not developed the full implications of their position; that they were still members of one party with us; that they represented 40 percent of the membership; and that we could still entertain hope that the instruction of events would come to the aid of our arguments and influence the petty-bourgeois opposition of 1940 to modify their position and reintegrate themselves in the movement. But life has passed that by. We now have new times, a new situation, deeper differences, even sharper antagonisms, and a far different relation of forces.

Our policy must be based on the present reality. In 1940 they were inside the Socialist Workers Party. This gave them rights and privileges and entitled them to concessions which we would never dream of offering to a rival group outside the party. Permitting a group to remain inside the party on condition of discipline, and inviting an outside group to come into the party to conduct an organized factional struggle from within—these are not the same things. And 1940 and 1945 are not the same year.

The factional manifesto of the minority explains that they want to bring the Shachtmanites as an organized faction into our party in order to "strengthen" the SWP. That sounds like irony. They evidently think we need a bigger and better factional fight in the party. We don't think that would strengthen us and aid in the development of our ambitious expansion program adopted by the recent convention and now going forward with full speed on all fronts. Obviously they are thinking that the entry of the Shachtmanites into our party would strengthen our present minority through the medium of a "bloc," of the type which we saw in the 1939-40 fight. But it would be very difficult for anyone to prove the advantages of such a "bloc" to the party itself.

Someone may ask, "But would not unity under present conditions at least increase our membership and thereby strengthen us numerically?" To such a question we can only answer, "Yes—and no; more no than yes." We are now recruiting new members at the rate of 300 per year and the rate of recruiting is increasing from month to month. That is, a year's new recruits equals the maximum total membership of the Shachtmanites; and the quality is better because our new recruits are predominantly proletarian trade union militants, the very type out of which the future party of the revolution must be constructed. A *principled* unity with another ideological grouping, even a very small one, even a group of ten members, would undoubtedly help and strengthen us and would be well worth our time to achieve. But a false unity of the type proposed by our minority, followed immediately by an internal factional struggle and paralysis of party work, would be more apt to stop recruiting and drive the new workers away from the party. That we don't want. That we will not permit under any circumstances.

Our basic orientation is proletarian. We want a party of workers, a party where the worker feels at home. We want a party where the worker feels himself to be the master of the house. We want a leadership that is predominantly proletarian. We are building such a party and such a leadership and we intend to continue on this course—the course which has brought us such good results since the split of 1940, and which promises far greater successes in the coming period.

Max Shachtman

THE DOWNFALL OF BROWDER[45]

August 3, 1945

The following are major excerpts from a speech given at Webster Hall in New York to an audience of 400. The version appearing here was first published in The Militant, *September 8, 1945. The full text is no longer extant.*

What has transpired in the ranks of American Stalinism in recent weeks is something more than a "change of line," as they say. It is a confession of failure of a policy carried out in the United States by Browder, but inspired and directed from Moscow: the policy of selling out the American workers in the interests of the Soviet bureaucracy, of harnessing them to the imperialist war machine, and of attempting to represent that policy as service to the workers and to the cause of socialism.

The Stalinist party, which during the current war has been the most enthusiastic advocate of the cause of the imperialists, the worst enemy of the workers, the most criminal strikebreaker, did not arrive at this depth of degradation and treachery at one step. When the bureaucracy in the Soviet Union consolidated itself on the basis of the reaction which set in after the failure of the German revolution in 1923,[46] it began to renounce the theory and practice of international revolution in favor of a new theory of socialism in one country.

Trotsky and his collaborators, the best of the leaders of the Russian revolution, warned the workers of Russia and the world that this theoretical revision of Marxism, this turn from internationalism to a narrow-minded national policy, would result in the downfall of the Communist International and the social-patriotic degeneration of all the parties. That prediction seemed remote and farfetched in those days, but how truly it was fulfilled. Year by year, step by step—once the Comintern, and the American Communist Party with it, got off the theoretical rails of Marxism, they departed further and further from the original program of the Communist International. This theoretical deviation led to a complete betrayal of the interests of the workers of the world in the second imperialist war.

These traitors counted upon the hysteria of patriotism, the repressions of the government, and the befuddlement of the workers to give them the opportunity to dispose, once and for all, of that hated group of Trotskyists who remained true to the ideas of Marx and Lenin, true to the ideas of communism. And for a time it appeared that they might have success. The leaders of the American Trotskyist movement were finally imprisoned. But the enthusiasm of the workers for the war and for patriotic strikebreaking did not measure up to the expectations of these finks at all. Quite the contrary. The American workers accepted the war very sullenly. They had not forgotten World War I and they already had in their minds the specter of World War III. And they did not believe the workers should surrender all their rights during the war.

They maintained the right to strike in case after case, and to the great surprise of the Stalinist strikebreakers and superpatriots, great numbers of workers manifested sympathy and admiration for the genuine communists in this country, the Trotskyists of the Socialist Workers Party. Union after union gave us moral and financial support.[47] There was so much sympathy for us the government did not deem it expedient to keep us in jail too long. And the net result of the war experience has been that the Socialist Workers Party, instead of being crushed and driven out of existence, gained by leaps and bounds, precisely in the mass workers' unions in the country where the Stalinists formerly had been so powerful. The Stalinist traitors finally had to realize that they had overplayed their hand a little bit. Browder is the scapegoat for this mistake.

They made a great success in Washington. They even did pretty well in Wall Street. Even J. Pierpont Morgan, if he didn't accept Browder's offer to shake hands, accepted Browder's offer to grovel before him, and said, "Good boy, that is all right."[48] But the Communist Party began to lose thousands and tens of thousands of militant workers, and tens of thousands of Negroes whom they had deserted and betrayed in the war. And they began to realize that if they wanted to stay in business as a bargaining agent for Stalin, they had better repair their fences and get an organization together that would have some real influence among the workers. That is the real reason for the so-called change of line in the Stalinist party, in the course of which a little man named Browder, who was standing on the stair, wasn't there anymore.

The order for cutting off Browder's head came straight from Moscow via Paris. You know the Comintern was dissolved; so instead of sending cables direct from Moscow, now they send letters to Paris and print them in a magazine and transport them by boat to the United States. But the authenticity of the direction, the origin of it in Moscow, was known to all the dearly beloved collaborators of Browder in the National Committee of the Communist Political Association.

And strangely enough, every single one of the national and district leaders of the Communist Political Association, every editor and organizer, every functionary and every flunky, who in May 1944 had voted unanimously for Browder as the leader of the party, as the representative of Marxism—every single one, without exception, voted in July 1945 against Browder as the representative of what they call "revision of Marxism." But that really isn't what it was at all. Browder is a victim of Stalinist reconversion. He was caught in the cutback to peacetime production.

Another victim of the cutback is a very prominent scoundrel of an especially unattractive type, named Robert Minor. Robert Minor was leaning too close to Browder, was his alternate and deputy when Browder was in Atlanta.[49] Minor was one of those functionaries in the Stalinist hierarchy who combined the repulsive traits of sycophancy toward those above him and brutality toward those below him, each in the highest degree imaginable. Minor was one of the most despicable of all the functionaries of the Communist movement who entered into the service of Stalin.

Browder once told a story about Minor in one of the old faction fights. I always remembered it because it was the only witticism I ever heard this pompous jackass perpetrate. He said Minor used to be an anarchist, which is true, if I may say so without meaning to offend any anarchists who may be present. But, said Browder, as an anarchist he had the idea, which is part of the antipolitical teachings of anarchism, that politics is a very dirty business; and then Minor became converted to communism without changing his idea of the nature of politics and engaged in it in a very dirty way. It was fitting that Minor and Browder should be the two chief partners in that game of crime and betrayal which passed as political leadership in the Communist Party. And it is rather poetic justice that they should go out together.

I was reading the other day, in preparation for these remarks, a book which previously had not come to my attention. It is a very well printed official record of the convention of the Communist Political Association of May 1944. Looking through this volume, I could see that in May 1944 one leader after another was called on to speak at the convention. Browder spoke in favor of his policy; then Minor, then Dennis, then Williamson. Then all the rest of the trained seals of the Communist apparatus got up, one after another, and expressed complete approval of everything Browder had said. I turned from that book to the file of *Daily Worker*s containing the recent discussion and convention reports. The very same people who spoke so devotedly in echo of Browder in 1944 said the exact opposite in 1945. All, without exception, denounced Browder as a revisionist of Marxism, as a peddler of bourgeois ideas, etc. And Browder, who had unanimous support in May of 1944, had not a single vote in July of 1945.

Now, what kind of a movement is it and what kind of leaders are they who can be unanimously elected one year and unanimously rejected the following year without any change on their part whatsoever? That is the type of leader who is not elected, but is appointed from above. Such people are all the same type; they are fit to run a bureaucratic machine but never to lead a real struggle. I can't imagine anything more personally degrading than to be in a formal position of "leadership" by the sufferance of another; to have all the external trappings of office and yet to know that there is nothing real or solid about it; to know that the whole thing is a fake and a buildup; that one does not represent a real movement; that one's position is not based on the confidence of comrades gained in struggle, but on the appointment of someone higher in power. That is the fate of Browder, as it has been the fate of all others who succeeded the genuine leaders of the early Communist movement.

Stalin needed people of this type, not only in central positions, but all the way down the line. In the course of years of struggle, all the independent, honest, and revolutionary types of worker-leaders, who could not fit into the machine of Stalin, who could not obey the instructions to betray the workers, were expelled from the party, slandered, hounded, and their places taken by manufactured leaders. These leaders have no personal authority, no independence. When Stalin wishes to depose one of them as a scapegoat, it is not necessary to do more than send a letter, a note, and the job is completed.

In sacrificing Browder they have tried very hard to make it appear that this time there is really a change of line; that Foster, who has been dug up out of the reserve list and placed in Browder's seat, really represents something different from Browder; and that they are not going to betray the workers anymore. They say openly now that the whole policy of Browder was a policy of betrayal, but "We are going to change that now. We are going to be honest for a change. Foster is the representative of real Marxism."

What did Browder do? Browder's policy was to send the workers into the war; to tell them they should follow the leadership of the Wall Street gang; that they had a vital stake in the war adventures of the imperialists; that they should not strike, they should not protest; that they should hunt down and even lynch the incorruptible communists who called upon the workers to defend their rights even in the war. Under Browder, the Stalinists tried to break every strike of the workers, no matter how great were the wrongs.

What did Foster do? Foster supported that whole basic policy throughout the war, and even today his first pronouncement upon entering the place of Browder calls for the same program, supporting the imperialist war in the Orient. On what grounds? As a war for the liberation of the colonial peoples! Never could a more scoundrelly lie be told than that. Can you imagine a more monstrous lie than that—to say that the imperialist war machine is going into the Orient, burning and destroying the people of the Orient, for the purpose of their liberation?

Yet that is the first plank in Foster's program. Foster pledges no strikes while the war is going on.[50] Just last week there was a strike of the workers at the Wright Aeronautical plant in New Jersey. The Stalinists in this plant, under the leadership of Foster, acted in the strike as finks and strikebreakers, just as they acted under Browder in the Detroit strikes, in the coal strikes, and in all others. In principle the policy of Browder and Foster is the same thing. They both lie and they both betray.

But Browder wants to pledge also for the future, beyond the present war in the Orient. On the other hand, Foster says—and herein comes his "radicalism"—"That is going too far. That," says our uncorrupted Marxist, "that is revision and I won't stand for it." What a travesty, what a farce, what a deception of the hundred-times-deceived workers in the Stalinist party! The whole thing is a skin game; an attempt to continue the same policy with a change of faces and the promise that in the future, perhaps, if Stalin gets into a conflict with Truman, they may get a little more radical as a form of pressure on Truman.

This sham battle between Foster and Browder appears to me like an argument on the price of virtue between two cut-rate prostitutes. Foster says, "After the war we should make a small service charge." That is about the worth of the disagreements between them.

The fundamental reason for all this stage play, for this chopping off the empty head of Browder, for sacrificing the little man who wasn't there, is to call a certain halt to the idea that the American Communist Party, which is an agency of the Soviet bureaucracy, should become too completely merged with the governmental apparatus in this country.

Stalin has need of the Communist Party in this country, as in other countries, for only one purpose—as a bargaining agency in the diplomatic conflicts with the various imperialist powers. But in order to fill this mission the Communist Party must keep a certain influence over the workers. If it becomes a stench in the nostrils of every independent militant, as the CP did under Browder, then it has no bargaining power left. In order to keep it from becoming completely discredited, they had to go through this comedy of repudiating Browder, to denounce him as a "revisionist." They had to dig up Foster from the reserve list and put him forward as a labor leader who is in favor of strikes sometime in the future, and so on, in order to overcome the demoralization and discouragement in their own ranks and to find a new basis for deceiving the awakening militant workers.

The necessity for this stratagem was emphasized in the reports of the district organizers. One report after another explained: "Under the policy we have been following we have been losing influence in the trade unions, and the Trotskyists have been gaining with their policies. As we have been fighting against strikes and following the government too uncritically, the Trotskyists who kept agitating on the same program as before have been making gains. We have got to correct our policy a little in order to head off the Trotskyists."

That is the real basis for their change in leaders and their so-called change of line. By adopting a new facade and a little more radical phraseology they hope to gain a new credit with the militant workers of America. They are coming too late. The crimes of Stalinism have gone too far and are too widely known. Corruption has entered too deeply into the bones and marrow of that party for anyone to have any realistic hope of reforming it. They cannot and do not mean a return to the policy of the proletarian revolution. The degeneration of the cadres of that party, of its officials—national, district, and local—is not only political, it is moral, too. They have not been able in seventeen years—since they expelled us from the party—to train any new cadre of leaders. So corrupt, so sterile is the life of the Stalinist party that the whole party has to be dominated and controlled by the same old gang of case-hardened hacks. Old functionaries and pensioners that we haven't heard of for years reappear, crawling out of forgotten corners of the party like cockroaches out of old woodwork. This is the "new leadership" which is supposed to regenerate the party.

Stalinism, with all its power and all its money, can train only functionaries, never independent leaders; whereas the Socialist Workers Party, which began as a small persecuted group, in seventeen years has developed on a national scale a whole new staff of younger leaders who have been trained exclusively in our movement. They have come forward and developed their capacities in the free, democratic atmosphere of an honest revolutionary party. When our eighteen leaders were put in prison for a whole year, the party did not lack for qualified younger people to take their places.

Our whole party life has been a constant process of selecting, educating, and training new people, younger and more revolutionary than any the Communist Party can dream of. These Stalinist functionaries, who have been selling principles for more than seventeen years—how can anyone have the slightest hope that they will turn revolutionary, suddenly become honest and virtuous again? That is impossible. A political error can be corrected, but moral degeneration has to run its course. These people are traitors to the marrow of their bones.

They betrayed the United States workers in the war. They betrayed the workers of Europe. They betrayed the Negroes of this country in the most shameful and cynical manner. Then, on top of that, at the very moment when they are promising to be good and honest and revolutionary again, we read of this cynical and despicable alliance of the Communist Party in New York City with Tammany Hall. They put up Davis, this cynical traitor to the Negro people, as a candidate of Tammany Hall.[51]

They say to the people of Harlem: "We and Tammany Hall will fight for your freedom and liberties." Could there be a greater cynicism, a more shameful betrayal than that? No, you cannot hope for any regeneration of this thoroughly corrupt party.

It is not a question of "revisionism" at all. It is a question of complete degeneration, complete abandonment of vital principles of the proletarian revolution which are represented by Marxism.

We are the real communists, the Trotskyists. And in that we are the polar opposites of the Communist Party of Stalin and Browder and Foster and all the rest of them. Some people make a great misidentification; some people are inclined to consider Stalinism and communism as the same thing. That is false to the core. In one case, it might be passed off as ignorance of the

It's Still the Same Answer

Laura Gray

general public who have not studied the question closely. In the other case, it is conscious misrepresentation and miseducation. They point to the American Communist Party and Browder and Foster and say, "that is communism," in order to discredit the very idea of communism in the eyes of the workers. That is not true. We denounce the Stalinists, not because they are communists but because they have betrayed the cause of communism.

The Socialist Workers Party goes straight back to Lenin and Trotsky. We uphold the old program. We carry on the great tradition of the Russian revolution and the Comintern. All those members of the Communist Party who may have been shaken out of a coma by the present discussion, who are looking for the real party of communism, must come to our party and they will find it there. Our party stood up under persecution in the war and grew stronger in the struggle. We build our party on the organizational principles and methods of Lenin. The spirit of our party is the spirit of socialism. Socialism is the only salvation of humanity. The Stalinists are the greatest obstacles in the fight of the workers toward socialism.

The Socialist Workers Party is confident of the future in Europe, in the colonial countries, and in America too. The workers of starving and tortured Europe and the great colonial peoples—they see America today as the most predatory of all the imperialist powers, casting a dark and menacing shadow over the whole of humanity. That is the America these people see throughout the world today.

But we shall make it our task—and we invite you to join us in it—to show the people of the world another America, a different and better America—the America of the people, the America of the workers, the America of the proletarian revolution, which will lead the way to peace and cooperation of all peoples and all nations in the Socialist United States of the World.

THE BOMBING OF HIROSHIMA AND NAGASAKI

August 22, 1945

The following speech was given at Webster Hall in New York. It was scheduled as a memorial meeting for Leon Trotsky. Cannon took the occasion to comment on the atomic bombing of Hiroshima, August 6, and Nagasaki, August 9. The text is taken from The Militant *of September 22, 1945, where it was published under the title "The Heritage of Leon Trotsky and the Tasks of His Disciples."*

Five years ago today, when the world stood in the depths of the reaction engendered by the imperialist war, our great leader and teacher, Comrade Trotsky, perished at the hands of a Stalinist assassin. We memorialized him then as the great man of ideas, not yet acknowledged by the world, but a man whose ideas represented the future of mankind. Today, on the fifth anniversary of his tragic and most untimely death, as we stand at the beginning of the greatest revolutionary crisis in the history of the world, when thoughts and words must be transformed into deeds—today we pay our grateful tribute to Trotsky as the man of action.

When we celebrated the tenth anniversary of our party in 1938, at a great jubilee meeting, Comrade Trotsky was one of the speakers. He couldn't come to New York, but he spoke to us on a phonograph record which he had made for the occasion—a greeting to our party on its tenth anniversary. Many of you no doubt have heard that speech.[52] You will recall that he said we have the right to take time out to celebrate past achievements only as a preparation for the future. In the same sense we can say that if we take time tonight to memorialize our noble and illustrious dead, we do it primarily as a means of preparing and organizing the struggle of the living for the goal which he pointed out to us.

The main ideas of Trotsky, the ideas for which he lived and died, are comparatively simple. He saw the great problem of society arising from the fact that modern industry, which is necessarily operated socially by great masses of people, is hampered and constricted by the anachronism of private ownership and its operation for private profit, rather than for the needs of the people. He saw that the modern productive forces have far, far outgrown the artificial barriers of the national states. These two great contradictions—the private ownership of the means of production and their operation for private profit, and the stifling of industry within the outlived framework of the national states—are the sources of the great ills of modern society—poverty, unemployment, fascism, and war.

Trotsky saw the only way out for humanity in the revolutionary overthrow of outlived capitalism. Industry must be socialized and operated on the basis of a plan, for use and not for profit. The national antagonisms of the separate capitalist states have to give way to an international federation—the Socialist United States of the World. Socialized and planned economy can produce and provide an abundance for all the people—not only in one nation, but in all nations. The separate socialist nations, having no need or incentive to exploit others, having no conflicts over markets, spheres of influence, and fields of investment, no need of colonies to exploit and enslave—these separate socialist nations will necessarily unite in peace and cooperation based on a worldwide division of labor. The strength of one nation will become the strength of all, the scarcities of one will be made up by the plethora of others. Humanity will organize the cooperative exchange of all the conquests of art and science for the use of all peoples of all lands.

Trotsky taught that only the workers can bring about this revolutionary transformation. Only the working class, the only really progressive and revolutionary class in modern society, standing at the head of all the oppressed and deprived and exploited and enslaved—only they can bring about this great revolutionary transformation and reorganization of society. The workers are the only progressive class, and they are the most powerful class by virtue of their numbers and their strategic position in society. All the workers need is to become conscious of their historic interests and of their power, and to organize to make it effective.

Trotsky taught that this struggle for the revolutionary transformation of the world, which is on the historic agenda right now, requires the leadership of a party. But—Comrade Trotsky emphasized—not a party like other parties. That was his message to our tenth anniversary meeting: "not a party like other parties," not a halfhearted, not a reformistic, not a talking and compromising party, but a thoroughgoing revolutionary party, a thinking and acting party. A party irreconcilably opposed to capitalism on every front and to capitalist war in particular. Such a party, he said, is required to lead this grand assault against an outlived social system.

The workers of the world needed the ideas of Trotsky in 1940. All the material conditions for the transformation of society from capitalism to socialism had long since matured. What lagged behind was the consciousness and the understanding of the masses of the workers and their organizations. They had need of Trotsky's ideas when he spoke out—the one great voice in the world—against the slaughter of the second imperialist war. But they were not yet ready, they were not yet properly organized, to understand the ideas of Trotsky and to act on them.

The great organizations of the workers, political and industrial, had fallen under the leadership of men who were, in effect, not representatives of the interests of the workers, but agents of the bourgeoisie within the labor movement. The Social Democratic parties; the Communist parties of the Comintern, which had turned traitor to communism and to the proletariat; and the great trade unions—they all rejected the revolutionary program of Trotsky. They all supported the capitalist governments; and the governments plunged the people into the bloody shambles of the war.

Trotsky died confident of the victory of the Fourth International, as he said in that last message which we carry above our platform tonight. He died confident of the victory, but without having the opportunity to live and participate in it.

We have had six years of the war. The war that was supported by the labor leaders. The war that was defended by the professors and the intellectuals. The war that was blessed by the church. And now we can count up the results. What are the fruits of this war which, it was promised, was going to bring benefit to mankind? Look at Europe! Look at Asia! Or, closer home, look at the closing factories and the long lines before the unemployment offices, lines that will grow longer and hungrier, lines in which the returning soldiers will soon take their weary places—if they come back alive and able to walk from the battlefields.

Under capitalism the factories ran full blast to produce the instruments of destruction, but they cannot keep open to produce for human needs in time of so-called peace. The whole of Europe, the whole of great cultured Europe, is a continent of hunger and despair and devastation and death.

The victors at Potsdam announced to Europe the fruits of the victory and the liberation. They decreed the breakup of German industry, the most powerful and productive industry on the continent of Europe. They announced that the living standards of industrialized Germany, the workshop of Europe, can be no higher than those of the devastated backward agricultural states. Not to raise the lowest to the level of the highest, but to drag the highest and most developed and cultured countries down to the level of the lowest and least developed countries—that is the explicit program of the makers of the so-called peace. Such is the program for Europe.

And what are the results in terms of human beings? I read a dispatch in the *New York Times* today from Frankfurt. It is a casual, matter-of-fact informational piece from which I quote a reference to an official report of the situation in that area. "The figures," says the correspondent of the *Times,* "show that the average consumer in this zone is living on 1100 to 1300 calories a day, in contrast to the army's ration of 3600." Less than one-third of the food estimated by the army to be required to maintain the soldiers at a level of efficiency is allotted to the "liberated" people of Germany in the American zone. Surely the European people will develop a great love and appreciation for the liberators.

Surely the foundations are being laid for the peace of a thousand years. Capitalism in its death agony is dragging humanity down into the abyss. Capitalism is demonstrating itself every day more and more, in so-called peace as in war, as the enemy of the people. Bomb the people to death! Burn them to death with incendiary bombs! Break up their industries and starve them to death! And if that is not horrible enough, then blast them off the face of the earth with atomic bombs! That is the program of liberating capitalism.

What a commentary on the real nature of capitalism in its decadent phase is this, that the scientific conquest of the marvelous secret of atomic energy, which might rationally be used to lighten the burdens of all mankind, is employed first for the wholesale destruction of half a million people.

Hiroshima, the first target, had a population of 340,000 people. Nagasaki, the second target, had a population of 253,000 people. A total in the two cities of approximately 600,000 people, in cities of flimsy construction where, as the reporters explained, the houses were built roof against roof. How many were killed? How many Japanese people were destroyed to celebrate the discovery of the secret of atomic energy? From all the indications, from all the reports we have received so far, they were nearly all killed or injured. Nearly all.

In the *Times* today there is a report from the Tokyo radio about Nagasaki which states that "the center of the once thriving city has been turned into a vast devastation, with nothing left except rubble as far as the eye could see." Photographs showing the bomb damage appeared on the front page of the Japanese newspaper *Mainichi*. The report says: "One of these pictures revealed a tragic scene ten miles away from the center of the atomic air attack," where farm houses were either crushed down or the roofs torn asunder. The broadcast quoted a photographer of the Yamaha Photographic Institute, who had rushed to the city immediately after the bomb hit, as having said: "Nagasaki is now a dead city, all the areas being literally razed to the ground. Only a few buildings are left, standing conspicuously from the ashes." The photographer said that "the toll of the population was great and even the few survivors have not escaped some kind of injury." So far the Japanese press has quoted only one survivor of Hiroshima.

In two calculated blows, with two atomic bombs, American imperialism killed or injured half a million human beings. The young and the old, the child in the cradle and the aged and infirm, the newly married, the well and the sick, men, women, and children—they all had to die in two blows because of a quarrel between the imperialists of Wall Street and a similar gang in Japan.

This is how American imperialism is bringing civilization to the Orient. What an unspeakable atrocity! What a shame has come to America, the America that once placed in New York harbor a Statue of Liberty enlightening the world. Now the world recoils in horror from her name. Even some of the preachers who blessed the war have been moved to protest. One said in an interview in the press: "America has lost her moral position." Her moral position? Yes. She lost that all right. That is true. And the imperialist monsters who threw the bombs know it. But look what they gained. They gained control of the boundless riches of the Orient. They gained the power to exploit and enslave hundreds of millions of people in the Far East. And that is what they went to war for—not for moral position, but for profit.

Another preacher quoted in the press, reminding himself of something he had once read in the Bible about the meek and gentle Jesus, said it would be useless to send missionaries to the Far East anymore. That raises a very interesting question which I am sure they will discuss among themselves. One can imagine an interesting discussion taking place in the inner circles of the House of Rockefeller and the House of Morgan, who are at one and the same time—quite by accident of course—pillars of finance and pillars of the church and supporters of missionary enterprises of various kinds. "What shall we do with the heathens in the Orient? Shall we send missionaries to lead them to the Christian heaven or shall we send atomic bombs to blow them to hell?" There is a subject for debate, a debate on a macabre theme. But in any case, you can be sure that where American imperialism is involved, hell will get by far the greater number of the customers.

American imperialism has brought upon itself the fear and hatred of the whole world. American imperialism is regarded throughout the world today as the enemy of mankind. The First World War cost twelve million dead. Twelve million. The Second World War, within a quarter of a century, has already cost not less than thirty million dead; and there are not less than thirty million more to be starved to death before the results of the war are totaled up.

What a harvest of death capitalism has brought to the world! If the skulls of all of the victims could be brought together and piled into one pyramid, what a high mountain that would make. What a monument to the achievements of capitalism that would be, and how fitting a symbol of what capitalist imperialism really is. I believe it would lack only one thing to make it perfect. That would be a big electric sign on the pyramid of skulls, proclaiming the ironical promise of the Four Freedoms.[53] The dead at least are free from want and free from fear. But the survivors live in hunger and terror of the future.

Who won the war that cost over thirty million lives? Our cartoonist in *The Militant*,[54] with great artistic merit and insight, explained it in a few strokes of the pen when she drew that picture of the capitalist with the moneybags in his hands, standing on top of the world with one foot on the graveyard and the other on destroyed cities, with the caption: "The Only Victor." The only winner is American imperialism and its satellites in other countries.

What are the perspectives? How do our masters visualize the future after this great achievement of the six-year war?

Before the Second World War, with all its horror and destruction of human life and human culture, is formally ended, they are already thinking and planning for the third.

Don't we have to stop these madmen and take power out of their hands? Can we doubt that the peoples of all the world are thinking it cannot go much further, that there must be some way to change it? Long ago the revolutionary Marxists said that the alternative facing humanity was either socialism or a new barbarism, that capitalism threatens to go down in ruins and drag civilization with it. But in the light of what has been developed in this war and is projected for the future, I think we can say now that the alternative can be made even more precise: The alternative facing mankind is socialism or annihilation! It is a problem of whether capitalism is allowed to remain or whether the human race is to continue to survive on this planet.

We believe that the people of the world will waken to this frightful alternative and act in time to save themselves. We believe that before American imperialism, the new master of the world, has time to consolidate its victories, it will be attacked from two sides and defeated. On the one side the peoples of the world, transformed into the colonial slaves of Wall Street, will rebel against the imperialist master, as the conquered provinces rose against imperial Rome. Simultaneously with that uprising, and coordinating our struggle with it, we, the Trotskyist party, will lead the workers and plebeians of America in a revolutionary attack against our main enemy and the main enemy of mankind, the imperialists of the United States.

Five years ago today we first mourned and commemorated our great man of ideas, Comrade Trotsky. Today, as revolutionary action is becoming a life-and-death necessity for hundreds of millions of people, as we prepare to go over from ideas to action—to action guided by ideas—we commemorate Trotsky as the great man of action, the organizer of workers, the leader of revolutions. That is the spirit in which we commemorate Comrade Trotsky tonight.

He enjoined us above everything else to build a party. And again I repeat what he said: "Not a party like other parties," but a party fit to lead a revolution, a party that does not dabble, does not go halfway, but carries the struggle through to the end.

If you are serious; if you mean business, if you want to take part in the fight for a better life for yourself and for the salvation of mankind, we invite you to join us in this party and take part in this great struggle.

There is no place for pessimists or fainthearted people in our party, no place for self-seekers, careerists, and bureaucrats. But the door is wide open to resolute workers who are determined to change the world and ready to stake their heads on the issue.

Trotsky has bequeathed to us a great heritage. He gave to us a great system of ideas which constitute our program. And he set before us the example of a man who was a model revolutionist, who lived and died for the cause of humanity, and who, above all, showed how to apply theory in action in the greatest revolution in history.

With this heritage we are armed and armored for struggle and for victory. All that we, the disciples of Trotsky, need for that victory is to understand those ideas clearly, to assimilate them into our flesh and blood, to be true to them, and, above all, to apply them in action.

If we do that we can build a party that no power on earth can break. We can build a party fit to lead the masses of America—to answer the imperialist program of war on the peoples of the world, with revolution at home and peace with the peoples of the world.

AGAIN: ON "UNITY WITH THE SHACHTMANITES"

September 2, 1945

This speech was given to a meeting of the New York membership of the SWP. The text is taken from the SWP's Internal Bulletin, *vol. VII, no. 9, September 1945.*

1. The Letter of the Workers Party[55]

This is the second discussion of the question of our attitude toward the Workers Party, and it coincides with a second stage in the development of our relations toward them. The first stage was marked by the proposal of our minority that we should offer unity proposals to the Shachtmanites, that we should approach them. That was not a unity proposal; we had nothing from the Shachtmanites, no sign at that time of any change in their attitude toward us upon which to base a change in our position.

Now we have something different. It might be called a follow-up letter of the Workers Party on the resolution of our PC minority. We must analyze this letter also and see what it really is. Let us understand what it is. First, the letter of the WP is not a unity proposal. It would not be intelligent for us to discuss it from that point of view. It is an offer on their part to "discuss" unity with us. Let us examine the letter and see what it says. You have all received copies, and I presume you have read it.

The letter of the Workers Party contains two new points. The first one is contained in the last sentence of paragraph four of their letter, in which they say that "the interests of uniting the Fourth Internationalists in the United States on a sound foundation are more important than the regime in the Socialist Workers Party." Now that is something new and we must recognize it as such. The position of the Shachtmanites that they could not tolerate the regime in the Socialist Workers Party was precisely the point upon which they based the motivation for their split five years ago. They consistently maintained this position for five years. Even as late as May of this year, in the article of Shachtman in the *New International* summing up the five years' existence of the Workers Party, this was the issue he gave as the obstacle to unity: the regime in the Socialist Workers Party. Now, if this statement in their letter here means what it says, if it is sincerely made, then we must recognize that the Workers Party leaders have renounced the justification for their split of five years ago and their independent existence as a party for the past five years. That is something new and we must take due note of it.

The second new point of the WP letter is contained in paragraph five, in which they offer for the first time in five years to discuss unity with us. Up to now and in the past they have wanted to "discuss" with us only as implacable enemies, party against party. They now say they are ready to discuss unity with us.

These two new points constitute a change in the situation which we must recognize. We must approach the question on the basis of this new situation, created by a change of position on their part; at least an ostensible change of position.

2. Our Answer to the Workers Party

We sent a very quick answer to the Workers Party. We didn't take very much time to decide how to answer it either. Our answer to the Workers Party contains six points, and I think I am justified in saying that each point goes right to the point. You will note that the tone of our letter is polite, partly friendly. Why? That is because their letter indicates a change of attitude toward the Socialist Workers Party. We communist politicians are not subjectivists. Our attitude toward political groups and individuals in the general labor movement is determined not by their attitude toward us as individuals personally, but by their attitude toward the Socialist Workers Party. To those who are friendly to the SWP, however unfriendly they may be to any of us as individuals, we are friendly. To those who are hostile to our party, we are hostile. In this case we are polite in adjustment to the change of attitude represented by their letter.

There are six points, I said, in our letter. Let us mention them briefly point by point.

First, we say we are in favor of the discussion they propose and will so recommend to our National Committee. Nobody will object to that, I am sure, because I don't recall when our party or its leadership ever refused anybody's offer to discuss unification with us.

The second point, we ask the Shachtmanites, in view of the long conflicts that have prevailed between us, if they don't think they should indicate more precisely and more concretely their view of how the unification should be brought about and what form it should take. They didn't indicate that in their letter. I don't know if they had even thought about it or made up their minds. But if they are going to discuss unity they must soon reach a stage where proposals are concretized. So we helped them out, so to speak, by politely asking them: "What do you want; how are you going to do it?"

The third point is the statement that "we have always proceeded from the point of view that programmatic agreement is the only sound basis for unification; and that where divergences of opinion occur, unity can be maintained only by the scrupulous observance of the democratic principle of the subordination of the minority to the majority, and strict discipline in public activity and action."

The fourth point is our answer to their proposal that we should begin practical cooperation between the parties before we have discussed their programmatic differences. We say, "No, that appears to us to put the cart before the horse. Let us first discuss the program, and if it appears in the course of the discussion that we are approaching a unification and have reasonable grounds to believe that we can unite, then practical cooperation in all fields of work will follow as a matter of course. Let us begin, however, at the beginning and not at the end."

The fifth point is that we say that unity is a question which must be discussed frankly and seriously. We don't play with unity any more than we play with splits. The only aim of a unity discussion must be to effect a serious and long-lasting and firmly based unity that leads to the strengthening of the party and the building up of the party. A unity not firmly based, hastily prepared, and then followed by a paralyzing faction fight and another split—that would not help to strengthen and build up the party, and we are not interested in that kind of unity.

The sixth point in our answer to the very careful and somewhat hesitant letter of the Shachtmanites politely formulates the blunt proposal: "If you want to talk business with us, even in an exploratory way, just call Comrade Stein, our organization secretary, on the telephone and we will arrange a meeting in short order. Let's get down to business without beating around the bush."

These are the six points in our answer to the Shachtmanites.

3. Unifications and Splits

I believe the party will recognize our letter as the correct answer. It says everything that should be said at this stage of our new relationship with them. It does not reject them out of hand; offers to discuss any proposals that they may concretize; tells what we consider to be the main aims of unification and the main prerequisites to bring it about; and announces at the very beginning that we are not interested in any maneuverist unity. We want a real unity that will build up the party or none at all.

It was easy for us to write this letter because we are animated by certain general conceptions of unifications and splits. I believe it would be very useful, if nothing else comes out of this discussion, if the younger members of the party will put themselves to school during the course of the discussion and learn these basic principles which have guided us and our teachers in the building of a revolutionary party through a complicated process of unifications and splits.

It may seem strange to some of you that I put unifications and splits on the same level. But that is where they belong. We communists are neither light-minded splitters nor unity sentimentalists. Either method can be a means of developing the revolutionary party in a given situation. The important thing is not to split when unity is on the order of the day and not to get bogged down in a false unity when a split is indicated.

Light-minded, subjectively motivated splits have done great harm to the movement in the past. This was the case in the early days of the Communist movement in the United States. There was not a single one of the splits—and a number of them took place in the first five years of the American Communist Party—that was properly based except possibly the split of the extreme ultraleftists who left the Communist Party for good, the undergroundists.[56] All the other splits which kept the movement in turmoil and division with an unnecessary loss of blood in the first few years were unjustified splits. The splits which took place in the British Trotskyist movement over a period of years—which were only finally healed last year—were devastating in their effects on the movement, because they were not justified in principle.

There are situations in which splits in one direction and unifications in another take place almost simultaneously. We had such a situation in 1933-34. After the German events, after we had fought five years as an expelled faction of the CP, we simultaneously proclaimed a definitive split with the Stalinist party and at the same time approached new centrist groupings, moving to the left, for unification.[57] We made the definitive split with the American Communist Party in 1933 and a few months later were discussing and negotiating with the Musteites for unification, which was finally carried out in the fall of 1934.

Our great teachers were neither splitters nor unity shouters. We can learn much from old Engels. In the Marx-Engels correspondence we have numerous references to the Marxist policy toward unifications and splits and the building of the party in the process—now using one tactic and now another.

4. Engels on Unity and Splits

Let us take, for example, a quotation from a letter of Engels to Bebel about the split in France:

> Unity is quite a good thing so long as it is possible, but there are things which stand above unity. And when, like Marx and myself, one has fought harder all one's life against self-styled Socialists than against anyone else (for we regarded the bourgeoisie only as a *class* and hardly ever involved ourselves in conflicts with individual bourgeois), one cannot be greatly grieved that the inevitable struggle has broken out.[58]

Another letter of Engels to Bebel said:

> One must not allow oneself to be misled by the cry for "unity." Those who have this word most often on their lips are the ones who sow the most dissension, just as at present the Jura Bakuninists in Switzerland, who have provoked all the splits, clamour for nothing so much as for unity. These unity fanatics are either people of limited intelligence who want to stir everything into one nondescript brew, which, the moment it is left to settle, throws up the differences again in much sharper contrast because they will then be all in one pot (in

> Germany you have a fine example of this in the people who preach reconciliation of the workers and the petty bourgeoisie)—or else they are people who unconsciously (like Mühlberger, for instance) or consciously want to adulterate the movement. For this reason the biggest sectarians and the biggest brawlers and rogues at times shout loudest for unity. Nobody in our lifetime have given us more trouble and been more treacherous than the shouters for unity.[59]

Of course, that was back in 1873. We don't take these quotations as applicable in every detail to our present situation. But they are very useful for general guidance. Here is what he said in the same letter to Bebel. Bebel was the leader of the German Social Democratic Party, as you know, and Engels was his teacher:

> Moreover, old man Hegel said long ago: A party proves itself victorious by *splitting* and being able to stand the split. The movement of the proletariat necessarily passes through different stages of development; at every stage part of the people get stuck and do not join in the further advance; and this alone explains why it is that actually the "solidarity of the proletariat" is everywhere being realized in different party groupings which carry on life-and-death feuds with one another, as the Christian sects in the Roman Empire did amidst the worst persecutions.[60]

Profound words. "A party proves itself by splitting and being able to stand the split." Our party has proved its right to life precisely by this test.

From these letters we can see—and one could quote other remarks along the same line—that Engels was no sentimentalist on the question of unity. Unity shouters never bowled him over or stampeded him. He appreciated the value of unity, but insisted on a principled basis for it.

That was the position taken by Marx in his famous criticism of the Gotha program. He and Engels objected violently to the unity which Bebel and Liebknecht carried out with the Lassalleans without having a clearly defined program of Marxism.[61] Marx stated that in the case of such differences they should not have united into one party on a confused program, but should have made a compact to carry out a series of joint actions instead. But these were mass organizations and it was possible for them, had they agreed on a practical program of action, to really carry out mass actions. We are not a mass party yet. We are primarily a propaganda party, and it would be a great error to take this expression of Marx as having literal applicability in the present relationship of our small propagandist party to the still smaller propagandist party of the Shachtmanites.

5. The Method of Lenin

Unity is a good thing, there is no question about that, but the fetish of unity is extremely harmful. The best example of the harmful effect of the fetishism of unity is the Social Democratic parties of the Second International before the First World War. I believe the greatest mistake of the German left, headed by Rosa Luxemburg, was their hesitancy to carry the fight against the reformists up to the point of split and the formation of a revolutionary party out of the left wing. As a result, the outbreak of the war found the left wing imprisoned in the discipline of the opportunist party.

Lenin was the only one, as far as I know, of the great leaders before the First World War who defied the fetishism of unity and did not hesitate to carry through the split with the Mensheviks. In that period Trotsky's greatest error, the error which Trotsky had to recognize and overcome before he could find his way to unity with Lenin, was his insistence that the Bolsheviks and the Mensheviks had to unite. Trotsky's conciliationist position, which he repudiated in his later writings, was what separated him from Lenin during those fateful years. Lenin's policy was vindicated in life. Lenin built a party, something that Luxemburg was not able to do with all her great abilities and talents; something that Trotsky was not able to do precisely because of his wrong estimation of the Mensheviks.

Lenin built a party! And let there be no misunderstanding—either between us here or between us and any other party in the labor movement—that when it comes to organization we are Leninists. That means, we are for unity when it is possible. But we don't fear splits when they are politically indicated and necessary. Our aim is to build a Leninist party and all of our tactics are subordinated to this aim.

6. The Concrete Problem

In every case we approach the problem concretely. We are guided by general concepts, but we apply them concretely according to the situation as we see it. We strive to ascertain the facts as they really are, not as they are represented but as they are in actuality. It is from this point of view that we approach the letter of the Shachtmanites—as a concrete case. We have to examine this case and see what it is.

Here is a rough outline of the background. We had a nine-month faction fight inside the SWP in 1939-40. This faction fight led to a split five years ago. When the Shachtmanites were suspended by the Political Committee for their refusal to accept the decisions of the convention, they were given a period of time to consider the question and return to the party. They didn't avail themselves of it. In the fall of 1940 we held a plenum-conference. They presented no appeal, and were formally expelled. Since then we have held two conventions of the party. There was no appeal from the Shachtmanites to either convention. On the contrary, if you study the material you can say that the antagonism of the Shachtmanites toward us rather increased than decreased over the whole period of five years up until last week.

Now, however well-disposed we may be toward healing the split, however far we may wish to go within the bounds of principle to help the Shachtmanites find their way back to the party—it would be very foolish for any of us to think that this five-year struggle can be resolved in one day at one stroke. That is not the reality of the situation. The party interest—and that for us is paramount—demands a very careful and even cautious approach to the latest letter of the Shachtmanites, and any subsequent ones they may send us. We must be careful; we must be cautious; we must not gamble; we must know what we are doing and do it with our eyes open. I am not saying this in definitive rejection of the possibilities of changes for the better. Not at all. But we want to know in each case, at every step, just what our actions are based on.

7. The Amendment of the Minority

Our letter was not completely satisfactory to the minority in the Political Committee. Comrade Morrow introduced an amendment—I am sorry that through an oversight it was not mimeographed—but the amendment proposed that we add a paragraph in our letter declaring that the differences between us and the Shachtmanites are compatible with common existence in one party. That is the gist of the amendment. We rejected it. By that we did not mean to say that we insist upon the contrary. No.

We said, it is not for us to say whether the Shachtmanites' differences with us are compatible with unity or not. You know in 1940 we offered them the right to remain in the party and retain the views they held at that time, on condition of discipline, but *they* found the differences incompatible. That is the crux of the question.

It is turning the whole question upside down, comrades, to represent matters as though it is up to us to establish what is compatible for the Shachtmanites as a minority. We never expelled anybody from our party for a difference of opinion. I don't recall a single case in seventeen years. We didn't expel the Fieldites or the Oehlerites because they differed with the decisions of the party. We said to them: "You can have your opinion. Stay in the party and be loyal, be disciplined."

But *they* found the differences incompatible with membership in the party as a minority and broke discipline. We expelled them for that. Such was the case with the Shachtmanites. They passed judgment on the differences as incompatible. If they have changed, we will see and we will see to what extent they have changed and consider the matter after further examination.

8. Trotsky's Method in Building the Fourth International

Comrade Trotsky gave us many lessons in the long period of developing, first the International Left Opposition and then the Fourth International, from 1929, when he first got his hands free in Turkey, up to his death eleven years later in Mexico. Trotsky, in the formative period of the Left Opposition, refused to unite with anybody who did not accept the whole program of the Left Opposition on Russia, on the Anglo-Russian Committee, on the Chinese revolution, and the other basic points.[62] He was urged by many to unite with the Brandlerites, who had a false position on the Russian question, on the ground that they stood for party democracy and were very sensible on the trade union question and that we should cooperate with them in practical work. Trotsky said no. We are building a movement on a principled basis, and, just as I would not discuss the different tendencies in materialism with a man who makes the sign of a cross when he passes the Catholic Church, so I will not discuss trade union tactics with a man who does not take the right position on the questions of principle.

This was the harsh, narrow, "intolerant" line that Trotsky

followed in those years. He made an attempt, over several years, to find unity with the Bordigists, the left-wing communists of Italy, a very resolute and determined group inspired by the ideas of the great Italian left communist Bordiga. At the end of the experiment, although there was general agreement with the Bordigists on the most important principled questions of communism, their rejection of Bolshevik tactics, their rejection of democratic demands, constituted in the mind of Trotsky an insuperable barrier between us and them in the formative period of the International Left Opposition. He said, we cannot live in the same party with the Bordigists at the present time. They are too rigid and too narrow in their conception of tactics. In that very same article, where he declared that he couldn't live in the same international faction with the Bordigists, he made a very interesting comment. Paying tribute to the revolutionary devotion of the great majority of the Bordigists, he said, undoubtedly in a mass party the Bordigists could find a place on the condition of discipline in action, but our movement in its present stage of development as a propagandist faction cannot be paralyzed by this eternal dispute with them.[63]

Reading that article again the other day, I thought very important for us that last remark, to the effect that differences which are incompatible in a small propagandist faction can be tolerated in mass party. We are at a certain stage of our development in this country. I believe it is safe to say we have gone over from the propagandist circle and have taken a resolute course toward the building of a mass party. But we haven't reached that goal yet. We are neither a propagandist circle nor a mass party, but something in between. The question of what is compatible or incompatible with membership in our party has to be decided by an in-between criterion.

Trotsky, it has been said, frequently tried to reunite sections of the Fourth International after splits had taken place. That is true, but one should study each case in its context. Trotsky tried to bring about unity between the Molinierists in France and the official French section.[64] But, as he explained in *In Defense of Marxism* in answer to some questions raised by Shachtman, the condition for his attempts at reunifications with the Molinierists was that they did not maintain any principled differences with the Fourth International. He said, "I never made a single concession in principles to Molinier."[65] Their disagreement, they maintained, was over the "regime." They didn't like the regime in the Fourth International—the Trotsky regime. They accused us of "bad methods," etc. I personally participated, at Trotsky's direct request, in an unsuccessful attempt to bring about a unification with the Molinierists in 1938. I was the agent of the International Secretariat and the official French section. I never approached Molinier until I had first talked to my own people, my own party, my own comrades in the official French section of the Fourth International, and secured their consent. I reported back everything that transpired in discussions with Molinier and his comrades. But I told Molinier nothing about what had transpired in discussions with my own party in France. That was the rule back in 1938. Shachtman, who took part in the negotiations, also followed the rule.

Similarly, in 1938, Trotsky asked me to go to England to try to bring about the unification of the four different Trotskyist groups in England. The basis of the assignment was that all of them acknowledged the program of the Fourth International, that the differences were over secondary tactical questions. I heartily agreed and made the attempt, with partial success. In the same year, at the time of the founding conference of the Fourth International, the International Secretariat supervised and brought about a unity agreement between two organizations of Greek Trotskyists. But in all these cases there was no question of accommodating ourselves in principle to any group that objected to the program of the Fourth International.

I repeat: The differences which are "compatible" with membership in a common organization vary according to the stages of its development. What is incompatible with membership in a faction may be compatible in an independent propaganda circle existing as the embryo of a party. What is incompatible in a propaganda circle may be compatible in a party which has broken out of it but which has not yet attained a mass basis. And similarly, in our present stage of development we cannot even dream of accommodating the divergent tendencies which a mass party can tolerate, either to the right or to the left. We cannot do it at the present stage of our development. We are in between, as I said. We hope we have turned away definitively from the propaganda circle. We are recruiting new workers almost daily now, but we have not yet attained a broad mass basis. And when we are approached with the problem of accommodating ourselves to broadly divergent tendencies within our ranks we have to examine the question carefully before we give our answer.

9. The Aims of Our Discussion with the Shachtmanites

We are going to discuss with the WP as we readily agreed. What should be the aims of this discussion? Shall we lose our bearings and rush pell-mell into an ill-prepared unity because somebody is getting impatient? I don't think the leaders of the SWP are going to take such a line. We must first set down for ourselves certain aims. We must aim to clarify in the discussion all the important differences which caused the split and prolonged it for five years, to ascertain what changes have taken place, and see if we can agree on a common program. That is the purpose of the discussion in the first place—to explore the new situation and find out what it is in reality, in all its concreteness, not to enter it with a preconceived decision.

It is quite false for comrades of the minority to think or say that we are opposed to discussion. You don't understand us. On the contrary, we insist on discussion before we act. We insist on developing the discussion to the very end, until nothing ambiguous remains. That is the necessary precondition for unity with the Shachtmanites. We must ask ourselves: Why did they change their attitude toward unity with us? That is a very important question. Why do people who split from the party five years ago, and remained split for five years because they couldn't stand the regime, as they said—why do they now say that the regime is less important than unity? If that is a real change, it is a very important one. But they have not given their motivation yet. In our opinion the discussion must bring this out clearly. What is the motivation? We will find it out one way or another.

Lenin was a man of unification and a man of splits, too. He took them as they came, as the interests of the movement indicated. I was reading again the other day his writings in the early *Iskra* period, when they first started the paper and the question of uniting all the socialist circles and groups in one party was on the order of the day. Lenin approached the question with this formula: "Before we can unite, and in order that we may unite, we must first of all draw firm and definite lines of demarcation."[66] We have comrades in our party, I am sorry to say, who don't understand that that is the right way to approach the question of unity with people who have differences.

It is very wrong to blur differences, to minimize them, to represent that they don't really exist or that they have no significance. Such a method can only prepare a "unity" which is in turn a preparation for a new factional explosion and a new split. The way to get a firm unity is to probe the differences to the bottom, draw the lines of demarcation clearly and definitely, and then see if we can approach agreement. That is the way we are approaching the discussion with the Shachtmanites and we will continue it that way. That does not presuppose at all an irreconcilable refusal of unity. We don't deny the Shachtmanites the right to change, nor do we deny the possibility that we can change in their direction. All things are subject to change. Neither do we exclude in advance the possibility of a working compromise being arrived at without sacrificing principle. We are simply proceeding by the principle that in order to unite, and before we can unite, we must clarify the causes which brought about the split and the long division.

We have not yet reached the stage of negotiations with the Shachtmanites. Not yet. We are in the stage of discussion. And, so far, only an exploratory discussion. At a certain stage we will go over to negotiations if the prerequisite conditions are present. In that case you can be sure we will make it our business to know what we are doing. In negotiations between two political parties or groups the most important things are, first, to know what you want, and second, to know what the relation of forces is. I believe we know those two things.

We know what we want. We want a genuine workers' party with an unambiguous program of Bolshevism. That is what we want. We want a party with a firm discipline in action and public activity.

I believe we know what the relationship of forces between the two parties is; and I can tell you that the relation of forces between the two parties is one of the most important reasons for the turn that the discussion of unity has taken up till now. And the third thing: I believe that you have a right to expect of your party leaders, whom you have elected and trusted with great responsibility, that we represent our own side, always and under all conditions represent our own party and fulfill the trust you have placed in us.

I said that we are going to approach the Shachtmanites cautiously and carefully; I might even say, suspiciously. Trotsky repeated over and over again in connection with united fronts, that the first rule of the united front is to be distrustful of your allies. Now if we have to be distrustful of allies, how much less ground is there for us to have a naive confidence in opponents, those who have for five years sought to destroy the party? That would not be good political leadership.

When we took this attitude—which I have always considered axiomatic—we were given the astounding criticism, both in the Political Committee and in my last debate with Comrade Goldman, that we are taking a "shopkeeper's" attitude. Well, that is a little farfetched, because a shopkeeper is a petty bourgeois and we are revolutionary communists. But you might say, by stretching a point, that to a certain extent every representative of every party, elected to represent the interests of his party, is a "shopkeeper." In that sense I believe Goldman also is a shopkeeper. The difference between us seems to be that we are taking care of different shops. That is where the conflict comes in between us. We are vigilant caretakers of the interests of the Socialist Workers Party, which we were elected to represent. And you can bank on one thing: whatever comes out of the discussion and possible negotiations with the Shachtmanites and any other party, we are going to represent the interests of our own party through to the end.

10. New Issues in Dispute

The issues between us and the Shachtmanites have been discussed in our previous meeting. I will not repeat them here—the main lines of difference. I believe we have to add now a new difference: How to fight fascism in the United States. I believe the Los Angeles experience will bring very sharply to the fore in the movement the whole concept of the struggle against fascism.[67] It is very important symptomatically. Our party categorically rejects the idea of putschist "hit and run" methods of fighting the menace of fascism. We base our policy squarely on the mobilization of the labor movement against the fascists. We insist on approaching the Stalinist party and the Stalinist unions in order to stir up the rank and file to push them into action.

Another difference has arisen, I am sorry to say, in the last week. I mentioned in the last debate that we apparently had differences with the Shachtmanites on the labor party question whenever it comes to a matter of practical application, although in general we appear to be in agreement. I read to my astonishment in the current *Labor Action* that they are opposed to our critical support of Frankensteen in the Detroit elections. It is really astonishing. They are for the labor party, just as we are, but we are never able to find a time or a place when we can support the same candidates in an election. Our Political

Committee couldn't find the slightest reason for not accepting the motion of our Detroit branch to support Frankensteen critically in the election. We are prodding our people there not to take too lackadaisical an attitude. We are discussing the idea of them getting deeper into the campaign, of going on the radio and making it known all over Detroit that we are for the labor candidate. *Labor Action* says: No, that is wrong. "The truth is that labor does not have a candidate in the election."

And they give a very dubious reason. They say: "If the same Frankensteen, however, were a candidate of a Labor Party and thereby subject to its program and control, we would support him." Program is not the basis on which we give our critical support to labor candidates. What we are supporting in the election is the principle of labor in politics independently. That is the class basis of our labor party policy.

I think we will have to clarify this question in the discussion with the Shachtmanites. It is a tactical question—that I grant you—but it may be very important in the next period. Such a question alone could cause a split in the movement if it were persisted in seriously enough by a minority.

In order to examine the possibility of unity with the Shachtmanites with the necessary thoroughness, we have to get some more information about their party. I presume we will. We haven't paid much attention to them in the recent years. We have been busy with other activities which we considered more important. We don't even know what the nuances, tendencies, and factions are at the present time. We hear they have one faction against the labor party in principle; another in favor of the "Three Theses"; another in favor of the conception that the Russian state is fascist; another that it is ruled by a new bureaucratic class, and so on.

They know all about us. We ought to get some exact information about them. I wonder how it is that we don't get any reciprocity—that people who carry our internal bulletins to them don't carry their internal bulletins back to us. Shouldn't they conduct a two-way package service? However, we don't really need it. Perhaps, in one of our next letters we will ask the WP to send us a full set of their internal bulletins, and we will offer to pay for them at the full price. Surely such a reasonable request will not be refused, if unity is seriously contemplated.

Would it be too much if in the course of the discussion we should ask Shachtman where he stands now on his bloc with

Burnham in 1940 against us, against Trotsky, against Marxism? That was the beginning of the downfall of Shachtman. Our youth must be taught that blocs with anti-Marxists against Marxists are not permissible. This bloc paved the way for the criminal split.

11. The Analysis of Stalinism

The question of our attitude toward the Stalinist party and the Stalinist unions is, in our opinion, a decisive question. And this leads straight to the Russian question from which, no matter how impatient you may be, you can't get away. If Russia is simply a new class state of exploiters, then the CP, and the unions controlled by the CP, are, as the Shachtmanites are more and more describing them, not workers' organizations, but pure and simple instruments of a foreign enemy class. The logic of this is that we have to treat them as we treated the German Bund, as Burnham wanted us to treat the CP back in 1939. This tendency would be fatal for us, comrades, because the key to the penetration of the labor movement of America, in many respects, is through the Stalinist unions. Why, the great demonstration that was organized in Los Angeles against Gerald L. K. Smith was made possible primarily by the Stalinist unions—in large measure through the pressure of our fraction working upon them. The Shachtmanites proposed a united front of the WP and the SWP, the Socialist Labor Party, the Socialist Party, and the IWW to fight fascism. Our comrades said, "No, the ones you left out are the most important." We said, the key to the fight against fascism is to get into the Stalinist unions, which control the CIO, and through them to put pressure on the other unions, in order to organize the class united front against fascism.

We have to clarify the analysis of Stalinism, of the Stalinist party and the Stalinist unions. While our minority have been concentrating their whole thought in this period on the Shachtmanites, as though this is the whole key to the development of the revolution in the United States, we have been paying more attention to the CP and the unions under their influence and control. As a result, we have established valuable connections with Stalinist workers in two different sections of the country. We consider this work of the greatest importance for the development of the party. It cannot be done if we fail to make a correct analysis of Stalinism and the Stalinist organizations.

Up till now, in our opinion, the real orientation of the Shachtmanites was to the right. Their approach to the YPSL for unification clearly showed it. Their repulsion from the Stalinist workers showed it—a form of adaptation to the Social Democracy. The general friendliness of rightist elements toward them showed the rightward trend of the WP in inverted form. In every case, when there is a difference between us and the Shachtmanites, look at the right-wing elements and see where their sympathy lies—with them, not us. You might say Shachtman can't be blamed for such people liking him better than they like us. But Lenin didn't have that opinion. In one of the most remarkable books ever written in the history of our movement, Lenin's book called *One Step Forward, Two Steps Back*—which is an account of the struggle in the 1903 congress and the split—Lenin attacked Martov for an opportunist tendency because, whenever they had a difference in the congress, all the right-wing elements in the congress supported him against Lenin. When Martov protested that he was being misrepresented, Lenin answered: I didn't say you had a formal bloc with them. I would never accuse you of such an abomination. But every time there was a disagreement they supported you against us, and that showed they felt an instinctive affinity with you. Historical developments showed that Lenin's interpretation had a sound basis.

12. The Prospects of Unification

Their trend has been to the right. The discussion will show whether the trend is reversed. I don't deny the possibility. We have always known that the Shachtman organization is a combination of all kinds of tendencies; some of them are antagonistic. The Shachtman organization is, you may say, a perfect representation of the consequences of unprincipled combinationism in politics. From the beginning they were united only on one thing: against the "regime" in the SWP.

I don't doubt that there may be appearing in the Workers Party some sentiments for unity in good faith with us. We will see how the trend develops. Certainly, if there is a genuine unity sentiment in their ranks it is a trend toward the left, toward revolutionary Marxism, and we certainly should not repulse such a tendency.

But we have plenty of time. We have time; and please don't try to push us, because we are not going to be pushed. If it took the Workers Party five years to discover the necessity of discussing unity with us, we can take a little time to scrutinize the new proposals. That is what we are going to do. We are not going to sabotage the discussion. We are not going to play abstentionist politics with them. We will answer every letter. Maybe later we may change.

You might ask what, in our opinion, is the perspective? Are we going to have unity with the Shachtmanites; or is their approach a maneuver which will be exposed and frustrated? We are not going to give a categoric answer in advance. The prospects of unity depend on how much and how seriously the Shachtmanites mean the change which they have indicated in their first letter, and what guarantees can be established in the course of the discussion for a firmly based unity that will strengthen the party and build the party.

I will admit that we had a different opinion at the beginning of the discussion, and I state this frankly so that the minority comrades, when they take the floor, can know what our analysis was. We thought at first that it was more likely that our minority would leave the SWP and join the Shachtmanites than that the Shachtmanites would come to us and join the party. That is the way we appraised their ideological rapprochement with the Shachtmanites, combined with their bitter estrangement from us and their scandalous disloyalty to our party.

Perhaps the minority have thought it over and are shrinking back from such a course, because the Workers Party is a bankrupt organization and they know it. They know, when they have to face the issue point-blank, that these people can't build a party, neither by themselves nor with the aid of our minority. They know that the only hope either one of them has to function effectively in the expanding revolutionary movement is on the basis of the Socialist Workers Party, because we do know how to build a party and we are proving it in action every day. We are proving it by the proletarian forces that are coming to us in steadily mounting numbers.

I could read here the statistics of the new members joining our party week to week, month to month; the new successes we are achieving with our press, our trade union fractions, etc. But I don't have time to do that. Maybe I can give you a little of this information in my summary.

I will wind up with this. Our orientation is going to remain what it is and has been: a proletarian orientation. We are going to concentrate first of all on our expansion program for the development of our party as a workers' party. We will discuss with the Shachtmanites, as much as they want to discuss, but not as the main element of our activity; only as a small part of it. And, similarly, we will continue the discussion with the minority as long as they want to discuss; but also not at the expense of the development of the party in the class struggle, and the recruitment of new workers who are the basis of the future revolutionary party in America. That comes first. And that, if you stop to think about it, is the best way to prepare the party for unity with the Shachtmanites—or any other eventuality.

Felix Morrow and Albert Goldman

SUMMARY SPEECH AT THE NEW YORK MEMBERSHIP MEETING

September 2, 1945

The following are Cannon's summary remarks after the discussion that followed his report, "Again: On 'Unity with the Shachtmanites.'" The text has been slightly abridged from the version published in SWP Internal Bulletin, *vol. VII, no. 9, September 1945.*

1. We Must Put Our Own House in Order

We had two characteristic speeches from Goldman. The first in the fishwife tone packed with hysteria, insults, denigration, and slander. Then we had a summary speech in the patronizing grandfather tone: "Think, children, listen to Grandpa. You are on the wrong road. All your work is no good. The party is in terrible shape. You must do what we say and do it within two weeks. We must bring in the Shachtmanites in order to intellectualize the party." Goldman was even more insulting, even more offensive than usual today. That is saying a great deal.

Goldman does not introduce insults, condescension, and unbridled abusiveness into the party discussion because he lacks "manners." On the contrary, he is well schooled in this respect; and in discussions with people whom he considers equals and superiors—intellectual opponents of the party, free-lance litterateurs, prominent renegades, etc.—he behaves with Chesterfieldian courtesy. What he lacks is not "manners" but respect for the party, for its proletarian cadres, for the intelligence of its members.

It took the minority five years to discover the merits of the Shachtmanites, and they give us two weeks to jump on the bandwagon. Pardon us if we take a little more time. [. . .]

Our minority have been doing a lot of discussing, a lot of talking, and a lot of writing. Don't you think it would be a good idea now for us to develop this discussion and carry it through to its conclusion in our own ranks? Before we unite with any other party, wouldn't it be a good idea to put our own house in order, stamp out disloyalty in the ranks, and restore discipline in the party? Wouldn't that be the most serious and responsible way of preparing for any eventuality with regard to the Workers Party—whether it is to be a unification or another period of warfare as we have had for the past five years? I believe so.

What good is a party that has no discipline in its ranks? What respect will workers have for such a party? And above all, what respect can workers have for a party that has no discipline for its leaders? We say to the worker who joins the party, that he must be disciplined; that he must obey the decisions of his fraction; that he must operate under the control of the party in his union work and all party activities. Can we do that and then permit leaders to flaunt the discipline of the party, to sneer at the idea of loyalty to the party?

The anarchistic leaders of the minority overestimate the virtues and powers of "direct action." They think that by openly breaking discipline and laughing at party loyalty they have thereby eliminated these concepts from party life. I believe they are going to be disappointed; the party is going to pass judgment on them. The party is going to proceed as it always has in such cases: justly, but firmly. [. . .]

Goldman tries to dispose of party loyalty—something that every communist worker feels in his bones—by saying, you can't make people loyal by rules. That is true. Loyal people don't need rules. Rules are made to restrain the disloyal and prevent them from disrupting the party. That is why we have a constitution, that is why we have rules and regulations. I believe the party is going to insist that they be observed; that all members without exception—especially the leaders—must subordinate themselves to the discipline of the party. [. . .]

Goldman said in the fishwife section of his discourse: "You can't scare us." What he meant to say was: "You can't discipline us. You can't prevent us from negotiating behind the backs of the party. You can't prevent us from collaborating with political opponents of the party against our own party's Political Committee." Why, he stood up here today and admitted that they had already been discussing a split from the party, and now he says the split question is eliminated. Why? Because they have decided to be loyal and disciplined? No. Because we are going to have unity in two weeks, consequently they don't have to bother about a split anymore. Perhaps what took the split idea out of their minds temporarily was the realization that it wouldn't be a very big split; that the ranks of our party would be consolidated strongly against them; and that even in their small faction they couldn't take the few workers with them in such a treacherous adventure. Perhaps their new idea is, unity first and then a bigger split.

2. Special Pleaders for the Workers Party

Whom was Goldman speaking for here today? The Socialist Workers Party or the Shachtman party? He, and Williams [Oscar Shoenfeld] repeating after him, said, "examine the letters." Pardon me. They examined one letter. They examined the letter of the Political Committee of the Socialist Workers Party line by line to see if there is a "maneuver" in it. The letter from the Workers Party they take for good coin. There is no possible maneuver on the part of the Shachtmanites. The Shachtmanites are entitled to full credit because, after all, all they did was split our party and try to destroy it. But if we show the slightest doubt, the slightest desire to proceed cautiously and carefully, to test them out in action and probe them deeper—then we are against unity.

I don't think that is the correct way to present the question. Goldman says that if we don't appoint on our negotiating committee to talk with the Shachtmanites a member of the minority who has already been negotiating with them for weeks, day and night, behind our backs, then he will not trust the report of the committee. I tell you, I don't give two hoots whether you trust our committee or not. What I am concerned about is whether the rank and file of the party will trust it. We will test that out by taking the issue to the rank and file of the party. [. . .]

You ask us, "Are the differences compatible?" Suppose I ask you: "Will the Shachtmanites be loyal this time? Will they be disciplined? Have they changed to that extent? Have they changed that seriously?" We don't know. We know that you are not loyal; we know that you are not disciplined. And you are very poor recommenders for other people that we are going to have to put trust in.

I believe these issues, these accusations, and these abominable slanders that have been raised by our minority require a discussion in our ranks. And I mean a real discussion, one that is carried to a decision by the party. If that entails a delay in any organizational steps toward unity or otherwise with the Shachtmanites, it is not our fault. We have got to fix up our own party first. Does anybody think that we are crazy enough to make unity with the Shachtmanites without establishing absolutely clearly and firmly our own party position on every point? No, we wouldn't even talk about such a thing.

3. The Party Convention Must Decide

And among the positions we have got to establish by convention decision are precisely these points which have been raised by our minority, as well as those which have separated us from the Shachtmanites. The accusations must be answered not merely by us in debate with you, but by the party membership in convention, deciding. That is the way we are going to answer the questions in the last analysis. The falsified issues have to be set straight; and the slanderers have to come before the judgment of the party. And we absolutely must discuss and decide once again the question of questions, which was at the bottom of the split in 1940 and which is at the bottom of our fight with our present minority: the question of *what kind of a party!*

You say here tonight: "The party is on the wrong road. The party's organization system is wrong." Very well. Let us take it to the convention and let the party convention decide this question. [. . .]

Every reasonable, serious person must know that an attempt to heal a five-year split will take time and careful deliberation. Any attempt to rush the party into a speculative unity, to "stampede" the party, will be regarded as an act of hostility and will be met by hostility. If anyone wants to sharpen the fight, then let him say he wants to sharpen the fight and dispense with hypocritical sermons about unity. Nobody will believe them.

4. Advantages and Dangers of Unification

There are a great many dangers attached to the unification with the Shachtmanites, even under the best conditions, and there are advantages too. We have to weigh them carefully. We have time. It is not we who are in a crisis and panic. It is you, the minority. Our party is rolling along. Our party morale is away up on the peak. Our party is growing and expanding on all fronts. What have we to be panicky about? It is you who are in a panic and demanding a quick answer, within two weeks! I believe the Shachtmanites are in a rather bad way too. I don't know much about them. We have no agents in their ranks. We didn't have anybody to spare for that kind of a job. We sent all our militants out into the trade union field where we thought they could get better results. That is one of the reasons why we have grown, because we have sent our activists out where the awakening workers could be reached.

There are certain advantages to unification, provided it is securely and firmly based. But there are certain dangers too. One of them that I would like to pose to you is that the admittance of the Shachtmanites into our party now—and, in view of the relation of forces, that is the only realistic form that unification could take—would tend to dilute the party. Wouldn't it? It isn't a question of differences on one point or two points, but of systematic differences on many points. Grant, in the best case, if they have goodwill—which is an absolutely necessary aspect of any serious unification—that with our increased strength and our expanding movement, we could tolerate that dilution. But that might not be the end of it. Diluting the party to the right—admission of the Shachtmanites would be diluting it to the right—would carry with it a certain pressure to dilute it still further to the right, which they might propose and insist upon, with the best will in the world, as corresponding to their ideology.

Since I made my speech at the first discussion, I got the convention proceedings of the Yipsels, to whom a bare few weeks ago the Shachtmanites addressed a fraternal letter, proposing unification. I didn't have the exact text before me at that time, but I got it since. And reading that, I was astounded. These people had a fraction inside the Yipsels of three or four people. And knowing the trend of this organization, they addressed a fraternal letter of unification to them. I believe the letter they sent to the Yipsels was a really sincere letter. It wasn't a maneuver. It was really a proposal for unity. Now, here is the programmatic position of the YPSL. It is the political resolution of their convention, "On the Road to Power." The Yipsels reject reformistic Social Democracy. That is good, as far as it goes, but every centrist group does that. But that is not all they reject. They also reject Bolshevism. That is not good at all.

They say:

> *No more than reformist Social Democracy can Bolshevism achieve our goals.* This approach was utilized by the Bolshevik Party in Russia in their seizure of power in 1917. It is an approach which Bolsheviks would have us imitate in other countries. The basic fault of such a program is the failure to recognize the relationship of means and ends. The Bolshevik revolution of 1917 was a coup d'etat, carried through by a party which had no majority. This same party considered all other socialist parties their "enemies" and proceeded to liquidate each one upon their assumption of power. The result is well known—a brutal dictatorship of one party which has completely regimented and terrorized the Russian people. This result—the Soviet Union today—is not only not a socialist country, but is one of the greatest enemies of socialism throughout the world. We reject the notion that this set of tactics shall be imitated in our attempt to achieve socialism.

If that isn't a perfect and classical formulation of anti-Bolshevism I would like to have one presented. I don't object, mind you, to the YPSL having that opinion, and I don't propose putting them in jail for it. But I strongly object to any suggestion of unity with them in one party. They don't have our communist ideology. And I would like to inquire, in the course of the discussion with the Shachtmanites, what prompted them to propose unification with these Souvarinist Yipsels.

5. What Kind of a Party?

[. . .] We want a party that is dominated by the workers. We want a party that disciplines the leaders. If the Shachtmanites come back to our party eventually, they will come back to that kind of a party, if we have our say about it. There can be no compromise on this question. The minority has been repeating more and more, idea for idea, and lately, even word for word, all the concepts of "War and Bureaucratic Conservatism" on the nature and character of the party. [. . .]

We are against that and we demand of you now, since you are presenting so many demands: Formulate your theories of party organization in a resolution! Quit nibbling at little questions. Put down in black and white, in the form of a resolution, what kind of a party you want. Whether we have unity with the Shachtmanites or don't have unity—if the Shachtmanites join us or if they don't join us—what kind of a party do we aim to build? We don't have to write a resolution. Ours are already written. The documents of the big fight with the Shachtmanites, collected in the book *The Struggle for a Proletarian Party,* contain our program. If you never mention that book, it is not because you don't like its author. It is because you don't like the party resolutions on organization contained in the book and you haven't enough courage yet to formulate counterresolutions. We don't have to write a resolution, but we are going to write another one anyway. And we are going to direct it against you and all the ideas of organization you have developed in the discussion during the past year, and submit the dispute to the judgment of the party and later to the international movement.

And speaking of the International, I can only repeat what Comrade Stuart [Sam Gordon] said. You will be defeated there too. You are trying to threaten us with the Fourth International, which allegedly is going to support you and your ideas and give sympathy to the Shachtmanites. You even introduce into the atmosphere of our party the suggestion of a letter or "cable from Moscow" which might change the policy of the leadership. As if our Political Committee is governed by cables and letters of individuals. You are doing a very bad service to the party and to the International to make even such a suggestion as that.

What is the Fourth International? Is it a few isolated individuals in different parts of the world pronouncing edicts for us to carry out? Not at all. We are not formally affiliated to the Fourth International, but we are part of the international movement, and a very important part of it too. The Fourth International is an association of parties, and these parties cannot have formulated their opinions on our fight yet because they haven't had the opportunity to study the essential material.

I know this, that the Fourth International in the past has always supported the proletarian majority of our party every time. On what do you base the assumption that the whole Fourth International will change its basic views after the experiences of five years? I believe that the harsh experiences of the comrades in Europe will condition them harder against the idea of a talking club, a petty-bourgeois discussion circle, such as they had too long in France, and in favor of a workers' party with loyalty and discipline in its ranks. We respect the opinions of all comrades of the International, even when we disagree with them. If there are differences of opinion in the Fourth International what will we do? Will we sit around and wait for a cable? By no means. We think for ourselves and fight for our ideas. If necessary, we will fight for our opinions in the international party as we fight in the national party. We haven't any doubt about the outcome; we are sure that we are right, and we are sure that we will get the support of the majority. [. . .]

6. The Proletarian Orientation

I want to close the way I think it is right to close—on the basic line that governed our fight against Burnham and Shachtman in 1939-40. The proletarian orientation—that is our line. Relations with the Workers Party, unity with them or a further split with them—that is not our main axis as it was in 1939-40. It is a secondary issue. So also is our internal faction fight with Goldman, Morrow, and Company. All these concerns are secondary to our basic work of penetrating the awakening movement of militant workers in America and bringing them into our ranks. That is the way we have been proceeding ever since the split with the Shachtmanites. It is the right way, the only way for us.

I read in this magazine which Goldman slanders so maliciously, the *Fourth International,* for August, the reprint of Trotsky's old letter called, "Closer to the Proletarians of the 'Colored' Races!" This was based on a letter that had been received from a group of Negro workers in Johannesburg, proclaiming sympathy for the Fourth International, who didn't yet know all the fine points of the program. Trotsky said, their approach to us is very important and very symptomatic, and we must accept them with open arms. He had a different criterion for the acceptance of oppressed workers than for worldly wise and world-weary intellectuals. He said:

> When ten intellectuals, whether in Paris, Berlin, or New York, who have already been members of various organizations, address themselves to us with a request to be taken into our midst, I would offer the following advice: put them through a series of tests on all the programmatic questions; wet them in the rain, dry them in the sun, and then after a new and careful examination accept maybe one or two.[68]

That was the Old Man's advice. He continued: "The case is radically altered when ten workers connected with the masses turn to us. The difference in our attitude to a petty-bourgeois group and to the proletarian group does not require any explanation." He wanted to take in these workers who had applied, confident that their class instinct and the added pressure of their national oppression would facilitate their assimilation of the basic ideas of the International Left Opposition.

When that letter was written, we had not one single Negro worker in the party. At the time of the split with the petty-bourgeois opposition, notwithstanding the fact that we had then a very talented and eloquent Negro comrade at the head of our work in this field, I don't think we had a dozen in the party.[69] Now we have more than a hundred Negro workers in the party! They have been recruited in the struggle of the party in the last five years. And all the reports from Detroit and Los Angeles and other basic industrial centers of the party report an influx of workers of which there is a goodly percentage of militant Negro trade union comrades.

We are recruiting workers into the party; and don't accuse me of switching away from the "political" question when I report it, because that is the essence of the political question—that we are building a genuine workers' party, a party where the worker feels at home and stays. That is what we are fighting for. The recruitment figures tell the story of a rapidly expanding proletarian party.

That is what is taking place in this party, and that is why we are not in panic about unity with the Workers Party. You know about the sub campaigns of *The Militant*. The circulation of *The Militant* is held down to 31,000 now only because the printshop can't handle any more. But as soon as we make the necessary mechanical arrangements, we are going to put on another subscription campaign for 10,000 new readers. We are all confident that by January 1 we will have a *Militant* circulation of 50,000. By the next convention we expect to reach the goal of 100,000 circulation. That is the way this party, which you so shamelessly denigrate until the party members are sick of listening to you—that is the way the party is developing into a popular mass party of the workers.

The relation of forces is entirely in our favor with regard to the Workers Party and with regard to the minority in the party, and there is a profound reason for it too. It arises from the nature of the party—its proletarian composition, and its attractiveness to workers. [. . .]

The opposition of the membership to you is not due to their ignorance and their inability to think, as you represent with despicable snobbery. It is due to their revolutionary merit, their revolutionary spirit, their proletarian composition. Such a spirit, and such a composition of the party will be the strongest safeguard in the future against any repetition of what we had in 1939-40.

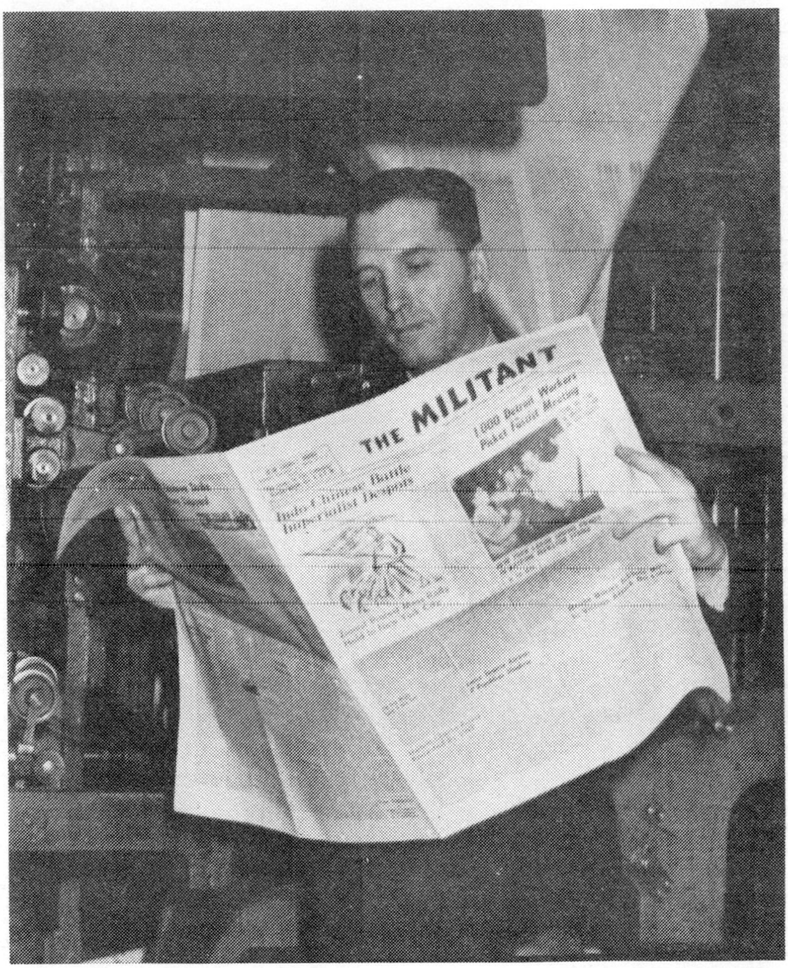

Farrell Dobbs, 1945

A LETTER TO NATALIA SEDOVA[70]

September 4, 1945

This letter from Cannon's archives has not been previously published.

Dear Comrade:

Usick just handed me a translation of your letter of August 28 with the reference to the Workers Party and the standpoint of Goldman. Your viewpoint in these respects has been known to us for some time. You are equally aware of our opinions on these matters.

The purpose of this letter is to ask explicit direction from you as to what disposition you wish to have made of your letter of August 28. The salutation "Dear Friend" would indicate that it is intended for some individual, but the name is not specified. The contents of the letter could indicate, however, that the letter was destined for the consideration of the committee as a whole, or possibly for the internal bulletin. If this is the case please inform me promptly and we will publish your letter in the internal bulletin with our answer. On the other hand, if you wish to restrict the discussion, for the time being, to personal correspondence, we will answer you in that sense.

It would be useless to try to confine the letter, even during a period of preliminary discussion with you, to the confines of the committee. All matters and all documents which come up for consideration in our Political Committee these days are promptly transmitted to the Workers Party for publication in their press. This situation necessitates absolute precision as to the intended destination of your letter of August 28 or any others which you may address to us.[71]

We do not want any repetition of the incident connected with the first letter which came from you last year on the Russian question. Roland in his notorious "document" made the assertion that you had intended this letter "for the party" and that the party leadership had "suppressed" it, a foul falsification which you unfortunately did not promptly denounce. Needless to say, the Shachtmanites repeated this falsification in their press on the basis of Roland's "information."

Yours fraternally,
J. P. Cannon

Rose Karsner, Natalia Sedova, Grace Carlson

U.S. TROOPS OUT OF INDOCHINA![72]

September 26, 1945

The following telegram was sent to President Truman on behalf of the SWP. The text is from the October 6, 1945, issue of The Militant.

United Press dispatch dated September 16 reports that American troops have intervened in the struggle of the Indochinese people for freedom from the oppressive rule of French imperialism and that United States troops in Hanoi broke up a demonstration by Annamese demanding the independence of their country. In Saigon, British and French troops in collaboration with the Japanese garrison are reported shooting down the Indochinese people.

The Socialist Workers Party protests vigorously against these Allied attempts to suppress the independence movement of the Indochinese people and to deny them the freedom which the United States and other Allied powers promised to all peoples in the Atlantic Charter.[73] We request from you, Mr. President, a public assurance that the armed forces of the United States will not henceforth be used to oppose and frustrate the just demand of the people of Indochina for full freedom and independence.

THE WORKERS PARTY AND THE MINORITY IN THE SWP[74]

October 7, 1945

These remarks were made during the discussion period of a special plenum of the SWP National Committee held in New York October 6-7 to take up the question of unity with the WP. They have been slightly abridged from an unpublished and uncorrected stenogram.

I think Comrade Morrow demonstrated two things for us in his speech. The first is that he doesn't understand the resolution that is before the plenum. The second is that he doesn't understand our party and how its leadership functions.

I will explain how he misunderstands the resolution secondly, but first I want to point out that his objections to the calling of the plenum and his remark about our "maneuver"—how we will fool the comrades in "the sticks"—show that he doesn't understand the party. He doesn't understand that the people from "the sticks" are the people who rule the Socialist Workers Party.

The functionaries in the center have the duty to initiate policy. That is their function of leadership. But they cannot carry out policy without the support and sanction of the representatives of the districts. That is the way it is; and that, in our opinion, is the way it should be. That is why we construct our leadership the way we do. That is why it is a broad committee. That is why it is dominated, when matters of decision are concerned, by representatives from the field, who represent the proletarian cadres of the party.

Morrow and Goldman would never get the idea in their heads that this is a deliberate policy of our party, and that the plenum is called in order to submit to the full leadership of the party the proposals which the political functionaries in the center have initiated. The purpose of the plenum is to fix and decide the policy of the leadership. That is what it is for. Not to fool anybody at all, but to make sure that nobody fools the party.

This whole issue of unity with the Shachtmanites has arisen artificially. It did not arise, after five years of warfare, through any need felt by the SWP for unity with the Shachtmanites. Neither did it arise through any need felt by the Shachtmanites for unity with us. I don't need to tell you this, as far as our party is concerned, because you know it. As far as Shachtman is concerned, he told us frankly in the discussions that they had not thought of the question of unity with us until the minority issued their "unity" resolution.

The orientation of the Shachtmanites toward unity is based entirely upon the emergence of a "unity" faction in our organization. The proof of this is formally indicated by the fact that their first reference to unity in their press begins with the publication of the resolution of the minority, courteously handed over to them before it was published even in our internal bulletin.

You have only to read Shachtman's article entitled "Five Years of the Workers Party," which was published in the May or June issue of the *New International,* to confirm this fact once again. This article clearly shows that as late as May and June the Workers Party leadership had no idea of unity with us and, as a matter of fact, stated that it is excluded by the regime in the SWP. The issue of unity was dealt with even in their Active Workers Conference in the following terms.[75] I have here a document called "The Task Before the Party," one of Shachtman's theses for the Active Workers Conference, in which he said:

> A sharp division is being created in the S.W.P. It is difficult to say at present just how it will develop. One thing is already clear, however: the minority has developed a most friendly attitude toward our party. It is already speaking in terms of unity between the S.W.P. and the W.P., an idea which is received with the greatest hostility by the Cannonite leadership. Naturally, we for our part do not exclude in advance and under all circumstances and conditions the possibility of unification of the two Trotskyist organizations in this country. At the same time, desirable as unity is in general, we are too deeply devoted to our own principles and program and above all to our conception of a democratically centralized (as against a bureaucratized) party, to surrender them for the sake of good fellowship. As matters stand now, we cannot, therefore, speak too optimistically about unity. *A regrouping, on the other hand, is possible, even if we cannot yet*

> *speak with any exactness about the way it may take place.* What we can speak about with confidence is that whatever does take place in this field in the next period will not be to the detriment of our party, its ideas and its future. [Emphasis added—J.P.C.]

At the Active Workers Conference, in preparing the material, Shachtman had in mind the logic of the development of this friendly faction in our party, not as a unity with the SWP but as a regroupment.[76] Well, I think he is quite logical about that.

> We have a doctrine; we have a tradition; we have a program; we have worked out, after painful experience, a method of working in the class struggle, and a method of building the kind of party we believe is necessary for leading the fight for the socialist revolution. These we must maintain. They make up our party.

That is the conception that the Shachtmanites discussed at their Active Workers Conference. In another document of this conference, they state:

> In the course of the past five years, the number of these political differences between the S.W.P. and the W.P. has increased, and they range all the way from theoretical to tactical-practical questions.[77]

That doesn't read much like the formulations that have been given to us by the minority. It shows that the Shachtmanites put the thing straight. They have a program. They have a tradition. They have a method of organization which they intend to maintain. And this is not what they said five years ago; this is what was said a few weeks ago.

Discussing unity, like everything else, we should discuss it with a full understanding of all the facts and circumstances, and that is part of the facts, part of the circumstances. Now, having that attitude—which was confirmed to the hilt in our discussions with them—we have to ask: What does the proposal, the so-called unity proposal, of the Shachtmanites really amount to? Is it a proposal for unification in any form that we have ever experienced before in the history of our movement? No. It is absolutely unprecedented in the Trotskyist movement; in the entire revolutionary movement, as far as we know.

And that is not merely our opinion; that is Shachtman's opinion, stated frankly in the discussions and incorporated in the letter which he sent to our plenum, a copy of which you all have. It is not a proposal to unite on a common program. It is a proposal to apply toward the SWP the tactic which we applied to the Socialist Party in 1936—that is, an entry. They propose to enter the Socialist Workers Party with all their ideas and methods, as an organized body with an organ of their own.

The only difference between their proposal to the SWP and our proposal to the SP was that we called it by its right name. When we united with the Musteites on a program, we said, that is a unity. When we joined the Socialist Party with our different ideas, we said, that is an entry. This is a fact that we have to establish at the very beginning.

I don't mean to say that that, in itself, rules out the acceptance of it. You know that the Bolsheviks are absolutely inexhaustible in their adaptation of organizational forms to their political needs. I only recite this to establish what the facts are, and then to discuss whether it is advantageous for us and politically necessary to accept that proposition at the present time. [. . .]

Now, this was the great purpose that our discussions with them served. It served the purpose it was designed for. Not negotiations in any sense of the word; they were exploratory discussions. We wanted to get behind the formal letter they sent and find out a little more accurately the feel of their attitude. And the discussions that we had with the Shachtmanites confirmed the fact that they have not only not changed their attitude toward us, our ideas, and our methods, but they have hardened them and developed them over a period of five years.

We would be in error if we judged the Shachtmanite conceptions of politics and of organization solely on the basis of what they said and did in 1940, because then they were only in a stage of their evolutionary development, still under certain pressures from us, and from Trotsky, and from membership in a common organization with us. And since then they have been five years completely on their own, uninfluenced by us or by Trotsky or by the Fourth International, and they have developed their half-formed conceptions and hardened them into greater antagonism to us, more frankly stated, more freely developed. Even the document entitled "The War and Bureaucratic Conservatism" contains sections which they have thrown overboard in the interim. I will demonstrate that in the course of the discussion.

Morrow mentioned the fact that we, in our discussions with the Shachtmanites, talked a good deal about the so-called tendency bulletin. We did. Because that was a sort of touchstone for us.

And the discussions with them on this point, and the further discussions and elaborations of the question here by Goldman yesterday, show that that is a question, an issue, of extraordinary symptomatic importance.

You know—I repeat again—that the Bolsheviks are capable of bending organization rules in any direction in an abnormal situation. We have no immutable principles of organization. We have norms, and in abnormal situations we bend the norm one way or another; but then, when the situation becomes normalized, we try to come back to the norm. We have a criterion, we have a conception that we don't always succeed in applying in practice, but which we aim for.

You might say that our conception of the press, in the Bolshevik conception of the centralized party, has as its most basic consideration the principle of the party-owned press.

The Socialist Party in the United States before First World War was dominated by the privately owned press. This, perhaps, may be news to some of the younger comrades here of the newer generation who did not participate in the movement before the First World War, and do not know what an enormous gulf separates communism from Social Democracy in the field of organization as well as in the field of politics and theory.

The Socialist Party was a party of unlimited freedom of tendencies, which is a rather fancy word for factions. The right wing of the party controlled and dominated the party through the press. And what a press! The biggest propaganda weekly of the Socialist Party before the war was the *Appeal to Reason*, a private enterprise owned by J. A. Wayland. For a long time the most popular monthly magazine of the party was called *Wilshire's Magazine*, a private enterprise of Gaylord Wilshire, which he used to preach socialism and to advertise mining stock.

In later years the most influential monthly magazine was the *International Socialist Review* owned by Charles H. Kerr and Company in Chicago. Not by the Chicago branch, not by the National Committee of the party, but by Charles H. Kerr and Company. It was the informal center of the radical wing of the party, but they didn't control it; they had the privilege of buying and selling it in bundles. The big dailies like the *Milwaukee Leader*, in later years the *Oklahoma Leader*, the New York *Call*, were owned by rigged-up stock companies such as the *Jewish Daily Forward*, outside the control of the party, controlled by the stockholders.

Only in isolated locals was the press owned by the party, and those were the cases where no one else would put up the money for them and they were a losing proposition. The big press was privately owned.

That is, you may say, the ultimate extreme of decentralization in the field of the press. Against that, when we formed the Communist Party in 1919, we wrote on our masthead from the very beginning, "Party-owned press." From the very beginning we never heard the suggestion in the early Communist Party of such a thing as a privately owned organ. There was no such thing.

The party was unanimous in its conception that the party had to own the press. That we have carried over into the Trotskyist movement. Our press has always been the press of the party and we never have tolerated, not only privately owned organs; we never have tolerated local organs unless we found the necessity for them. In every case the issuance of a paper locally by our party would have to be approved by the National Committee and would have to be under the control of the National Committee. The purpose of that is, of course, obvious, that we want one uniform line of policy from New York to California.

In the old days, every paper preached its own brand of socialism. The *Ohio Socialist* was a "red" paper. The *Milwaukee Leader* was a "yellow" paper. The Chicago *International Socialist Review* was a sort of mildly "red" magazine. The New York *Call* had a slightly different centrist line. Complete local autonomy in one sense, and individual autonomy in the other. This kind of business was cloaked over with the slogans of democracy and free press, free expression.

The conception of a multitude of organs is a perfect formula for a brand of spurious democracy which gives irresponsible intellectuals absolutely free play to write whatever they damn well please. And that is the beginning and the end of their conception of democracy. The idea that the rank and file of a proletarian majority has the right to dominate the press and to control it, and to subordinate the intellectuals to it, is completely alien to them.

The question is put: Why don't we say in so many words that we reject in principle the idea of the Shachtmanites moving into our party, getting themselves all set with a paper of their own? Well, we don't have that immutable principle. It is not normal with us. We never, in the seventeen years of American Trotskyism—which is not the worst section of world Trotskyism by any means—had any such thing as that. From the very beginning in 1928 we had one public paper for the party, owned by the party, and one internal bulletin, owned by the party.

But when, as happened in 1935, a militant, split-threatening faction, the Oehlerites, began to publish a paper of their own, a bulletin of their own, we did not immediately proscribe it. We were then confronted with the problem—we were in the midst of a principled discussion with them—should we forbid the separate bulletin, and expel them from the party, or should we tolerate their direct action in order to keep the discussion on a political plane, and leave discipline out of it for the time being? We decided on the latter course. We who considered it an absolute outrage, when they had free access to the party's internal bulletin, to publish a bulletin of their own, we decided to put up with it.

But now, after the Bolsheviks have demonstrated their capacity, in one case, to adapt themselves to the abnormal situation of a bulletin published by a group outside of the control of the party, the present minority want to make that into a precedent and say that it is the normal, natural right of a tendency to do that. Every time there is a violation of organizational norms, they want to say that is the norm for all time.

Let us take this theory expounded by the Shachtmanites—and they, like we, want to discuss the question in its broadest sense. We said, it is not a question for us, as Shachtman correctly pointed out in the letter, we haven't any immutable principle. There are times when we would have to permit such a thing although we don't agree with it. I said in the fight of 1940—I think I wrote it in one of the letters in my book, in a letter to Comrade Trotsky—that I don't exclude under all circumstances granting their demand for a public organ. It is a question of weighing which costs you more—a split or a temporary toleration of a rival public organ. We know Lenin tolerated a daily paper in the fight over Brest-Litovsk. He tolerated it because he couldn't help himself, but as soon as the situation cleared up and the party returned to normal, they put a stop to it.[78]

But let us take the principles they are enunciating: that they don't want this as an abnormal right. They want this as a natural right, and not only for them, but for any other tendency that wants it.

All right, now, let us develop that idea a little further. Goldman has already explained to us—in the Political Committee and again yesterday—that he doesn't believe in secrecy; he doesn't really believe in internal bulletins. "Why should they not be distributed to people who are interested in the party?" So that we have not simply a question of permitting, in an exceptional circumstance, one faction, the Shachtmanites, to have a bulletin of their own for a period in order to allay their suspicions. We are confronted with a principle that that is the norm and shall not be challenged, and not only they, but anybody who wants to do it. And then the step which goes further than that: that internal bulletins are, after all, an "absurdity." [. . .]

Let this thing develop now. The Shachtmanites have a bulletin. Goldman and Morrow have a bulletin, if they don't become joint owners of the Shachtman bulletin. Johnson has a tendency; why shouldn't he have a bulletin? Perhaps some other tendencies in our ranks would develop. These bulletins are not confined to the members. No. That is not Bolshevism. You are stupid. Bolshevism means: take the public into your confidence. Let the advanced workers, at least, know what you are talking about.

Let the thing develop a little further. This party is growing. It is not going to be a small party all the time. And when the party gets bigger it becomes more and more difficult to confine party discussions to the closed circle of the party. I know that is correct. Then every one of these tendencies has a printed paper.

Goldman says that they would not distribute it to the public if it contains "agitational" material. But who determines what is agitational? The bulletin is under their control. They will explain to you: "You are mistaken. That is not agitation." Shachtman will point out this article in the last number of the *New International*, in which he demands that the theory of Trotsky on the Soviet Union be killed: "That is not agitation. You are stupid. That is just explanation." Or, you object that they are giving out their paper on Fourteenth Street indiscriminately. They reply: "The workers on Fourteenth Street are all advanced workers." Who decides who are advanced workers or not? They own the paper, they distribute it, they control it, and they do as they damn please with it—and what are you going to do? Expel them? No, you can't expel them. You are in the middle of a political discussion. And so on, and on, and on.

No, it breaks down the whole concept of democratic centralism. That is what they are driving at. It is from that point of view that we have to discuss the question of the tendency bulletin. We have the conception of a certain norm of the centralized party press, and of a discussion bulletin. The party gets bigger; this discussion bulletin will be printed. If the party sees fit it can be publicly sold. It is no principle with us that all discussion has to be internal. When the party reaches the size, for example, of the CP it would be impossible in any case to keep it absolutely internal.

And then the question arises of establishing a norm which sometimes is violated, in a severe faction fight, but which we try to come back to. But with your conception of the party, there would be no coming back. [. . .]

Suppose I turn anarchistic and don't like the way the party is being run, and have some money of my own, or can get money from sympathizers, why can't I run a little paper of my own for distribution to the party and to the radical workers who are interested? I wouldn't sell it in the sticks, of course, but only to the people who are interested. And who would judge who are radicals and interested? Why, naturally, my tendency.

That is the picture of a madhouse, the picture of a norm in the Social Democratic movement. That is what we once had. That was beneficial to everybody but the workers. They got the worst of it because the accumulative power of privately owned and semiprivately owned press was able to shape the party in a reformistic direction and to strangle the workers.

I think the best way to deal with this question, as well as all others, is to judge the Shachtmanite proposal from two points of view. One, from the point of view of their theory of the party, which is not our theory of the party. As Shachtman explained to us in a twenty-five or thirty-minute speech, it is a conception of a party of tendencies, and of course everybody knows that tendencies, if they are not led by pacifists, become in critical moments militant factions, a federation of factions.

That is not our conception of the party. Their conception of the press flows from their conception of the party. What does this unity proposition of the Shachtmanites really amount to? The Shachtmanites are offering to move the Workers Party inside the Socialist Workers Party, with their own press and their own program. That is their unity proposition.

Do we want to encourage that idea? What would be the result of it? Morrow assures us, and so does Goldman, "Oh, there would be no faction." Of course not. All they say is that our basic theory of the Soviet Union must be killed. All they say is that the International is dead and we killed it. All they say is that our conceptions are false.

And they want to come into the party as an organized body,

and they want to have their own press to fight for their ideas.

And they give us notice in advance that they are going to fight for a majority. Okay. In an educational way, I take it. All right, that is clarified. They are going to fight for a majority.

Now we have the majority. We are not going to fight to keep it? You know we are just a bunch of scissorbills who don't know anything but mass work. We think the secret of the revolution is doing honest, constructive work in the field—like Muste used to do—and then letting some other tendency come along and take it away from us.

No. That is not us. We are mass workers, we believe in mass work and recruitment, but we are also faction fighters, and when somebody tries to take the majority away from us and change the course of the party. They are in for a battle.

So the Shachtmanites are going to fight for a majority, and we are going to fight to keep it, and we are going to have a faction fight. Isn't that clear? It is as clear as day. I don't say, well, that proves we shouldn't have them in the party. No. We had them before and we took care of them, and I think we could do it again. But would it be advantageous for us—will it create a better arena for us?

Trotsky gave me some great lessons on this question when I was in France in 1934. I visited Trotsky prior to the unity with the Musteites to get his opinion. I was attending a plenum of the International Communist League where the turn toward mass work was formalized in a resolution, and I carried to him a report of a conversation I had had with Sneevliet of Holland, in Paris.[79]

We were negotiating with the Musteites. Sneevliet was beginning negotiations with the OSP [Independent Socialist Party] headed by Schmidt in Holland. The question of unification was being discussed by the German Trotskyists and the SAP (Socialist Workers Party). The two groups were in emigration after the coming of the Nazis, and the London Bureau had been set up.

Sneevliet put forth the theory: Now you are going to unite with the Musteites. We will unite with the Schmidt people. Let us unite the German group with the SAP, and let us move the whole bunch into the London Bureau and take the leadership of the London Bureau away from the centrists. I admit I was intrigued with that idea. I thought that would be pretty good. I explained it to the Old Man.

He said, "No. Partly right and partly wrong." He said, what do we make unity for? Not because we are professional unity sentimentalists or because we are afraid of splits when they are necessary.

I never saw anyone more cold-blooded on the question of unity or splits. He didn't care which it was because he didn't proceed from the point of view of unity or splits, but from the point of view of what was advantageous for the movement at the time. "You in America should by all means unite with the Musteites, if you can induce them to on a program. . . ."

I am not absolutely sure about this, but I was of the opinion at that time—and so was Shachtman—that even if we couldn't agree on the theoretical program, that we would unite with the Musteites on a limited program that would leave some questions for settlement later. And I am not sure the Old Man sanctioned that, but I believe he would if it would be necessary. He said, what we need is unity, an increase of communist forces in the groups split off from the Comintern because it is a getting-together of communist forces. We should be united.

Another reason for unification is to create for ourselves a broader arena. And consider what you have in America. You have in the Muste organization, according to your report, a great number of militant workers who are revolutionary in their feeling, although they are not very well experienced in politics. By uniting with the Musteites you create an arena for the comradely education and assimilation of excellent new recruits for the party. The same is true in Holland.

But the SAP—you know the Old Man was not in favor of unity with the SAP although they were much more political than the Musteites were. He said, let us go slow. Why? Because both our group and the SAP are separated from the German workers. They are in emigration. Although they are formally communists, they are in reality hardened centrists. Uniting with the SAP would only put us in a circle with unassimilable centrists in emigration, and not give us a new arena of workers. He said, if the SAP were in Germany and had thousands, it would be different, but in the present situation, he said, let us "keep our elbows free" with regard to the SAP, and then discuss political questions with them. And as you know, it never came to unification.[80]

That is why the Old Man was opposed to going into the London Bureau. He said there are no workers there; there is no arena for us. He said, I am in favor any time of ten communists joining the Norwegian Labor Party to look for workers in the ranks, but I am opposed to joining in a common committee with the reformist leaders who don't have any workers present when we are talking to them. There is no arena there.

Now, what do the Shachtmanites and ourselves offer to each other in a projected entry on their part? Who creates the arena for whom? Isn't that a good question? The Shachtmanites have got seventy-five new workers, that I grant you. I read that in their internal bulletin. They recruited them approximately over the period when we recruited 300. They are having some trouble assimilating them, but grant they have them. Is that an arena for us? We recruit that many new workers of the same type in two months and less.

What is the rest of their arena: the hardened, the young, miseducated college students from New York. No, that is not an arena for us. We have the arena we need right now—the arena of the militant labor movement from which we are recruiting forty and fifty a month. Art Wood [Arthur Burch] just told me they have thirteen applications in Detroit that haven't been passed on yet.

We have an arena, and by concentrating on this arena in the past period instead of wasting our time with the Shachtmanites, we sizably increased the membership of our party and have every prospect of increasing it more. I say here, as a very realistic and conservative estimate, that we are going to recruit one thousand workers in the next year. One thousand workers in the next year is not an unrealistic perspective.

The Shachtmanites, however, haven't done so well in the arena of the broad labor movement, although I grant you they tried. They tried their best to make *Labor Action* talk like they thought the workers talked. A great many of their young people went to work in the factories, and that does them credit. They went in there to educate the workers and to recruit them. But I look through their internal bulletins—it is one long complaint of their poor results, of their inability to assimilate the new workers. Problems which I have never heard raised in our party of the great difference in the level of the raw workers and the politically educated student-turned-worker-for-the-duration, etc.

The branches don't function very well. By God, you may not believe it, but you find they are writing theses now on what are the duties of a financial secretary of a branch, and how meetings should be conducted, what an organizer's tasks are, etc. They have shown no capacity to do any serious work except in a flashin-the-pan way in the labor movement. Compared with our solid, integrated work they made a poor showing in the mass movement.

The Shachtmanites have every reason to want to join our party, because there they will find an arena. There they will find 1,200—by next year 2,000—what they consider raw workers, raw material to work on. They will absolve themselves of the onerous responsibilities of trying to maintain a party with a big public press and a headquarters and a staff, and just move the whole thing over into our party. Let us take care of the organization, the mass work, and the press, and they will go to work on their new arena, the membership of our organization. Well, I think they would have something to gain by it and I don't blame them for proposing it. And I would not blame the leadership of our own party for saying, "Not yet, boys." And if they say hurry, because somebody is pushing us, we say, No, we don't feel that. We don't feel the push.

I said Morrow didn't understand our resolution. He was talking against the wind. Our resolution doesn't say a word about negotiations with the WP. Our resolution says the task now, for the next period, is to draw the lines of demarcation between ourselves and the Workers Party. That is what our resolution says. That we have to clarify every point in which they challenge our program and organization methods. "And what is our answer?" you said. "You have to give an answer to the Shachtmanite proposal." That is our answer. Discussion, clarification, drawing the lines of demarcation—that is our answer. And then we will see.

The purpose of the discussion is not only to establish with absolute precision the differences between us and the Shachtmanites. That is a prerequisite for unification in any case. But the purpose also is to educate our party, its new generation, on the program that we stand for; to reeducate them, to take all the new members of the party back again through the experiences of the political, theoretical, and organizational struggle from 1939 to date, where we trace the differences down to the roots, and educate our people on our position. [. . .]

You say, if you don't take the Shachtmanite offer of entry now, you will never take them. That doesn't follow. One of the important things is the relationship of forces. If we had 10,000 workers and they had 300, the problem would not be the same as when we have 1,200 and they have 300.

In addition to the political differences, and the different conception of the party which also has to be debated, there is another way of testing. Why, in view of the fact that we and the Shachtmanites have such sharply different conceptions of what the party is and how it should function, why should we believe that everything is settled by dispute and debate? Why not apply the test of experience, too? Why not say, let us take another six months, or a year, in view of the fact that the whole future of the movement depends on what kind of a party.

You know that is correct, Morrow. You state that in your article, that the question of what kind of a party is the overpowering, decisive question. All right, let us accept that. Let us test it out in action for another period. Let us see what the Shachtmanites can do with their theory and what we can do with ours, and periodically take stock. Say, every six months or so, come together and take stock.

(*Morrow:* "Try it with the Stalinists.")

Oh, it is a question of the Stalinists? In the early days the Stalinists used to cite our isolation from the mass movement as proof that our ideas were no good. Too many workers were saying the Trotskyists have very good ideas but they are only critics, their theories don't work out in practice.

That was a very good question. And how did we answer it? We answered it by saying that they had a big advantage. They began with a tremendous apparatus. They had a lot of money, the prestige of the Soviet Union, and we had nothing but a handful. But we said that in spite of that, we will turn to mass work, and prove we can beat them in mass work, and that is what we are trying to do. We accepted their challenge and went into the mass movement.

The Shachtmanites, however, didn't begin with such handicaps. They began with as many members as we had, almost. They began with smarter people, more talented, more educated, more intellectual, and with better theories too. At least that's what they thought—and said. So the empirical test has been completely fair to them.

They had a fair test. And let us test it out a little while longer, and if it turns out that their method is better than ours it will be a powerful argument in favor of their theory. [. . .]

We want the minority to participate in the work of clarification and demarcation. We want the minority to take a position with us or the Shachtmanites or in between and submit the question to the party convention.

You challenge us on many points. Your elementary duty is to put your theories down in a resolution. Why do you delay it? You can write all kinds of statements but you don't seem able to sit down and formulate your conceptions of party organization in a resolution. That is your absolute duty. I am sure you can do it and I hope that you will do it. I am confident that you will get a good hearing in the party for it. You know we have a very democratic party and we go for discussion. If someone wants to discuss. I am certainly anxious to begin the discussion of your organization resolution.

We provide for a certain amount of collaboration with the Shachtmanites, clearly delimited, defined. Where it serves practical ends we will go for it. Where it muddies up and doesn't serve practical ends, we don't go for it.

I would like to say a few words about our minority, what is the matter with them. I would characterize the minority in our leadership as a faction which has lost its head. So much so that they are not able to debate in the highest body of the party from the point of view of the interests of the party. They wonder why they got so badly isolated in the party.

I heard they had a discussion recently and some thought it was because of their bad tone. No, it is your bad ideas, bad conceptions. Your tone, of course, didn't help you, but modifying your tone won't make your ideas any more palatable to our party. This faction feels a blood-kinship with the petty-bourgeois opposition. I am willing to modify that expression—and I hope the minority will take note of my change of mind on it. I am willing to take off the opposition part and say it is independent and separate from us and in opposition to our party at the present time.

But the minority wants to reconvert it, the petty-bourgeois party of the Shachtmanites, into a petty-bourgeois opposition in the SWP. They feel a blood kinship with them and they are driven by some sort of inner compulsion to get together with them and they want to jump over the head of their own party. [. . .]

You denigrate the Socialist Workers Party and build up the Workers Party. You operate in our party, even though perhaps not fully consciously, as agents of the Shachtmanites. [. . .] And then you say blandly, you should have minority representation on the negotiating committee also. Well, I am in favor of the participation of a minority representative even on negotiating committees. [. . .] If this was a loyal minority, I would say, why not? But the reason you can't be on any negotiating committee of ours with the Shachtmanites is because you are not loyal to the Socialist Workers Party and we don't trust you there, and you have no right to be there because you are negotiating behind our backs. And tell that to the Fourth International. Tell the Fourth International why you are kept off the committee and we will tell them why you were kept off, and you will see how far you will get with it.

Goldman told us some history of our party—when he didn't belong to it. That is not correct. That is not right. We conducted no negotiations with the leaders of the Socialist Party until after the right wing [of the SP] had been expelled here in New York. It was after the Oehlerites were outside the party. The first meeting that we held with the leaders of the Militants was after we had adopted among ourselves a decision to turn toward the Socialist Party. We couldn't negotiate with them before then because we didn't have the orientation of joining the Socialist Party, as I explained in my *History* account, because we were only probing.[81] We couldn't join the Socialist Party because the right wing was in control of New York and didn't let us join. We couldn't do as Goldman did: sneak in as an individual.

We wanted to join as an organized body so that was why in the midst of all that fight, when we were accused of wanting to join the Socialist Party, we said, no, we want to keep the question open. And the negotiations that we began with them were after the Oehlerites were expelled from the Workers Party and we had established a firm and overwhelming majority in the Political Committee and in the membership itself. That doesn't mean we didn't have some people scouting the Socialist Party and getting some information for us, but that was in the interests of our party, not for the Socialist Party. You have the thing turned upside down. [. . .]

Now, you are beginning to talk very boldly about the International. Prophets who have no honor in their own country always hope to make the grade in another country where they are not so well known. In my opinion when they get to know you as well in the International as we know you in this country, you will have no more standing there than you have here—and that is not very much. In connection with the International—and this I believe to be the most important aspect of the whole question of the Shachtmanites—I believe that appears to us in a different way than it appears to you. I consider the Shachtmanites as an enemy of the Fourth International. The Shachtmanites in 1940 split the party and tried to split the Fourth International. Isn't that a fact? They absolutely rejected all the discipline of the International. They didn't just make the split here locally and then appeal to the Fourth International. Not at all. They split here in America and then set up a committee of Shachtman . . . and called it the Committee for the Fourth International. They tried to carry the split to every section of the International.

What is their position on the Fourth International now? I think you read something in their magazine, didn't you? They pronounce the Fourth International as having died during the war and they want to come into our ranks and conduct an educational discussion as to who killed it and who is responsible for it, meaning the Socialist Workers Party. [. . .]

Now you take that program to the Fourth International and we will go with you and fight it out in the International, and let us see whether they want to be regrouped around the Shachtmanites and the so-called German section, or whether they want to be grouped around the people of a different stripe, of whom we are a part. We have a duty to the International. The International is not, as you try to picture it in your minds and your speeches, as "they" and "we." [. . .]

That is not the Fourth International, not at all. We are part of the Fourth International. We are, leaving out the Russian section, the oldest and strongest, and perhaps the most experienced, section of the Fourth International, working under favorable political conditions. We have got a big responsibility to the International not to permit isolated individuals to arrogate to themselves the authority of the International, to assert our own point of view. And I know that the workers of the Fourth International throughout the world listen attentively to our point of view and take our party seriously. And why shouldn't they? We are not only the oldest and the strongest, and in some respects the most experienced, section; we have always been loyal to the Fourth International. We always put the interests of the International highest every time since 1928. Never once went against the interests of the International. Always supported the progressive line of the International from beginning to end.

Under the difficult conditions of the war we did everything in our power to keep the flag flying and assist the comrades in other countries under the most difficult conditions. You will go there in the midst of organizing the international bloc against the SWP, the bloc of the right and the left—more correctly called, the bloc of adventurers, the individuals who have not yet been subject to verification—with Munis in Mexico and the leaders of the RCP in England, with anybody you can pick up anywhere, no matter what his differences, what his errors, so long as he is against us. All you are doing is just running into a fight, that is all.

You talk about the regime in our party. You have got a bloc-partner in England called the leadership of the RCP. You know what kind of regime they have got? Jock Haston stood up in the last conference of the RCP and defended Morrow and Goldman against the methods of Cannon. [. . .] And by the methods, of course, they mean the regime under which these people are being so cruelly persecuted. Do you know what kind of regime your pals in England have? They have a minority led by Healy whose crimes consisted in the fact that he supported the unity line of the International Secretariat, that he broke with the sectarian nationalism of the WIL and became a real internationalist, rejected their nationalistic taint, and has been sympathetic in general to the Socialist Workers Party political position.

Do you know what this regime calls Healy? A quisling of the Socialist Workers Party; that is, an agent of an enemy country. Healy had 25 percent of the delegates supporting him at the conference, but he only got a little better than 10 percent representation on the National Committee. That is the regime. But that isn't the half of it. Then out of this National Committee, just as we do, they constructed a Political Committee. You know how we construct ours, don't you? At the present time it consists of everybody in New York, which means, when Goldman was in town, that a 5 percent minority in our party had two voting members and one consultative member on our Political Committee; that they have almost double their proportionate representation on the National Committee.

But in the RCP, a part of this international pressure that is being mobilized against us and that we are supposed to flee from to a storm cellar, they constructed a Political Committee in London—where Healy lives—and he is left out of it. The National Committee only meets every three months. He is deprived of representation on the Political Committee. He is not permitted to attend even as a spectator. It is a closed committee. And he doesn't even get the minutes of the Political Committee. He has to wait for the plenum to find out what is going on.

That is the regime in the RCP who are supporting Goldman and Morrow against our regime, and with whom they have concluded a bloc. And I challenge them to deny it. Talk about unprincipledness. You will deny it and we will prove it because we have the dope on you. You are helping Haston and [Ted] Grant to fight Healy right now. You are sending personal letters to Haston to help them in the fight against Healy—to utilize against Healy. You are in a bloc and you are already ashamed of it openly, but we will expose that bloc and all the rest of it. And we will take the fight on the international field. You go ahead and line up your bloc. We will work with those people who believe in the same principles, the same program and methods, that we do. And we will fight it out and see what happens in the International.

A REPLY TO GOLDMAN ON THREE POINTS

October 7, 1945

This is the second speech Cannon made at the October 6-7, 1945, plenum of the SWP NC. It is from an unpublished and uncorrected stenogram.

I want to speak briefly only on three points.

The first is on the question that was raised earlier in the discussion: How is it explained that our party has outstripped the Shachtmanites in the mass movement and in recruiting? Goldman originally answered that by saying it was very foolish—something like the argument, why did the Stalinists get the majority over Trotsky and why did they outstrip us in the mass movement in this country. Now that was not only a good question, but it was a very effective question, and we found it necessary to make an answer to it.

Trotsky, as you know, gave the classic answer, that the strength of Stalinism was the strength of the reaction sweeping through the world and reflected in the Russian working class. We answered it in this country by stating that we began as a small handful, victims of this reaction. They had the big party, a big apparatus, a daily press, money, the prestige of the Soviet Union, of which they appeared to be the representatives. And we had the rather thankless task of explaining what appeared to be rather abstruse theoretical questions, such as socialism in one country. For that reason we had difficulty in making headway in the mass movement, but nevertheless we realized we had to face that question by our. . . .

That is why we made a determined turn to the mass movement and when we got our opportunity in Minneapolis we demonstrated that we could do mass work, and that was the condition for our further development.

We put the question then as to why we, who began with relatively the same numbers as the Shachtmanites five years ago, have surpassed them. You can't say this is on the level of the differences between the old Communist League of America and the Stalinists, and you have to explain how it is that one party proved superior to the other, at least for the first five years.

Goldman offered three reasons: one, that we had the help of Trotsky; second, that we had the trade union cadres; third, that we had the Minneapolis trial.

Well, it seems to me that that is not a complete answer, because if you say we had Trotsky up until August 1940 you have to say why did we have Trotsky. Trotsky, if I am not mistaken, was a very critical thinker. He took his position on the basis of a thoroughgoing examination of the problem at hand. He took a deliberate stand in favor of us and against them, not by accident at all but deliberately and with knowledge beforehand. So I believe it isn't sufficient to say we had the support of Trotsky in the faction fight—and that was a big factor, there is no question about it—but to see why did we have that support?

Was Trotsky mistaken or deceived, or were we then worthy of his support and are we not good enough now, worse now? Were the Shachtmanites unworthy of it then and more worthy of it now? I believe this question can be pursued along these lines. But we had the support of Trotsky only in the inner-party fight. He played no role externally at all. We had the support of Trotsky in gaining the majority inside the party.

Then, after the death of Trotsky five years ago, we had to go out into the mass movement on even terms with Shachtman and it didn't do us any good to have the support of even the great name of Trotsky because the great mass of workers that we go to know about Trotsky only what we tell them, because they have not joined the party on the basis of Trotsky in the first place. They have joined on the basis of our concrete activities in the class struggle.

They say we prevailed there because we had the trade union cadres. Again I say it is only half the answer. *Why* did we have the trade union cadres? Like attracts like. The smart people get only the smart people. The stupid leaders got the stupid trade unionists. But these stupid trade unionists proved to be superior in the field to the Shachtmanites. But that was not the case everywhere. We had the bulk of the trade union cadres, but in Akron they had everything. When the split occurred we had one member there and they had important trade union contacts in the unions and they had the standing of being the Trotskyist group known for years there. The work of Widick and the others was well known. He was in contact with many of the leading militants there, and in the course of five years we have had to go into Akron, you might say, empty-handed. [. . .]

In five years the situation has been reversed, even there in Akron, so that the trade union hegemony in Akron now belongs to the Socialist Workers Party in the rubber industry and the Shachtmanites have signaled their new turn by withdrawing the leader of their forces in the rubber union and sending him to Chicago as organizer of the Chicago branch in preparation for the entry.

So that we not only had the trade union cadres to begin with, but we built them up. But in this particular case we made up, and went over them, and without a cadre to begin with. How do you explain that? I believe it would be reasonable to say that our method and our program had something to do with it.

Now the second point is about Zinoviev. You know I have had a practice for twenty years in the movement of making very few answers to personal attacks because I always have the good luck to have so many personal attacks made against me that if I took time to answer them all I would never have time to get down to the issues in dispute, never get to the meat of the situation. [. . .]

But this question about Zinoviev I want to answer briefly because I think it has some historic importance. Zinoviev was not one man. There were four Zinovievs at least—I would say there were six Zinovievs. There was the Zinoviev who was the most intimate collaborator of Lenin in exile during the war, who did great historic work. Then there was the Zinoviev who, [. . .] together with Kamenev, lost his nerve on the eve of the insurrection. [. . . Then there was the] Zinoviev who corrected himself after that, who became the chairman of the Comintern and Lenin's agent, really, in leading the Comintern.

All the great worldwide propaganda against Zinovievism and Zinoviev was set in motion by the group of centrists who were attracted to the Comintern in its first years and recoiled from it in its first years under Lenin: Balabanov and others of that sort who gave to the whole organization and method of Lenin, the organization of the Comintern, the twenty-one points, they gave the name of Zinoviev, making it synonymous with Leninism.[82] When anybody waves the flag of Zinovievism you can do very well to trace it back to which Zinoviev they mean. [. . .]

Then there was a fourth Zinoviev, the Zinoviev of the troika with Stalin and Kamenev after the death of Lenin. This is the Zinoviev who began to backslide, and it is correct, as Goldman said, that the organizational methods that began to be introduced into the Comintern, in contradistinction to the earlier years, were sort of a bridge toward Stalinism. Not Stalinism by a long way, but a bridge toward a beginning of the bureaucratism. In that period Zinoviev was chairman of the Comintern. All the most influential pronouncements and articles coming from Moscow came in the name of Zinoviev. He was the leader of the Fifth Congress. The writings of the Left Opposition under Trotsky were suppressed. We got only faint snatches of them here and there and I, like every other leader of the American party in those days, could be said to be a Zinovievist. We were taken in by that campaign of the troika.

In that time, the campaign twenty-one years ago, when my sin is cited, I would say it would be very safe to say at that time I was a Zinovievist in the sense that every other leader of the party was, in the sense that they were taking for good coin the whole line from Moscow and not examining it too critically.

But then there is another Zinoviev, the fifth Zinoviev, who in 1926-27 broke away from the bloc with Stalin and concluded a bloc with Trotsky, and made as one of the issues of his campaign [democratization of the state] and of the party, the demand for party democracy. Now I was not a Trotsky-Zinovievist in that period, but I began, as I recounted in my history, to be very disturbed about that question. But I didn't become a Trotskyist until 1928 and that was when the bloc of Trotsky and Zinoviev had been broken and the sixth Zinoviev, the capitulator, appeared and went back to the camp of Stalinism, and I, on the other hand, supported Trotsky. I didn't support Zinoviev number six.

My reeducation on all the principles of Marxism, including party organization, took place under the tutelage of Trotsky from 1928 on. And if you blame me for having been a sort of Zinovievist for the period of 1924-25, you have to find me, I think some one of my accusers who was wiser.

I don't know what the organizational and political views of Goldman were at that time as I am not familiar with his writings at that period. [As far as I know, he was a] supporter of the official line and swallowed it whole; but I became a Trotskyist.

And it might be said in exculpation of the sin that is alleged against me, I was the first leader of American Trotskyism to become a Trotskyist and I think that should counterbalance. And I remained a Trotskyist, since 1928 up to the present, up to 1945. [. . .]

Now the third point I want to speak about is the comment made by Goldman on my reply to that slip of Morrow's about putting over our line in "the sticks." If Morrow had stopped to think, he wouldn't have done it. It was only because it was a slip of the tongue that it rang so true about his thinking about the role played by the comrades out in the country. And when I answered that and characterized it for what it is and gave my view of what party control is, Goldman characterized that as demagogy.

I said the workers in our party are the bosses and the real controllers of the party. And when the boys come in from the field, the people who come into the plenum here from the field, in our system of organization they are in reality the dominating force in the committee, because they actually represent the workers in the party. He thought I was making a demagogic appeal to the scissorbills. That is not a very good reflection on me and on the people from "the sticks," to consider them being taken in by rib-tickling demagogy.

No, I wasn't demagogic. I really mean that and this is what you don't understand. I really mean that we should have a party that is predominantly worker in its composition and a party in which the workers control the party, not fictitiously but in reality. A party in which, although the initiative, the central leadership, of necessity comes from the functionaries and intellectuals in the center, the real control and the real power rests in the hands of the plenum. And that is why we have evolved this concept of organizing the leadership. That doesn't happen by accident.

It is by design that we have twenty-five members and thirteen alternates in the committee, and not by accident that we have this leadership distributed over the different districts. The reasons, I explained in my preconvention thesis on the question of the NC,[83] is that by this means we insure that there comes into the plenum of the party the elected and truly representative leaders of the workers in the district, and that their position is not decorative, but controlling; that they are in a position to really control the actions of the Political Committee. And when we were confronted with making a decision on the Shachtmanites we didn't call in the people from the country merely for decoration, but for consultation.

Our conception of the role of intellectuals in the movement is that they have to be part of a larger group of worker-leaders and subordinate to them. It is not going to be a party of a couple of smart guys in New York running it as they please. The workers are represented in the plenum by delegates from the districts.

I have had occasion to hear this idea more than once in the past history of the party. Workers! We are really the smart people in New York! The smart boys in New York really run things. But I never hesitated to say the plenum is really the highest body in the party. And whenever I didn't agree with the PC—which was quite often—I didn't hesitate at all to appeal to the plenum against the Political Committee.

In 1939 when the fast-talkers in New York were in the majority in the Political Committee, that didn't settle the policy of the party. We called a plenum and the plenum changed the composition of the Political Committee just to give them a demonstration of who is boss in this party.

Now then, this thing has great pertinence from the point of view of the position the minority finds itself in now. They don't perhaps fully realize it, but they don't believe in this talk about a workers' party with a worker leadership. They can't get into their heads the idea that intellectuals can only function in the leadership of this party if they learn how to subordinate themselves to the workers.

They are right up against this proposition now. After all, it is nearly two years [since we began this] discussion; we come to a plenum and nobody would dare to say that this plenum doesn't represent the party in view of the fact that the members from the districts have all been elected by their own delegations and are at the head of the locals.

After two years of debate in the party [the minority comes] to the plenum and find themselves completely isolated. If they have any hope whatever of getting a majority in the party, they must know that the road to the majority in the party is through the body sitting in this room. And when they find themselves against a stone wall here, they have to do one thing or another. This is the hardest of all for a petty bourgeois to do, [to admit] that I haven't been able to convince and I must submit. I must wait until I get a majority because otherwise I have no party behind me, and without a party you can't carry through a policy.

Their reaction so far isn't a good one, in my opinion. Their reaction, instead of asking themselves, as Sam [Gordon] put the question: What is wrong with us that we can't get the workers? they are asking: What is wrong with these workers? They are stupid, the whole bunch of them; they have been misled by demagogues.

That is only a rationalization of your own unfortunate position. Unless you learn how to subordinate yourself to the workers, you can never be leaders of this movement. If we were in your position and the positions were reversed and we saw that 90 percent of the plenum was lined up against the position we brought in, we would have to recognize: Well, we still think we are right, but we can't do a damn thing about it because the majority won't go for it; so we have no alternative except to submit, wait for another chance to discuss the question, prove our loyalty to the party, and try to win them over next time.

The alternative to that is jump over the head of the party, try to play politics without a party. You can't have any success in this broadly democratic party. Try some other party or one of your own. Unfortunately that is the road the petty-bourgeois intellectuals often take, and that is one of the reasons that our. . . .

The capacity to subordinate oneself to one's own party and its worker cadre is the first mark of a revolutionist. It is questions like that that we want to elaborate in our discussions as to what kind of a party we want to have. You can put me down as one who wants not only a workers' party predominantly [but a party in which the nonproletarian minority] learns how to subordinate themselves and discipline themselves to a workers' organization. The greatest weakness of the intellectuals—many of them we had in the past and many we still have today in the Fourth International—is that they have never learned to do that.

Their leadership is all pretension. Why, they can't even organize ten workers. They try to operate without any force behind them, which is just as foolish in politics as it is in military science. I recall the Old Man laid special stress on this point. The intellectuals have got to learn how to work in a workers' organization and be disciplined in it. I recall two incidents in which the Old Man stressed this point, to my knowledge.

You remember when Harold Isaacs came back from China in 1934. He was a newspaper man who had been converted to Trotskyism, I think by Li Fu-jen, in newspaper circles in China, and had become a very responsible figure. By virtue of his legal position he became a liaison man and, if I am not mistaken, was in contact with the underground committee. He joined the movement much the same as our remarkable T. P. [Terence Phelan] did—at the top—and had dealings with the upper circles of this underground movement without having any experience whatever with its basic organizations.

He learned all the formulas of Trotskyism and knew them very well, so well that he could come back here and sit down at a typewriter and knock out an article on any subject of current interest, with only a slight consultation with the editors. He had assimilated the formulas, but the Old Man had special advice for him. He had gone to visit the Old Man and asked the Old Man's advice about what he should do in this country. And his advice to him, as Isaacs told it to me, was: The most important thing for you to do is to join a workers' organization. Learn how to work in a workers' organization very humbly and learn discipline. He recommended that Isaacs join a branch of the Socialist Party, if the Political Committee agreed, which had workers in it, and work there a year or two and learn how to work under the discipline and control of a workers' organization. Well, Isaacs never got around to that. For some reason or other he never found it feasible to join the Socialist Party.

He joined our organization and for the years that he worked with us he hardly ever attended a branch meeting. He neglected that. He was busy. He did a lot of fine work for us. [But he never assimilated the] control and discipline of a workers' organization, and in the critical moment we found that our ties to him, to this man who knew our ideas so well, were just mere threads that were snapped under the first pressure of personal difficulties, when he got a baby, some difficulties, etc. He had not assimilated the qualities of a real proletarian revolutionist, and left our ranks. As far as I know, he was the only casualty of the war.

The second instance is the case of Logan [Jean van Heijenoort]. Logan was six or seven years in the secretariat of Trotsky. He had a great, rich experience, you may say at the very top of the general staff of the world revolution. And he saw all the moves, all the strategies, all the tactics of the great masters of Marxism employed by Trotsky. But he never had any really serious experience in a workers' organization, and began to imagine that others could do what Trotsky did without knowing that Trotsky's background was a background of participation in the struggle. Trotsky joined the party as a young man, not as the General of the Revolution but as a simple organizer of workers in a Ukrainian town. He wrote afterward that what he learned from his experience in Nikolayev from the workers stuck with him all his life. After he had gone through that experience he knew what workers were and thought he knew how to work with them.

When the May attack occurred on the Old Man in 1940 we rushed down there,[84] Farrell and I and [Sam] Gordon, and several other people, and Logan sent word by me that he was willing to come back. He had in the meantime been in the United States a few months and finished his service. He was willing to come back and assist in the guard if the Old Man wanted it. The Old Man said he appreciated his spirit and readiness to come but didn't think he should do it. He said he was very much afraid for him just as he was for Keller [Jan Frankel], because he had been too long in the secretariat. And just like Keller, despite his years of experience under the direct tutelage of Trotsky, he proved to be washed out in the American movement.

What Logan needed more than anything else was experience in a workers' organization and for the sake of development of Logan himself he should attach himself to a workers' organization and learn how to work in it. And my greatest criticism of all the intellectuals we are now confronted with, both nationally and internationally, is that the great majority of them have remained intellectuals too long. They are not learning the message that the Fourth International has got to be a workers' organization, that the workers have got to dominate its leadership, and that the intellectuals have got to learn how to fit into a workers' organization and serve it and not lord over it.

FREE THE IMPRISONED INDOCHINESE REPRESENTATIVES IN FRANCE!

October 13, 1945

The following telegram was sent to Charles de Gaulle, president of the French provisional government in Paris. The text is from The Militant, *October 20, 1945.*

Socialist Workers Party strongly protests arrest of Dr. Tran Duc Thao and delegation of forty-two representing twenty-five thousand Indochinese living in Paris. We demand their immediate release. We demand they be given full opportunity to put the case of the Indochinese people fighting against imperialism to the French people and the peoples of the whole world. Imprisonment of the forty-two will be interpreted only as attempt to prevent understanding and cooperation between masses in Indochina and the people of France. Let the people of the world hear the voice of Free Indochina.

James P. Cannon
National Secretary
Socialist Workers Party

THE RUSSIAN REVOLUTION —TWENTY-EIGHT YEARS AFTER

What Has Been Lost and What Saved

November 4, 1945

The following speech on the twenty-eighth anniversary of the Russian revolution was given to an audience of 300 at the Hotel Diplomat in New York. The text, slightly abridged, is from The Militant, *November 17, 1945.*

The development of socialism from a utopian conception to a scientific doctrine was accomplished with the publication of the *Communist Manifesto* in 1848—ninety-seven years ago. The development of socialism from science into action was accomplished sixty-nine years later by the Russian Bolshevik revolution of November 7, 1917. On the fusion of these two great historic achievements—the formulation of the principles of scientific socialism and their verification in action in 1917, the union of theory and practice—we stand today, as we have stood in the past, and once again assemble to celebrate the anniversary of the great revolution.

Socialism cannot be established in one country. That requires international action and cooperation. A workers' revolution, started on national ground, cannot be completed unless it is extended to other countries. The Russian revolution was the beginning of the international revolution, but only a beginning. Only from this point of view can it be properly judged. Every year for twenty-eight years we have had to answer impatient and disillusioned people who demanded more from the Russian revolution than it could give, and withdrew their approval from it; who prematurely announced the end and the death of the revolution; who wanted to close the account and write it off as a bad debt. But the Russian Bolsheviks did not promise the millenium. They only said: "We will begin the international revolution in Russia, but you, the workers of Europe and America, must finish it."

The Russian revolution was national only in form, but in the essence it was the beginning of an international action. That is what we have to understand about it first of all. The leaders of the great Russian revolution were internationalists through and through, incapable of thinking in limited national terms. The guiding theory of the Russian revolution came not from Russia but from a German Jew, Karl Marx, who lived in exile in England. The victory of the revolution was made possible by the international contradictions of capitalism in the First World War. It was kept alive in the postwar period by the international support and solidarity of the workers in the capitalist countries, above all those in Europe. The workers of Europe were not strong enough to carry through their own revolution in the postwar years, but they were strong enough to prevent a full-scale military intervention against Russia by their own governments.

Lenin and Trotsky linked their revolution directly to the German revolution. They said: "We live in a beleaguered fortress until the European revolution comes to our aid." None of the leaders of the Russian revolution believed it could last very long if it remained by itself, alone and isolated in a capitalist world.

But the Russian Bolsheviks built better than they knew. The revolution proved to be stronger than they or anyone else ever dreamed it could be. The Russian revolution could not complete itself within the national borders of a single country. But in spite of that, in spite of the drawn-out delay of the European revolution to which they had looked with such hope, the revolution in Russia didn't die. It survived and struck deep roots into the soil. The property foundations laid down by the revolution—the nationalization of industry and the planned economy—proved to be far stronger than any previous calculations, even the most optimistic.

But the isolated revolution, encircled by a hostile capitalist world, could not escape the ravages of a terrible reaction which set in on Russian soil. This reaction led to the renunciation of the international perspective and a nationalistic degeneration all along the line. The regime of workers' democracy based on the soviets was replaced by a brutal totalitarian tyranny. The revolution was beheaded, and a whole generation of Bolsheviks was massacred. The political rule of the workers was overthrown, but the economic conquests of the revolution displayed a great vitality. Thanks to that, the revolution survived twenty years of bureaucratic degeneration and betrayal and revealed an enormous power on the field of battle in the war with Nazi Germany, as Trotsky had predicted it would.

Trotsky alone analyzed and explained this phenomenon, hitherto unknown and unforeseen, unique in history, of an isolated workers' state in a capitalist encirclement, mutilated and betrayed by a usurping bureaucracy, but surviving nevertheless, although in a horribly degenerated form. [. . .]

Social revolutions in history, which represented the greatest, the most colossal exertion and expenditure of the creative energies of the masses, concentrated on a single point, have always been followed by periods of reaction. We have seen that in the last twenty-odd years in the Soviet Union. But the reactions against the great basic revolutions have never swung back to their starting point. Observing that fundamental fact of history, one has to be very cautious and careful about writing off any part of the achievements of the Russian revolution before it is time to do so.

The Great French Revolution, the revolution that destroyed feudalism and laid the basis for the tremendous expansion and development of the productive forces of mankind on a capitalist basis—this great revolution had its Thermidor; its Napoleonic dictatorship; it even saw the restoration of the Bourbon dynasty.[85] But the reaction never was strong enough to restore the feudal property system that had been swept away by the revolution.

The American Civil War—a genuine revolution—was followed by a reaction which restored political power to the expropriated slaveholders in the South, but it could not go back far enough to restore private property in slaves.

The revolutionary changes in property forms, which enabled mankind to increase its productive powers, have been the fundamental basis of human progress. These have have been the achievements of the great revolutions. The abolition of capitalist private property in the means of production, and the nationalization of industry and the institution of a planned economy made possible by this abolition of private property—that is the great conquest of the Russian revolution which has not yet been overthrown. That is what we see yet in Russia. That is what we see through all the monstrous betrayals of the Stalinist bureaucracy. And that is what we defend. Not Stalinism, not the treacherous and corroding bureaucracy, but the economic conquests of the great revolution which still remain. That is what we defend against the imperialists and against the Stalinist bureaucracy too.

Marxism asserts that the capitalist system of production is decayed and doomed. Marxism asserts that the workers' revolution must and will sweep away the capitalist order and reorganize world economy on a socialist basis. That is what Marx and Engels proclaimed in the *Communist Manifesto* of 1848. But neither Marx and Engels, nor the disciples who came after them, ever promised a free and easy road to socialism, without defeats, and setbacks, and even catastrophes, along the way.

We have had nothing but defeats, and setbacks, and catastrophes for twenty-two years. Our movement has had to make its way in the face of defeats ever since 1923, the defeat of the German revolution. That is why our movement remained comparatively small in numbers and isolated. But the important thing is not that the Marxist movement, in the face of the defeats and catastrophes, was small and isolated. The important thing is that, in spite of all, we made our way and are still fighting.

We Marxists-Trotskyists can still fight and we are still fighting, not because we cherish illusions; not because we wish to deceive ourselves and others; but because we see the whole reality in the world and not just a part of it. We recognize the defeats, but we do not recognize the total defeat of humanity. The war was a terrible defeat for mankind. Fascism was a terrible defeat. The degeneration of the Soviet Union under the Stalinists is a defeat. The failure of the first stage of the war to produce victorious revolutions in Europe is, in a sense, a defeat. These are facts, big and important facts, and we recognize them. But the death agony of capitalism is a bigger and more important fact, and we see that side of the picture too. We see that capitalism, in this period of its decay and death agony, is utterly and completely incapable of organizing the economy of the world to provide, not abundance, but even a living for the masses of the people.

We see not only the weaknesses on the side of the workers, but we also see the fatal diseased weakness of the capitalist world order. We do not close our eyes to defeats. But in each case

Trotskyism seeks to establish precisely, in every situation, what has been lost, what has been saved. Trotskyism searches in every defeat or setback, and the altered situation created by it, to find a vantage point for a new development of the struggle. And Trotskyism alone proceeds this way. That is why Trotskyism is the only revolutionary political current in the whole world today.

Fascism could survive only with victory after victory. The great vaunted military power of Mussolini and Hitler could not stand up under a few military defeats. Social Democracy and Stalinism are both capitulatory currents which survive only because of working class defeats. They renounced faith in the proletariat and converted themselves into servitors of the class enemy. But the Trotskyists, the modern Marxists, have lived now through more than twenty years of continuous defeats and continued to fight. That is the surest indication that Trotskyism is the doctrine that will flower and expand in the days of the coming victories of the workers, and prepare the way for them.

The party that made the Russian revolution didn't begin with victory. The Bolsheviks really began with the defeat of the 1905 revolution and persevered through the long years of the tsarist reaction from 1906 to 1917. It was precisely in that period, when all the fainthearted people, when all the disillusioned, ran for cover, when they all gave up the fight and renounced it as hopeless—it was precisely in that period that Bolshevism showed its caliber. In the depths of darkest reaction and defeat the Bolsheviks forged the party that was destined to lead the victorious revolution in 1917.

The accusation has been made against us—and not for the first time—that our theory is a religion with which we console ourselves; that our analysis of the Soviet Union, of what has been lost and what has been saved and what is still worth defending, is a religion. Those who made that accusation in the past—and there have been many of them—nearly always ended by placing their own faith in "democratic" imperialism. We want nothing to do with that kind of religion in any case.

Marxism and the Russian revolution represent the union of theory and practice; the union of the word and the deed. Every tendency toward capitulation to the class enemy which we have known in the past—and we have known many—every one began with a revision of the theory and ended in repudiation of the deed. After the first flush of victory in 1917, each and every setback of the struggling revolution, every difficulty, every defeat, brought new waves of disillusionment, and with them new experiments and new revisions of theory; and, finally, new capitulations in principle to the class enemy. The case of Professor Burnham is only the latest example.

The case of Professor Burnham is recent enough to be remembered. He began with a revision of the Marxist theory of the state and the Marxist analysis of the Russian revolution, and ended in the camp of American imperialism. That is the most disgraceful and shameful capitulation that one can make. It represents a real betrayal of humanity because American imperialism is the enemy of humanity. One who goes over into that camp has a "religion" which no self-respecting worker ought ever to become infected with.

Stalinism itself began as a revision of Marxist theory and ended in class betrayal. Trotsky began his struggle against Stalin in the realm of a theoretical dispute over the revisionist theory of "socialism in one country" and the renunciation of the international character of the Russian revolution. The Trotskyists understood the nature of Stalinism better, and explained it earlier, and fought it longer and harder than any others. Therefore nobody needs to incite us against Stalinism. But vulgar "anti-Stalinism" is no more revolutionary, and no more attractive to us. We know where this "anti-Stalinism" leads. Up to now it has always led to the camp of "democratic" imperialism.

We can have no quarrel whatsoever with those who denounce Stalinism for its bloody crimes against the workers—and they are legion. But excessive zeal in criticizing and denouncing the Soviet Union and those who still defend it—that part of it which is worthy of defense—against imperialism is subject to suspicion. The unbridled antagonism bordering on Russophobia—which one can notice in the atmosphere these days—is a very dangerous sentiment, especially at the present time. Because it is perfectly clear to everybody that before any peace is concluded, the mobilization for the next stage of the war, a war against the Soviet Union, is already taking place, and proceeding at a feverish pace. Why, the preparations are going forward openly on all fronts.

Who can be so blind as not to see them and understand them? On the diplomatic front American imperialism is mobilizing its forces and lining up allies. On the economic front American imperialism is granting or withholding loans and credits to serve its diplomatic aims. On the propaganda front, why, the American people are being bombarded by a calculated campaign of prejudice to prepare them for another war of "democracy"—God help us!—against the Soviet Union. And even on the military front we read the brazen announcements in the papers every day now that the armies of Chiang Kai-shek engaged in the civil war in Northern China are armed, equipped, and even partly trained by American militarists.

A tremendous wave of public sentiment against Russia, reminiscent of the early days of 1917-19, which some of us remember, is being set into motion. The present agitation recalls again the days of the Soviet-Finnish war when every democrat, every liberal, every Russophobe, every anti-Stalinist, was waving the flag for war against the Soviet Union in the service of American imperialism.[86] It was a little difficult, and it took some courage and independence of judgment, to stand up against that terrific anti-Russian wave of sentiment and propaganda at the time of the Soviet-Finnish war. We see the same thing developing again today, helped along, as before, by the bestial crimes of Stalin. The crimes of Stalin inside the Soviet Union, in Poland, in Eastern Europe, and now in Korea, deal mortal blows to the prestige of the Soviet Union. In the occupied territories the Red Army, under Stalinist leadership, behaves in such a way as to tear the hearts out of the workers and disillusion them with the Soviet Union, and weaken their allegiance and friendship for it, and thus open the way for a more effective eventual mobilization of the capitalist world against it.

Denouncing these crimes with all our souls, we must still strive to keep our balance, to see the picture whole, to see behind the crimes and filth of Stalinism the Soviet Union and the stake which the workers of the world still have in it. Trotsky predicted that the fate of the Soviet Union would be decided in the war. That remains our firm conviction. Only we disagree with some people who carelessly think that the war is over. The war has only passed through one stage and is now in the process of regroupment and reorganization for the second. The war is not over, and the revolution which we said would issue from the war in Europe is not taken off the agenda. It has only been delayed and postponed, primarily for lack of leadership, for lack of a sufficiently strong revolutionary party. The Fourth Internationalists all over the world are working to build that leadership, to build that party. [. . .]

The Russian revolution appears only as a part, and not even

the biggest part by any means, of a colossal worldwide conflict of forces which cannot be reconciled. The Russian revolution of November 1917 showed the workers of the whole world the way to power, to the overthrow of the capitalist property system, to the reorganization of economy on a rational basis. There is no other way to save mankind on an international scale then the Russian way. From that point of view we salute the great revolution tonight, as the initiator and inspirer of greater things to come. Therein lies its greatest significance.

If we view the Russian revolution in the right perspective we must see it for what it really was: an international action of the working class, started in a backward country, the most backward country of the great powers, tsarist Russia; and destined to be concluded in the most advanced and powerful country, the United States of America. That which was begun in the domain of the tsars will be finished in the domain of the American monopolists. And regardless of victories or defeats in one country or another, or even one continent or another, the central issue of our epoch—capitalism or socialism—will not be finally decided until it is decided in the United States of America. [. . .]

Just as the Russian Bolsheviks gave us the model of a victorious revolution, so also they gave us the model of a party fit to lead and organize the revolution. If we take the Russian Bolshevik party for our model—and there is no other model worth even talking about—this means a party that is orthodox Marxist in its theory, that is firm in principle, and strong in its unity and its discipline. Only such a party is fit to organize and lead a revolution.

We are striving to build such a party in the United States, and we invite you to join us in the task. If you can foresee, as we do, the grandiose perspectives of the American revolution, we invite you to join us in preparing for it. [. . .]

Here in the United States is the greatest imperialist power, a monster exploiting and oppressing the whole world. That is true, and we take full account of it. But here also is a still greater power—and that is the militant and undefeated American working class. Great historic responsibility surely rests on our shoulders. The two greatest powers of the world—the power for evil and destruction, and the power for the regeneration and salvation of mankind—are both here.

There is only one way for us to do our duty. That is to foresee the revolution and to prepare for it. And the way to prepare for it is to go to the American workers with the message of the party. Go to this source of power that is greater even than the power of American imperialism and teach them the lesson of the Russian revolution. Organize them and inspire them. And lead them to the socialist victory in America which will insure the socialist victory throughout the entire world.

Cannon gives Mayday speech at Webster Hall, New York, 1945.

LETTERS TO ROSE KARSNER

November 1945

Following are excerpts from three previously unpublished letters to Rose Karsner, Cannon's companion from 1924. Cannon was on a speaking trip to Chicago, writing to Rose Karsner in New York.

November 12, 1945

Dearest:

The meeting last night—the twenty-eighth anniversary celebration—was quite successful. The largest crowd and the largest collection yet in Chicago—150 people and $150 collection. It was much different from the old audiences I used to have in Chicago—mainly tired radicals, lunatic fringers, and "ex's" of various kinds. This was, in the main, a new audience of freshly attracted workers. The front rows, for example, were dominated by a delegation of steelworkers who traveled twenty miles by streetcar to come to the meeting. *Seven* new members made application for membership after the meeting. I [. . .] would gladly take a train this afternoon to arrive in New York tomorrow. However, I still have a number of meetings and conferences to go through before I can leave. [. . .]

Love ever,
Jim

November 14, 1945

Dearest:

[. . .] I debated with Goldman last night. This business is becoming very boring to me. The monotony was relieved a bit last night by the fact that I lost my temper and told Goldman face to fact what we thought of his conduct at Sandstone. I always feel a bit sorry for such indulgences afterward, but it did me good at the time. [. . .]

Jim

November 15, 1945

Dearest:

[. . .] I met with the majority caucus last night. This about completes my work here except for some personal talks with individual comrades. Everything seems to be in pretty good shape here. [. . .]

I think we straightened out the main difficulty in the caucus—the antagonism between the "old guard" and the later recruits. [. . .]

Love ever,
Jim

Oscar Shoenfeld, Rose Karsner, James P. Cannon, 1941

CALIFORNIA NOSTALGIA

November 27, 1945

This letter to Murry Weiss in Los Angeles was written in reply to a suggestion that Cannon and Rose Karsner spend the winter in Southern California. It has not been previously published.

New York

Dear Murry:

I got your letter of November 13. I think you're taking advantage of me. You knew very well that my California nostalgia would be working very strongly at this time of the year; it was wrong for you to play on my sentiments when it was your duty to confine yourself to facts, logic, political exigencies, and so forth and so on.

I don't think the comrades here would object very strongly to my leaving New York. They run things pretty well without me. But just the same, I feel a sort of compulsion to remain here for a while longer just to make sure that the attempt of our disloyal minority to organize a split is smashed to splinters, and to make doubly sure that the Shachtmanites don't steal anything from our party. As things stand now, however, neither prospect appears to be very serious, and if I could just summon the energy and willpower to make a decision, Rose and I would soon be on a train for the land where the sun and the comrades' faces are always bright and shining.

My real wish would be to set up shop in California and do the rest of the work that I have to do for the party there. Sooner or later I have to make the decision because I don't seem to be able to get started with sustained writing projects here. The little that I do in the direction of the party here is just enough to divert me from sustained literary work and probably not enough to make any serious difference in the course of the party. What I give in the way of consultation and advice could very probably be given just as well by correspondence from California, as was the case during my year's absence from the center in 1944.

I must confess again that the real problem is one of decision. Since I am too weak-willed to make it myself, I suppose the whole project will just hang fire until somebody decides for me.

A half dozen of our leading comrades spent a few days in the country a short while ago, devoting the whole time to a discussion of fundamental questions in general, and the preliminary "Theses on the American Revolution" in particular.[87] Arne [Swabeck] and I had a talk about the same thing during my visit to Chicago. You will see some of the results of our reflections in my speech on the anniversary of the Russian revolution.

Do you think we could do some fruitful work on this theme in California? I have in mind a bold reorientation along the lines of the *Americanization* of the party, not only in its "approach," tactics, and methods of working—this has already been pretty well accomplished and is not the least reason for the advances we have made—but in its theoretical thinking, outlook, and perspective. In other words, we must begin to think of America as the decisive battleground in the world struggle of socialism and capitalism, and formulate our battle plan accordingly. I think this is the best contribution we can make to genuine internationalism in the next period.

Please give me regular reports about the results of the rest and health cure that you and Myra [Tanner Weiss] are taking. Needless to say, we all heartily approve of the decision of the Los Angeles comrades to afford you this opportunity. We must never forget that, according to our world view, today is important but tomorrow is still more important. There's going to be a good time coming, and a great gittin' up morning.

As ever,
[Jim]

LIFT THE BAN ON "LA VÉRITÉ"!

December 3, 1945

The following telegram was sent to French President de Gaulle and André Malraux, then de Gaulle's minister of information, to protest the refusal of the French government to legalize the publication of La Vérité, *the newspaper of the Parti Communiste Internationaliste, the French section of the Fourth International. The text is from* The Militant *of December 15, 1945.*

The Socialist Workers Party learns with astonishment that *La Vérité,* central organ of the Parti Communiste Internationaliste, is refused authorization to appear as a fully legal newspaper. *La Vérité* was the first organ to be published in the underground in resistance to the Nazi invader. *La Vérité* has been fighting all forms of fascism and oppression. Refusal to grant this organ of the Parti Communiste Internationaliste full freedom of press appears to advanced workers in this country as unpardonable violation of democratic rights. We urently request you correct this injustice and grant full freedom to *La Vérité.* We propose to acquaint the entire labor movement of the United States with the conduct of your government in this important case.

James P. Cannon
National Secretary
Socialist Workers Party

A QUESTION OF DISCIPLINE[88]

December 4, 1945

The following remarks were made in a discussion in the SWP PC. The text is from the minutes of the PC.

I would like to say a word or two about this. It is true that Trotskyists traditionally don't begin with organizational measures when a political dispute is involved. They prefer to clarify the question in discussion first; that is the way we proceeded in this matter too. We have been discussing for one and a half years. The questions are pretty well clarified. Although there has not been a formal decision of the convention, the party has once more registered its decision in support of the majority and rejection of the minority. But I think that was a good procedure, that we didn't begin with disciplinary measures against the disloyal faction, as we had plenty of provocation to do months ago.

But for a party to permit a disloyal faction to take advantage of this method of procedure indefinitely in order to break up and demoralize the party—to permit that would only convict the leadership of failure to discharge its responsibilities to the party. We have to recognize a certain time when we call a halt. That is the way we proceeded in the past. We didn't begin with disciplinary action against the Oehlerites, but we finally expelled them from the party. That was before the decision was taken by the party. The convention was not held until March of 1936. The Oehlerites were expelled in November 1935 following the plenum at which they were given a warning. We had to do that because they were disorganizing and demoralizing the party. I don't think they were quite as dirty and flagrant as this faction, but they openly defied the discipline of the party.

Even the expulsion of the Shachtmanites didn't fall at the end of the discussion, because after the party convention we still provided for a continuation of the discussion. We expelled them for disloyalty. If you don't do that at a certain point, the party gets demoralized and you will begin to lose the worker elements. If we tolerate this any longer, the worker elements in the party will begin to fall away. That would be a far worse loss to us than the loss that will ensue from disciplinary action against the antiparty minority.

I believe that the party membership will vote by 96 percent to support the decision of the committee in proceeding now to act against the disrupters. I haven't any doubt about that. I think, on the other hand, that if the committee tolerates these infractions any longer, it will begin to lose authority and prestige in the party and it will be impossible to enforce discipline in the fractions and so on.

This will be a salutary lesson, not only for our party but for the whole international movement, that we can't permit petty-bourgeois anarchist elements to disrupt the party and defy its discipline. An International that would permit that would never be capable of developing a revolutionary movement.

James P. Cannon, Felix Morrow, Albert Goldman

HOW "THE HISTORY OF AMERICAN TROTSKYISM" WAS WRITTEN

December 21, 1945

The following is a previously unpublished letter to Anthony Ramuglia.

New York

Tony Ramuglia
New Haven, Conn.

Dear Ram:

Sam [Gordon] is away on a long trip and his mail—according to agreement—is turned over to the national office. That's how I received your letter of December 17. I will save it for Sam until he gets back.

You really have a justifiable beef on the Allentown business considering all that you did and put up with there to help the party in a tough time. I feel very bad about my carelessness in failing to mention you and the part you played in the fight.[89] However, I wish to assure you that it was only carelessness and not design.

Your letter prompted me to look through the index of the book, and I saw with dismay that many, many comrades who did great work for the party over a long period of years, some of them from the very beginning, are not mentioned by name. This gives me the uneasy feeling that perhaps they are all sore at me and feel that I intentionally slighted them. This pains me more than I can say, for I am really a man of good intentions and goodwill.

The writing of this history book came about in a peculiar way without any well-prepared plan or design of mine and without much work being put into it. In the winter of 1942 I was asked by the New York local if I would give a few lectures on the history of the party. I agreed, and originally planned to compress the whole thing into three or four lectures, dealing only with the outstanding events. However, when I began to brush up my memory by checking the old bound volumes of *The Militant* and other material, and making notes as I went along, the project seemed to stretch out endlessly. It finally required twelve lectures just to bring the subject up to the end of 1937 and the formal launching of the SWP. By that time I was sick and tired of the business and called it quits.

I had emphasized in the lectures that I was only hitting the high spots and making no pretense of giving a definitive and documented history of the movement. The lectures were taken down stenographically, and some comrades thought they ought to be published for the benefit of the new members of the party. I, however, was somewhat conscious of their inadequacy and let the manuscript lay around without making any attempt to edit it for publication for a year and a half.

In November 1943 we got the notice that the Supreme Court had refused to review our case and that we had to serve our sentences. That forced me to realize that a decision had to be made, once and for all, whether to publish the stuff or not. I then set to work, but I had no time to do anything more than edit the manuscript, correct the grammar, etc., and let the thing go as it was.

I know better than anybody that the final product contains many flaws and omissions, but I console myself with the thought that I never originally promised to do anything more than to give a few lectures touching the high spots; and that, in any case, something on the history of our movement is better than nothing.

I will say one thing, however, in behalf of my little book. I consciously tried to deal justly and truthfully with all those people whose names I mentioned, regardless of any quarrels or conflicts that had taken place between me and them in the past, and I think I succeeded in this undertaking.

Fraternally,
J. P. Cannon

THE MINORITY IS AIMING TOWARD A SPLIT

December 27, 1945

This letter to the organizer of the San Francisco branch of the SWP has not been previously published.

New York

Bob Chester
San Francisco

Dear Bob:

I think the main point in the attack on the minority now should be their split program. Additional proof of this policy is now furnished by the letter of Jeffries resigning from the minority faction, copy of which you have received from Morris.[90] Your local Goldmanites should be put right up against the wall on this issue and compelled to state clearly where they stand. If they say they are against the split, demand that they issue a statement to the party as Jeffries and Alberts did. It should be clearly explained to the local comrades, some of whom are new in the movement, that if our party survived and grew strong in the face of all kinds of attempts to disrupt it during the past seventeen years, not the least reason was that we never had any tolerance for splitters and fought them mercilessly. We take the same attitude toward the Shachtmanite agents who are trying to engineer a new split in our ranks under the hypocritical slogan of unity.

Profound political differences were implicit in the position of the minority from the beginning, although not openly stated. Opportunists nearly always begin with secondary questions and organizational grievances and only later reveal what they are driving at in a political sense. It was so in this case too. The revisionist tendencies of the minority are quite clearly revealed now, especially in the last two articles of Morrow in *Internal Bulletin* no. 12, and are already meeting with strong condemnation from the Marxists on the international field. The driving force behind the minority's hysterical campaign for unity with the Shachtmanites is first of all their blood relationship to them in a social sense and a rapidly approaching rapprochement with them in a political sense.

I don't know much about Fisher.

The indication that your local minority will base themselves on the letter of Natalia duplicates the pattern which has already been shot to pieces in the New York and Chicago discussions.[91] Natalia does not introduce any new arguments which were not already heard from Goldman and refuted. If we rejected these arguments when Goldman put them forward, why should we accept them when Natalia repeats them? That, as we explained in the New York and Chicago discussions, is nothing but an appeal to "authority." But didn't Goldman himself instruct us to be critical independent thinkers? And to accept no arguments from "authority" which do not stand up on their own merits? Our respect for Natalia as a comrade does not obligate us to take political instruction from her.

More than that, the best answer to the argument that we should have made an election bloc with the Shachtmanites in the New York election is provided by the results of the election itself. Have your local minorityites read the figures?—they were printed in *The Militant*.[92] These results in our opinion prove pretty conclusively that we had no need of any election combination with the Shachtmanites and that the alleged "confusion" among the advanced workers about the two parties apparently wasn't very great in New York. 4,267 of them seemed to have no difficulty in distinguishing the genuine Trotskyist party from the counterfeit. In our opinion, the results of the election demonstrate quite conclusively that our tactic was right and that we should stick to it in other elections. Our election policy is motivated primarily by our determination to popularize our ideas and build up our own party in struggle against all other parties. What's wrong with that?

As for Munis, what political authority can he have for the membership of our party? They have already had a good example of his political thinking in his criticism of the Minneapolis trial.[93] As far as I know, nobody in our party with the exception of [Sam]

Joyce found any merit in his farrago of sterile formalism and ultraleftist phrasemongering. Joyce agreed with him and expressed the same kind of criticism because his mind works the same way. Our party, however, has been trained and educated in a different political method. Munis's demand for "unity" with the Shachtmanites—he is, in fact, one of the authors of this badly conceived maneuver—is inspired in large degree by his Yankee-phobia. Besides that, the factional bloc of the ultraleftist Munis with our right-wing minorityites is an unprincipled combination which discredits both of them in the eyes of all our party members who have learned something about principled politics from the history of our party.

This great "unifier" Munis has just succeeded in manipulating a split in the Mexican section of the Fourth International. That does not give him very good credentials as a "unifier" of the movement in the United States.

Let us know how the internal situation develops in San Francisco. It is perfectly clear that the minority on a national scale is moving rapidly toward a split from the SWP. We are going to fight this split without mercy and reduce it to a splinter.

Fraternally,
J. P. Cannon

THE PC'S ANSWER TO THE MINORITY'S ULTIMATUM

February 12, 1946

The following motion was presented by Cannon to the SWP PC in reply to a January 26 letter from the Goldman-Morrow minority threatening to quit the SWP and join the WP if action were not taken rapidly on the fusion question. The motion was adopted by a vote of 8 to 1, the negative vote cast by Morrow. The text is from the previously unpublished minutes of the PC meeting of February 12, 1946.

Under date of January 26 the minority faction in the National Committee presented the majority with the demand that it change its position "in the coming weeks" on the question of fusion with the Shachtmanites under penalty of withdrawal from the party by the minority. Specifically, they stated:

> If in the coming weeks we can see any sign that we can reasonably consider as a move on your part toward resumption of negotiations for unity with the Workers Party, we shall remain in the Socialist Workers Party in order to work for the cause of unity. If, on the other hand, you give no sign of a desire to reconsider your stand against unity, then our place will be with the Workers Party.

The only answer the Political Committee can make to this ultimatum is the following:

1. The course of the Political Committee on the question in dispute is determined by the resolution of the October plenum.[94] The Political Committee has neither the desire nor the authority to change the line of this plenum resolution. Under date of January 1946 the European Secretariat adopted a resolution on the question of fusion between the Socialist Workers Party and the Workers Party, endorsing the general line of our plenum

resolution and making specific recommendations for the further consideration and discussion of this question. The Political Committee is in full agreement with the resolution of the European Secretariat and intends to proceed along the line indicated therein.

2. Under date of December 28 the European Secretariat addressed a letter to the party leadership declaring that "there is not at the present time any valid political reason to hang the threat of a split over the American party and thereby over the International as well." The letter of the European Secretariat further appealed to both factions in the leadership "to safeguard the unity of the party, to abstain from any measure which might appear bureaucratic, from any threat of expulsion, as well as from any abuse of national and international discipline."

3. The Political Committee fully agrees with the position taken by the European Secretariat in this matter and assures the minority that its democratic rights of free expression will be safeguarded and guaranteed in the future as in the past, and that all their party rights will be respected in the further course of the discussion. At the same time we insist that the minority respect the discipline of the party.

4. We strongly urge the minority to reconsider the position stated in their letter of January 26, to avail themselves of the opportunity to continue the discussion on the question of fusion with the Shachtmanites and other important questions in dispute, and at the same time to respect the principles of democratic centralism and refrain from any further violations of party discipline.

THE PUBLICATION OF TROTSKY'S SUPPRESSED BIOGRAPHY OF STALIN

February 16, 1946

The following press release by Cannon was issued in response to an announcement from Harper and Brothers publishers that they were about to release copies of Trotsky's Stalin, *which had been printed during the war but withheld from distribution as a favor to Stalin. The text is from* The Militant *of February 23, 1946.*

According to press reports, Harper and Brothers have announced the publication of Leon Trotsky's biography of Stalin for this April. Although this book was ready for publication over four years ago, it was suppressed by the publishers early in 1942 owing to pressure exerted by the U.S. State Department. Washington obviously moved to suppress the book as a favor to its ally in the Kremlin who feared the appearance of this book.

The lifting of the ban upon the book at this time is a sign of the changed political relations between Moscow and Washington.

Trotsky was struck down by an assassin of Stalin's GPU in Mexico in August 1940, before the book was completed. The printed text is only in part the product of Trotsky's own pen. At the time of his assassination Trotsky had completed only seven chapters of his biography of Stalin. The remainder of the manuscript consisted of a rough draft of the five final chapters and notes for an introduction.

Instead of publishing this material in the shape left by its author, Harper and Brothers arbitrarily appointed Mr. Charles Malamuth, who had been hired solely as translator, to "edit" the manuscript. The latter thereupon proceeded to make unauthorized alterations and interpolations which express views contrary to those held by the author and, in effect, pervert and falsify Trotsky's political standpoint.

In protest against this "unheard-of-violence committed by the translator on the author's rights," Natalia Sedova Trotsky wrote on September 23, 1941, regarding these interpolations that Malamuth "had not been authorized to do so either by L. D. Trotsky or myself." She insisted that "everything written by the pen of Mr. Malamuth must be expunged from the book" and instituted legal action.

However, the present printed text contains all the objectionable material.

The public should therefore be advised that the latter part of the Harper edition of the biography of Stalin is not the work of Trotsky himself. Nevertheless, its appearance after more than four years of official suppression will enable the world to judge in part why the Kremlin was so anxious to assassinate the author before the book was completed.

RELEASE THE TROTSKYISTS ARRESTED IN PARIS![95]

March 8, 1946

The following telegram was sent by Cannon to André le Troquer, the Socialist minister of the interior (police) of the French government. The text is from a copy of the telegram in Cannon's files.

Indignantly protest March 6 Paris police raid on public meeting of the Internationalist Communist Party and arrest of audience, reported in American press, as outrageous violation of democratic rights of assembly. United States labor public opinion will be aroused against these antidemocratic actions. Demand immediate unconditional release of all arrested, end to interference with PCI meetings and publications. Please inform us action of your government on this protest.

James P. Cannon
National Secretary
Socialist Workers Party

STOP THE TENNESSEE LYNCH MOBS![96]

Published March 9, 1946

The following message was sent to Governor McCord of Tennessee. The text is from the March 9, 1946, Militant.

Governor Jim McCord
Nashville, Tennessee

We vigorously protest the outrageous wholesale atrocities and violations of civil rights committed by state troops and local police against the Negro citizens of Columbia, Tennessee.

All the facts clearly prove that the invasion by your troops of this Negro community was a calculated move to terrorize and repress the defenseless Negro citizens of Columbia who had been threatened by lynch mobs.

Eyewitness reports reveal that your troops blasted away at Negro dwellings and businesses with machine guns and carbines, invaded and ransacked homes without search warrants, manhandled men, women, and children, and arrested at random scores of Negroes, many of whom are still being held in jail in violation of their constitutional rights. Two imprisoned Negroes were shot down in cold blood by guards.

Together with other working class political parties, unions, and civil rights organizations, the Socialist Workers Party demands that you immediately end the reign of terror in Columbia, withdraw the state troops, and release all the innocent victims who are being held illegally in prison.

We hold your administration directly responsible.

James P. Cannon
National Secretary
Socialist Workers Party

MAJORITY AND MINORITY RIGHTS IN THE INTERNAL BULLETIN AND THE PARTY PRESS[97]

April 9, 1946

Following are excerpts from a discussion in the SWP Political Committee, taken from the PC minutes.

Walter [Cannon]: First, I don't think the minority has any legitimate grounds to complain at all about the way the discussion has been conducted in the internal bulletin or in the magazine. None whatever. We never opened the magazine for unrestricted discussion. We opened it only for a selection of articles which summarize the conflicting points of view. The unrestricted discussion has been relegated to the internal bulletin, and that is correct. Otherwise the magazine would lose its value as a rounded journal.

Point two: We are governed by certain conceptions in the selection of material for publication in the public organ. There the last word belongs to the majority. We haven't the slightest objection to publishing Angel's stuff, as you know, but we have the right to say when it will be published and to publish it with the answer of the majority every time. The magazine is not a discussion organ in an unrestricted sense, but is an organ for the presentation of the views of the majority, and the extent to which we publish the material of the minority is governed by that, keeping clear what the line of the majority is all the time. I don't believe there can be any legitimate objection to that.

We printed one critical article by Morrow by itself, then an answer by Simmons [Swabeck]. So it became clear to everybody that while we are permitting the minority to express itself, we are at the same time giving the last word to the majority. That is what I think we should do in this given case. I take it that this answer [by Morrow] has been sent to Europe. Comrade Sloan [Breitman] informs us that they are planning to give a final answer to your answer. It will be more appreciated by our readers and conform to our conception of the magazine if we hold it up.[98]

On the internal bulletin: There is no ground I know of for complaint whatsoever.[99] As a matter of fact, there was no need especially for consultation after the first few numbers because we followed the principle of publishing everything in the order it was received. The only exception to that was when the minority leaders came in with some late stuff and asked us to push it in ahead of other material submitted by their supporters.

Of course, that didn't stop them from complaining about delay in publishing some of the articles that had been pushed back by the submission of this other minority material. The general, overall impression must be to any fair person that the minority has had a square deal.

I don't know what Angel's idea is that this [Morrow's letter] was not submitted to the internal bulletin but to the magazine. All your previous discussion with the ES [European Secretariat] was printed first in the internal bulletin and then in the magazine. That is the way we conceive of the discussion. Everything goes in the internal bulletin and then selections of it go in the magazine. I believe my motion is the better one.

We have no desire whatever to be unfair to them. Joint editorship with a minority of this size is a little bit ridiculous, in my opinion. We had joint editorship with the Shachtmanites, but they had 42 percent of the party. But a minority of this size that has a delegate on the editorial board of the bulletin—taking into account the method by which we proceeded up to now, I think [our procedure] will be recognized as fair enough.

Angel [Morrow]: I object to the whole conception of the so-called limited discussion in the *FI.* When you are dealing with political ideas, there are obvious criteria which should be employed by the leading body to determine whether a given article is suitable—tone, etc. We have had this question over and over again and we know what those criteria are. But once you open a discussion in the *FI,* then that discussion should actually be a discussion.

Now consider what picture is created. I write an answer which, however, is not to be published until the IS answers. I have no reply from them. I have no knowledge whether they are ever going to answer it. If they don't ever answer it, it announces to the readers of the *FI* that I didn't answer them. The idea that we must wait for their answer is obviously an unfair method of discussion. The least the committee can do is to explain in the magazine the basis for publication and make clear the minority is not free to answer when it answers but is compelled to wait until the majority in its own sweet time prepares a reply, and only then will the minority's answer appear in the *FI*.

Barr [Dobbs]: Comrade Angel is evading the whole point that Comrade Walter made. He proceeds on the assumption that the *FI* is an internal bulletin.

Angel: Then explain that to the readers.

Walter: There is a different conception of the public magazine. You want to claim the same rights there that you have in the internal bulletin and we don't grant that. The magazine is the organ of the majority. What the readers will gather from it—to use your phrase—the only impression they can gather is that the minority point of view is fairly presented in the magazine at adequate length by themselves, and the only advantage the majority takes is that they have the last word. Angel seems to think that the privilege of the last word belongs to him. He places himself in the same position as the IS. We don't print any attacks on the IS without their having their answer to it there at the same time.

Angel: We are not arguing the difference in conception. I am saying that in all decency when you present this, you. . . .

White [Cochran]: I don't like to have any rule here, any idea that we are bound by any rule that before a minority is permitted to publish its article we are going to have to have a rejoinder. I stick by the idea that the magazine is an expression of the party and has to be used to suit the party needs. The party can decide to do it one way at one time and another way at another time. Maybe we can publish Angel's reply and the IS reply, or maybe we don't publish it at all and confine it to the internal bulletin, depending on our own needs. That has been the conception that has governed our periodicals all along. [. . .]

Walter: This talk about falsification sounds to me like a revival of the hunt for Stalinism which up to now has never been made by anybody but enemies of our movement. What happened in this case was that Angel submitted his motion for the internal bulletin. That was printed, wasn't it? Usually we don't bother to answer a lot of the stuff of the minority, but since in this case the motion made assertions that we were supporting Reuther, we took the action of inserting Short's [Morris Lewit] answer to it, which was a formal part of the minutes. . . .

The very title, "Against Supporting Reuther, etc." is an insulting slander to the committee, and Short's brief statement made that very clear, that that was not involved as far as we were concerned. What you are giving us now is an argument against a joint committee [to edit the internal bulletin]. We couldn't publish an internal bulletin because you would exert the right of veto on everything concerning our rights. Joint editorship of the bulletin can only be extended to a minority that is willing to cooperate reasonably. [. . .]

THE MINORITY IN THE SWP AND THE FOURTH INTERNATIONAL[100]

May 19-20, 1946

These remarks were made at a plenum of the SWP National Committee, held in New York, May 19-22, 1946. Cannon was given extended time in the dicussion period of the first point on the agenda, on developments in world politics and in the Fourth International. His speech was interrupted by the end of the first day's session and he continued on the following morning. The text, slightly abridged, is from a previously unpublished and uncorrected stenogram.

The bible was right on quite a few things, especially that point where it says open confession is good for the soul. We had a very long, detailed, open confession here tonight, and I assure you it wasn't extorted by us. It was a free confession. More powerful factors than we are behind that. Our pressure was quite secondary. Comrade Morrow gave us a characteristic performance of a man who is running away from Marxism and its program and its perspectives. We have seen it so often that it falls into a recognizable pattern: Brazen revision of all the most fundamental considerations upon which our movement has been founded and built, personal denigration of the orthodoxists, and a bitter, irreconcilable-enemy tone in which the argument is pitched. You would think Morrow here today was talking in an assembly of class enemies. And you wouldn't be far wrong.

Morrow speaks very boldly in attacking the program of the movement. And boldness is a new attribute on his part. As he admitted here today, he said, "Cannon used to scare me." But today he spoke boldly as though he feels a real power behind him, and indeed there is a power behind him that at the moment is greater than the fear of Cannon. But that power is not in this party and it is not in our International. It is outside us. Morrow in his confessional today revealed that he is just finding out what has been ailing him for several years.

When he voted for our resolutions and then at the same time started a very bitter faction fight against us there were some people, inexperienced, who hadn't seen that phenomenon before on the part of others, predecessors of Morrow. They wondered what is it all about? If he agreed on the resolution, even so much so that he insisted on voting for it whether the convention wanted to let him vote for it or not, and is still fighting, there must be something personal involved here. We didn't think so.

Morrow voted for the resolutions because he was scared, he says, and then he started to fight because he didn't believe in what he voted for. That was the real explanation. Because he has developed himself in stages. First he was a shamefaced and scared revisionist who accused us of slander when we intimated that was behind it, and now he is an open bold revisionist, bold because he expects to find support outside our ranks—and in that, I must admit, he will not be disappointed. The support is there, and powerful, and waiting for him.

He says, "We compromised with the majority in 1942 at the convention." That is not quite literally accurate and doesn't befit a man with the meticulous command of language that Morrow has. A compromise implies concessions on each side. There was no compromise on our part. You "compromised" by voting for our resolution. And then he adds that after the 1942 convention we didn't get along very well. Do you recall that? What a revealing confession that was. Before that, as you know, he said we got along very well together but after the 1942 convention we didn't get along.

By that Morrow confesses before this body of communists that the fight was not a personal fight as it appeared to be, that all the talk about bureaucratism and our bad manners and methods was a fake from the start, that from the very beginning the fight had a political content hidden in it and that content is clearly disclosed here today and I believe that indicates progress.

Now we can quit fighting about trivials and incidentals. [We can get down to the basic questions] upon which the existence of our movement depends. Listen to this. The perspective was false not only in Europe, and in Russia. The analysis was false. But this analysis and the perspective that flowed from it were shared by all of us through the war. He gave us a list of all the various papers that had spoken in the same tone—French, Indian, Chilean, Belgian, etc. The perspective and the analysis was common to all of us and its chief author, as you know, was Trotsky. And if the fundamental analysis of the epoch and the perspectives derived from it were false, then Trotskyism is no good and something different, a substitute for it, must be found. Isn't that the conclusion?

The whole analysis was wrong. The perspective was wrong. The whole movement shared it, the movement educated and trained by Trotsky. Trotsky was the author of it and that is what he should say—that Trotskyism has failed the historical test. And that is what he would say if he were not scared. He is getting rid of his fears and phobias in stages—first the fear of Cannon and after that comes Trotsky. All opportunists go in stages and that is next. You will get rid of the phobia of Trotskyism in the not-too-distant future.

The real phobia behind all the revisionists throughout the world is the fear of the greater power that is pressing down upon them. You will not get rid of that. You are capitulating to that. That is the whole meaning of your attack upon the program of the international conference and upon the conference itself, which means upon our organization.

There is a kernel of truth in his statement that Trotsky's death was bound to provoke a crisis in our international movement. That is so because when Trotsky lived a great many congenital but not very courageous revisionists were afraid to open their mouths with the kind of stuff we heard here today. Burnham was the rare exception and he only got the courage when he was ready to leave the movement, which followed a few months later.

All I could make out of his whole analysis of the international resolution today is anti-Stalinism. I believe the question about the slogan of withdrawing the Russian troops also is a debatable question in our ranks, although I would approach it from a fundamentally different point of view from Morrow and consequently would have no basis for agreement with him in any case. But I believe the slogan we should emphasize in the United States is the slogan of withdrawing the American troops. That is our task. I believe the main enemy and the main power that has to be overthrown in the world before humanity can be liberated is the power of American imperialism. That is located not in the Kremlin, but here in America.

One-sided, vulgar anti-Stalinism—there is plenty of empirical proof of what that means. Anti-Stalinism according to a great array of accumulated evidence in the person of people who have left our movement under that banner is the anteroom to pro-Americanism. If you doubt that, just pick up any issue of the *New Leader,* and read the list of anti-Stalinist, ex-Trotskyists who are vociferously demanding war on the Soviet Union.

Morrow didn't speak about his resolution on the conference. He decided after he had revealed its content to us to put it back into his briefcase.[101] But that doesn't prevent us from taking it out of the briefcase and discussing it, and that is the side I want to emphasize in my remarks. After five years of war and devastation, our international movement succeeded in assembling a conference larger in scope and representation than the founding conference in 1938 in times of peace. In spite of all the losses, the difficulties of transportation, which are still far greater than then, and without the guiding hand of Trotsky, we succeeded in assembling a conference in Europe with the power and the capacity to speak in the name of our world party and its program.

Here is a remark, I want to quote it again—what George [Breitman] referred to in his report: "I consider that if the move against the German comrades succeeds, that is only the beginning. By the very same method we here and the French minority can be treated the same way, and then the British leadership, the same way. It is the beginning of the end of the Fourth International if this prevails."[102]

I should quote some of the interjections that were aroused by people who had heard that before and had it still ringing in their ears. I said, "Only now the beginning of the end? We heard that in 1940, remember? And we just heard that a few months ago from Shachtman, that it was not only the beginning of the end but the finish."

I haven't any doubt that Morrow and all the others following him on the revisionist path have declared war on the Fourth International, beginning with its program and ideology, and concluding with its organizational existence. And naturally we take that as a declaration of war, not a squabble, not a personal argument, not a piddling difference about bureaucratic methods but a declaration of war on everything we stand for and have stood for in our long struggle. We on the other hand are supporters of the resolution of the world conference, of the conference itself, and of the executive bodies set up by it. [. . .]

You know that the Fourth International began as an ideological current in the Russian party, the Left Opposition of Trotsky.

Concomitantly with the degeneration of the Communist International under Stalin, a countermovement began. First in Russia as a minority faction, and eventually through a long series of struggles and historical experiences, it evolved into the world organization which celebrated its fourth international conference a short time ago. If we should mark out this historical evolution from 1923 up to the present time, twenty-three years, I think we can recognize definite stages. Even though the one overlaps the other in each case, there are certain distinguishing features of each case that I would like to call to your attention.

While the Left Opposition was bottled up in Russia and suppressed and had neither the organizational nor the publishing facilities to extend its sway outside the borders of Russia, the first and original movement of Left Oppositionists, presumed Trotskyists, took shape in the form of groups throughout the world who were in conflict with the bureaucracy on various and different questions, sometimes contradictory questions. When you stop to realize that Souvarine was a leader of the first Trotskyist group in France; and Treint, a disappointed bureaucrat; and Rosmer; and that lawyer whose name I can't remember; and [Ruth] Fischer and Maslow in Germany; and Urbahns; Lore in this country—those were the first people who rallied to the support of the Soviet Left Opposition. Not a one of them is in the movement today. The only one who remains so far as I know a sympathizer is Rosmer and he has been organizationally separated from us for about fifteen years.

What was the basis of this first, presumably Trotskyist movement, the first nuclei of the Fourth International, the movement that evolved into the present Fourth International? The first basis was democracy, dissatisfaction with the bureaucratization of the Communist International regime and the regime of the party. It was characterized by a confused ideology. It contained in it both opportunists and ultralefts. It was scattered, disconnected, split, and demoralized, and practically the whole of this original cadre of Trotsky supporters fell by the wayside in the course of further developments. That is the period, you may say, from 1923 to 1929. When we rallied to the banner of the Russian Opposition in 1928 we had very little contact. The leading representative of the Trotskyist movement in France at the same time was the lawyer Paz, who a short time later just threw off his Trotskyism as though he were changing his coat and went over into the Social Democracy.

A second stage began in 1929 with the exile of Trotsky to

Turkey, which for the first time gave him the chance to communicate with a free hand with co-thinkers and disaffected elements throughout the world. During that period Trotsky set out to do away with the mishmash that called itself Trotskyist and to lay down clear programmatic lines as conditions for association with him. Right and left he hammered at every deviationist tendency. Everybody who was in the Left Opposition by mistake was challenged by him. He didn't call for everybody to get together against the Stalin regime. He didn't try to unite anybody who had a grievance against the party leadership. He said no. We have a program that we are fighting for and he laid down his conditions. It appeared for a time that Trotsky was really hard to get along with. He split here with . . . and split there with Souvarine. People who are inclined to make a fetish of unity think you are stronger if you have more numbers, regardless of the differences between you. Such people wondered if there wasn't something in the accusation of the Stalinists that Trotsky was a hard man to get along with. But pretty soon the pattern began to come through. He wanted to get along with people who had the same general ideas of Marxism, and he wanted to break off relations with those who were using the banner of Trotskyism as an excuse to get away first from the Communist International and then from class struggle altogether.

From 1929 to 1931 there were two years in which we had not even the semblance of an international organization. All we had were small groups in various parts of the world and Trotsky in Constantinople. Trotsky was the central committee, in effect, of the international Trotskyist movement. It wasn't until 1931 when a small conference—if you try to compare the [recent] conference in size, homogeneity, etc., with the conference in 1931 you would see how the group has progressed in that time.[103] You would see what a great work has been accomplished in the meantime.

A few representatives of small groups who weren't very clear on what they wanted, who had no qualified leadership, new young people who had stepped up and taken the places of all the oldtime leaders who had fallen by the wayside, Paz, etc. There was a new leadership everywhere of inexperienced young people, many of them who had no benefit of the rich experience of the Communist International. They gathered in a small conference and formed the International Communist League and set up what was called an International Executive Committee and an

International Secretariat.[104] If you call the roll of the leaders of that time—Naville, Molinier, Nin in Spain, a preacher whose name escapes me but who later deserted the movement and went over to the labor party, and then what later became the SWP in the United States. Out of all that leading cadre—if you could speak of a leading cadre in the case of people who had very little qualification for leadership—that was international Trotskyism in that period. They not only were not qualified to lead the international movement, they were not qualified to build and lead a movement on national soil anywhere. In the political essence of the matter, Trotsky was not only the executive committee; he was the leader of each and every individual party. Less so in the United States, but in Europe he used to intervene on every kind of question, organizational as well as political ones. And with the people he had to contend with—without experience or special qualifications, and with many of them, almost all, intellectuals without any knowledge of the mass movement or ability to penetrate the mass movement, and with great pretensions—it was with that material that Trotsky tried to hammer out an international organization with an international leadership.

The internal literature of our movement during that whole period is full of the battles waged by Trotsky for a uniform program, for a proletarian composition, and for the emergence of the movement out of its sectarian isolation onto the road toward a mass movement. [. . .]

Urbahns developed a theory which he thought was very new and original. The same theory that we have heard adumbrated here today about Russia. That it was a *zwischen* state. It is neither bourgeois nor proletarian, but something in between. And Trotsky declared war on the theory of the in-between state because he said that is not Marxism. One has to first reject Marxism before one can set up a theory of a state that is neither proletarian nor bourgeois in this epoch. I said we heard that theory adumbrated here today. Not clearly stated. What we got was the political conclusions from the Urbahns theory of the in-between state, and after they have drawn their political conclusions they will remind themselves sooner or later that it is necessary to say what is the nature of the state. They will remind themselves to describe the character of the state. They will get around to that.

Why don't we publish Logan's document? I will tell you what it is—"The Eruption of Bureaucratic Imperialism"—the same thing we heard from Burnham in 1939 and from Urbahns in 1929. And we were going to publish it and we promised to. In the meantime it was published in Shachtman's magazine.[105] So we said that is going too far. We said to him, as we say to our opposition, "You can break into our house, you can steal our belongings, and you can assault our wife, but have a care, Sir Belvedere, someday you will go too far." And Logan went too far when he published a document intended for us to discuss in the press of an opponent party.

We believe in monogamy in the political field. We don't want any two-party people, any two-timers trying to belong to two parties. We won't tolerate that. And if anyone wants to read the world-shaking revelations of Logan, he can buy the *New International*. Morrow says that is his document. Then he has developed the theory of a bureaucratic imperialism without defining its class base. Logan left entirely aside the class analysis of the Soviet Union and in a typical shamefaced revisionist manner tried to draw political conclusions. It had nothing new or even interesting.

Trotsky waged a war against Urbahns, then the leadership of Landau led to another split. Then the betrayal of Roman Well, another German intellectual litterateur. At that time, way back in 1933 when the crisis of Landau was followed by the crisis of Well. . . . Trotsky put forward the slogan for the German section: "It is time to have a workers' leadership. It is time for the workers of the German section to take control of their organization and put up no more with these irresponsible and unworthy people."[106]

We had in that period in the International Secretariat more than one secretary who in the midst of a crisis and scandal left the movement. One of them was the Greek [Demetrios Giotopoulos], who later left the International and went over to the London Bureau. Another was Mill, who after all kinds of unprincipled combinations and abuses of power jumped the fence and went over to the Stalinists.

The task Trotsky had in those days was certainly incommensurate [with ours]. Out of the tremendous confusion and demoralization generated by the reaction in Russia and the Comintern, he had to fight for ideological clarification on the fundamental questions, not on the tactical questions. [. . .]

Some of you may have read in the *Fourth International* a month or so ago some of the historic letters that Trotsky wrote in that period. His letters to Souvarine and to other comrades. . . .

[One of these was in answer to a letter] in which Souvarine had urged him to unite with Brandler; others had written him, asking why don't you take in this group, and that group, and so on. He seemed to be an arbitrary person. In a letter to comrades, Trotsky laid down three points of principles upon which one had to agree in order to be included in the organization he was founding. You will recall, it was the Russian question; the question of the Anglo-Russian Committee, which involved the question of the role of the party; and the Chinese question, which involved the problem of the colonial revolution and also the question of the role of the independent revolutionary party. And he left out of his platform for the formation of his faction the one thing these people put for the formation of their faction—the question of the regime.[107]

[And that was the] Stalin regime, not the Cannon regime. He said the regime question has no independent significance whatsoever.

That was a rich historical period. Surely the future historians will say that was the heroic period of the Fourth International, when Trotsky out of virtually nothing but chaos and confusion was hammering together the future cadres of the proletarian revolution, the cadres of the Fourth International, attempting to squeeze them, find out what was in them. That was when Nin, one of the original leaders of Russian and world Trotskyism, jumped the track and went over to centrism. That is the time when the entry tactic was devised, that is, the tactic of joining the Social Democratic parties with the objective of forming a broader basis of organization for our movement.

The entry tactic had nothing in common whatever with what Morrow is talking about today.[108] The Trotskyist entry tactic was designed to go into the centrist formations, unite with their left wing on the basis of our platform, and create a party on a broader basis. Your tactic is to go into reformist organizations with your revisionist program and stay there. That is your program when you get around to stating it fully. With the program you elucidated today you would go into a reformist organization and organize a revolutionary left wing? You are coming to the wrong address. You belong with the others more than with us. We are Marxists.

In 1936, ten years ago, Trotsky prescribed for all the parties as a matter of life-and-death necessity the turn from propaganda circle to mass work, the turn from discussion clubs to penetration of the mass movement and the recruitment of a proletarian membership in the party. Ten years ago. And that was a recognition of the utter inadequacy both of the leadership and of the composition of the Trotskyist organizations of that time. The revolutionary movement after a great defeat can't begin otherwise than as a discussion circle. But those who want a discussion circle in permanence where people have nothing to do but listen to fast-talkers cannot become a revolutionary organization. It has to grow out of that and become a workers' organization which knows not only how to learn from these leaders, but to control them and subordinate them. [. . .]

Now, 1938 brought the Fourth International to a new stage, that is, to the stage where it was able to hold an international congress for the first time. Not a big one. Only ten parties, I think, were represented, but most of the European parties and the American party were represented there. Then was set up, as the successor of the International Communist League, the Fourth International as a world organization with an Executive Committee and an IS.

During all that time, from 1929 to 1940 when Trotsky died, the end of another stage, another epoch in reality, there never was a time when the International Communist League or the Fourth International had a capable and authoritative Executive Committee and IS. In explaining the weaknesses of it—it brought constant criticism—Trotsky explained time and time again: the leadership cannot rise higher than the parties that make up the leadership. We have young, inexperienced people without great capacity, but they are all we have and that is the international leadership. But in reality the international leadership in all that period never took upon itself the political responsibility for leading the movement. The formal structure was the same as now, but the reality was that Trotsky, first in Turkey, then in France, then in Norway, then in Mexico, was the political and organizational leader and director of the world movement. Trotsky could play that role not because he wished to do so but because he concentrated within himself such capacity as an individual and collective experience that he could lead the movement not really as an individual, but as a whole collection of leading people concentrated in one man.

The period from 1938 to 1940 consolidated the forces in the founding world conference. At least we brought some organizational order and responsibility into the movement. But that proved to be a little too optimistic. It wasn't more than a year after that, with the approach and outbreak of the war, as you know, that we were plunged into the most fundamental fight of the Left Opposition since its beginning. And that, as you know, had its center right here in the United States, and it began over nothing else than an attempt—as Trotsky stated—to overthrow and disqualify our program and our tradition, to revise our whole ideology. That is what it began about. And Trotsky devoted the entire last year of his life almost exclusively to the fight in the Socialist Workers Party, and he said more than once that the whole future of the international revolutionary movement depended on the outcome of this fight against the Burnham-Shachtman revisionists.

I don't need to tell you that we shared that opinion and joined him and supported him in the fight against revisionism with the same militancy and irreconcilable determination that we are going to maintain in the fight against revisionism that has grown up since the conclusion of the war. And in that struggle our party became transformed and began to look like something, really looked like a party. [We accomplished that in] the fight against revisionism, unprincipled combinationism, and petty-bourgeois politics, all of which characterized the Burnham-Shachtman combination, just as it characterizes the opposition we have in our party today. To be sure, our opposition didn't begin with an unfurled banner of revisionism, but today they have confessed to us that that is what they have come to. That must be what was at the bottom of the fight and explains its terrible bitterness. [. . .]

[Session adjourned for forum—remarks to be continued in next session.—Stenographer's note]

I spoke yesterday at some length about the historical development of the Fourth International and the efforts that were made by Trotsky over a period of years to construct an international center and give it the semblance of authority. And I spoke of the great weakness which this international center always had because of the weakness of the development of the young cadres of the movement. And the attitude that Trotsky always took toward those people who recognized the weakness of the International Secretariat and who exaggerated it and used that as an excuse for leaving the movement or for indiscipline, for violations of one kind and another.

Trotsky always answered them: Don't ask more from the

international leadership than the international leadership can give. The thing to do is to send our best forces from the various parties to it to strengthen its authority and build it up because that is the connecting link which ties our world movement together organizationally and we must not allow it to be discredited or broken. And every time, as a result of the actions of irresponsible individuals like Landau and Naville, every time, Trotsky said, the link that ties our world chain together is broken, let us forge a new link. Let us tie it together again.

He would painfully try to assemble a new International Secretariat, not out of ideal material, but of what material there was on hand in Europe. I can say proudly for our part that throughout the entire history of the International since 1929 our attitude toward each succeeding international body that was set up was always loyal, always responsible; that we always tried to help and support, never to denigrate and discredit, tear down. Although we were aware as well as anyone else of the weaknesses of each succeeding body that was set up, we realized that without such a body the International as an organization does not exist.

Now, we are going to continue that attitude. We are not going to accept any part of this irresponsible manifestation of disgruntled individuals who, dissatisfied by this or that decision or action taken by the international leadership, set out to discredit it, to undermine it, to deny its authority. [. . .]

The existence of the Socialist Workers Party in its present form in relation to the other parties of the International presents, one might say, a double anomaly. Here in the richest and most conservative country of world capitalism we have the strongest section of the revolutionary world party. A strict anomaly in contrast to all the previous developments here in America, because with its conservatism, its backwardness, its richness, America always offered the poorest and least fertile soil for the building of a revolutionary party. If someone explains the strength of our party in comparison to the international sections as a whole by the fact that America "is a rich country" one only needs to ask why did that phenomenon not manifest itself in the early days of the Comintern? In the early days of the Communist International, mass parties were constructed in Germany, Czechoslovakia, France, Italy, all over the European continent in the centers of revolutionary unrest, while the American party remained a very anemic propaganda sect composed in 90 to 95 percent of its membership of immigrants from Europe who brought the revolutionary traditions with them. It had only a thin layer of native American revolutionists in its ranks.

One might say today the Stalinist party in America is a baby in comparison to the Stalinist parties in Europe, and to the extent that the membership of the Stalinist party reflects a radicalism of the workers that comparison is very apt.

Or you might ask: If America because of its richness is the best field for radical organization, how does it happen that the Socialist Party of the United States is such a miserable caricature of the Social Democracy in Europe? I say our organizational strength in comparison to that of the sections of the International, while there are many reasons for it, presents a certain anomaly.

Another side of the anomaly is that here in America, where the pressure of conservatism arising from the domination of the all-powerful imperialism is strongest, our party in the United States is the firmest single bulwark of orthodox Marxism in the Fourth International. How is this to be explained in the long run, in the development of the historical process? I believe it is correct to say that the most advanced and developed capitalist country will eventually produce the most powerful revolutionary movement, but what happened in the United States was that we accelerated that process to a certain extent, we interfered with it and pushed it forward, and one of the great reasons for that was that we had the good fortune in America to carry over from the original communist movement some experienced cadres.

In Europe, and throughout the world in fact, all the old cadres of communism were lost in the Stalinist degeneration and Trotsky was compelled to build in Europe almost from scratch. [. . .]

We, in our party, carried over from the Communist Party some experienced cadres and retained the greater part of them throughout the entire eighteen years so that the leadership of our party is somewhat unique. There isn't anything comparable to it, as far as I know, in any section of the International at the present time. We have several generations of cadres in the party and in the party leadership.

Comrade Dunne and I were speaking about it last night and looking over the representative leadership we have here at the plenum. We recognized here at least four generations of people, each of whom embodies a certain experience and a certain talent and quality supplementing the others. There is the generation of the founders, one of whom is the distinguished chairman here today; Comrade Dunne; and the one who was yesterday in the chair; myself; Comrade Karsner, who belonged not only to the pioneer cadres of American Trotskyism, but to the pioneer cadres of American socialism, back in the days of the First World War and postwar period.[109]

We have a generation of people in their forties, represented by such men as Morris Stein and Wright, Warde [George Novack], and others, in their early forties or approaching forty.

We have a generation of people in the early thirties and even people in the National Committee in the generation of the twenties. The inestimable value of each one of these succeeding leading cadres in the party has been that, unlike so many countries in Europe, they did not have to come into the leadership and learn everything anew. Each generation as it developed came into a party that was solidly grounded and was able to benefit [by the experience] acquired by those of older generations. So they came into a school, so to speak, in which things could be learned in a telescopic fashion, assimilated from others, and didn't have to begin from scratch.

That long preparation we have gone through, the hard work we have put in over a period of eighteen years—to say nothing of the preceding preparatory period—the firm bonds that have been established by the various generations in the party and in the party leadership, our firm adherence to orthodoxy from A to Z, and our resistance to any attempt, directly or indirectly, to overthrow our program or our tradition—all that is beginning to bear fruit. And if I judge signs correctly, the Socialist Workers Party today is on the verge of a great leap into a new stage of its development.

When you hear the trade union and organization reports some of you will be astounded at the transformation taking place. Before our very eyes the party of American Trotskyism is really becoming transformed almost from day to day from the old propaganda circle into a mass workers' party. I believe that same process is underway in Europe now that they are really beginning to get a stabilized leadership in one party after another, now that they are beginning to settle accounts—and I believe definitively—with all right-wing and sectarian tendencies . . . and revisionists. They have set up an International that is able to lead and does lead. I believe the European sections will take the same road, and that the whole International is on the verge of beginning to realize that essential link in the chain of development that will lead it to the revolutionary victory, that is, becoming transformed from propaganda circles into genuine mass workers' parties.

Now on the issue between us and the right wing, both here and in the International. In addition to the fundamental problems of theory and politics which are now beginning to be correctly disclosed, there is also at issue a conception of what is the leadership and how does it function, how must it function. Is it to be an elected leadership of a collective body or are we to have the leadership of self-appointed individuals who, so to speak, by the force of their talents and their chances, to say nothing of their self-assertion, replace the elected functioning bodies of the parties and the International? I believe that is what is involved in part in our conflict that has arisen over the validity, the authority, of the international conference and bodies set up by it.

We have seen a conception grow in our party, and not only in our party, since the death of Trotsky, that what can save the Fourth International, the only thing that can save it, is to find a messiah somewhere. That is, collective work, in the process of which mistakes are corrected and the right answers are found, that the strict adherence to the program and collaboration between party members, the election of functioning leadership in parties and the collaboration between the leaders of one party and another in an international center, that that cannot suffice. We must have somebody who stands above that and leads in his personal capacity as an individual. That is the messianic complex. That has been at the bottom of all the grumbling we have heard for years, ever since the death of Trotsky.

We heard it for the first time openly in the Fifteenth Anniversary Plenum, two and one-half years ago. "Cannon does not replace Trotsky"—which is hardly an exaggerated statement. But behind that statement—"Cannon does not take the place of Trotsky"—lurks the feeling, *somebody* must take the place of Trotsky. We said, the International on an international scale must take the place of Trotsky because Trotskys don't grow on trees. And at the bottom of this assertion of self-misled individuals there lurks a feeling that perhaps they have been touched by the holy fire, there lurks a lack of confidence in the collective ability of the party to lead itself and to forge its leadership. That is wrong from beginning to end.

And the pretensions of these people who set themselves up above the party, above the international leadership appointed by the conference—their pretensions do not accord with reality. We are living in a different stage of the development of the Fourth International. We are living in the post-Trotsky stage. Five years, six years nearly now, since the death of Trotsky, and the whole thing, the whole international movement, has readjusted itself to the necessities of this new period. What do we have? We have the ideas of Trotsky and we have the cadres that were created by these ideas, and with that we are working and living with confidence in the future.

Why, you will recall, I think, some of you who either attended our memorial meeting in New York at the time of the death of the Old Man or read the published pamphlet, the speech I made at that time.[110] I posed there the frank question that was in everybody's mind, not only in our party but outside the party, that question which arose all over the minute the news of the death of Trotsky was announced, and that question was this: Will the movement founded by Trotsky survive his death? The whole philistine world was sure that the movement was finished when Trotsky died because it was so associated with his personality, his genius. And I answered the question affirmatively. I said the party will survive precisely because it is different from any movement created by individuals. Trotsky's movement was created by ideas and ideas live after their authors perish.

I believe my assertion there has been confirmed 100 percent in the endurance and capacity for survival shown by the parties here and everywhere else. Some people—unfortunately, including some who were close to Trotsky, some of them who observed what the situation was at the time that Trotsky was among us, who observed how he worked because there was no other way for him to work except as the embodiment of the international leadership—tried to duplicate the methods and proceedings of Trotsky. They are hopelessly wrong in two respects, in my opinion. First, the Fourth International today is not what it was in 1940. It is far more of a real organization, and even if Trotsky were alive he would function in it differently than in the days when the international leadership was only a formality, more or less.

They are wrong because they don't understand that the International itself has evolved to the point where no individual can or should seek to replace the elected leadership. And secondly—and this I say far more in sorrow than in anger—the pretenders to the mantle of Trotsky haven't got the qualifications Trotsky had. Trotsky did what he did and worked as he worked as the de facto executive committee of the Fourth International from necessity, not from choice.

His aim from the very beginning, didn't he say, was to create an international organization to lead the revolution, and he knew that his great and overpowering role was a transitory one. His task was to create an organization that would replace Trotsky when the time would come and the necessity for it. His aim was everywhere to build up organizations and function through them. Consider his attitude toward the SWP. You know that it is written in all the historical accounts that the Transitional Program of the Fourth International was the work of Trotsky.

The British Workers International League, who had seceded from the International, published it in fact not as the manifesto of the International but as a document by Trotsky. [. . .] Literally, that was correct. Trotsky did in fact write the Transitional Program. But he did not introduce it to the International in the name of Trotsky. He requested the SWP National Committee to sponsor the document and it was presented at the founding conference of the Fourth International as the resolution of the Socialist Workers Party of the United States.

Why did Trotsky do that? Did he do that because his personal authority wouldn't be sufficient to get a hearing for it? No. It was because he wanted wherever he had the chance to work through a party and in the name of a party and to help build up the prestige and authority of the SWP as an organization. That is the way real leaders work all the time. That is the way Lenin worked.

I often remember the story—I think it was related by Zinoviev who once compared Lenin, the organizer and leader of organized action, with Plekhanov, who tended toward individualism. Zinoviev said at one time that Lenin and Plekhanov both had an idea they wanted to bring to the attention of the party on some subject of current interest. Plekhanov sat down, wrote out his proposition and sent it to the Central Committee. Lenin sat down, wrote his proposition, and then went around trying to collect all the signatures of all the Bolshevik workers he could get in touch with to present it as a collective document. A very striking anecdote, [revealing the] difference between a man who tries to work through organization and one who tries to go over the head of organization and substitute himself for it. [. . .]

I believe this recent world conference more than anything else should be considered as a triumphant vindication of the struggle of Trotsky to create an organization and to carry on the ideas he formulated, after his death and do it adequately. [. . .] And that is where we come into conflict with people like Logan, like Munis, like Morrow, and others who try to act in this belated day in the capacity of individuals, ignoring the organization, ignoring our own party and its elected leadership, and even now having the unparalleled audacity to try to ignore the elected leadership of the world preconference. Absolutely absurd! The pretensions of a Logan, a Munis, a Morrow.

Let me give you one illustration of Morrow's messianic complex. Last April, a year ago I believe it was, Morrow sat down with us in the Political Committee and signed the truce agreement. You recall that it stated as its first point, there are no programmatic differences between the factions. We have agreement on the main lines of the European question. The difference is rather of emphasis than fundamentals. And because of that there is no justification for factional organizations in the party or factional struggle and we must agree to work together and collaborate harmoniously on the basis of the resolution of the convention. Words to that effect.

Two months later Morrow addressed a letter to the IS full of criticisms on the one side and of programmatic and tactical propositions on the other, and we did not even learn of that till about October. Here he had a National Committee, with which he had said over his signature he was in full programmatic agreement, the differences were only ones of emphasis. But when he wanted to contribute some ideas—whether good or bad—to the IS he did not even take the trouble to notify us that he was sending this. He didn't try to come to his National Committee and at least see—as Trotsky did in 1938—if the SWP wouldn't sponsor his proposals in the International. No. The great Morrow didn't even notify us about it, and I think it was only in October, when he handed in a copy of it, that we learned that he had sent this to the IS and to the parties in Europe, as "I, Felix Morrow."

Now compare that with the way a real leadership works, to the way Gabriel [Michel Pablo], newly elected the secretary of the International, works. He is a prolific writer, I judge. But we don't get any personal directives from him. He doesn't write any personal letters criticizing the SWP or praising it or telling it what to do. When he has something to say he tries to say it in an organized manner. He takes his proposition to the IS, discusses it, and tries to get an agreement. When he gets an agreement we get a letter. And that is the kind of letter we like to receive, signed from the IS, him merely as secretary. Because we are for organized action and would not take kindly to the attempts of Gabriel or anyone else to go over the head of his own organization and give us his personal advice.

Why, these people have so lost the sense of reality that a few weeks ago, on the eve of the referendum on the French constitution, Logan, Morrow, and I think Comrade Millner, if I am not mistaken, in their personal capacities sent a cablegram to the minority of the French party—at that time the proponents of voting for the bourgeois constitution were in a minority—with these words on it: "We consider the boycott of the referendum suicidal for the party. Why not make your position known publicly?"[111]

Here are three individuals, over the head of our party, over the head of the IS, counseling the minority in the French party to openly proclaim their opposition to the party's rule. In other words, split. That is what it means, or at least the first step toward a split. That is the way we construed it and Stein and Farrell and I and others talked with Morrow about this, about the dangerous road they are traveling, the incitement of a minority to make its position known publicly regardless of the position of the majority.

Morrow said, "If I were in France I would split the party over the question of the French referendum." I am one man who isn't afraid of splits. I have shown that in the past. I greatly admire Lenin who was willing to say to his Bolshevik Central Committee, If you take a social-patriotic position we part company. I admire Lenin who said at another critical stage of the revolution, when a really revolutionary issue was at stake, if you want to split go ahead. We will go to the sailors.

These people wanted to split because the French majority at that time wouldn't vote for the constitution. Lenin would split for the sake of the revolution. Morrow and Goldman and Company would split for the constitution that would protect bourgeois property. This is an absolute betrayal of Marxism in the first place and a very poor issue for splitting in the second place.

Now in their attacks on the conference, their attempts to belittle it, to deny its authority, to ridicule, denigrate, discredit, and overthrow the leadership elected by the international conference, they are coming into head-on collision with the march of progress in our movement. They are picking a fight on a ground where they are licked before they start. We are firm and ardent partisans of the conference and the bodies created by it and we are going to declare war on anyone who opposes it. [. . .]

The preconference provided, I believe, for a thorough discussion preparatory to a full-blown world conference. Everything done and decided by the conference is now submitted to the international organization for discussion, I understand, and for free criticisms. I believe we will have some criticisms although we support the main line firmly. We don't object to any ideas the minority may bring forward. They have a perfect right to do that. We will assure them in the future as in the past the fullest and freest expression, the more the better from our point of view. But we do not accept any attempt, direct or indirect, to disrupt, discredit, or break up the international leadership. [. . .]

What is taking place, comrades, if you look facts in the face, is that long process of consolidation. That is because of the struggle for this program which has taken place in our party over a period of eighteen years, and the fruit of which is our strength and firm organization today. That process is taking place throughout the International and particularly at an accelerated pace in Europe. A genuine, homogeneous Trotskyist cadre is in process of formation, the only way it could be formed, in the struggle against revisionism in the field of theory and politics and against anarchism and irresponsibility in the field of organization.

REPORT ON THE INTERNAL PARTY SITUATION[112]

May 22, 1946

This is Cannon's report to the May 1946 NC plenum on the findings of the Control Commission investigation of the minority's collabororation with the WP, initiated at the December 4, 1945, meeting of the PC. The text is from a previously unpublished and uncorrected stenogram.

Comrades: You have before you the report of the National Control Commission which the Political Committee requested for this gathering concerning the acts of indiscipline and violations of party loyalty by the comrades of the minority. This report of the Control Commission constitutes the written charges against the comrades in question. This is the first time, to my recollection, in six years that we have had a question of indiscipline before the leading committee of the party. We have had no occasion to discuss violations of party discipline because we haven't had any. Our party has a definite tradition which permeates almost through every pore of the organization. And it is strengthened and fortified by eighteen years through which our cadres have developed. That tradition is that of a genuinely democratic organization, a free democratic organization where every worker and every member has rights which are scrupulously respected by the party leadership.

Together with that we have an eighteen-year tradition of the strictest discipline, of party loyalty and party patriotism. One had only to hear the discussion which took place here yesterday and again today when the comrades from the trade unions and the field took the floor to see how deeply and profoundly this party is inspired by the feelings of party patriotism. And people who radiate these sentiments don't require formal discipline. It is in their blood. Since the last convention, where for the first time in four years we heard new accusations about the bureaucratism of the party leadership, since that time—which is now a year and a half—this party leadership has not expelled anybody from the party, has not suspended anybody, has not even censured anybody.

We took a survey of the branches a few months ago to find out how the question of discipline stands in the local organizations and all we could uncover through the whole extent of our organization in the period since the last convention is two or three local cases of discipline, one in Detroit where a comrade in the trade unions introduced a resolution not in accord with party policy without the authorization of the party. He was called up on charges, suspended for three months, not expelled, given a chance to correct himself. At the end of three months he had reconsidered his position, returned to the party, and according to our information, has done good work since that time. We had one single expulsion from the party in the past year. That took place in the Bayonne branch, where a comrade in the trade union acted in a manner contrary to his duties to the party and its program and the branch expelled him. The National Committee had no participation in it.

In six years not only have we had no disciplinary cases before us here in the plenum, but in six years since the split with the Shachtmanites we have never taken any disciplinary action against anybody in this party. So if our National Committee has a record of bureaucratism, it has not been manifested in actions of a disciplinary nature, expulsions, suspensions, or censures.

Our conception of the functioning of the party is the Leninist conception, that not only do members have rights of free discussion in the party, but they have duties. And one duty is this: that all their political activity has to be carried on under the supervision and control of the party. Does that mean that they cannot talk to members of other parties, as has been alleged against us; that they cannot fraternize with them; that they cannot collaborate with them? Not at all. Our comrades in the trade unions are talking, fraternizing, and collaborating with people of other political tendencies every day. Work could not be carried on without it. It is not the prohibition of talking, fraternizing, collaborating that has ever been at issue in our ranks. It is that the collaboration with other political elements—either Shachtmanites, or Socialists, or progressives, or labor partyites—that the collaboration, which is absolutely indispensable for the development of our work in many instances, has to be done as a party task.

That is the Leninist conception of the centralized party. That is concretized in our party constitution. That is not the demand of the bureaucrats in the center. This is the party law. Section VIII, Article 8 of the party constitution reads as follows:

"Political collaboration with nonmembers of the party must be formally authorized by the party committee having jurisdiction."

It doesn't say political collaboration is prohibited. It says it must be authorized and consequently regulated and controlled by the party. It is on this point of the party law—which was made not by the Political Committee or the national plenum, but by the party convention, that is, by the party itself—it is the violation of this law on the part of the comrades of the minority that we are considering here today. Have these violations taken place? On that I believe there cannot be any debate because the report of the Control Commission is a documented report which contains only those facts, out of a great multitude of facts, singled out only those for which documentary proof exists and which the minority members themselves have acknowledged in the greater part.

It has been going on now for a long time, nearly a year. And just because our party is a party of patriots who are loyal and devoted to the party this has caused the greatest indignation in the party membership. It is so contrary to our tradition. It is such a violation of all of our concepts of the Leninist party facing the outside world as a unit regardless of how we may be divided in our opinions in internal discussion, that the party members rose up almost in insurrection against the comrades who had so brazenly defied our tradition and our party law.

And if we were guilty of bureaucratism during this past year it was expressed only by the resistance which the party leadership put up against this pressure of the rank and file of the party for action against the violators of discipline. And that pressure was very great and at times it even penetrated into the leadership, represented by the leading comrades in Chicago. We had to resist the continuous demands and we did it for a reason. Why did we not expel the repeated violators of discipline? First, we wanted a political solution of the dispute. We don't like to fight over secondary issues. We don't like to conduct long explanations on small points. We were profoundly convinced that at the bottom of this indiscipline of our minority there lurked political differences of a profound character which had not broken through and been articulated by them. And we wanted to wait until the political content of the fight would be disclosed so that the members then could compare one program to another and learn something from the discussion. That is why we resisted the demands for disciplinary action.

A second reason was that we had just emerged from the wartime. New sections of the Fourth International were rising. Old ones with whom we had been out of contact for four or five years were reestablishing communication with us. They did not know any of the history of our dispute and we did not want to confront them with a split in the American party on simple organizational grounds. For their sake, in order to give them a chance to follow the discussion and the dispute and to participate in it and to study the documents of it, we delayed and delayed and delayed despite all the pressure put upon us to expel them.

We didn't want to throw them out of the party in the spirit of punishment and revenge. We wanted them to think the matter over and try to restore the attitude of party loyalty which they had manifested in the past and then within our communist family conduct the political dispute.

A fourth reason was not so benevolent: When they began this series of violations of discipline we were not sure but what it might be a method of provoking a split in the party by violating discipline and then starting a hue and cry to confirm the bureaucratism of the leadership of the SWP. We read in some of the documents which are quoted in the Control Commission that this was precisely the objective of the leading comrades of the minority. The Germans testified, in the document from which we quote in the Control Commission report, that the unity business was from the very start a maneuver designed to provoke expulsion in case it would not be accepted, a maneuver aimed at the leadership.[113] Shachtman, in his epistles to someone named Al, explained: "You keep on violating discipline and expect Cannon to expel you. Suppose he doesn't expel you? Suppose you keep on provoking and then instead of expelling you, he says only a censure and turns to you and says, comrade, what is your next provocation? And then you continue the provocations until finally you are expelled and everyone will say, the wisest ones, that was cooked up. They prearranged that. . . ."[114]

But a year has passed. The violations continue. The indignation of the party mounts. There is apprehension in many sections of the party that if we tolerate this monkey business any longer the whole sentiment of discipline in the party will be injured. That comrades in the rank and file and the trade unions, seeing the leaders violate discipline with impunity, will begin claiming these rights for themselves. Party morale will be injured, broken down, and we must do something about that.

Shall we expel them now at this session? The Control Commission report provides ample ground. Neither in our party nor in the International would anybody raise the slightest objection [even] of the most summary kind. And the entire International is apprehensive that this plenum will witness the justified expulsion of the leaders of the minority. But that is not our proposal. We don't propose to expel comrades Goldman, Morrow, and those associated with them. And that is also for definite reasons.

First, the political issues which were latent in the struggle from the beginning have broken through in full flower finally at this plenum. These are important issues, in the discussions of which not only our party but the whole International will be educated. You can't learn much just from expulsions, [or] from personal fights, except that one person is good, another bad, etc. That only creates demoralization and discouragement. But from the discussion of great political questions—the French constitution, the national question in Europe, the theses of the international conference, wages and prices[115]—from the discussion of such questions the whole new generation of party members can learn great lessons. And we want that discussion. The discussion between orthodox Marxism and revisionism has to unfold not only in our party but in the International. We sincerely desire to have it conducted within the framework of our party and the Fourth International.

A second reason is that we sincerely desire to give the comrades who have offended the party so grossly one more opportunity. Give them an opportunity to weigh the matter to the end, consider deeply, and return to the path of party loyalty. On that condition all punishments will be taken off; they will be given and granted all their rights; and we can proceed with the discussion. That is another reason that we don't propose today to expel them from the party. But we do propose a step toward the liquidation of the intolerable and scandalous situation where the discipline of the party of Leninism is no longer respected. And from that point of view the party Secretariat is proposing a resolution which I will read to you and submit for your consideration. It is called "A Statement of the National Committee of the Socialist Workers Party."

> The plenum of the National Committee of the SWP, at its meeting on May 22, 1946, established the following facts:
>
> 1. Comrades Goldman and Morrow and other party members associated with them in the faction have over a long period of time deliberately and systematically violated Section VIII, Article 8 of the party constitution, which reads as follows: "Political collaboration with nonmembers of the party must be formally authorized by the party committee having jurisdiction."
>
> 2. The Goldman-Morrow faction conducted its activities in direct collusion with the leadership of the Workers Party. The purpose of these activities was to disrupt the Socialist Workers Party and split away a section of the membership under guise of a demand for "unification" of the two parties.
>
> 3. The plan of operations was to provoke expulsion through a series of flagrant violations of discipline. In pursuance of this plan, Comrades Goldman, Morrow, and other party members associated with them in the faction, committed a long series of acts of indiscipline and disloyalty despite repeated warnings and appeals that they cease and desist.
>
> In order to restore party discipline and protect the party from disruption, while giving Comrades Goldman and Morrow one more opportunity to change their course and return to a party-loyal attitude, the National Committee resolves as follows:
>
> 1. To censure Comrades Goldman and Morrow and warn them that any further violations of the party rules will be met by further disciplinary action.
>
> 2. To instruct the Political Committee and the local and branch executive committees to take careful note of this resolution and see to it that it is promptly and rigorously enforced in case of any more violations of party discipline on the part of the above-named party members.
>
> 3. To publish this resolution.

Thus we present the question to the minority and it is up to them to say what they want to do.[116]

OUR ANSWER TO THE SKEPTICS AND DEFEATISTS

August 14, 1946

This letter, slightly abridged, on Cannon's work on the "American Theses" resolution for the November 1946 SWP convention was to Rose Karsner, who was on a visit to California.

Dear Rosie:

We have already started working on our convention thesis. Usick and I have already outlined the first eleven points and decided on their order. This in reality is the most important part of the work, as it reduces the general ideas which we discussed rather discursively to a systematic order. Usick has to do a little research work on the economic side of the question, but that will not take much time. I expect that we will have the first complete draft of the document as a whole ready within a week.

We have decided to cast the whole document in the form of numbered theses in the literal sense of the word. That is, the various propositions and contentions will simply be asserted without any amplifying data or argument. The reason for this form is to make the propositions themselves stand out clearly and even starkly without the encumbrance of lengthy amplification and argument. The exposition of the theses, the supporting data, and argumentation will be supplied first in the report to the convention and then later in even broader form by means of articles and speeches elucidating and supporting the different points in the main document.

Everyone that I have talked to here seems to agree that it is timely right now for the party to adopt such a document. It is just the appropriate moment to give a categorical and definitive answer to all skeptical and defeatist moods which arise from an absolutely unwarranted confidence in the strength of American imperialism, overlooking its frightful weaknesses and contradictions, and forgetting about the far greater power and potentialities of the great American working class.

Several comrades here have also expressed the opinion that the timely adoption of such a set of theses by the American party will have a most salutary influence throughout the Fourth International, balancing off their justified fears of the counterrevolutionary role of the American imperialist power with new hopes in the powerful reinforcement which will come to the oppressed workers and peoples everywhere from the development of a strong revolutionary movement in the U.S. [. . .]

Love,
Jim

Defendants (left to right) Albert Goldman, Oscar Coover, Sr., V. R. Dunne, and Harry DeBoer in Minneapolis SWP headquarters before going to prison (1943). Rose Smith at the piano.

THE HISTORY OF THE CHICAGO BRANCH

August 29, 1946

This was a letter to Hildegarde MacLeod in the Chicago branch of the SWP. The text, previously unpublished, is from a copy in Cannon's files.

Dear Hildegarde:

I received your letter of August 22 and was very glad to hear from you.

You can be sure that your point of view will be given the most serious consideration. I think about Chicago much more than you think I do; in fact, I have been worrying about this problem for eighteen years, ever since the first days of the Left Opposition. The "Chicago problem" has a history, and if one studies it from its origin through all the phases of its evolution up to the present period, following the departure of the Goldmanites—a distinctly new stage in the evolution of the Chicago organization—he can form a better judgment than if he proceeds by isolating the past year or so from all that went before. This method of approaching the problem—as all other problems—induces patience in dealing with the contemporary difficulty.

The Chicago branch from its inception in 1928 was composed predominantly of petty-bourgeois dilettantes, and this initial composition reproduced itself as the organization grew. That is the fundamental reason why Chicago was always a sort of plague spot in the party and the most solid and consistent base of support for the Abern clique.[117] The great faction fight of 1939-40, which culminated in the split, marked the beginning of a change in Chicago—but only a beginning. The struggle in Chicago did not follow the national pattern.

On a national scale the faction fight represented a pretty clear lineup of worker-Bolsheviks versus petty-bourgeois elements, and they fought consciously not only over the "political question" but also over the so-called "organization question"—the real touchstone of the struggle. The split took place along these lines. That is why "proletarianization" was not much of a problem for us after the split; it was 75 percent solved by the split itself. The decimated party was in its large majority proletarian in composition. These worker elements, in the course of their activities, also tended to reproduce themselves, and this further assured and reinforced the proletarian composition of the party as a whole.

This was not the case in Chicago. The two factions there fought each other furiously over the "Russian question" but they were both petty bourgeois in composition and mentality and the issues of proletarianization and the Bolshevik method of party organization were not fought out there at all. As a result, even after the split we still had a predominantly petty-bourgeois branch in Chicago, weighed down with a heritage of its past and sick with Menshevism on the organization question. If for the party on a national scale the split of 1940 was a sweeping "revolution" which cleared the road for the expansion and development of the party as a proletarian revolutionary organization, then Chicago required a supplementary "revolution" before the same process could take place there.

The uncompromising Bolshevik fight against the Menshevik clique of Goldman, Beidel, and Company—started in 1944 by a small minority, which eventually culminated in the isolation of the Goldmanites and their withdrawal from the party in 1946—was precisely this supplementary revolution. The final withdrawal of the defeated and isolated Goldmanites marked the completion of the fundamental struggle which began in 1939. Things and people at last fell into their right places. Not only did Goldman, Beidel, and Company join the Shachtmanite party, but the Chicago branch, for the first time, really joined the Socialist Workers Party.

That is the political essence of the Chicago situation as I see it. Of course one can't hope for perfection, for freedom from all defects, incidental difficulties, hangovers, etc. But it is important always to see the big things—the main line of development—and relate the little things, the hangovers, etc., to them in proper proportion. This, in my opinion, is the only way to approach any new difficulties which exist or may arise in Chicago, as in any other branch.

In the course of the long struggle the Chicago branch has been regenerated. One might better say re-created on new foundations. In my opinion there is not the slightest chance for a petty-bourgeois tendency to endanger the forward development of the Chicago organization. The sweep of the proletarian Bolshevik tendency on a national scale, now joined and reinforced at last by the Chicago organization, is so powerful that any new petty-bourgeois manifestation which might arise in any section of the party would be smashed like an eggshell.

The annihilating defeat of the Goldman-Morrow faction and the crushing answer which the party convention is sure to give to the Shachtmanite "unity" maneuver are assurance of this. If difficulties of the old kind arise in one branch or another, at least in the proximate future, we can be confident that they will be merely incidental or personal manifestations. It will be the part of political wisdom to treat them as just that—incidental and personal questions. That is our approach to local difficulties and frictions which may arise on a local scale among comrades who have fought on the same side with us in this great battle for the proletarian party. We value everybody who helped in the fight and reject nobody.

Most of all we honor and appreciate the small minority who initiated the heroic struggle in Chicago in 1944. It is monstrous to think for a moment that any one of them should fail to find a place in the central cadre of the new Chicago organization which we are confident is facing a great future. At the same time we insist—in Chicago as everywhere—that the leadership, which is united on the fundamental political line, must be broad and inclusive and hospitable to the comradely incorporation of comrades who may have had conflicts in the past and of new people of talent and energy who have lately joined us or who will join us in the future. This last point is most important of all. We want a party, not a faction; a genuine workers' movement, not a narrow circle.

I hope you will think as seriously over the points contained in this letter as I have considered yours, and I will be very glad to hear from you again.

With kind regards,
J. P. Cannon

THESES ON THE AMERICAN REVOLUTION

October 1946

This resolution, which constituted the SWP's basic programmatic document of the postwar period, was completed by Cannon at the beginning of October, 1946. It was adopted by the Twelfth National Convention of the SWP in November 1946. The text is from the pamphlet The Coming American Revolution *(New York: Pioneer Publishers, April 1947).*

I

The United States, the most powerful capitalist country in history, is a component part of the world capitalist system and is subject to the same general laws. It suffers from the same incurable diseases and is destined to share the same fate. The overwhelming preponderance of American imperialism does not exempt it from the decay of world capitalism, but on the contrary acts to involve it ever more deeply, inextricably, and hopelessly. U.S. capitalism can no more escape from the revolutionary consequences of world capitalist decay than the older European capitalist powers. The blind alley in which world capitalism has arrived, and the U.S. with it, excludes a new organic era of capitalist stabilization. The dominant world position of American imperialism now accentuates and aggravates the death agony of capitalism as a whole.

II

American imperialism emerged victorious from the Second World War, not merely over its German and Japanese rivals, but also over its "democratic" allies, especially Great Britain. Today Wall Street unquestionably is the dominant world imperialist center. Precisely because it has issued from the war vastly strengthened in relation to all its capitalist rivals, U.S. imperialism seems indomitable. So overpowering in all fields—diplomatic, military, commercial, financial, and industrial—is Wall Street's preponderance that consolidation of its world hegemony seems to be within easy reach. Wall Street hopes to inaugurate the so-called American Century.

In reality, the American ruling class faces more insurmountable obstacles in "organizing the world" than confronted the German bourgeoisie in its repeated and abortive attempts to attain a much more modest goal, namely: "organizing Europe."

The meteoric rise of U.S. imperialism to world supremacy comes too late. Moreover, American imperialism rests increasingly on the foundations of world economy, in sharp contrast to the situation prevailing before the First World War, when it rested primarily on the internal market—the source of its previous successes and equilibrium. But the world foundation is today shot through with insoluble contradictions; it suffers from chronic dislocations and is mined with revolutionary powder kegs.

American capitalism, hitherto only partially involved in the death agony of capitalism as a world system, is henceforth subject to the full and direct impact of all the forces and contradictions that have debilitated the old capitalist countries of Europe.

The economic prerequisites for the socialist revolution are fully matured in the U.S. The political premises are likewise far more advanced than might appear on the surface.

III

The U.S. emerged from the Second World War, just as it did in 1918, as the strongest part of the capitalist world. But here ends the resemblance in the impact and consequences of the two wars upon the country's economic life. For in other major aspects the situation has in the meantime drastically altered.

In 1914-18 continental Europe was the main theater of war; the rest of the world, especially the colonial countries, was left virtually untouched by the hostilities. Thus, not only sections of continental Europe and England but the main framework of the world market itself remained intact. With all its European competitors embroiled in the war, the way was left clear for American capitalism to capture markets.

More than this, during the First World War capitalist Europe itself became a vast market for American industry and agriculture. The American bourgeoisie drained Europe of her accumulated wealth of centuries and supplanted their Old World rivals in the world market. This enabled the ruling class to convert the U.S. from a debtor into the world's banker and creditor, and simultaneously to expand both the heavy (capital goods) and the light (consumer goods) industries. Subsequently this wartime expansion permitted the fullest possible development of this country's domestic market. Finally, not merely did the American bourgeoisie make vast profits from the war but the country as a whole emerged much richer. The relatively cheap price of imperialist participation in World War I (only a few-score billion dollars) was covered many times over by the accruing economic gains.

Profoundly different in its effects is the Second World War. This time only the Western Hemisphere has been left untouched militarily. The Far East, the main prize of the war, has been subjected to a devastation second only to that suffered by Germany and Eastern Europe. Continental Europe as well as England have been bankrupted by the war. The world market has been completely disrupted. This culminated the process of shrinking, splintering, and undermining that went on in the interval between the two wars (the withdrawal of one-sixth of the world—the USSR—from the capitalist orbit, the debasement of currency systems, the barter methods of Hitlerite Germany, Japan's inroads on Asiatic and Latin American markets, England's Empire Preference System,[118] etc., etc.).

Europe, which defaulted on all its prior war and postwar debts to the U.S., this time served not as an inexhaustible and highly profitable market, but as a gigantic drain upon the wealth and resources of this country in the shape of lend-lease,[119] overall conversion of American economy for wartime production, huge mobilization of manpower, large-scale casualties, and so on.

With regard to the internal market, the latter, instead of expanding organically as in 1914-18, experienced in the course of the Second World War only an artificial revival based on war expenditures.

While the bourgeoisie has been fabulously enriched, the country as a whole has become poorer; the astronomic costs of the war will never be recouped.

In sum, the major factors that once served to foster and fortify American capitalism either no longer exist or are turning into their opposites.

IV

The prosperity that followed the First World War, which was hailed as a new capitalist era refuting all Marxist prognostications, ended in an economic catastrophe. But even this short-lived prosperity of the twenties was based on a combination of circumstances which cannot and will not recur again. In addition to the factors already listed, it is necessary to stress: (1) that American capitalism had a virgin continent to exploit; (2) that up to a point it had been able to maintain a certain balance between industry and agriculture; and (3) that the main base of capitalist expansion had been its internal market. So long as these three conditions existed—although they were already being undermined—it was possible for U.S. capitalism to maintain a relative stability.

The boom in the twenties nourished the myth of the permanent stability of American capitalism, giving rise to pompous and hollow theories of a "new capitalism," "American exceptionalism," the "American dream," and so forth and so on. The illusions about the possibilities and future of American capitalism were spread by the reformists and all other apologists for the ruling class not only at home but abroad. "Americanism" was the gospel of all the misleaders of the European and American working class.

What actually happened in the course of the fabulous prosperity of the twenties was that under these most favorable conditions, all the premises for an unparalleled economic catastrophe were prepared. Out of it came a chronic crisis of American agriculture. Out of it came a monstrous concentration of wealth in fewer and fewer hands. Correspondingly, the rest of the population became relatively poorer. Thus, while in the decade of 1920-30, industrial productivity increased by 50 percent, wages rose only 30 percent. The workers were able to buy—in prosperity—proportionately less than before.

The relative impoverishment of the American people is likewise mirrored in national wealth statistics. By 1928 the workers' share of the national wealth had dropped to 4.7 percent, while the farmers retained only 15.4 percent. At the same time, the bourgeoisie's share of the national wealth had risen to 79.9

percent, with most of it falling into the hands of the Sixty Families and their retainers.[120]

The distribution of national income likewise expressed this monstrous disproportion. In 1929, at the peak of prosperity, *36,000 families had the same income as 11 million "lower-bracket" families.*

This concentration of wealth was a cardinal factor in limiting the absorbing capacity of the internal market. Compensating external outlets for agriculture and industry could not be found in a constricting world market.

Moreover, the need to export raw materials and agricultural products tended to further unbalance American foreign trade. This inescapably led to a further dislocation of the world market, whose participants were debtor countries, themselves in need of selling more than they bought in order to cover payments on their debts, largely owed to the U.S.

While appearing and functioning in the role of stabilizers of capitalism, the American imperialists were thus its greatest disrupters both at home and abroad. The U.S. turned out to be the main source of world instability, the prime aggravator of imperialist contradictions.

In the interim between the two wars this manifested itself most graphically in the fact that all economic convulsions began in the Republic of the Dollar, the home of "rugged individualism." This was the case with the first postwar crisis of 1920-21; this was repeated eight years later when the disproportion between agriculture and industry reached the breaking point and when the internal market had become saturated owing to the impoverishment of the people at one pole and the aggrandizement of the monopolists at the other. The Great American Boom exploded in a crisis which shattered the economic foundations of all capitalist countries.

V

The economic crisis of 1929 was not a cyclical crisis such as periodically accompanied organic capitalist development in the past, leading to new and higher productive levels. It was a major historical crisis of capitalism in decay, which could not be overcome through the "normal" channels; that is to say, through the blind interplay of the laws governing the market.

Production virtually came to a standstill. National income was cut into less than half, plummeting from $81 billion in 1929 to $40 billion in 1932. Industry and agriculture sagged. The army of unemployed swelled tenfold "normal," reaching the dizzy figure of 20 million. According to official estimates, based on 1929 averages, the losses in the years 1930-38 amounted to 43 million man-years of labor, and $133 billion of national income.

By 1939 the national debt soared to $40 billion, or $14 billion more than the highest point at the end of the First World War. The number of unemployed kept hovering at 10 million. Industry and agriculture stagnated. The foreign trade of the U.S. in a reduced world market fell to less than half of its "normal" peacetime share.

What all these figures really express is the fearsome degradation of living standards of the workers and the middle class, and the outright pauperization of the "underprivileged one-third" of the population. The wafer-thin layer of monopolists, naturally, did not suffer at all, but on the contrary utilized the crisis in order to gobble up even a larger share of the country's wealth and resources.

The bourgeoisie saw no way out of the crisis. They had no way out. They and their regime remained the main obstacle in the way not only of domestic but of world recovery. In its downward plunge, the American bourgeoisie dragged the rest of the capitalist world with it, and kept it down.

Decisive is the fact that despite all the "pump-priming," "brain trusting," and emergency "reforms," American capitalism was incapable of solving the crisis. The partial upswing of 1934-37 proved to be temporary and passing in character. The precipitous drop that occurred in 1937 revealed the abyss facing American capitalism. The threatening new downward plunge was cut off only by the huge expenditures made in preparation for the Second World War.

Only the war temporarily resolved the economic crisis which had lasted in both hemispheres for ten years. The grim reality, however, is that this "solution" has solved exactly nothing. Least of all did it remove or even mitigate a single one of the basic causes for the crisis of 1929.

VI

The basis of the current American postwar prosperity is the artificial expansion of industry and agriculture through unprecedented government spending which is swelling constantly the enormous national debt. In its fictitious character the war and postwar boom of the early forties far exceeds the orgy engaged in by European capitalism during 1914-18 and the immediate postwar years. The diversion of production into war industry on an unheard-of scale resulted in temporary shortages of consumer goods. The home and foreign markets seemed to acquire a new absorbing capacity. Universal scarcities and war havoc are acting as temporary spurs to production, especially in the consumers' goods field.

Overall there is, however, the universal impoverishment, the disrupted economic, fiscal, and government systems—coupled with the chronic diseases and contradictions of capitalism, not softened but aggravated by the war.

If we multiply the condition in which European capitalism, with England at its head, emerged from the First World War by ten times and in some instances a hundred times—because of the vaster scale of the consequences of World War II—then we will arrive at an approximation of the actual state of American capitalism.

Every single factor underlying the current "peacetime" prosperity is ephemeral. This country has emerged not richer from the Second World War as was the case in the twenties, but poorer—in a far more impoverished world. The disproportion between agriculture and industry has likewise increased tremendously, despite the hothouse expansion of agriculture. The concentration of wealth and the polarization of the American population into rich and poor has continued at a forced pace.

The basic conditions that precipitated the 1929 crisis when American capitalism enjoyed its fullest health not only persist but have grown more malignant. Once the internal market is again saturated, no adequate outlet can be hoped for in the unbalanced world market. The enormously augmented productive capacity of the U.S. collides against the limits of the world market and its shrinking capacity. Ruined Europe herself needs to export. So does the ruined Orient, whose equilibrium has been ruptured by the shattering of Japan, its most advanced sector.

Europe is in dire need of billions in loans. In addition to lend-lease, Wall Street has already pumped almost $5 billion in loans into England; almost $2 billion into France; and smaller sums into the other satellite countries of Western Europe—without however achieving any semblance of stabilization there. Bankrupt capitalist Europe remains both a competitor on the world market and a bottomless drain. The Orient, too, needs loans, especially China, which, while in the throes of civil war, has already swallowed up as many American dollars as did Germany in the early twenties.

At home, the explosive materials are accumulating at a truly American tempo. Carrying charges on the huge national debt; the astronomic military "peacetime" budget ($18.5 billion for this year); the inflation, the "overhead expenditures" of Wall Street's program of world domination, etc., etc.—all this can come from one source and one only: national income. In plain words, from the purchasing power of the masses. Degradation of workers' living conditions and the pauperization of the farmers and the urban middle class—that is the meaning of Wall Street's program.

VII

The following conclusion flows from the objective situation: U.S. imperialism which proved incapable of recovering from its crisis and stabilizing itself in the ten-year period preceding the outbreak of the Second World War is heading for an even more catastrophic explosion in the current postwar era. The cardinal factor which will light the fuse is this: The home market, after an initial and artificial revival, must contract. It cannot expand as it did in the twenties. What is really in store is not unbounded prosperity but a short-lived boom. In the wake of the boom must come another crisis and depression which will make the 1929-32 conditions look prosperous by comparison.

VIII

The impending economic paroxyms must, under the existing conditions, pass inexorably into the social and political crisis of American capitalism, posing in its course point-blank the question of who shall be the master in the land. In their mad drive to conquer and enslave the entire world, the American monopolists are today preparing war against the Soviet Union. This war program, which may be brought to a head by a crisis or the fear of a crisis at home, will meet with incalculable obstacles and difficulties. A war will not solve the internal difficulties of American imperialism but will rather sharpen and complicate them. Such a war will meet with fierce resistance not only by the peoples of the USSR, but also by the European and colonial masses who do not want to be the slaves of Wall Street. At home the fiercest resistance will be generated. Wall Street's war drive, aggravating the social crisis, may under certain conditions actually precipitate it. In any case, another war will not cancel out the socialist alternative to capitalism but only pose it more sharply.

The workers' struggle for power in the U.S. is not a perspective of a distant and hazy future but the realistic program of our epoch.

IX

The revolutionary movement of the American workers is an organic part of the world revolutionary process. The revolutionary upheavals of the European proletariat which lie ahead will complement, reinforce, and accelerate the revolutionary developments in the U.S. The liberationist struggles of the colonial peoples against imperialism which are unfolding before our eyes will exert a similar influence. Conversely, each blow dealt by the American proletariat to the imperialists at home will stimulate, supplement, and intensify the revolutionary struggles in Europe and the colonies. Every reversal suffered by imperialism anywhere will in turn produce ever-greater repercussions in this country, generating such speed and power as will tend to reduce all time intervals both at home and abroad.

X

The role of America in the world is decisive. Should the European and colonial revolutions, now on the order of the day, precede in point of time the culmination of the struggle in the U.S., they would immediately be confronted with the necessity of defending their conquests against the economic and military assaults of the American imperialist monster. The ability of the victorious insurgent peoples everywhere to maintain themselves would depend to a high degree on the strength and fighting capacity of the revolutionary labor movement in America. The American workers would then be obliged to come to their aid, just as the Western European working class came to the aid of the Russian revolution and saved it by blocking full-scale imperialist military assaults upon the young workers' republic.

But even should the revolution in Europe and other parts of the world be once again retarded, it will by no means signify a prolonged stabilization of the world capitalist sytem. The issue of socialism or capitalism will not be finally decided until it is decided in the U.S. Another retardation of the proletarian revolution in one country or another, or even one continent or another, will not save American imperialism from its proletarian nemesis at home. The decisive battles for the communist future of mankind will be fought in the U.S.

The revolutionary victory of the workers in the U.S. will seal the doom of the senile bourgeois regimes in every part of our planet, and of the Stalinist bureaucracy, if it still exists at the time. The Russian revolution raised the workers and colonial peoples to their feet. The American revolution with its hundredfold greater power will set in motion revolutionary forces that will change the face of our planet. The whole Western Hemisphere will quickly be consolidated into the Socialist United States of North, Central, and South America. This invincible power, merging with the revolutionary movements in all parts of the world, will put an end to the outlived capitalist system as a whole, and begin the grandiose task of world reconstruction under the banner of the Socialist United States of the World.

XI

Whereas the main problem of the workers in the Russian revolution was to maintain their power once they had gained it, the problem in the United States is almost exclusively the problem of the conquest of power by the workers. The conquest of power in the United States will be more difficult than it was in backward Russia, but precisely for that reason it will be much easier to consolidate and secure.

The dangers of internal counterrevolution, foreign intervention, imperialist blockade, and bureaucratic degeneration of a privileged labor caste—in Russia all of these dangers stemmed from the numerical weakness of the proletariat, the agelong poverty and backwardness inherited from tsarism, and the isolation of the Russian revolution. These dangers were in the final analysis unavoidable there.

These dangers scarcely exist in the U.S. Thanks to the overwhelming numerical superiority and social weight of the proletariat, its high cultural level and potential; thanks to the country's vast resources, its productive capacity, and preponderant strength on the world arena, the victorious proletarian revolution in the U.S., once it has consolidated its power, will be almost automatically secured against capitalist restoration either by internal counterrevolution or by foreign intervention and imperialist blockade.

As for the danger of bureaucratic degeneration after the revolutionary victory—this can only arise from privileges which are in turn based on backwardness, poverty, and universal scarcities. Such a danger could have no material foundation within the U.S. Here the triumphant workers' and farmers' government would from the very beginning be able to organize socialist production on far higher levels than under capitalism, and virtually overnight assure such a high standard of living for the masses as would strip privileges in the material sense of any serious meaning whatever. Mawkish speculations concerning the danger of bureaucratic degeneration after the victorious revolution serve no purpose except to introduce skepticism and pessimism into the ranks of the workers' vanguard, and paralyze their will to struggle, while providing fainthearts and snivelers with a convenient pretext for running away from the struggle. The problem in the U.S. is almost exclusively the problem of the workers' conquest of political power.

XII

In the coming struggle for power the main advantages will be on the side of the workers; with adequate mobilization of their forces and proper direction, the workers will win. If one wishes to deal with stern realities and not with superficial appearances, that is the only way to pose the question. The American capitalist class is strong but the working class is stronger.

The numerical strength and social weight of the American working class, greatly increased by the war, is overwhelming in the country's life. Nothing can stand up against it. The productivity of American labor, likewise greatly increased in wartime, is the highest in the world. This means skill, and skill means power.

The American workers are accustomed to the highest living and working standards. The widely held view that high wages are a conservatizing factor tending to make workers immune to revolutionary ideas and actions is one-sided and false. This holds true only under conditions of capitalist stability where the relatively high standard of living can be maintained and even improved. This is excluded for the future, as our whole analysis has shown. On the other hand, the workers react most sensitively and violently to any infringement upon their living standards. This has already been demonstrated by the strike waves in which great masses of "conservative" workers have resorted to the most militant and radical course of action. In the given situation, therefore, the relatively high living standard of the American workers is a revolutionary and not, as is commonly believed, a conservatizing factor.

The revolutionary potential of the class is further strengthened by their traditional militancy coupled with the ability to react almost spontaneously in defense of their vital interests, and their singular resourcefulness and ingenuity (the sit-down strikes!).

Another highly important factor in raising the revolutionary potential of the American working class is its greatly increased cohesiveness and homogeneity—a transformation accomplished in the last quarter of a century. Previously, large and decisive sections of the proletariat in the basic industries were recruited by immigration. These foreign-born workers were handicapped and divided by language barriers, treated as social pariahs, and deprived of citizenship and the most elementary civil rights. All these circumstances appeared to be insuperable barriers in the way of their organization and functioning as a united labor force. In the intervening years, however, these foreign-born workers have been assimilated and "Americanized." They and their sons today constitute a powerful, militant, and articulate detachment of the organized labor movement.

An equally significant and profound development is represented by the transformation that has taken place in the position occupied by the Negroes. Formerly barred and deprived of the rights and benefits of organization by the dominant reactionary craft unions and, on the other hand, regarded and sometimes utilized by the employers as a reserve for strike-breaking purposes, masses of Negroes have since the twenties penetrated into the basic industries and into the unions. Not less than two million Negroes are members of the CIO, AFL, and independent unions. They have demonstrated in the great strike struggles that they stand in the front lines of progressiveness and militancy.

The American workers have the advantage of being comparatively free, especially among the younger and most militant layers, from reformist prejudices. The class as a whole has not been infected with the debilitating poison of reformism, either of the classic "Socialist" variety or the latter-day Stalinist brand. As a consequence, once they proceed to action, they more readily accept the most radical solutions. No important section of the class, let alone the class as a whole, has been demoralized by defeats. Finally, this young and mighty power is being drawn into the decisive phases of the class struggle at a tempo that creates unparalleled premises for mass radicalization.

XIII

Much has been said about the "backwardness" of the American working class as a justification for a pessimistic outlook, the postponement of the socialist revolution to a remote future, and withdrawal from the struggle. This is a very superficial view of the American workers and their prospects.

It is true that this class, in many respects the most advanced and progressive in the world, has not yet taken the road of independent political action on a mass scale. But this weakness can be swiftly overcome. Under the compulsion of objective necessity not only backward peoples but backward classes in advanced countries find themselves driven to clear great distances in single leaps. As a matter of fact, the American working class has already made one such leap which has advanced it far ahead of its old positions.

The workers entered the 1929 crisis as an unorganized, atomized mass imbued with illusions concerning "rugged individualism," "private initiative," "free enterprise," "the American Way," etc., etc. Less than 10 percent of the class as a whole was organized on the trade union field (fewer than 3 million out of 33 million in 1929). Moreover, this thin layer embraced primarily the highly skilled and privileged workers, organized in antiquated craft unions. The main and most decisive section of the workers knew unionism only as "company unionism," remaining without the benefit, the experience, and even the understanding of the most elementary form of workers' organization—the trade union. They were regarded and treated as mere raw material for capitalist exploitation, without rights or protection or any security of employment.

As a consequence, the 1929 crisis found the working class helpless and impotent. For three years the masses remained stunned and disoriented by the disaster. Their resistance was extremely limited and sporadic. But their anger and resentment accumulated. The next five years (1933-37), coincident with a partial revival of industry, witnessed a series of gigantic clashes, street fights, and sit-down strikes—an embryonic civil war—the end result of which was a leap, a giant leap, for millions of workers from nonexistence as an organized force to trade union consciousness and organization. Once fairly started, the movement for unionism snowballed, embracing today almost 15 million in all the basic industries.

In one leap—in a brief decade—the American workers attained trade union consciousness on a higher plane and with mightier organizations than in any other advanced country. In the study and analysis of this great transformation, rather than in vapid ruminations over the "backwardness" of the American workers, one can find the key to prospective future developments. Under the impact of great events and pressing necessities the American workers will advance beyond the limits of trade unionism and acquire political class consciousness and organization in a similar sweeping movement.

XIV

The decisive instrument of the proletarian revolution is the party of the class conscious vanguard. Failing the leadership of such a party, the most favorable revolutionary situations, which arise from the objective circumstances, cannot be carried through to the final victory of the proletariat and the beginnings of planned reorganization of society on socialist foundations. This was demonstrated most conclusively—and positively—in the 1917 Russian revolution. This same principled lesson derives no less irrefutably—even though negatively—from the entire world experience of the epoch of wars, revolutions, and colonial uprisings that began with the outbreak of the First World War in 1914.

However, this basic conclusion from the vast and tragic experience of the last century can be and has been given a reactionary interpretation by a school of neorevisionism, represented by the ideologues, philosophers, and preachers of prostration, capitulation, and defeat. They say in effect: "Since the revolutionary party is small and weak it is idle to speak of revolutionary possibilities. The weakness of the party changes everything." The authors of this "theory" reject and repudiate

Marxism, embracing in its place the subjective school of sociology. They isolate the factor of the revolutionary party's relative numerical weakness at a particular moment from the totality of objective economic and political developments which creates all the necessary and sufficient conditions for the swift growth of the revolutionary vanguard party.

Given an objectively revolutionary situation, a proletarian party—even a small one—equipped with a precisely worked out Marxist program and firm cadres can expand its forces and come to the head of the revolutionary mass movement in a comparatively brief span of time. This too was proved conclusively—and positively—by the experience of the Russian revolution in 1917. There the Bolshevik party, headed by Lenin and Trotsky, bounded forward from a tiny minority, just emerging from underground and isolation in February, to the conquest of power in October—a period of nine months.

Numerical weakness, to be sure, is not a virtue for a revolutionary party but a weakness to be overcome by persistent work and resolute struggle. In the U.S. all the conditions are in the process of unfolding for the rapid transformation of the organized vanguard from a propaganda group to a mass party strong enough to lead the revolutionary struggle for power.

XV

The hopeless contradictions of American capitalism, inextricably tied up with the death agony of world capitalism, are bound to lead to a social crisis of such catastrophic proportions as will place the proletarian revolution on the order of the day. In this crisis, it is realistic to expect that the American workers, who attained trade union consciousness and organization within a single decade, will pass through another great transformation in their mentality, attaining political consciousness and organization. If in the course of this dynamic development a mass labor party based on the trade unions is formed, it will not represent a detour into reformist stagnation and futility, as happened in England and elsewhere in the period of capitalist ascent. From all indications, it will rather represent a preliminary stage in the political radicalization of the American workers, preparing them for the direct leadership of the revolutionary party.

The revolutionary vanguard party, destined to lead this tumultuous revolutionary movement in the U.S., does not have to be created. It already exists, and its name is the **Socialist Workers Party**. It is the sole legitimate heir and continuator of pioneer American communism and the revolutionary movements of the American workers from which it sprang. Its nucleus has already taken shape in three decades of unremitting work and struggle against the stream. Its program has been hammered out in ideological battles and successfully defended against every kind of revisionist assault upon it. The fundamental core of a professional leadership has been assembled and trained in the irreconcilable spirit of the combat party of the revolution.

The task of **Socialist Workers Party** consists simply in this: to remain true to its program and banner; to render it more precise with each new development and apply it correctly in the class struggle; and to expand and grow with the growth of the revolutionary mass movement, always aspiring to lead it to victory in the struggle for political power.

REPORT ON "THE AMERICAN THESES" TO THE POLITICAL COMMITTEE

October 4, 1946

This is Cannon's report on the "Theses on the American Revolution" to the PC, prior to its publication in the party's internal bulletin for the preconvention discussion by the membership. This speech was first published in the October 1974 issue of the International Socialist Review.

These theses are the result of thoughts and informal discussions which have been taking place for a long time in our ranks. What is new about the theses is that for the first time we are sort of summing up and generalizing the ideas and perspectives which have governed our work for a long time—from the beginning as a matter of fact. As far as I know, all of our people both in the center and throughout the country have expressed agreement with them, which shows that the ideas are not new amongst us. What is new, I repeat, is that for the first time in generalized form an attempt is made to grapple with the perspectives of the revolution in the United States in a concrete manner.

Why is it necessary at this moment to bring this perspective forward? Well, first of all there is nothing artificial about it. All of our thoughts have been flowing together this way. The very fact that the theses met with universal approval in the leadership is an illustration of that. But there is an additional reason why it is especially timely right now. The attempt to build a revolutionary party in the United States, and to draw into it a mass of workers outside that very thin stratum of politically educated communists and socialists, requires an affirmation of a perspective. The workers who are called to join the party have got to be told in rather precise terms what this party is expected to accomplish.

Not what it is fighting for as an ultimate and remote goal, but what is in store for them, what they can expect to achieve by their struggle. I think this is the only way you can build a revolutionary party on a broad basis—if you have a very clear view of your perspective and frankly state it.

Without having the theses, we have spoken more or less along these lines, and I have noticed—and perhaps you have—that the new workers who have been recruited into the party in the last couple of years take the revolutionary perspective very seriously. They understand what they are joining—a party that is going to make a revolution. There is much more revolutionary optimism among the new workers than there is in a lot of people who imagine themselves to be super theoreticians, who haven't got any real faith in revolutionary possibilities in the United States. It is necessary now for our movement to state this precisely, and I believe it is necessary also for the sections of the Fourth International throughout the world. I believe that nothing can do more to lift them up and inspire them with new hopes; nothing can do as much as a declaration from the American party of its confidence in revolutionary prospects in the United States.

The theses represent a new stage, in my opinion, in the development of the concept of internationalism in America. If you go back through the history of the American movement, you can see that this concept of internationalism has gone through a process of evolution. Prior to the First World War the concept was rather nebulous, as were nearly all of the socialist ideas. The concept of internationalism as international solidarity, etc., was pretty strongly developed. What it meant in terms of revolution, what it meant in terms of the order in which the revolution would develop on a world scale, was never approached precisely.

The beginning of the Russian revolution brought a new stage. It seemed as though the victory of the Russian revolution in 1917 and subsequent years came at a time of the greatest reaction and the strongest upsurge of conservatism and prosperity in the United States. It was a pretty hardy Bolshevik who was able to see the prospects of revolution in the United States in the early years of the Russian revolution. Our internationalism in those days could be expressed primarily as solidarity with the Russian revolution—to support the Russian revolution, defend the Russian revolution. For example, one of the three main agitational slogans of the Communist Party in the early twenties was *recognition* of the Soviet Union by the United States.

By way of digression—to give you an idea of how far we have developed since that time—the three agitational slogans of the Communist Party in the early twenties were: Recognize the Soviet Union; Amalgamate the Craft Unions (and Organize the Unorganized, which was connected with that); and Build a Labor Party. Very elementary and very primitive.

So reactionary and conservative was the trade union movement in those days that we didn't dare to hope for the organization of the unorganized as a revolutionary breaking up of the monopoly of the craft unions, but saw it only as the process of amalgamating them.

In 1928, as you know, we split with the Stalinists fundamentally over the question of internationalism. But it is interesting to note that the issues of our fight were not American. They dealt with the policy in the Soviet Union, the Anglo-Russian Committee, the problems of the Chinese revolution; later on, the question of fascism in Europe, etc. Again, our internationalism, insofar as it expressed itself in practice, was that of a group outside the actual developments, fighting over and clarifying issues and questions dealing with other parts of the world, primarily with Europe and Russia and the Orient. It was not until the economic crisis broke in full force in the United States that the concept of revolutionary possibilities in this country began to interest rather wide circles of people. This crisis, which was a conjuncture, changed almost overnight the attitude of thousands and tens of thousands of people—especially among the intellectuals who generally react quicker than the mass of workers—toward American capitalism, which up to then had appeared to be completely invincible, not only to us but also to the Europeans.

The theses mention that marvelous honeymoon of the twenties when both here and throughout Europe, with the exception of the Bolsheviks, everyone was of the opinion that the American capitalist genius had solved the problems posed by Marx. In the early days of the crisis in the thirties there was a tremendous influx of intellectuals toward Marxism, or what they thought was Marxism. When capitalism showed its weaknesses most glaringly, they began to lose faith in it. They swelled the ranks of the Stalinist party and quite a few of them came to us.

Sometimes we are apt to forget that we had for a time almost a mass movement of Trotskyism, or pseudo-Trotskyism, in the radical intellectual circles in New York, which was based primarily on their reaction to the conjuncture of the crisis and their opinion—which was largely self-delusion—that they had become revolutionists and even Trotskyists. Suffice to recall that we had in the early thirties a fraction of New York high school and college teachers of between twenty and thirty members. We had a periphery of a hundred or two hundred intellectuals whom we counted on as sympathizers of Trotskyism. As you know, we don't have them today. The beginning of the economic upturn, combined with the events in Russia, Spain, and Europe generally, brought about a mass desertion of these people.

But even in that period of deepest crisis in America when the terrible cracks in the economic and social system were revealing themselves, it is important for us to remember that the big disputes in our party, in our movement here in the United States, the ones with which the great majority preoccupied themselves, were disputes over Russia, Spain, Germany, etc. The incipient split between the proletarian and the petty-bourgeois tendencies was indicated in those days not so much by a formal and affirmative posing of questions as by the orientation each side took. The very fact that the proletarian tendency oriented itself very deeply toward the American labor movement and the trade unions, while the petty-bourgeois intellectuals preoccupied themselves almost entirely with foreign affairs was, so to speak, an unformulated beginning of a fundamental difference of conception of the role of our party and its potentialities on the American scene. We were acting according to these theses before we really formulated them as concretely as we have done today.

I said these theses should have a profound effect on the thinking, and especially on the morale, of the sections of the Fourth International. The shadow of this terrible power of American imperialism is undoubtedly very heavy over every section everywhere. France, Italy, England, South America—wherever it may be—the revolutionary workers of the Fourth International cannot fail to feel that they have not only the problem of overthrowing their own bourgeoisies, which they may feel fully competent they can do; they must feel that "this alone will not guarantee us anything because we will have to fight this colossus in North America." And I don't think anything can do more to round out and clarify their thoughts and struggle and morale than a positive assertion by the American party that we see the prospects of revolution in the United States and that we are organizing for that. That we are not playing the role of mere commentators on affairs in Europe and we are not going to be a

Red Cross society to collect funds for someone else to make a revolution somewhere else, but our main contribution to the European movement is the making of a revolution in the United States which aims at victory.

These theses in their theoretical part are strictly Trotskyist. There isn't any innovation there. And I say Trotskyist in the sense of expressing the real thought and conviction of the Old Man himself. That goes way back. In the recent period I have been studying his writings from this point of view and it is remarkable how far back Trotsky, above all, saw the Achilles heel of this apparently invincible monster in the United States. At the Third Congress of the Comintern in 1921, referring to the feverish development of the American economy during the war and afterward, he expressed the opinion that it was bound to lead to a convulsive crisis. And he used the expression, as I recall it, that the revolutionary development of the American workers can proceed at an American tempo equal to its feverish economic development during the war and postwar period.[121]

In 1929, in the first letter he sent to the Communist League of America from Constantinople, he said there were many indications that America would not be the first country to follow the example of the Russian revolution. In fact it was rather common in those days to say and to think that America would be the last—that following Russia there would come Germany; it would spread over Europe and from Europe to the Orient, interacting on each other, and that America would be the last capitalist country to succumb to revolution. The Lovestoneites put a decoration on top of that with their theory of "American exceptionalism," which in essence amounted to the idea that America was outside of revolutionary developments for a whole epoch. But in that first letter Trotsky said that while there was much to indicate that America would not be the first, a course of development would be possible in which this order would be sharply reversed and America could take first line in the revolutionary process.[122]

From that point of view, he said, it was necessary to prepare a party with that in mind. The Transitional Program of 1938—it is very interesting now in retrospect to recall the origin of this document—was written in Mexico after consultation and to a certain extent collaboration with a delegation from the United States.[123] And at that time, I venture to say, the Old Man's main preoccupation already was with America, and he intended the Transitional Program as applicable to America as well as to

Europe. The Transitional Program does not have any meaning unless one has in mind a revolutionary perspective. The very fact that you go over from the concept of the maximum and the minimum program—that is, the minimum program of daily small change, the maximum program of ultimate goal that you talk about on Sunday—to a transitional program presupposes a development of a revolutionary nature, with the prospects of a showdown struggle in sight. And the Transitional Program applies to America. As a matter of fact, if you recall the conversations and articles of the Old Man, I think he wrote more about America in its relation to the Transitional Program than about any other country.

Again, in his introduction to *The Living Thoughts of Karl Marx* he develops very categorically the theme that America is heading toward great revolutionary explosions and to a revolution.[124] More than once, confronted with the sweep of fascist reaction in Europe—which all those people who thought of internationalism and revolution solely in European terms took to be a sort of death sentence on the European movement—Trotsky said, "If fascism conquers Europe, then that means only that the center of Marxism will be transferred to American soil, and that the revolution in the United States would establish a new balance."

So from the point of view of the teachings of Trotsky and of the ideas by which we have been operating without stating so in precise terms, there is nothing new in the theses except that it is all brought together and generalized. But I believe it will be something new in its effect on the work of the party, and should be. The theses should be the starting point of a complete reorientation of our agitational and propaganda work. The whole party and its periphery and all the new recruits should be saturated with the ideas outlined in this document.

Just as in the early days of our movement—at least in the first ten years—we rearmed the movement with education and discussion and agitation around the basic principles of the Russian Opposition, the Anglo-Russian Committee, the policy in the Soviet Union, problems of the Chinese revolution, later on the problems of fascism in Europe, so now I believe we should go through that same process again of organizing our educational work, our literary and propagandistic work, in terms of popularizing and expanding on each one of the basic ideas gathered together here in the theses, so the whole party becomes saturated with the concept of the theses and the whole outlook that flows from it—that we are actually building a party to make the revolution in the United States.

Not the least of the results of the adoption of this document and the reorientation that will follow from it—the clarification of everything hazy as to what we mean, what we are driving at, what we hope to accomplish—is that it will bring out more clearly and fundamentally than ever the irreconcilable difference between us and the Mensheviks of all shades, including the Shachtmanites and our minority. During the summer, while we were discussing these ideas and formulating some of them out in California, Murry [Weiss] and Charlie Curtiss and I took occasion to study very attentively the bulletins of the Shachtmanites to see to what extent they have occupied themselves with this question of the perspectives of the American revolution. And it is really astonishing to see that they haven't given it a thought. They are far more interested in Stalinism and the national question in Europe. In fact, they are almost exclusively interested in that. Their resolution on the American question does not go any farther than we went in the heights of capitalist prosperity in the twenties, before the crisis—that is, of speculating on the next turn in the conjuncture and drawing some small-change conclusions with regard to tactics.

Johnson [C. L. R. James], who brought in a counterdocument in which he, in his own way, tried to assert that the Transitional Program has application for America and that there are revolutionary perspectives in the foreseeable future in America, was just laughed out of court by the Shachtmanites. They don't ever see it; they don't think about it. It is noteworthy that our own soul-sick Mensheviks have never given that a thought, and that is one reason why they are so pessimistic, why they are crawling under the bed. It has never entered their heads, evidently, that the American working class can compensate in one or two blows for any number of defeats in Europe. And it is interesting also that our conflict with them on secondary questions—I don't think this has been formulated before, we have only felt but haven't stated it—had at its root a difference of perspective and goals in the United States.

We have always believed in the American revolution, and it is from that concept—even though we did not generalize it—that we derived our conception of the party: for example, of a revolutionary combat party, of a professional leadership, of an optimistic morale, of harsh demands upon the membership. Goldman, and later Morrow, and others attack us on these derivative conceptions. They are against the homogeneous party. They are against this combat nonsense. They are against discipline. Morrow, at the last plenum, called our revolutionary exhortations "dope." We dope up the party with fantasies, etc. Now, if you stop to think about it, this debate about the conception of the party is a rather sterile debate if you isolate it from your milieu and your perspective. If socialism is only a remote aspiration, a moral ideal, or an ultimate goal that you hope for as men of goodwill hope for the moral regeneration of the world, what in the hell do you want a tightly disciplined combat party with a professional leadership for? It becomes a caricature.

As a matter of fact, you couldn't have organized such a party as this in America before the First World War. The prospect of the final struggle for the dictatorship of the proletariat was so far off that it seemed like playing soldiers to have that kind of a party. On the other hand, if you foresee a development of the class struggle that is leading to revolutionary collisions and a fight for power, then our conception of the party flows very logically and necessarily from that. It is not accidental that the one place where a Leninist type of party was organized before the First World War was in Russia, because the Russians, especially the Bolsheviks, expected a revolution, and Lenin was preparing a party to lead a revolution. The Social Democrats in Europe, who had a perspective of long, drawn-out, evolutionary development, saw no need of such a party.

Trotsky remarked in his autobiography that the difference between the Bolsheviks (which included Trotsky in this respect) and many others stemmed from the fact that there developed in the socialist movement, after one generation had succeeded another, a tendency toward conservatism of outlook as to prospects. People who recognized socialism as a desirable and eventually inevitable outcome postponed it to future generations, and that affected the whole life and concept of the party, its daily work, etc. The thing that characterized the Bolsheviks is that they were deliberately preparing for a revolution, and from that, as a derivative, flowed their type of party, their morale, etc.

You may say that for all these years we have been fighting both openly and in a muffled form with the petty-bourgeois tendency in our movement, we have been fighting over derivatives of a fundamentally different view of prospects in the United

States, and all we are doing now is turning things upside down, or rather, right side up, and developing our revolutionary perspective from which we derive our conception of professional leadership, the heavy demands we make upon ourselves and others, etc.

I had a discussion with Comrade Dobbs just before the meeting about section XI [of the theses], which deals with the question of what the real problem in the United States is—whether it is a question of the struggle for power or the danger of bureaucratic degeneration afterwards. I believe that has to go in there because the common argument of all varieties of Menshevism is the danger and the possibility—or, as they think, the certainty—that the revolution, once achieved by our program, will go the way of the Russian revolution. Munis even wrote, incredible as it may seem, in an article purportedly dealing with the most fundamental questions of the revolution which was reprinted by Shachtman, that the fundamental problem is the prevention of Thermidorian reaction after the revolution. That is the theme upon which all our opponents harp—that the program of communism leads to totalitarian tyranny as in Russia. I think it is necessary to state in our theses, with the object of arming our comrades and new recruits in advance with the conception, that the problem in the United States is the problem of the conquest of power; that the danger confronting the American workers is that they won't take the power when the time comes, not that the power will degenerate, as in Russia, afterwards.

There is a section in thesis XV about the labor party which Comrade Dobbs also raised, in which he expressed the opinion that we state perhaps too categorically that a mass labor party based on the unions would arise. I would agree to make that a bit more qualified, to say that if in the course of this development there will be a mass labor party, etc., without giving the impression that we consider this a necessary and inevitable phase of development. I personally do not consider this inevitable at all. Another course of action is possible. If the growth of a labor party is delayed too long and the SWP continues to grow and expand, another development is possible. It is only the most probably indicated one at the present time.

There is the question also of the necessity of a program or thesis on the tremendous anti-red campaign that is developing. It might be argued against the theses that a new wave of repressions is being prepared: J. Edgar Hoover's speech at the

American Legion convention; Attorney General Clark's speech before some lawyers' organization in Chicago in which he called for a tough attitude against red lawyers, which might indicate that they're all prepared for a new series of prosecutions; and the press campaign which encompasses practically the whole press and at least the AFL bureaucracy. It might be argued that a big wave of persecution would alter this perspective. We have to have a section in the document, if only a small one, asserting that our perspective is not based on the contemporary policy of the ruling class but upon more fundamental considerations of the weakness of the system economically and that it cannot be changed by persecutions—as a matter of fact, might be even accelerated by them. We must not concede at any place or any point to that school of thought now very popular among our neorevisionists that revolutionary possibilities are decided by subjective factors—the existence or nonexistence, the strength or weakness of the party, or the reactionary or liberal policies of the ruling class at a given moment, etc. The revolutionary perspective of the Russian revolution was not based upon a liberal regime and was not arrested by the most reactionary tsarist regime; and I believe it is necessary to have perhaps a small section stating that; that even if we encounter really ferocious persecution—and that seems more likely than not—that will not halt revolutionary developments or succeed in breaking up the party.

The point about the assertion of the role of the SWP, I think, follows from everything written in the document before. I think nothing condemns a party more than a lack of faith in its own future. I don't believe it is possible for any party to lead a revolution if it doesn't even have the ambition to do so. That is the case with the Shachtmanites and the case with Goldman and Morrow. The Shachtmanites assert that neither their party nor ours is the party of the future revolution. Somewhere, somehow, out of something or other, it will arise, they hope.

We must assert as a matter of course that our party is going to lead the revolution.

OUR RELATIONSHIP WITH THE FOURTH INTERNATIONAL

October 21, 1946

This letter to Michael J. Myer, a Chicago attorney who represented the Socialist Workers Party in legal matters, was in response to a demand by the federal government that the party register as a foreign agent linked to the Fourth International. This previously unpublished text is from Cannon's files.

Dear Mr. Myer:

Enclosed you will find a letter we received from N. T. Elliff, chief of Foreign Agents Registration Section.

We would like you to reply to Mr. Elliff in our behalf that we have no relationship with the Fourth International or any other body that would require us to register with the Foreign Agents Registration Section.[125]

The Socialist Workers Party is an autonomous independent organization and has no affiliation with parties or groups outside the United States. Our views are in many ways similar to the views of the Fourth International as expressed in the press of the Fourth International and its sections throughout the world, but this is only a matter of coincidence since we derive our views from a common socialist program.

Please send us a copy of your reply to Mr. Elliff.

Sincerely yours,
James P. Cannon
National Secretary

A FINANCIAL RETRENCHMENT

October 25, 1946

This letter to Charles Curtiss, a member of the National Committee in Los Angeles, reported proposals by the PC for cutbacks in party press and staff as a result of the extreme postwar inflation. Copies were sent to NC members and branch organizers. The text is from a copy in the archives of the SWP.

Dear Charlie:

I am enclosing a copy of an editorial which is to appear in next week's *Militant,* announcing the reduction of the size of the paper to six pages.

We have no choice in this matter and you will notice that we do not even promise to do better in the near future. Quite the contrary, we will have a hard battle even to maintain six pages at the rate prices are climbing. The printing costs since the time we projected and started the eight-page paper have nearly doubled, and now we have notice of another 40 percent increase to take effect next month.

We have been running up a big deficit on the paper for a long time, and this has upset our budget so badly that when we get through with the convention we will be flat broke again. We have been hit three ways by the conjuncture of the inflation with our greatly expanded program of activities. Many comrades, affected by the strikes, part-time layoffs, and increased cost of living, have had to curtail their contributions to the party. The great expansion of local activities, election campaigns, etc., has diverted considerable sums which used to come directly to the center. Then on top of all that, we encounter murderous increases in the cost of everything we have to spend money for in the national office, especially publications.

We had a session the other night and after a thorough discussion of all the facts in the situation, came to the conclusion that we have to take some drastic measures to reinstate a semblance of balance in our financial position.

1. The paper is to be reduced to six pages.
2. Absolutely all free distributions of *The Militant* are to be discontinued as soon as the election campaigns are over, and all branches will be asked to cut their bundles to the minimum amount they can sell and pay for.
3. The magazine will be either cut to sixteen pages or else printed in a cheaper form on newsprint.
4. All projected publications of Pioneer Publishers are to be suspended.
5. The staff everywhere, both in the center and in the field, is to be cut to the absolute minimum. There is one thing we cannot do—that is, reduce wages of the functionaries, as they are already the "forgotten men" of the inflation.
6. We must ask the convention to authorize the collection of another fund of $20,000.
7. Another step we may find absolutely necessary is to reestablish a partial printing establishment of our own—but on a more modest scale and with more sensible arrangements than was the case with the venture which was liquidated so ingloriously in 1940. We are thinking about merely getting a linotype to set our own copy on the paper and magazine, as well as on the pamphlets and books, and have all the presswork done elsewhere. The plan would be to pay full union wages for the actual work done on the typesetting and conform in every way to union regulations so as to have no difficulty about the label. However, we would need one reliable comrade to do the bulk of the typesetting and manage the modest enterprise in general from a technical point of view.

Let me know what you think of such a project and whether you would be in a position to take hold of it.

Fraternally yours,
J. P. Cannon

PS: We are approaching this problem in a businesslike manner without panic or even any nervousness. We are simply making a retreat on the financial front in time and in good order so as to avoid a serious rout later. The question should not be presented to the membership in any spirit of panic and defeat, and we do not want to throw a cloud over the convention. The funds to cover the convention have been laid aside and discounted as part of the overhead. We want all the comrades who have been planning to go to the convention to do so and make it a thoroughgoing demonstration of party solidarity and fighting morale and confidence in the future. A successful convention will be the best preparation to solve the present difficulties and prepare new advances.

George Breitman

OPENING SPEECH TO THE TWELFTH NATIONAL CONVENTION OF THE SWP

November 15, 1946

The Twelfth National Convention of the SWP was held in Chicago, November 15-18, 1946. The text of this speech is from The Militant, *December 14, 1946.*

In the name of the National Committee, I announce that the Twelfth National Convention of the Socialist Workers Party is now in session.

Our first thoughts and our first words are dedicated to the memory of those comrades who have fallen in the struggle. Since we last gathered in national convention we have suffered the great and irreparable loss of the veteran of our movement, the honorary member of the National Committee, Antoinette Konikow. We have suffered the loss of Comrade John Harrington of Lynn, Massachusetts. We will miss the friendly counsel of these comrades and the inspiration of their example, their dauntless enthusiasm and courage.

Since the convention two years ago we have reestablished communications and intimate relations of our party with the various sections of the Fourth International throughout the world who were cut off from us during the dark and terrible days of the war. We have learned with great joy that in spite of everything, the cadres of the Fourth International everywhere survived the terrible ordeal, continued their activity under all conditions, and continue to work and struggle. But our joy at the reestablishment of contact with them has been sadly tempered by sorrow at the news of the loss of so many comrades who perished in the fight.

In France, in Germany, Holland, Belgium, China, Greece—from all these countries—we heard reports of the decimation of our forces during the war by our enemies on every side. We learned of the death of Comrade Blasco, pioneer Italian Trotskyist and one of the founders of the Fourth International, who was assassinated in a Nazi concentration camp by Stalinists.[126]

We learned of the death of Comrade Lesoil, pioneer Belgian communist and also one of the founders of the Fourth International, who died in a Nazi concentration camp. We learned of the death of the Greek leader, Comrade Pouliopoulos, and the shocking assassination of more than 100 members of the Greek section of the Fourth International by the Stalinists,[127] and scores of others by the fascists.

But no hardships, no persecution, no terror could break the Fourth International. This was due to the dauntless spirit and the unshakable conviction manifested by our cadres of the Fourth International, which included those who have fallen in the fight.

Heavy indeed has been the toll which the struggle for the liberation of humanity has taken from the ranks of the Fourth International. Our martyrs are many. Long live their great innumerable names! Even in death they participate invisibly in our work and inspire us to greater efforts.

The presidium proposes that the convention should rise and stand for a moment in silence in honor of the martyrs of the Fourth International. [The audience rises and stands in silence.]

While the martyred dead can participate only invisibly in our deliberations, the work which they had to cease has been continued and fructified by the living. Since the last convention of the Socialist Workers Party we have inducted into our ranks a total of 1,013 new members. Here at the convention we formally welcome the new recruits into the ranks of the party.

The party offers to them hard work, heavy sacrifices, and many hazards. The party demands from them unconditional and undivided loyalty. But in return for that the party promises to the new recruits the satisfaction of struggling jointly with many others for great goals; the satisfaction of living a life that is inspired by purpose and meaning, a satisfaction that can come only from serving a cause that is greater than self.

And this great cause which we serve is on the march. Yesterday we counted only scores and at most hundreds under our banner. Today this cause commands the allegiance of thousands in the United States alone, and tomorrow it will mobilize millions in the grandiose struggle for the liberation of mankind.

History is working on the side of our victory. Our victory is assured if we also work for it. This Twelfth National Convention of the Socialist Workers Party, celebrating at the same time the eighteenth anniversary of our glorious party, will help to prepare the victory. In this confidence we begin the work of the Twelfth Convention, with the consideration of the recommendations for the organization of our work which have been prepared by the National Committee.

Antoinette Konikow

THE COMING AMERICAN REVOLUTION

November 15, 1946

This was Cannon's report to the Twelfth National Convention of the SWP on the "Theses on the American Revolution." The text is from the pamphlet The Coming American Revolution *(Pioneer Publishers, April 1947).*

We have undertaken as our central task at this Twelfth Convention of the Socialist Workers Party to analyze the present stage in the development of United States imperialism as it emerged from the Second World War—and its further perspectives—and to draw the necessary conclusions from this analysis.

In our main thesis we deal exclusively with the perspectives of the American revolution. Secondary questions of tactics, and even of strategy, are left for consideration under another point on the agenda after we have discussed and decided the main question of perspective.

The question might be asked: Why are the theses on perspectives needed now? In order for the party to see clearly on the road ahead it is necessary to have a main orientation and a long-range view of future developments. The theses we have presented are needed at the present moment for a number of reasons.

First, the whole Trotskyist concept of our epoch as the epoch of revolutions has been challenged by a new school of revisionists of Marxism. What answer do we give to this challenge, with specific reference to the United States of America?

What conclusions do we draw from the war and its consequences; from the new power of American imperialism; from the postwar prosperity; and from the retardation of the European revolution? What conclusions do we draw from these great events for the conduct of our own work and for our own future outlook in the United States?

Secondly, what shall we say to our co-thinkers in other lands about revolutionary prospects in the United States? They are surely waiting to hear from our convention on this question, for it is of the most vital and decisive importance for them. This applies to the workers of Europe, but not only to them. It applies to the workers of Russia, of South and Central America, of China, Japan, Asia as a whole, India—in fact, to the workers of the whole world which lies today under the shadow of American imperialism.

And finally, what shall the party teach the new members who today are streaming into our ranks by hundreds and who will come to us tomorrow in thousands? What shall we tell them concretely about the prospects of the revolution in the United States? That is what they want to know above everything else.

Our document undertakes to give straight answers to all these questions.

Another question may well be asked: What is new in the "Theses on the American Revolution" presented by the National Committee?

In one sense it can be said that nothing is new; for all our work has been inspired by, and all our struggles with opportunist tendencies have been derived from, a firm confidence on our part in the coming victory of the American workers.

In another sense it can be said that everything is new; for in the theses of the National Committee on the American revolution we are now stating, explicitly and concretely, what has always been implied in our fights with opportunist organizations, groups, and tendencies over the questions which were derivative from this main outlook of ours.

That has been the underlying significance of our long struggle to build a homogeneous combat party. That has been the meaning of our stubborn and irreconcilable fight for a single program uniting the party as a whole; for a democratic and centralized and disciplined party with a professional leadership; for principled politics; for the proletarianization of the party composition; for the concentration of the party on trade union work ("trade unionization of the party"); and, if I may say so without being misunderstood, for its "Americanization." All of this derived from our concept of the realism of revolutionary prospects in America, and of the necessity to create a party with that perspective in mind.

In short, we have worked and struggled to build a party fit to lead a revolution in the United States. At the bottom of all our conceptions was the basic idea that the proletarian revolution is a realistic proposition in this country, and not merely a far-off "ultimate goal," to be referred to on ceremonial occasions.

I say that is not new. In fact, it has often been expressed by many of us, including Trotsky, in personal articles and speeches. But only now, for the first time, has it been incorporated in a programmatic document of the party. That's what is new in our "Theses on the American Revolution." We are now stating explicitly what before was implied.

For the first time, the party as a party is posing concretely the fundamental question of the perspectives of the American revolution.

You will note in your reading of the theses that secondary questions of tactics and even of strategy, with all their importance, are left out. And this is not by accident or negligence, but by design. The theses deal only with analysis and perspectives—and these only in the broadest sense—*because that is the fundamental basis from which we proceed.*

Tactical questions and even questions of great strategical importance—such as the alliance of the labor movement and the Negro people, the role of the returned war veterans, the relations between the workers and the poor farmers and the urban petty bourgeoisie, the questions of fascism and of the labor party—these questions with all their great subordinate importance are left out of the main theses for separate consideration in other documents. They will be considered at another time in the convention, because the correct answer to all of them depends in reality on a correct answer to the main question of general perspective posed in the theses of the National Committee.

Of course, a general line, a general perspective, does not guarantee that one will always find the right answer to the derivative questions, the secondary issues. But without such a general orientation, without this broad overall ruling conception, it is quite hopeless to expect to find one's way in tactical and strategical questions.

The theses have been criticized already by people who deal exclusively in "the small coin of concrete events." We have been criticized because we "do not mention concrete tasks" and "pose no concrete problems."

That is true. But what is wrong with that procedure?

We are Marxists; and therefore we do not begin with the small questions, with the tactics, or even with the strategy. We first lay down the governing line from which the answers to the secondary questions derive.

Those who preoccupy themselves primarily with tactics reproach us for our procedure, and allege that it reveals the difference between their political *method* and ours. That is quite correct. We proceed from the fundamental to the secondary; they proceed by nibbling at the secondary questions in order to undermine the fundamental concepts. There is indeed a difference in method.

Our theses specifically outline the revolutionary perspectives in America and require the party to conduct and regulate all its daily activity in light of these perspectives.

Our preoccupation at this convention with American affairs and American perspectives does not signify a departure on our part from the time-honored internationalism that has always distinguished our tendency. Rather, we are taking a step forward in the application of our internationalist concepts to American affairs. That means to bring them down from the realm of abstraction and give them flesh and blood.

We began in 1928 with a struggle for internationalism against the dogma of "socialism in one country" which had been imposed on the Comintern and all its sections by the Stalinist revisionists. That was the most fundamental of all the principled questions which have shaped and guided the development of our movement in America for the past eighteen years.

We said then, and we still believe, that the modern world is an economic unit; and that not a single important social problem—and certainly not the most important problem, the socialist reorganization of society—can be definitively solved on national grounds.

With the presentation of the theses of the National Committee on the perspectives of the American revolution, we are adding a correlative idea to the following effect: it is no longer possible to speak seriously about the world socialist revolution without specifically including America in the program. Today that would be almost as utopian as was the theory of "socialism in one country" when it was first promulgated by Stalin for Russia in 1924.

This was always true, but it is truer now than ever in the light of the Second World War and its outcome. The United States has emerged from the war as the strongest power in the world, both economically and militarily. Our theses assert that the role of the

United States in further world developments will be decisive in all respects.

If the workers in another country, or even in a series of other countries, take power before the revolutionary victory in the United States, they will have to defend themselves against the American colossus, armed to the teeth and counterrevolutionary to the core.

On the other hand, a revolutionary victory in the United States, signalizing the downfall of the strongest bastion of capitalism, would seal its doom on an international scale.

Or, in a third variant, if the socialist revolution should be defeated in other countries or even on other continents, and pushed back and retarded, we can still fight and win in the United States. And that would again revive the revolution everywhere else in the world.

The world situation makes it quite clear that platonic internationalism is decidedly out of date in this country. Internationalism, as the Trotskyists have conceived it, means first of all, international collaboration. But in our view this international collaboration must signify not only the discussion of the problems and tasks of co-thinkers in other countries—this is where platonic internationalism begins and ends—but also the solution of these problems, above all our own specific problems, *in action*. That is our conception of internationalism as we mean to apply it and as we have expressed it in the theses.

One-sided internationalism—preoccupation with far-off questions to the exclusion and neglect of the burning problems on one's own doorstep—is a form of escapism from the realities at home, a caricature of internationalism. This simple truth has not always been understood, and there are some people who do not understand it yet. But our party can justify its existence only if, beginning with an international program, it succeeds in applying this program to the conditions of American life and confirming it in action.

This presupposes first of all an attentive study of America and a firm confidence in its revolutionary perspectives. Those who are content with the role of commentators on foreign affairs—and it is surprising how many there are—or that of a Red Cross society to aid other revolutions in other countries, will never lead a revolution in their own country; and in the long run they will not be of much help to other countries either. What the other countries need from us, above everything else, is one small but good revolution in the United States.

Trotskyism—which is only another name for Bolshevism—is a world doctrine and concerns itself with all questions of world import. But let us not forget—or rather, let some of us begin to recognize for the first time—that America, the United States, is part of the world; in fact, its strongest and most decisive part, whose further development will be most fateful for the whole.

It is from this point of view that we deem it necessary now to outline more concretely and more precisely than before our estimation of American perspectives, and to concentrate on the preparation for them. When we speak of the "Americanization" of the party in this sense we are not speaking as vulgar nationalists—far from it—but as genuine internationalists of the deed as well as of the word.

Our theses on the perspectives of the American revolution proceed in accord with the Marxist method and the Marxist tradition by analyzing and emphasizing first of all the objective factors that are making for the revolution. *These are primary. These are fundamental.* Any other approach than that which begins with the objective factors is unrealistic, mere wishful-thinking utopianism, no matter how revolutionary-minded its proponents may be.

This characterization of unrealism applies also to the new revelation of those who have exalted the subjective factor—meaning thereby the party and its strength or weakness at the given moment—to first place.

It would be incorrect, however, to add the supplementary qualification that these latter-day experts of the subjective factor, these latter-day revisionists, are "revolutionary-minded." They are unrealistic, but not revolutionary-minded, for they employ their new "theory" exclusively for the explanation of past defeats and anticipation and prediction of new ones. I don't see anything revolutionary about that.

Our theses pay due acknowledgment to the great strength of United States imperialism. Let no one accuse us of failing to give the American imperialist power its due. We paid due acknowledgment to it. This is correct and proper in a document which aims at scientific objectivity; for the might and resources of the Yankee colossus are so imposing in relation to all other countries, and in relation to anything that has ever been seen in the world before in the realm of material power—and have been so well advertised in the bargain—that no one could possibly overlook them.

But our theses—and here we demarcate ourselves from all those who are hypnotized by the superficial appearance of things—

point out not only the strength of American imperialism but also its inherent weaknesses; the contradictions from which it cannot escape; and the new, even greater, power which it has created and which is destined to be its gravedigger—the American working class. That is also part of the American picture which has to be observed and noted if one wants to have a completely true and objectively formulated document.

A one-sided view of the American capitalist system—overestimation of its power and awestruck prostration before it—is the source of many illusions. And these illusions, in turn, are the chief source of American labor opportunism in general; of the capitulation and treachery of the radical intellectuals en masse; of Stalinism; and of all varieties of reformism and Menshevism.

In considering the perspectives of the American capitalist system in general and of the present postwar prosperity in particular, we observe a peculiar and rather interesting anomaly. The capitalist masters of society, and their ideologues and economic experts, enter the new period with doubts and fears which they do not conceal; while the greatest confidence in the long life and good health of the present order of society in America is either openly expressed or tacitly implied by those who set themselves up as representatives of the workers—namely, the official leadership of the labor movements and the Mensheviks of all grades.

The American bourgeoisie entered the great boom of the twenties with the exuberant confidence and enthusiasm of alchemists who had finally discovered the philosopher's stone which turns everything into gold. In that golden age of American capitalism a new school of bourgeois economists came from the colleges to proclaim the glad tidings that Marx had been refuted by Henry Ford; that American business genius had discovered the secret of full employment and permanent prosperity without interfering with the private ownership of the means of production, but on the contrary, strengthening it and aiding its concentration.

They continued to beat the drums on this theme up to the year, the month, and even to the day when the stupendous myth of the twenties was exploded in the stock-market crash of 1929. The very week in which the whole structure came tumbling down, the most learned articles were published in the name of the most eminent college professors explaining that this prosperity was going to go higher and would continue endlessly.

It is true that the labor leaders and the Social Democrats in this country and throughout the world were captivated by the myth of permanent prosperity in the twenties and were enlisted in the great parade. But they only followed; they did not lead. The capitalists were in the lead, full of confidence and optimism in those days. The capitalists and their economists were fortified in their faith by their ignorance, and that is a wonderful fortification for some kinds of faith.

They simply observed that profits rolled in and productivity increased at a rate and on a scale never known before, and that this continued year after year. Hypnotized by the marvelous empirical phenomenon, they mistook a passing phase for a permanent condition.

This misunderstanding was widely shared. The myth of the twenties penetrated deeply into all social strata in the United States and imbued even the great mass of the workers with future hopes of prosperity and security under capitalism. Those were the conditions under which the pioneer communists had to lay the foundation for a party aiming at the revolution. The confidence and illusion in the permanence of the prosperity of capitalism penetrated down into the depths of the working class itself.

The great boom of the twenties developed under the most favorable conditions. The American sector of capitalist economy was still in its healthy prime, relying on a vast internal market of its own which extended from coast to coast and from Canada to the Gulf, and on an expanding foreign trade. All other conditions were most favorable then.

But in spite of that, it is now a matter of historical record that this great boom ended with the stock-market crash of 1929. It is a matter of record that the crisis lasted, with some fluctuations, for ten years.

The salient facts and figures about the crisis of the thirties are recited in our theses. They show the depth and intensity of the crisis, its horrible effects in terms of human misery, and the irreparable blows it dealt to the American capitalist system. National income was cut in half, and with it the living standards of the workers were cut in half. Unemployment reached the figure of twenty million out of a working class population of no more than forty million at the time.

The partial recovery, brought about in large measure by huge government expenditures, only led to a second sharp drop in 1937, a crisis within the crisis. The crisis as a whole lasted for ten solid years. And even then, a way out to the revival and increase of production and the absorption of the unemployed was found only in the war and the colossal expenditures connected with it.

And this artificially induced recovery, which greatly expanded the productive plant of the country and the numerical force of the working class, has only deepened the contradictions and has prepared all the conditions for the explosion of another crisis, far worse than the thirties and fraught with far more serious social implications.

So, in surveying the future prospects of American capitalism, we simply heed the counsel of realism by putting the question: If American capitalism was shaken to its foundations by the crisis of the thirties, at a time when the world system of capitalism—and America along with it, and America especially—was younger, richer, and healthier than it is now; if this crisis lasted for ten years, and even then could not be overcome by the normal operation of economic laws; if all the basic causes and contradictions which brought about the crisis of the thirties have been carried over and lodged in the new artificial war and postwar prosperity, with new ones added and old ones multiplied many times; if all this is true—and nobody but a fool can deny it, for the facts are clearly to be seen—then what chance has the capitalist boom of the forties, that we are living under now, to have a different ending from the boom of the twenties?

Marxist realism tells us that it can be different only insofar as the crisis must go far deeper, must be far more devastating in its consequences, and must come sooner than it came in the boom of the twenties.

The specious theory expounded by the foolishly optimistic bourgeois economists in the heyday of the capitalist boom of the twenties, to the effect that Marx had been outwitted by American business genius, was refuted by the ten-year crisis of the thirties—and that crushing refutation remains in the memory of all.

How inexcusable, then, how absurd, how downright reactionary is the cultivation of this myth under the new conditions today!

In justice to the bourgeoisie and their ideologists it must be admitted that they, instructed by the experiences of the past, now take a far more sober and cautious position in their prognostications of the future. The burnt child fears the fire—that is, if he is a bourgeois economist, a businessman, and not a theoretical trifler.

The bourgeois economists and businessmen talk today far more of "boom and bust" than of boom without end. Any businessmen's economic review you may pick up at random expresses dark forebodings for the economic future. They speak quite casually--as though it is a matter of course, to be taken for granted—of an impending "shake-out" which will slow down the wheels of production and bankrupt the smaller firms which have flourished on the fringes of the boom.

At first, they referred to this process as a "shakedown," but that expressed their thoughts too truthfully. And since bourgeois economists cannot live without lying and dissimulating, they stopped talking about the "shakedown" and finally hit on the euphemistic substitute of a "shake-out."

That sounds better but it will not be one cent cheaper.

The sole chorus of optimism, where the economic prospects of American capitalism are concerned, is that raised by the American variety of Mensheviks. And that is a thin, piping chorus of trebles and tremolos, without a bass voice in it, or a baritone, or even a first-class tenor. It is a eunuchs' chorus.

Our fundamental theses on the American revolution do not tie themselves to the economic prospects of the next month or the next year. They deal exclusively with the long-range inevitable outcome of the present artificial prosperity. From the point of view of our theses it makes no difference whether the deepgoing crisis begins in the early spring of 1947, as many bourgeois economists are predicting; or six months later, as many others think; or even a year or two later, as is quite possible in my opinion. Our theses do not consider immediate time schedules, but the *general perspective*. That is what we have to get in mind first.

We take the position that the crisis is *inherent* in the situation; that it may not be escaped or avoided; and that this crisis, when it strikes in full force, will be far deeper and far more devastating than was the crisis of the thirties. As a consequence it will open up the most grandiose revolutionary possibilities in the United States. That conception must be at the base of the policy and perspectives of our party from now on.

I proceed from the discussion of the objective factors in the broadest sense, as our theses do, to go over to another of the most fundamental factors making for the coming American revolution and its victory.

The American working class which confronts the next crisis

will not be the disorganized and helpless mass which met the crisis of the thirties in bewilderment and fear, and even with an element of despair. Great changes have taken place in the meantime, and all these changes redound to the advantage of the revolution.

The proletariat greatly increased in numbers with the expansion of industry during the war. Millions of Negroes, of women, and of the new generation of youth have been snatched up out of their former existence and assimilated into the process of modern industry. Thereby, they have been transformed from a multitude of dispersed individuals into a coherent body imbued with a new sense of usefulness and power.

Most remarkable of all, the most pregnant with consequences for the future, is the truly gigantic leap which the American workers made from disorganized individual helplessness to militant trade union consciousness and organization in one brief decade. The trade union movement in the early thirties embraced barely more than three million members. Today the figure stands at *fifteen million members of organized labor in the United States.*

One can point to this fact and say that this represents a remarkable growth. But these bare figures, eloquent as they are, do not in themselves tell the whole story, the true story. For of the three-million-odd members of the trade unions in the early thirties, the great majority were composed of the thin stratum of the most skilled and privileged workers, who are the most conservative in their social thinking. The great bulk of workers in the mass-production industries—the most decisive section of the proletariat—were entirely without benefit of organization and had never even known the experience of it.

In spite of that—or more correctly, because of that—when these mass-production workers took the road of trade union organization, with the partial revival of industry in the middle thirties, they were not impeded by the old baggage and deadening routine of the conservative craft unions. They started from scratch with the modern form of organization—the industrial union form—and with the most militant methods of mass struggle, which reached their apex in the great wave of sit-down strikes in 1937.

The benefits these mass-production workers derived from trade unionism were wrested from the employers in open struggle, and therefore were all the more firmly secured. The stability and cohesiveness of the trade union organizations created in these struggles were put to the test in the strike wave of the past year. Here we saw a clear demonstration of the great difference in the relationship of forces between the workers and the capitalists at the end of World War II from that which prevailed at the end of World War I, a difference entirely in the favor of the workers.

After the successful termination of the First World War "to make the world safe for democracy," the ruling class of America embarked on a furious reactionary campaign to break the unions, to establish the open shop, and to suppress all forms of labor radicalism. In the "Palmer Red Raids" of 1919, hundreds of political meetings were broken up and thousands of radical workers were arrested; hundreds were sent to prison; whole shiploads of foreign-born workers were deported. The newly founded Communist Party was savagely persecuted, its leaders were arrested and indicted, and the party was driven underground.[128]

Simultaneously, the steel strike was broken, in part by ruthless violence and in part by the wholesale importation of strikebreakers; unions newly formed during the war were broken up and scattered right and left; the railway shopmen's strike was defeated in 1922. American capitalism, smashing all opposition before it, marched confidently into the strikeless, open-shop paradise of the great boom of the twenties.

The same thing was attempted, or at least contemplated, for the period immediately following World War II, but the result was a miserable fiasco. This time it was the organized workers who were victorious on every front.

The great industrial unions of the steel, auto, oil, packinghouse, electrical, and maritime workers demonstrated their capacity to bring production to a complete stop until the employers came to terms. So great was the new-found solidarity and militancy of the workers that neither violence nor the importation of strikebreakers—the decisive factors in the defeat of the strikes following World War I—could even be attempted by the bosses.

Millions and tens of millions of workers in other industries, profiting by the example of the auto, steel, packinghouse, electrical, and other strikes, and riding on the wave created by them, gained wage increases by "collective bargaining," while keeping their unions intact and even strengthening them.

Where did this marvelous labor movement come from? Who created it?

Here we must pay due acknowledgment to American capitalism. By the blind operation of its internal laws and method of operation, it has created the greatest power in the world—the American working class. Here is where Marx takes revenge on Henry Ford. Capitalism produces many things at a rapid rate and in great quantities. But its richest contribution to the further and higher development of human civilization is the production of its own gravedigger—the organized working class.

American capitalism, as we know, could not work the miracle of boom-without-crisis. But in the period of the twenties and thirties, working blindly and unbeknownst to itself, it wrought some other wonders which border on the miraculous.

American capitalism took millions of barefooted country boys from the bankrupted farms of the country, put shoes on them, and marched them into the regimented ranks of socially operated modern industry; wet them in the rain of the man-killing, speedup exploitation of the twenties; dried them in the sun of the frightful crisis of the thirties; overworked them on the assembly line, starved them on the breadline, mistreated and abused them; and finally succeeded in pounding them into a coherent body which emerged as a section of the most powerful and militant trade union movement the world has ever known.

American capitalism took hundreds of thousands of Negroes from the South and, exploiting their ignorance, and their poverty, and their fears, and their individual helplessness, herded them into the steel mills as strikebreakers in the steel strike of 1919. And in the brief span of one generation, by its mistreatment, abuse, and exploitation of these innocent and ignorant Negro strikebreakers, this same capitalism succeeded in transforming them and their sons into one of the most militant and reliable detachments of the great victorious steel strike of 1946.

This same capitalism took tens of thousands and hundreds of thousands of prejudiced hillbillies from the South, many of them members and sympathizers of the Ku Klux Klan, and, thinking to use them, with their ignorance and their prejudices, as a barrier against unionism, sucked them into the auto and rubber factories of Detroit, Akron, and other industrial centers. There it sweated them, humiliated them, and drove and exploited them until it finally changed them and made new men out of them. In that harsh school the imported Southerners learned to exchange the insignia of the KKK for the union button of the CIO, and to turn the Klansman's fiery cross into a bonfire to warm pickets at the factory gate.

You won't find Ku Kluxers or Black Legionnaires [white racists] in the auto and rubber factories today—or at any rate, not many of them. But there is a mighty sight of first-class shop stewards and picket captains who orginally came down out of the hills and up from the bayous of the backward South at the summons of American capitalism.

The American working class covered the great distance from atomization, from nonexistence as an organized force, to trade union consciousness and organization in one gigantic leap, in one brief decade.

What grandiose perspectives this achievement opens up for the future! What are the limits to the future possibilities and powers of this remarkable class? There are no limits. All things are possible; and all things that are necessary will be achieved.

If someone had predicted in 1932, at the depths of the crisis, that in ten years' time ten million new workers who had never known unionism would organize themselves into industrial unions of the most modern type and demonstrate their ability to force the absentee owners of the steel and auto and rubber and other mass-production industries to come to terms and not even to dare to attempt to break the strikes—the skeptics would have said: "This is fantasy. This is ultraleft radicalism."

But it happened just the same.

The American workers do not always move when impatient revolutionists call them, as many of us have learned to our sorrow. But they do move when they are ready, and then they move massively.

Industrial unionism is not a new idea. It was projected long before it found its realization on a mass scale in America, and the pioneers of industrial unionism in America suffered many disappointments. In 1930, the IWW dolefully observed its twenty-fifth anniversary. At the end of a quarter of a century, the organization which had proclaimed the program of industrial unionism twenty-five years earlier was completely defeated, a hollow shell comprising far fewer members than it had started with in the bright year of promise, 1905, under a great galaxy of leaders. Industrial unionism seemed to be a defeated program in 1930. But only ten years later the majority of the most important basic industries were completely organized in industrial unions under a new name.

The workers did not move when the IWW called them in 1905. They didn't move when many of us called them later than that.

But they moved when they were ready and when conditions were mature for it, and then they moved on a scale and at a speed scarcely dreamed of by the pioneers of industrial unionism.

The scale of the difference is remarkable. Bill Haywood, the great captain of the IWW—I love to mention his name—used to dream and speak in his intimate circle of the goal of a "million members" in the IWW. As a matter of fact, the organization never had more than 100,000 at any one time in all its history, and most of the time only a fraction of that number. The great strikes of the IWW which took place in its heyday, those great pioneer battles which heralded and blazed the way for the CIO—Lawrence, Akron, Paterson, McKees Rocks, the lumber strikes in the Northwest—never involved more than ten to twenty thousand workers at any one time.

But in 1946 nearly two million workers of the CIO, with only a few years of trade union experience behind them, were on strike at one time!

These comparative figures show not growth, not simply progress, but a veritable transformation of the class. And what has been seen up to now are only the preliminary movements, the promise and the assurance of far greater movements to come. Next in order—and not far away—comes the political awakening of the American workers. That will be at the same pace and on the same scale, if not greater. The American workers will learn politics as they learned trade unionism—"from an abridged dictionary." They will take the road of independent political action with hurricane speed and power.

That will be a great day for the future of humanity, for the American workers will not stop halfway. The American workers will not stop at reformism, except perhaps to tip their hats to it. Once fairly started, they will go the whole way.

He who doubts the socialist revolution in America does not believe in the survival of human civilization, for there is no other way to save it. And there is no other power that can save it but this almighty working class of the United States.

The younger generation entering the revolutionary movement today, with the goal of socialism shining bright in their far-reaching vision, come at a good time. A lot of pioneer work has been done. Many obstacles have been cleared out of the road. Many conditions for success have matured.

The young generation coming to us today comes to a party that foresees the future and prepares for it. They come to a great party with a glorious record and a stainless banner, a party that has already been prepared for them and awaits their enlistment. They come to a strong party, firmly built on the granite rock of Marxism. This party will serve them well, and is worthy of their undivided allegiance.

This Twelfth Convention coincides with the eighteenth anniversary of the party. The experience and tradition of the party are the capital of the new generation. The work of many people for two decades has not been done in vain. And, besides that, the new recruits can find in a realistic examination of the objective facts many assurances that the course of development is working mightily in favor of the realization of their ideal.

Our economic analysis has shown that the present boom of American capitalism is heading directly at a rapid pace toward a crisis; and this will be a profound social crisis which can lead, in its further development, to an objectively revolutionary situation.

Our analysis of the labor movement has shown that the workers have already demonstrated the capacity to move massively and rapidly forward in the field of trade unionism; and we have every right to confidence that they will move even more massively and with even greater speed on the political field in the days to come.

The objective prerequisites for the social revolution in America will not be lacking. Capitalism itself will provide them. The manpower of the revolution will not be lacking either. The many-millioned masses of the organized workers of America will provide this manpower. It is already partly assembled and partly ready.

The rest is our part. Our part is to build up this party which believes in the unlimited power and resources of the American workers, and believes no less in its own capacity to organize and lead them to storm and victory.

SUMMARY SPEECH ON "THE AMERICAN THESES"

November 16, 1946

The following are major excerpts from Cannon's summary remarks following the discussion on his report on the "Theses on the American Revolution" at the Twelfth National Convention of the SWP. Felix Morrow had been given equal time for a counterreport opposing adoption of the theses. The text is from an uncorrected and previously unpublished stenographic transcript.

Comrades:

The convention is the highest point of party life. At the convention all the work of the party for two years and all its perspectives and plans for another two years are concentrated together. At the convention all the best thinkers and the best activists of the party are gathered. And consequently here when one presumes to speak and to report before the convention everyone is duty-bound to prepare well and to do his level best. Good enough will do on ordinary occasions. Even some negligence and laxness can be tolerated under normal circumstances, on other occasions. But at the party convention the delegates have the right to expect of everyone no excuses, that he gives everything he has.

Now, feeling that, having that opinion of the convention in my duty as a reporter, I listened most attentively to the criticisms of my report. I heard that it was a mere mass meeting speech, that it was a soapboxer's demonstration—although the author of that winged phrase doesn't know the great role that soapboxers will play in the mobilization of the revolution. I heard from a young man that it was moonshine from which the party will get a hangover, an emotional outburst, etc.

Now these are grave accusations, in my opinion, and I ask you, was my economic analysis wrong? Did I falsify or exaggerate the achievements and strength of the American workers? I don't think so. I believe that I related the economic facts and perspectives in a strictly orthodox manner with rigid allegiance to facts and figures that are known and established and demonstrated in the theses. And if I drew conclusions, they were not in the least on the exaggerated side, but I left a qualification even on the conservative side as to the rate of development of the crisis.

I believe that the emotionalism was all on the side of Morrow. I believe that Morrow's whole speech was a rationalization in terms of economic analysis of his own mood of capitulation and defeat. He cannot see any hope of the American workers developing on the revolutionary road, so he underplays—responding to that emotion of pessimism—he underplays the working class movement and the party. And having no hope of any serious convulsions of American capitalism that will confront them with revolution, at least in our time, or our children's time, or our grandchildren's time, he describes the economic prospects of American imperialism with unbounded and unbridled optimism.

I don't believe, as I heard some comrades say, that Morrow ought to get a job as economic analyst on a bourgeois financial or economic paper. They wouldn't hire you. They don't want that kind of dope. They want facts. You couldn't write in an economic review to be circulated among businessmen. The best that could be done with your stuff, as Warren Creel so aptly said, is a propaganda sheet for the front page to dope the masses, but for themselves they want economic realism insofar as they can get it.

He says that we are constantly exaggerating the economic situation. Wherein? How? If we did, we must correct that, because you can't make a revolution by seeing what you want to see. I don't think so. All I did and tried to do, and all the theses of the National Committee did and tried to do was, one, to recite the economic facts which are demonstrable and which nobody has challenged successfully. Second, to give a true picture of the transformation of the American working class in the last decade or so—and I would like someone to challenge those facts which we recited: the development from three million members of the trade unions organized in craft unions to fifteen million, the bulk of them in the mass-production industries.

I recited the strikes. I didn't exaggerate the figures. I said the strikes couldn't be broken and they couldn't dare import strikebreakers and use violence. These are facts, and from these facts and the state of American economy and its history over the past twenty years, the transformation of the American working class, revolutionary optimism and hope were derived. That is true both in the theses and in my speech. But that is not emotionalism, Comrade Morrow, that is Marxism. That is Trotskyism. [. . .]

Did I demand a crisis before it is due? I did not. Did I predict a crisis to come before the conditions are matured for it? I did not. And why? Because I am a Marxist; at least I try to be. And neither we nor Morrow nor anyone else knows when this crisis will strike in full force, and that is why we don't predict it with too much precision. Not even Marx himself—who from his analysis of the mainsprings of capitalism, propounded the theory of the inevitability of productive rises turning to crises in the course of the cycle—could predict crises with accuracy. That is one reason he couldn't make a fortune on the stock-market even if he tried. As a matter of fact, Marx and Engels at the time when they did make some predictions made errors in time schedules. But that didn't alter the fundamental fact that their analyses and their prognoses in the essentials and in the long run were correct.

Now will the coming crisis, which appears rather near—six months, a year, or two years—will that be a crisis of the 1921 order which will result in a temporary recovery before the real plunge on a 1929 scale or greater comes, or will the first crisis be the real one, the deep one? We don't say because we don't know. And it does not matter in the long run, does not touch the essentials of our economic prognosis, whether the first crisis is tentative or whether the conditions and contradictions have matured so much that once it begins to topple it will go to the very bottom. I believe you will find more support [for the latter position] from bourgeois economic circles, if they tell you the truth in four walls, than for the other prediction that it will be a more moderate crisis. But that doesn't matter.

I had a talk with a businessman a little while ago who is connected with economic affairs and we discussed the economic situation and I gave him our theses to read. He is interested in what we think. And he said: When do you think the crisis is going to come? I said, well, I don't know. He said, They are talking about the spring. I said, it might be in the spring or the fall. It might be two years. I couldn't confine myself to a strict prediction in time-space on such a question. All I know is that the conditions are maturing for it and it is going to be terrific. But he said, "Two years, you say? There isn't a businessman in my acquaintance that takes such a conservative view of the situation. They are all scared to death."

The trouble with Morrow, however, is that he is not allowing himself any leeway. This emotionally inspired politician sees what he wants to see, apparently, and he is following formalistically the pattern of the crisis of 1921. We know that in the postwar prosperity following World War I there was a dip in 1921 that lasted a year, nearly two, and then rose to new heights again on the basis of the internal market and the fundamental health and strength of American capitalism. He can't see or acknowledge anything more severe than that. There has to be a temporary crisis but he would never call it a crisis or depression or a recession or a "shakedown" or a "shake-out." The most he will allow is "price adjustment." And then it must "rise" again for a period of years. He commits himself to that. I wouldn't do that.[129]

I say it is possible that the first crisis will not be the real one, but I will not guarantee anyone to that effect because I don't think it is realistic to follow the pattern of the twenties, because American capitalism today is far weaker and in a far more vulnerable situation, and the whole world situation is far worse than it was then. But I don't demand an immediate crisis, and if you are under that impression, I will withdraw any such implication. We are in no hurry for that crisis. And we are in no hurry to hop up the delegates here to a crisis just around the corner. That would work to our disadvantage.

Why, out in Montana once I heard a story told me by the late Rodney Salisbury, the Communist sheriff in Plentywood, when I was out there on one of my tours. I had a wonderful visit with the comrades there and was entertained in the county jail by the sheriff there—not behind the bars, but in the office. And he told me a story about our comrade, Senator Taylor, who is now one of the active members of the Seattle branch and at that time was a Communist state senator in Montana, elected on a Farmer-Labor ticket. And the CP at this stage—to which he then belonged—had not, as we have, a realistic Marxist attitude toward crises, but some ultraleft and exaggerated idea that it must go out and preach the coming of an immediate devastating crisis. So, obedient to the party's instruction, Comrade Taylor made a speech in a town at the other end of the state and began to expound the thesis of the party about the coming crisis.

And he presented such a picture of the depths of this crisis and its miseries and the effects it would have on agricultural products and everything, that when it came time to take up the collection, everybody present was so damned scared that he would be broke that he wouldn't part with a nickel and Taylor had to wire to Plentywood to get carfare to come back home.

Now you know that at conventions, as in life, one thing follows another. After the discussion of the theses comes a discussion of the practical tasks, and then comes the organization report, and then comes the trade union report, and then a couple of other piddling little questions about unity with the Shachtmanites and the internal situation, and then comes the question: How much money are you going to give to us to carry on party work? And we don't want to terrify you with the economic prospects so you say you have no money for us. No, outside of that the party can use very well another period of prosperity, a prolongation of it. And just as we predict war against the Soviet Union, we don't demand it in a hurry. The party needs and can very well use an interval of economic prosperity and peace that will give us more time to build our cadres and prepare the future. [. . .]

These people see a defeat some place here or there in the world and conclude that everything is going to pot. They just discovered America since this discussion started. They see some defeats in Europe and say, "Oh me, oh me, humanity is going back some hundreds of years." They forget that humanity in the United States has been going forward.

Trotsky said about Europe, when all the advance guard of the Morrow brand were moping and whimpering and whining, when fascism was marching across Europe, he said, "The victories of fascism are important, but the death agony of capitalism is more important."[130] And if fascism conquers Europe, he said, what does that mean? That means the center of Marxism will be transplanted to the United States and America will produce the greatest Marxists of all because it is going to produce the greatest revolution. That is how Trotsky analyzed the prospect of revolution when nothing appeared on the horizon anywhere but defeats. [. . .][131]

Look at that shameful document presented here by Morrow, by the authors of the "Three Theses" and touched up a bit by him.[132] They dismissed this profound document which codifies and regularizes for the first time the fundamental thoughts of Trotsky and of all revolutionists on the American perspectives. They dismissed it with a sneer, and they are violently antagonized by it and are completely alien to it. I said it is Trotskyist on the economic side and it is also Trotskyist on the party side because we say there that our party, small as it is, will have every opportunity to develop in revolutionary situations and come to the head of the masses. That is Trotskyist. They sneer at that. They say, that is the nine-months theory of revolution.[133] By God, if you would ever put down your theory of revolution and put it down by months, I wonder where you would get the figures in the whole dictionary. You couldn't find astronomical figures big enough to describe [the pessimism] that you have at the bottom of your miserable souls.

Trotsky was confident of revolution in Spain and its victory in 1931 when there were only about six Trotskyists there, returned from exile. He said, "Go directly there and build and you will come to the head of the movement." In 1936 he was confident of the revolutionary prospects in France when they had a party far smaller than ours numerically, and nearly all intellectuals with weaknesses and vacillations, foibles and idiosyncrasies, and the unreliability of intellectuals.[134]

Trotsky was confident of the possibility of revolution in Russia in 1905 when the party was pretty small, pretty weak, and he walked right into the avalanche as an individual and right into the Soviet and became elected chairman of the Soviet. And it was not led by the Bolshevik party—as a matter of fact the soviets were created without even the participation of the Bolsheviks as a party in the first stage of 1905.[135] Lenin and Trotsky were confident of the ability of the small Bolshevik party to come to the head of the masses and lead and organize the revolution in Russia [in 1917] when Kerensky was in power, and even before Kerensky. When the great millioned masses were completely under the domination of the Mensheviks and the SRs, Lenin and Trotsky were confident of it, but hardly anyone else. And that is exactly why the revolution was successful in Russia—because they had some resolute men who believed in it. Even the Morrows, all the Morrows . . . lost their faith and capitulated in their ideology to the democratic revolution, and it required the will and the faith of Lenin and Trotsky to transform the domination of the SRs and the Mensheviks over the millioned masses over to the leadership of the Bolsheviks and a successful revolution.

There is a certain law about revolution—maybe you never heard of it—that in order to organize and lead a revolution you must first have faith in your ability to do so.

Morrow, speaking here, compared us to the POUM. A very interesting comparison in more ways than one, and will be doubly interesting when it is set in its truthful aspect. He said, thinking to denigrate us once again, "The cadres of the POUM were just as good as the cadres of the Socialist Workers Party." In one sense, although not in the sense perhaps that he meant, I would grant that—if you speak in terms of the personal ability of the leaders, of Nin, and a group of others, I would say we have absolutely no reason to constantly demand a recognition that we are more clever than they, that we speak better or are personally more talented or able. They were able men.

The trouble with the POUM was—and here is where the difference between them and us comes in—that Trotsky blamed them for the defeat of the revolution in Spain and said that if they carried a correct policy they could have won the revolution in Spain. They had cadres enough to do it. From a small group at the beginning of the 1936 civil war, they bounded to a great group, with daily papers and armed detachments and I think not less than 50,000 members, if not more. And Trotsky said that is enough, given a correct policy, to lead and win the revolution. But the trouble with Nin and the others was that they did not believe in their ability to lead that revolution and they took the road of the People's Front. They took the road of entry into a bourgeois government, together with the Stalinists and the Social Democrats and even the Anarchists, who don't believe in governments, in Catalonia.[136]

And the reason for the failure of the revolution in Spain was not the lack of cadres in the POUM, although they didn't have as large a party as ours before the revolution, by a long shot, but because they didn't follow a policy of revolution. They got infected with a dose of Martovism at the critical moment and lost faith in the ability to carry through. As Comrade Roberts, in his magnificent speech on the first point on the agenda, pointed out, it is characteristic of all Mensheviks that they believe in the revolution up to the time when they have to make it, and then they always find a reason why you cannot do it. Morrow of course improves on the classic Mensheviks by coming to the conclusion long in advance that you can't do it.

How did Trotsky characterize the leaders of the POUM who had once been his close collaborators? Did he say they are on a par with the cadres in America? He did not. Andrade, who was the best of them, the left wing, wrote a little pamphlet—I forget what it was about—and he sent a special copy to Trotsky and inscribed it, "To my teacher, Comrade Trotsky." And Trotsky answered him in the press. This was after they had entered the People's Front. Trotsky answered Andrade who inscribed himself as a pupil, and said, "I would be only too happy if that inscription told the truth because nothing gives me greater pleasure than to see a young man recognize that I helped him to learn something. But I am not Andrade's teacher because I never taught anybody to betray the working class."[137] That is the way Trotsky spoke of the best one of the leaders of the POUM. And what did the betrayal consist of? Of joining the People's Front government.

I would like to know if anyone would dare to say that these people who voted for the capitalist constitution in France, they would never have the occasion, if Trotsky were alive and in the flesh, to get that kind of rebuke over the inscription. They would never dare to inscribe themselves as pupils of Trotsky. Trotsky never taught anybody to betray the working class.

The POUM did not arrive at the participation in the bourgeois People's Front government in Catalonia in one bound from having been members of the International Left Opposition. And Nin himself, a member of the Opposition in Russia even, who came to Spain, as Trotsky said, with a halo around his head as a pioneer Trotskyist in Russia, and with that great record of authority he did not carry out a Trotskyist policy. He made a combination with Maurín's Menshevik party in Catalonia and united with the Mensheviks on a program that was not Trotskyist.[138]

Are we comparable to the cadres of the POUM in that respect? Do we look for Menshviks to unite with? Just the contrary. This cadre, this party, declares irreconcilable warfare against Mensheviks of all description including the Morrow description and we are not looking for unity with them but war to the end with them. That is the difference between us and the POUM. The POUM's initial mistake of sanctifying unity with the Mensheviks culminated in the betrayal of the People's Front and the participation in a bourgeois government and the paralysis of the revolution and its defeat.

You say Nin was as good a revolutionist as we. No! Trotsky said he was a revolutionist subjectively, and an honest and a most honorable man. I knew him myself personally from as far back as 1922 when we sat together in the Executive Committee of the Red International of Labor Unions in Moscow. Trotsky said the trouble with Nin was that in a revolutionary situation, although he understood Marxism in all the formulas, he could not rise above the level of Martov. He couldn't be like Lenin. He had the Menshevik disease of explaining perfectly in classical terms all the formulas of Marxism, but when the time came to act he was paralyzed by that fatal sickness known as Menshevism, indecision, lack of confidence in the party and in the class. Enough of that.

Now, in viewing the coming crisis we do not want to create the impression—and I hope we have not done so—that the crisis will come sooner or later and this will produce the revolutionary situation and that will solve everything. Far from it. It is not even the crisis alone that creates the revolutionary mood of the masses. Trotsky explained brilliantly in his speech at the Third World Congress of the Comintern, it is neither crises nor prosperity that revolutionizes the working class, but the constant and abrupt changes. From steady work and the habitude of fairly good standards of living, a sudden crisis throws them out of work, they are hungry, cannot find food for their families; then they go through a period of revival of industry, and they go into that revival of industry with all that resentment upon them and they translate their resentment in the form of strikes and union organization. And then another crisis. It is the constant changes, the insecurity of American capitalism, that is the Marxist guarantee of the rapid revolutionization of the American working class. And from that everything depends on the party. Everything depends on the party. And why are we assembled here in convention, and what are we working night and day for, and what have we been working for, some of us, for years and even decades, except to build a party to take advantage of the revolutionary situation which will be created by the crisis of capitalism? [. . .]

Now, what is your perspective? Isn't that a brutal question to ask? The Socialist Workers Party is no good. The program is wrong, misapplied. We don't know politics. The leaders are no good, and are scoundrels into the bargain. The cadres are no good. The membership is politically inexperienced and is doped up by the leaders. And if this cadre is no good and there is no hope for it because it is too small and too miserable, what are the prospects of your cadre, which is even smaller and almost as miserable? Where then are your hopes of a revolution and what confidence can anybody place in you when you say, of course, of course, we all believe eventually in the revolution? Eventually is a long time. The ultimate goal—why even Bernstein in the Second International believed in the ultimate goal of socialism, only he said the movement is everything and the goal is nothing.

They misunderstand everything, these clever lads, including us. They can't even analyze us correctly although they see us every day, even more than they want to. They try to prove we are sectarians. If that were true, out of this party and out of this convention there would surely be some people able to detect it and turn against the leadership, because serious and even half-educated revolutionists know that sectarians cannot make a revolutionary party successful.

Their analysis is false. They say that we are ignorant and stupid, while they on the contrary are very clever and well-educated. Now of course, far be it from me to say whether this part of the analysis has a grain of truth in it or not. But all I can call to the attention of these people who think the function of leaders is to teach and never to learn from the party is that they have been talking to the party for three years and now they are in the presence of about 500 of the leading activists of the party and they have been talking now for two days. And the party, out of the immense audience that we have here, has only given them three votes for their cleverness and their education, and those are three votes they had before they came here—and three votes they are fully entitled to, by God.

Now what kind of a reflection on the intelligence of this audience is it if you can't convince one of them that you are the clever boys and we are the dopes? [. . .]

Morrow condemns us of violent demagogy. I believe there is no one so reprehensible as a leader who will resort to demagogy to mislead and disorganize the workers. I say the one thing the workers have a right to demand of the leaders is that they at least tell them the truth as they see it and not play upon their prejudices, but fight them and try to overcome them. But you add to your accusations against us that we have a politically inexperienced membership that cannot distinguish between being doped up and being given a correct analysis of economy, of politics. And by that you hurl a whole bucket of filth in the face of this whole convention and the whole party. You show that contemptible ingrained snobbery of the petty bourgeois, colored with contempt for the workers and an ingrained conviction that they can never learn, that they are a different order of beings and cannot know or do anything unless somebody tells them. Do you call that a Marxist ideology?

Marx said the workers will conquer the world and he said the work of the emancipation of mankind will be the work of the working class itself. Marx was no snob. He counted not only on the contradictions of capitalism, but he counted on the working class for intelligence enough to do it. And one who has no faith in the intelligence of the workers is no Marxist. [. . .]

The condition for the growth and development of our party in its present form and with its present magnificent prospects, the condition for that was a political one. That was the definitive fight with the petty-bourgeois opposition in 1939 and '40 and the definitive break with the Menshevism of this group. Our slogans in that fight, you will recall, were two: One, programmatic orthodoxy. Second, proletarianization. The fight won us the victory for the program and that victory created the conditions for the proletarianization of the party. And what a different party we have now from then. When you hear the trade union report, then you will begin to get an intimation of what really magnificent work has been done and what progress has been recorded in the recent times in the basic organizations of this country, the trade unions. Trotskyism in the early part of its existence in this country was cursed and held back as a result of historical conditions, by its predominantly petty-bourgeois composition. [. . .]

The very first test of pressure of the war was sufficient for them to return to bourgeois democracy by way of the Shachtmanite halfway house. That is the role Burnham and Shachtman play. They provide a halfway house for people who are leaving the movement—teachers, groups of writers, and professionals of various kinds. Henry Luce has a whole stable full of ex-Trotskyists in his editorial stables and I wouldn't be surprised if it would grow bigger rather than smaller. You can't build a party on a petty-bourgeois composition if you mean a revolutionary party. Now let that get saturated in the flesh and blood of our party. The social base of the intellectual is such that it is only the exceptional individual who can make the complete and inevitable break with his social background and identify himself with the proletarian revolution for life or death. The intellectuals of the passing generation certainly made a sorry showing. Judge them, workers, look them over, don't be bluffed by them.

Nobody is any better than a revolutionary worker and the very idea that was propounded two years ago that someone who has the virtue and merit of writing novels is entitled to give advice to our party on how to conduct its politics—that whole business of slavishly backing down has got to be burned out of the proletariat before it can become self-sufficient and really revolutionary.[139]

Why should we kowtow to them and why should we take any guff from them outside the party or inside the party? Look at the showing they made. Look at that enormous mass of formerly radical intellectuals in New York, from Max Eastman and Sidney Hook through James Burnham to Solow. It would make a roster almost as big as those sitting here at these tables, of people who went back like whipped curs into the camp of American imperialism.

Look at that house of prostitution called the *New Leader*. Why it is full to overcrowding of inmates who came from our party and our periphery.

Sometimes a whole generation of workers look for leadership. They have to find it in their own ranks, in their own party, and they get it nowhere else. These teachers and these journalists, these professors, they promised to teach and instruct the youth, but they lied and betrayed the youth and they are entitled to no confidence. The lost generation—that is a euphemism. The New York intellectuals are a generation that is rotting away, that hasn't a bit of hope or capacity or fighting optimism in it.

The workers on the contrary have shown in the same period, as I recited yesterday, progress and militancy and hope for the future. Marx was vindicated surely when he said the working class is the only revolutionary class in society. That is the motive force. Lean on that for organization and the revolution will be secured. This party must be firmly built on a proletarian Marxist program and a proletarian composition. And that is not easy to do.

If you will permit me to take an extension of time. We have been listening to this sniveling for three years and we didn't say too much in answer. It is a hard job, comrades, to build a revolutionary party. As a matter of fact, it is the hardest job in the world. The building of a revolutionary party of the workers on a mass scale is nothing less than the unsolved problem of humanity. The only thing that has stood between the transformation of society in the whole of Europe from capitalism to socialism years ago was the nonexistence of a strong enough Marxist revolutionary party to lead the masses in the great opportunities that were presented to them. And that is testimony to the fact that it is a hard job and that it takes a lot of time and it takes intelligence, it takes thought and study and work and sacrifice, and in addition to that it takes courage and faith. And if you haven't got all of these qualities you have no right to burden down the party with your presence. You are an obstacle, not a help.

The great unsolved problem of humanity is the building of a Marxist party fit and capable of leading the masses to the socialist revolution. We have undertaken to solve this problem and we fear no obstacle from the outside, nothing that they can do can break us, nothing they can do can stop us. Individuals may falter here and there but the party as a party is too firmly built now to be broken by any force the bourgeoisie can hurl against it. And if we won't permit it to be broken from the outside, we will not allow anybody to disrupt it from the inside. [. . .]

Now, what tasks specifically flow from the theses which we are adopting today with such unanimity? It follows from this that the party leadership must reorganize in a sense all of its propaganda work. It must begin now a new, organized system of propaganda, something like that we undertook at the origin of our movement in 1928 when we reconstituted all of our activity around the basis of expounding the fundamental principles of the Left Opposition which we discovered and hadn't known before. [. . .]

Now, on a higher level as the party is making several big changes from propaganda into mass action, we are going to take the theses to inspire and infuse all the branches and all the study circles and schools of the party with the education of the membership old and new, on the basis of the theses; classes illustrating and elaborating the theses, supplying facts and figures to prove all the points. And imagine that! What a grand undertaking this is for the young Marxists in the party. We want and we need young intellectuals, college-trained boys who have not been. . . .

But we don't want any of the old and the worn-out, the tired and the weak and the cowardly. We want to catch them young before they are spoiled and make party intellectuals out of them, party professionals, and tell them we value to the highest degree specialized college training and education. And we want them to come to us young and new and full of hope to help us in our propaganda work, to dig up material to confirm this point, diving into the archives and into the statistical volumes to confirm and elaborate another point. We want to catch them young and new and full of hope at that stage in their life which is so critical for everyone when the young man and the young woman ask themselves, What is the meaning of life? What is the purpose of life?

And if the party can find them when they are putting that question and give them the answer, that the meaning of life and the purpose of life in this epoch is the union of one's energies and talents with the working class, which is the great motive power of salvation—that is the way Trotsky taught us to think of the party. He said, the party takes us, each of us, in our individual weakness and helplessness and combines us with others in the party and thereby the talents of one are added to the talents of others, hundreds of thousands, and becomes a gigantic collective intelligence that can deal with every problem. The party, he said, without the party in this epoch we are nothing, but with the party we are all and with the party we can storm earth and heaven.

And who will make that party? Will somebody make it for us? Will we find it somewhere already created? Will it spring up spontaneously? In other words, the great unsolved problem of history—will somebody else solve it for us? No, said Trotsky, in his great speech to the Tenth Anniversary Celebration of our party and for the Conference of the Fourth International.[140] He said, "Nobody will prepare it and nobody will guide it but ourselves." If we have the confidence and the faith and the courage to do that, then we will build the party and the party will lead the workers and the workers will make the revolution and nothing will stop them.

PROTEST PARIS POLICE ATTACK ON INDOCHINA DEFENSE RALLY[141]

December 27, 1946

The following message was sent to French Premier Léon Blum. It was published in the January 4, 1947, Militant.

Léon Blum, Premier
Paris, France

Sir:

The Socialist Workers Party vigorously condemns the action of your government in arbitrarily banning and breaking up a December 6 mass meeting in Paris, organized by the Parti Communiste Internationaliste (French section of the Fourth International) to protest the slaughter of the Indochinese people by French imperialism.

When the police charged into the crowd, a number of North Africans and Indochinese as well as members of the PCI suffered injuries and were arrested. This brutal police action shows what contempt the present French government holds for democracy.

Equally outrageous was the "legal pretext" for prohibiting the protest meeting—ordinances dating back to Napoleon Bonaparte and to Napoleon III, predecessor of the modern fascist dictators. These laws, enacted for the express purpose of violating democratic rights, are no less reactionary today when employed by a government in which the Socialist and Communist parties participate.

The denial of the workers to assemble and make public their grievances can pave the way for a fascist regime or military dictatorship in France.

The Socialist Workers Party is calling this attack on civil liberties to the attention of the whole American labor movement.

The interests of the American workers are involved wherever a threat to democratic rights occurs. The American workers are gravely concerned about the attack on democratic rights in Paris and about the brutal repression of the heroic Indochinese struggle for independence.

James P. Cannon
National Secretary
Socialist Workers Party

Laura Gray

STOP THE ATTACK ON THE FRENCH TROTSKYISTS!

January 31, 1947

The following letter to the French government was sent to protest continued repression of attempts by the French Trotskyists to hold public meetings in defense of the independence fighters of Vietnam. It was partially quoted in the February 8, 1947, Militant. *The text is from Cannon's archives.*

Paul Ramadier
Premier of France
Paris

The Socialist Workers Party vigorously condemns and intends to give the widest publicity to the repeated attacks by your government on the Parti Communiste Internationaliste, French section of the Fourth International, its right of assembly, and its right to publicly uphold the cause of Indochina's independence.

On December 6 your government banned a meeting in defense of the Vietnam Republic called by the PCI and then launched your police against the thousands of French and colonial workers there, beating and arresting numerous participants.

Since then we have learned that on January 24 your government again banned a meeting on Indochina called by the PCI at the Salle de la Mutualité. Three hundred police agents again forcibly dispersed the audience, beating up and arresting several members of the PCI, including its general secretary, Yvan Craipeau.

On behalf of the American workers opposed to the imperialist expedition against the Indochinese masses, we demand the immediate release of all PCI members and supporters of

Indochinese independence, and an immediate cessation of attacks on their right of assembly and the most elementary democratic liberties.

James P. Cannon
National Secretary
Socialist Workers Party

A NEW TURN ON THE QUESTION OF UNITY[142]

February 8, 1947

The following letter was sent to members of the SWP National Committee in preparation for a plenum of the committee to be held in New York February 15-16. It was later published in Internal Bulletin, *vol. IX, no. 2, May 1947.*

Dear Comrades:

New developments which will have to be considered by the plenum, to be held February 15-16, are as follows:

1. *Workers Party.* The decisive action of our party convention in rejecting and closing discussion on the previous unity maneuver of Goldman-Shachtman, together with the expulsion of Morrow, produced big repercussions nationally and internationally as was to be expected. Now that it has been made perfectly clear by the resolute action of our convention that the SWP will tolerate no more monkey business with discipline, and that unity maneuvers are firmly rejected and excluded for the future, new developments on a new basis are shaping up. As you know, we have had a visit from Ted [Sam Gordon] and Gabe [Michel Pablo]. Together with them we have discussed and prepared some new moves designed to put an end to all ambiguity and bring all questions to a head and a definitive settlement in connection with the world congress, now definitely scheduled for the fall.

Prior to the arrival of Gabe and Ted we had had a meeting with Johnson. He affirmed his complete political solidarity with us on all questions except the Russian question,[143] and his earnest desire to be given a formula that would facilitate his struggle and open the road for unification. At the same time, Shachtman had announced his wish to participate in the world congress and in the international discussion preceding it, and wanted to know under what terms and conditions this could be granted.

The information furnished us by Gabe and Ted made it clear that the genuine orthodox Marxist tendency is assured of a firm majority at the congress on all of the disputed questions. Previous experience and discussion has prepared this victory of authentic Trotskyism in the world movement. In the course of discussion we found complete agreement between ourselves and Gabe on all questions concerning the world congress. We agreed to stand jointly for the following program: 1. The congress should not only confirm the orthodox line as laid down in the previous documents of the preconference and the IEC, and now brilliantly amplified in the new theses of Germain on the Russian question, but should specifically condemn the theories of bureaucratic collectivism, national revolution, retrogressionism, and the conception of the Stalinist parties in capitalist countries as non-working-class bodies.

2. All discussion should be closed on these questions once they are decided by the congress, and may not be reopened without the authorization of the IEC. Membership thereafter should be conditional on acceptance of the political and organizational decisions of the congress and disciplined application of them in all political activity.

3. On the SWP-WP question, the congress should condemn the political line developed by the WP, condemn the split of 1940, the maneuverist character of the unity proposal, and the Goldman split which accompanied it.

Assuming the victory of this program, which seems to be absolutely assured, the question then arose as to what attitude shall be taken toward those elements inside the ranks of the International who hold one or more or all of the views which the congress will reject and condemn. Following the tradition of our movement, as well as political realism in the present situation, we could only arrive at the following conclusion: Those who *accept* the decisions of the congress and obligate themselves to carry them out in practice, may remain in the organization. Those who refuse to accept the decisions are to be automatically expelled. Any who may "accept" the decisions with tongue in cheek and then proceed to violate them, shall be expelled.

The next question then arose: what conditions if any can we offer to those groups formally outside the organization, including the WP or any section of it, who express a wish to participate in the world congress and the international discussion preceding it? On this point we worked out the following formula, in line with the already adopted resolution of the IEC:

Unaffiliated groups desiring to participate in the international discussion prior to the congress must give a *written* undertaking to recognize the authority of the congress and pledge themselves in advance to accept its decisions on both political and organizational questions. On that condition they may participate in the international precongress discussion and may have fraternal representation at the congress, without voting rights.

This formula was presented by Gabe to Johnson and promptly accepted by him. At the same time he announced that he would accept it and carry it out in any case, regardless of the position taken by the WP majority or any of its other factions.

Gabe then presented the same formula to Shachtman. Shachtman showed him a letter already drawn up by their PC which requested the right to participate in the precongress discussion but which stated the WP could not in advance agree to accept the congress decisions. However, after a six-hour discussion Shachtman announced that he would accept the conditions, and invited Gabe to attend a meeting of the PC of the WP where the question would be laid before them. At this meeting of the PC, after a long discussion and many protests from the right wing against the harshness of the terms and unavailing proposals for amendments or modifications, this body also voted unanimously to accept the conditions and to call a plenum within forty-eight hours to consider the matter.

This plenum of the WP, called on such short notice, was held Wednesday night. There the same process was repeated. Johnson aggressively defended the formula, condemned the split of 1940 and their whole course which had led up to the unity maneuver and second split of 1946, and announced that he would accept the conditions in any case. Shachtman, confronted by the resolute stand of Johnson, with the prospect of remaining alone in the party with the right wing, spoke for the acceptance of the terms. So also did Goldman. The right wing, protesting against the terms as a "capitulation" and characterizing the proviso that further discussion after the congress is to be prohibited as a "death sentence" on their tendency, finally voted to accept.

Yesterday we had another meeting with Johnson. He informed us that his faction has seventy members. They firmly agree with the SWP on all questions except the Russian question, and this they are willing to lay aside in order to concentrate all their efforts on hearty and loyal collaboration with us to build up the party in the USA.

Our PC has not taken a vote on the question. We are discussing the matter, both formally and informally, and plan to leave the decision open until the plenum convenes. I must tell you, however, that the majority opinion is definitely crystallizing in favor of going through with the proposition as outlined above. I personally am convinced that, taking everything into account nationally and internationally, it is a correct and necessary step and that we should proceed aggressively to its complete execution. Stein has the same opinion. Even those comrades in the PC who are inclined to emphasize the disadvantages and dangers of the proposition admit the difficulty of logically motivating a rejection of the formula, or of finding a better one.

I don't need to enumerate the negative aspects of a unification with the Shachtmanites, even under these harsh terms. They are quite clear to everybody. But the thing as a whole, in my opinion, is more of a plus than a minus; and this must determine our position.

It will be seen at a glance that this new formula is far removed from the original proposal of Goldman-Shachtman, which our convention correctly rejected. It is not the same thing at all. It is a new approach to the question, *made possible by the convention decision,* and is qualitatively different. *Then,* the Shachtmanites were the initiators, basing themselves on a disloyal faction in our own ranks and demanding a special bulletin of their own for *permanent* discussion after the unification. *This time,* after the original unity maneuver ended in a fiasco and boomeranged in the development of a strong faction in their own ranks putting the pistol of a split at their temples—this time, *we* are taking the initiative and we are laying down new conditions. The new conditions provide that all discussion of the disputed questions must be finished *before* the unification. Not only is there to be no special bulletin, but there cannot be any discussion whatever of the settled questions; and this must be agreed to and signed in advance, with the additional proviso that any violation of this agreement will result in the expulsion of the violators.

Under these conditions I think it would be very unwise for us to falter or haggle over the acceptance of the program, since it contains all the provisions which we could logically demand in the circumstances. That would be like chasing a streetcar that has already been caught.

There will be many difficulties and irritations in carrying out a unification after the seven-year fight, even if all the Shachtmanites come into the unification with goodwill. There will be even more irritations if a section of them come into the unification with bad will. On the other hand, if they come with goodwill and manifest it in a constructive attitude in the first period—and any other course would be absolutely suicidal for them—we have much to gain from the unification. The most important gain would be the elimination of the last remaining rival organization to the SWP as the organizing center of labor radicalism. After the elimination of the Lovestoneites, the Muste organization, the Socialist Party "Militants," Proletarian Party, the Oehlerites, the elimination of the WP as a separate organization—after a seven-year fight—would clear the field entirely for the SWP. This could not fail to make a strong impression on the minds of all radical workers, including the dissident Stalinist workers, and attract them more strongly to us.

At the same time, the unification would be a powerful blow against centrifugal tendencies throughout the International, and aid the International leadership in the task of unification and concentration. This would create the possibility for the first time of introducing a serious discipline to regulate and control the irresponsible individuals and groups who have been running wild up till now.

These, in my opinion, are the two main considerations. They far outweigh the minuses, serious and important as the latter may be. But if everything goes well there can be other pluses too. The WP is a much smaller organization than ours—they have about 400 members—but we shouldn't conceal from ourselves the fact that along with quite a number of fast-talkers and "discussion" fanatics, they have also some good activists who seriously want to build a revolutionary party to fight American capitalism. Johnson assures us there are many more than we are inclined to think. In any case, we should open the door for them and give them one final fair chance to integrate themselves in the party. A serious thought should also be given to the leadership of the WP. We know their faults and weaknesses, and their mistakes which have often amounted to crimes—all of which, from a political point of view, comes under the general head of *centrism*. But with the knife at their throats, confronted with a virtual ultimatum: capitulate to the Fourth International or definitively break with it, they decided—"under protest"—to capitulate. This action speaks for them, not against them. It entitles them also to one more chance—and a fair chance—to find a way to collaborate with us. This must be said in all seriousness if we are truly serving great political aims and are capable of subordinating everything, including personal sentiments, to the service of these aims.

2. *Morrow.* Following from the above, the same formula offered to the Shachtmanites should logically apply to Morrow. Having been expelled by the party convention, he naturally cannot be readmitted into the SWP by the plenum. But if he signs an undertaking to recognize the authority of the world congress and pledges himself to obey its decisions, he also should be given the opportunity to participate in the international discussion. We can easily agree to this, even though it is a bit "irregular." This concession on our part would help the International leadership to disarm the opportunist and unprincipled elements who represent our expulsion of Morrow as a device to deprive the right wing of an ideological representative in the discussion before the congress. But looked at properly, it is no concession at all. The more Morrow writes and the more his writings are translated into other languages, the simpler everything will become for the comrades in other countries.

* * *

We think it would be a good idea for the out-of-town plenum members to bring this communication to the attention of the leading comrades locally and have a preliminary discussion with them, so that the plenum can have clear reports of the first reactions of the party comrades to the new developments. It goes without saying that the new proposals, if endorsed by the plenum, must be submitted to the party membership for discussion and eventual decision by a special party convention.

Fraternally yours,
Martin [Cannon]

RESOLUTION ON UNIFICATION WITH THE WORKERS PARTY

February 16, 1947

The following resolution was drafted by Cannon, Morris Lewit, and George Clarke and adopted by a plenum of the SWP National Committee held in New York, February 15-16, 1947. It was circulated in mimeographed form to members of the SWP. The text is from the minutes of the plenum.

The plenum of the National Committee of the SWP, meeting in New York, February 15-16, considered a written declaration from the National Committee of the Workers Party, received February 10. In this declaration the leaders of the Workers Party obligate themselves and their organization, without qualifications or conditions, to accept the decisions of the extraordinary party convention projected for the coming fall and to obey its discipline politically as well as organizationally.[144]

This written declaration provides a realistic basis for the consideration of unity between the SWP and the WP. If it is carried out in good faith, it will make a unification of the two organizations possible and desirable, and give ground for confidence that the unification would lead to the strengthening of the party and the building up of the party. The National Committee has unanimously voted in favor of unification on this basis and is hereby submitting the proposal for the discussion and consideration of the party membership, with the definite recommendation for the unification.

In view of the disciplinary obligation undertaken by the leaders of the WP, the plenum on its part agrees that they shall have the right to participate in the preconvention discussion in a special discussion bulletin which will be distributed to the members of both parties. If the National Committee of the WP wishes to expedite matters and effect the unification even before the holding of the extraordinary convention, the NC of the SWP will be agreeable to the proposition and will favor an earlier unification on the condition that the discussion of the disputed questions in the party branches be completed before the unification.

As to the specific form of the proposed unification, the National Committee of the SWP will recommend that all members of the WP as of February 10, 1947, be admitted into the ranks of the SWP as a body without prejudice or discrimination, and that this proviso be extended to include any new members who may be recruited by the WP in the meantime, provided they have not been previously members of the SWP.

The Political Committee of the NC is fully empowered by the plenum to proceed with the implementation of this resolution and to take all the necessary practical measures, in cooperation with the leadership of the Workers Party, to organize joint activities with the WP and to work out all the organizational details of the unification, subject to the final approval of the party membership.

Joseph Hansen

Arne Swabeck and James P. Cannon, 1949.

REPORT TO THE NEW YORK MEMBERSHIP

February 17, 1947

Following are excerpts from Cannon's report to the New York membership of the SWP on the National Committee's discussion of proposals for unity with the WP at its February 15-16 plenum. The text is from a previously unpublished and uncorrected stenogram.

The results of the plenum on the point under discussion tonight have been concretized in the form of a resolution, which I take it you have all read, on the question of unification with the Workers Party. My assignment tonight as reporter from the plenum is to give you some information about the new developments and the reasons for the action taken by the plenum. In general the resolution speaks for itself and my report will be a sort of amplification.

The fight between our tendency and the tendency represented by the Shachtmanites had been smoldering in the party for a long time before it broke out into open struggle in September 1939. At the very beginning of that fight we and L. D. Trotsky with us characterized it as a struggle between the proletarian and the petty-bourgeois tendencies in the movement. Put in other, more precise, political terms, we called it a struggle of orthodox Marxism against revisionism. That characterization was completely correct when we made it then and its correctness was never clearer than it is today after seven years, nearly eight years, of struggle. [. . .]

Evidence of how deeply saturated our party was with the conception that the Shachtmanites represented a petty-bourgeois tendency and that ours was a proletarian Marxist tendency is indicated by the almost reflex action of the overwhelming majority of the party at the very first beginnings of the Morrow-Goldman opposition. The convention of 1944 in New York, held in the absence of many of the most prominent leaders, who were in prison, condemned the line of Goldman and Morrow in its very first tentative beginnings on the ground that it represented a tendency toward conciliationism with the Workers Party. [. . .]

We were finally confronted with the full-blown proposal of the Morrow-Goldman faction of unification with the Shachtmanites. [. . .] Bolsheviks are capable of all kinds of organizational adaptations and the justness of violating even precedent in the organizational field if it will serve political ends. So we did not reject it. We wrote a letter in reply to the Shachtmanites and we said for our part we think unity would be a good thing if it leads to the strengthening of the party and the building up of the party. On the other hand, a unification that would lead to a new faction fight and a split would be a bad thing for the party. [. . .]

In the course of the very first discussions with them through the joint committees you know they presented a demand that they should be allowed the right of an independent organ of their own controlled by their faction. The moment they said that, we understood that the unity was a false move. That was a proposal to perpetuate the faction in the party. That was a proposal to come into the party with a dagger pointed at its heart and the threat of a new faction fight and a new split. And we told them we didn't like that very much and we told them to think it over for a few days and we would meet again. We said to ourselves that if they really want unity in the spirit of our aim to strengthen the party and build up the party they will surely come into the next meeting and say, all right, we will withdraw this absurd, preposterous demand. Instead they came back to the second meeting and they said we have held a discussion in the Political Committee and we have unanimously reaffirmed our demand for an independent organ. So we passed a few jokes with them and called the meeting off.

And simultaneously with that, I don't know whether it was the same day or next day, we picked up a copy of the *New International,* with an all-out attack upon the Fourth International and its program and a truculent, belligerent demand that some of the basic principles of the Fourth International should be scrapped. Then we understood, of course, that the whole thing was unfeasible. [. . .]

The convention summed up the results of the whole experience of the unity maneuver of the Goldman-Morrow faction and made some decisions which introduced some new elements in the situation. One decision was the expulsion of Morrow from the party as a sabotager, disloyal, unworthy of being a member of our organization. The second was the rejection of the unity maneuver of the Shachtmanites and the order from the convention that this question should not even be discussed anymore now in our ranks. That put a stop to all possibility of maneuvering with unity between us and the Shachtmanites. And they drew the same conclusion. They said there is no more market here for a maneuver. They quit talking about unity. As a matter of fact they began to say also that unity is absolutely impossible.

Another new fact in the situation after the convention that crossed off all possibility of unity maneuvers was the resolution adopted by the International Executive Committee of the Fourth International a couple of months ago. I forget the exact date. And this was again a cruel blow to the maneuvering policy of Shachtman on the international field, because this resolution said the congress that is projected for later this year shall be open only to recognized sections of the Fourth International. Other groups who are for one reason or another not affiliated to the Fourth International must give a written undertaking to accept its decisions, the decisions of the congress, organizationally and politically, and must agree to this in advance as a condition for the consideration of their participation in the precongress discussion.

The whole thing was narrowing down and the WP was confronted on the national field with all doors locked against any kind of maneuverist unity. [. . .] The Shachtmanites, like these bizarre German politicians of the Three Theses, the IKD, etc., imagined the world congress was some kind of an international cafe, that one could walk in and take an aperitif and discuss the problems of the day there and if he didn't like what was said there he could walk over to another cafe with no obligation. We said no. This is not a cafe. This is an organization, a combat body, and if you want to participate in our affairs you must put yourselves under the discipline of our organization and agree with it as everybody else does.

Now those I say were the two new factors, the two new catalytic agents that brought everything to solution in the question of relations between the WP and the SWP. And in connection with the presence in this country of comrades who are authorized to speak for the International organization, it naturally arose that both we and the Shachtmanites, taking into account the new situation and the new development, had to take a position. For our part we thought the resolution of the IEC was a very correct and necessary one, completely in the tradition of our movement. [. . .]

I must tell you that we never did expect to make unity with the Shachtmanites in the near future. When we adopted our resolution at the convention we considered that a definitive settlement of the question for a long time to come, naturally not forever. We never discount the possibility of changes in our line or other people's. But as things stood at the time of our convention, we voted with complete unanimity, with the exception of two or three Morrowites, to close the door to any talk of unity with the Shachtmanites.

But as the time for the world congress developed, the Shachtmanites were confronted with a dilemma. You know they had been playing with theory for seven years. And that is more dangerous than uranium. Atomic energy is very good if you harness it and control it, but if you let it get out of hand it is terrible. Theory is still worse. It explodes. They started to play with a theory of bureaucratic collectivism. That is the theory that not the proletariat will be the successors to capitalism but some new class of bureaucrats and managers, as Burnham says. This is not a new theory; it was picked up by Burnham and then adopted in modified form by the Shachtmanites with relation to the Soviet Union. But anybody who knows anything about the theory of classes knows that it is impossible to confine classes to one country. If the theory of bureaucratic collectivism is correct, then, as Trotsky pointed out way back in 1939, if a new class is to be the successor to capitalism, a new exploiting class, and capitalism through its contradictions is not to culminate in revolution and the proletarian victory and socialism, then he said that means that a hundred years of Marxism has ended as a utopia. Then draw all the conclusions from that.

If that is true, give up the idea of Marxism, give up the idea of the proletarian revolution, and adopt a program of reforms to ameliorate the conditions of the slaves of the bureaucratic collectivist state. The Shachtmanites tried to play with the idea without drawing it to its conclusion. But as the years went by, this wing began to chafe at the national borders of the Soviet

Union and began to play with the idea of extending the theory of bureaucratic collectivism first to the occupied countries under the domination of the Red armies and later perhaps to the whole world. [. . .]

Now, in connection with the forthcoming world congress all these questions began to come to a head and the members of the Shachtmanite party had to begin to ask themselves, how, which way, shall we travel? Shall we draw the logic of our position to its ultimate conclusion and break with the Fourth International forever, or shall we turn back to it? That was presented to them in concrete terms when the representatives of the International laid on the table before them the conditions for participation in the forthcoming world congress.

Prior to that they had written a letter—they always write too much—stating that they wanted to participate in the international discussion before the congress and they wanted to have representation at the congress. And they agreed to all the provisions of the congress except one small point. They could not agree in advance to accept the decisions of the congress. And the International representative said, "The small point is the big one. That is what we want your answer to." And they were confronted, as I say, with the dilemma, an ultimatum—not in formal terms but in the essence of the matter it was an ultimatistic situation—yes or no. A break with the Fourth International and all further talk about a reconciliation with it or a turn in its direction.

We have been in a difficult situation in the course of the political struggle. We observed that ordeal of the Shachtmanites with considerable interest and, I must say, not entirely without some sympathy. Because you know, although we characterize their party as a petty-bourgeois tendency and as revisionist in its development, we never closed our eyes to the fact that these people had once been Trotskyists, or tried to be Trotskyists, and some of them were struggling valiantly against the revisionist, retrogressionist current, especially the Johnsonite faction in the Shachtmanites, [who hold a] rather false position, in our opinion, on the Russian question, but on all the other questions are very close to us and the Fourth International.

It was clear that the precipitation of this issue of acceptance or rejection of the conditions for participation in the congress would produce an eruption in the party—that was quite clear. And it was made known from the very start that the Johnsonite faction has been fighting, I say, a valiant fight for responsibility and loyalty to the Fourth International against the predominant tendency, which sneered at it and said it is dead, it is run by fools and bureaucrats and we should pay no attention to it. [. . .]

In my opinion that was a factor introducing the later developments. Shachtman thereby was confronted with the prospect of having his left wing torn off from his party. Not in the contemptible way that Goldman sneaked out of our party; a break of a faction bigger than the Goldmanites. In relation to the total membership of the WP, far greater than the miserable Goldman faction. And breaking under the banner of the Fourth International and leaving him alone with his right-wing, bureaucratic, retrogressionist, national democratic revisionists.

Now I don't want anybody to think that the National Committee of our party, either directly or by implication, had arranged the unity with the Shachtmanites. It is not so. There wasn't one in the leadership of our party who contemplated unity with the WP. We contemplated unity with the Johnson faction and were prepared to offer them the same conditions that the International laid down. But after Johnson had taken his position, a sort of chain reaction developed in the WP. Then Shachtman, who is not the centrist of the WP, but the center of the party which in all its wings is centrist, was confronted with the most important decision of his life. He knew what it meant. If he rejects the ultimatum of the IEC he has to definitively break with the Fourth International. No more maneuvers are possible. Maneuvers with the SWP were closed by the convention. Nothing further was possible on that road. A rejection of the conditions for participation in the congress would block all roads on the international field.

Shachtman, confronted with that dilemma, announced finally that he would accept those conditions even though he felt they were harsh and he would in writing agree to obey the decisions of the coming congress, organizationally and politically. And following him, the right wing, not having much else to do, did the same. Finally, [we have] the written statement of the whole National Committee of the WP. In this written declaration they say: We obligate ourselves to carry out the decisions of the world congress organizationally and politically. Now how could you characterize such a step on their part? I say you must characterize that as a step to the left—and a very decisive one. That at the last moment, almost, when they had to decide either to break with us and carry out the whole logic of their position and go to Social Democracy, or worse, into the open camp of the bourgeoisie, or come back and try once more to find a way to collaborate with the Trotskyists, they turned in our direction. And that is entirely in their credit, comrades, entirely in their credit. And if it is a capitulation, as they characterize it in their National Committee, and if, I say, it is a capitulation and change [. . .] that is a credit to them. To capitulate to the Fourth International—that is an honor to any revolutionist and a sign that he doesn't want to capitulate to the American bourgeoisie, that subjectively he still wants to be a revolutionist. That is the meaning of their turn.

Our committee, in discussing this at some length, called a plenum where the best representatives of the party from all parts of the country unanimously decided to recognize this as a new turn, to give them credit for the step they had taken, and to open the door once again for unity with the SWP on condition that they submit to discipline without any strings or qualifications, without any talk of an independent bulletin, without any faction fights, to come in to do work to build up the party. In that way, on that basis, we said we will receive them as brothers in a friendly way; we will give them fair treatment and fair representation, without discrimination. All of them can come without prejudice and discrimination. No vengeance will be taken on them, no spite work. On the contrary, to give them one more chance to find a way for collaboration with us.

That is now before us for discussion, before the party to discuss this. You know the plenum has no authority to decide it. You may begin discussion here tonight and in the branches. [There will be] no pressure campaign from the leadership, painting the thing up. It is a question that has many negative as well as positive sides, but in the opinion of the leadership of the party we have more to gain for Bolshevism, more to gain for the Fourth International, by accepting the proposition and trying the experiment, than by rejecting it. And that is why, if the party membership agrees with us, and the Shachtmanites carry out their agreement in good faith, there will be unity and in a very short time. The whole situation will be changed. And that is the way it is before you for discussion, with the definite recommendation of the National Committee that we should accept the situation and invite them to come into the party on that condition.

[A final comment] on Morrow: The plenum took into account the opinion of the International and adopted a resolution. In view of the fact that the expulsion of Morrow was being utilized by opportunist and unprincipled elements in the International to shift the international discussion from the theoretical and political to the organization plane and was representing his expulsion as a means of depriving the opportunist and unprincipled elements of an ideological representative, the plenum decided that while it cannot reinstate Morrow into the party, since it is a convention decision, it would have no objection if the international leadership permits Morrow to participate fully in the discussion prior to the congress so that the opportunist and unprincipled elements will not be deprived of their spokesman.

Trotsky, John MacDonald, and Jean van Heijenoort in Mexico during Dewey Commission investigation of Moscow trials, 1937.

JOINT STATEMENT ON UNIFICATION OF THE SOCIALIST WORKERS PARTY AND THE WORKERS PARTY

March 11, 1947

The following statement by Cannon and Shachtman was published in The Militant *of March 22, 1947, and in* Labor Action *of March 24.*

In 1940 an internal struggle in the Socialist Workers Party resulted in a split, the minority forming the Workers Party as an independent organization. The split has continued up to the present time.

Attempts made in recent times to find a basis for the unification of the two parties satisfactory to both sides, given the existence of the recognized disagreements on a number of important questions, did not meet with success and the discussions of the project were discontinued.

In recent days the question was opened again. New discussions between the leading committees of the two organizations have taken place. On February 10, the National Committee of the WP presented a written declaration in favor of unification. In this declaration the National Committee of the WP obligated itself to accept the decisions of an extraordinary party convention projected for the coming fall. This obligation was undertaken with the understanding that the WP, like the SWP, would have the right to participate in the preconvention discussion and to be represented at the EPC with full rights and in proportion to its numerical strength; and that fusion of the two organizations into a united party would be achieved. On this basis, the WP pledged itself to abide by the discipline of the united party, politically as well as organizationally, even if the EPC should adopt decisions which would place the members of the WP in the position of a minority.

The plenum of the National Committee of the SWP, meeting in New York, February 15-16, accepted this declaration as providing a realistic basis for unity and unanimously voted in favor of unification on this basis. In view of the WP declaration, the plenum of the SWP on its part agreed that the WP should have the right to participate in the preparatory discussion of the EPC in a special discussion bulletin which will be distributed to the members of both parties. This discussion is to be completed in the branches of the separate organizations before the final unification.

As to the specific forms of the proposed unification, it has been agreed by both sides that the members of the WP and the SWP, as of February 10, 1947, as well as all those recruited by each party subsequent to that date, shall be admitted into the ranks of the united party as a body, without prejudice or discrimination. However, while the unity negotiations are in progress, neither party will admit into its ranks any individuals or groups who are now or who have formerly been members of the other party, except by agreement. During the same period it is agreed that no exclusive measures will be taken by either party against any members or groups in its ranks in disciplinary cases arising out of the discussion on unity without consultation with the other party.

On the basis of the agreements and conditions outlined above, the two national committees are recommending the unification of the two parties. If this recommendation is approved by the membership of the two parties, as preliminary consultation indicates is most probable, the formal unification will take place as soon as the discussion now proceeding in the ranks of the two organizations is concluded. In the meantime a joint committee of the two organizations has been established, which is empowered to organize and arrange a program of cooperation and joint activities of the two parties in all possible fields of the class struggle, designed to lead up to and prepare the way for the formal unification.

James P. Cannon
For the National Committee
of the Socialist Workers Party

Max Shachtman
For the National Committee
of the Workers Party

RUTH FISCHER AND THE STALINISTS[145]

Published March 29, 1947

The following article was published in The Militant.

In the February 15 issue of *The Militant* appeared an editorial referring to Ruth Fischer and her testimony against the Stalinist GPU agent, Eisler, before the House Committee on Un-American Activities. The editorial was occasioned by the fact that the capitalist press, following the lead of the *Daily Worker,* had referred to her as a "Trotskyite." Since this is obviously not the case, the object of the editorial was to reject the false political identification of Ruth Fischer with the organized Trotskyist movement.

In the course of the editorial, Ruth Fischer was referred to, in passing, as an "informer." In view of the invidious connotation which is popularly attached to the word "informer," this was a most unfortunate and most inexcusable error. All the more inexcusable since we Trotskyists for many long years have been explaining the criminal character of Stalinism and its GPU murder machine, and have been denouncing it and "informing" against it, and alarming the workers of the world to its deadly menace. We have done this on every possible occasion and from every available forum, be it a public mass meeting, a Commission of Inquiry into the Moscow Trials, the capitalist press, parliamentary committees, or even capitalist courts. And we will gladly do the same again on any occasion where the opportunity presents itself.

In the long generations of the development of the world labor movement a well-recognized standard of ethics has made it a grave offense for representatives of rival parties, groups, or factions within the labor movement to submit their quarrels to the adjudication of bourgeois tribunals or to "inform" against each other. Every class-conscious worker, and even every ordinary trade unionist, instinctively recoils against such practices. But the professional killers of the GPU-Comintern apparatus, with the blood of so many tens of thousands of the best flower of the proletariat on their hands, have no right whatsoever to claim the benefits of this labor ethic when anyone points the accusing finger at them at any time or from any tribunal.

Ruth Fischer was right to protest against such a possible implication, in a letter to the National Committee of the SWP, and we sincerely regret the unfortunate and inexcusable incident.

Political assassination, the dread weapon introduced into the labor movement by Stalinism, is a standing threat to the free functioning and even to the very existence of every activist. All factions, all tendencies, all people who hope and strive for a better world must unite to expose and denounce such assassinations, no matter whom the victim may be at the moment. We have always taken this position, and not only in the case of Trotskyists, who contributed more than one drop to the rivers of blood shed by the Stalinist Mafia.

We did all we could to expose the Moscow trials and to defend the honor of their victims, including those who were not Trotskyists in the doctrinal sense of the word. Our party held a protest-memorial meeting for the martyred Andrés Nin, leader of the Spanish POUM, and spared no space in our press to accuse the Stalinist murder bund in the mysterious disappearance of the Socialist, Marc Rein, and the mysterious "suicide" of Krivitsky. And the columns of our press likewise remain always open to the Tresca Memorial Committee in its tireless efforts to keep alive his noble memory and track down his assassins.

There is no doubt whatever that Stalinism is the most formidable and dangerous enemy within the ranks of the labor movement and the greatest obstacle to the emancipation struggle of the workers. But who will defeat Stalinism, and what will take its place in those regions of the earth where it is consolidated in the form of state power? That is the question.

Ruth Fischer in the above-mentioned letter also protested against the reference in *The Militant* editorial to her "serving as a tool of American imperialism." If that is taken to signify any conscious and mercenary service to the American imperialist monster on the part of Ruth Fischer—as is the case with not a few professional anti-Stalinists—then such an interpretation must be emphatically disavowed. We know very well the long and honorable record of Ruth Fischer in the international labor movement, and the difficult conditions under which she has had to work as an emigré in wartime in America, and we do not wish to impugn her personal integrity in any way or to any degree.

Stalinism must be overthrown. By whom? Stalinism must be replaced wherever it is consolidated into a state regime. By what? These are political and not personal questions.

To put the issue positively: Either, the independent movement of the working class will defeat Stalinism and capitalism with it, and proceed to the construction of the socialist world order; or Stalinism, as represented by its state regime, will be overthrown by American imperialism in the course of its mad drive to reduce the people of the entire world to the status of colonial slaves. That is to say, those people who survive the atomic bombs, and the rockets, and the bacterial warfare, and the other harmless toys which the playful "democrats" at Washington are spending so many billion dollars to manufacture and prepare.

In our opinion, it is not enough to be an anti-Stalinist. One must also have a positive revolutionary program. In our opinion, those anti-Stalinists who do not unequivocally take the program of the independent movement of the workers, counterposing it to both Stalinism and capitalist imperialism, must inevitably fall into the service of the latter, regardless of what their subjective intentions may be. The question of Stalinism and how to fight it, and what to replace it with, is a problem of the greatest magnitude. It does not admit of any ambiguity.

This brief article has been written at the direction of the National Committee of the SWP to express its views. We hope to return to the question with much greater amplitude and detail in coming issues of *The Militant*.

Among other things, we want to explain why we make a distinction between the Stalinist workers and the unions led by the Stalinists, and the terrorist apparatus of the Comintern-GPU. We also want to show why we take flat issue with those "democrats" who, maddened by their hatred of Stalinism, would join the capitalist reaction in moves to suppress the Communist Party and deprive its members of their civil rights, thus preparing the destruction of the democratic rights of all workers' organizations and dissident groups.

C. L. R. James, 1938

Robert Chester

Carl Skoglund

George Novack

AMERICAN STALINISM AND ANTI-STALINISM

April-May 1947

The following articles, originally inspired by a disagreement between the SWP and Ruth Fischer over how to criticize Stalinism, became a major programmatic statement of the SWP on how to meet the deepening anticommunist witch-hunt. They were first serialized in The Militant *between April 5 and May 31, 1947, and then published as a pamphlet under the above title by Pioneer Publishers in July 1947. The text is from the pamphlet.*

1. Stalinism and Anti-Stalinism in Europe

Recent events afford us an occasion to present our point of view once again on the complicated and many-sided problem of Stalinism in the labor movement of the United States. The red-baiting drive on the one side, and the growth of anti-Stalinist sentiments in the ranks of the militant workers on the other, seem to require a reexamination of the question, and a more precise definition of the real nature of Stalinism. The blind fight against the Communist Party is unavailing. The workers must give thought to the why and how, in order to fight Stalinism in a manner that will serve their own interests. Otherwise they run the risk of falling into the trap of their worst enemies, who are currently raising a hue and cry against the Communist Party with other objectives in mind.

The Stalinist pestilence, like many other things good and bad, was imported from Europe; the American aspect of the question can be seen more clearly in its true light against a background review of the situation in the countries of Western Europe where Stalinism is now a burning and decisive question and is the subject of much discussion. For our part, we believe that a frank discussion among those anti-Stalinists who strive for the socialist goal should serve to clarify the issue and thus aid our cause.

It is known that we are and have been for a long time opposed to Stalinism, or to any conciliation with it whatever. We started on this theme more than eighteen years ago and have been hammering away at it ever since. We welcome cooperation with other opponents of Stalinism, but we believe that such cooperation can be fruitful only if there is some basic agreement as to the nature of Stalinism, and agreement also that the fight against Stalinism is part of the general anticapitalist struggle, not separate from it nor in contradiction to it.

So that there may be no misunderstanding, let us make our position clear at the outset. We believe that the greatest and most menacing enemy of the human race is the bipartisan imperialist cabal at Washington. We consider the fight against war and reaction in the United States to be the first and main duty of American revolutionists. This is the necessary premise for cooperation in the fight against Stalinism. Those who disagree with us on this point do not understand the reality of the present day, and do not talk our language.

An understanding of the perfidious character of Stalinism is the beginning of wisdom for every serious, class-conscious worker; and all anti-Stalinists who are also anticapitalist should try to work together. But anti-Stalinism, by itself, is no program for common struggle. It is too broad a term, and it means different things to different people. There are more anti-Stalinists now than there were when we started our struggle eighteen years ago, expecially in this country where Stalinism is weak and Trumanism is strong, and they are especially numerous in New York and not all of them are phonies. But very few of the current crop of vociferous anti-Stalinists have anything to do with us, or we with them. That is not because of exclusiveness or quarrelsomeness, either on their part or ours, but because we start out from different premises, conduct the struggle by different methods, and aim at different goals.

Many anti-Stalinists devote their arguments exclusively to the terrorist activities and totalitarian methods of the Stalinists. This is a rather common approach to Stalinism nowadays, but in our opinion it is an incorrect one. We believe it puts the question in too narrow a frame and provides neither an explanation of the monstrous phenomenon of Stalinism nor an adequate program by means of which the revolutionary workers can rid the labor movement of this plague.

Stalinism manifests itself in a totalitarian police state in the Soviet Union and a terrorist apparatus in the labor movement of the capitalist countries. But it is not only that. Stalinism has its social base in the nationalized property of the Soviet Union—the product of the great revolution. It is not the continuator and legitimate heir of Bolshevism, but its antithesis. The Stalinists, a privileged bureaucracy which fastened itself on the Soviet state in a period of its degeneration and decline, had to liquidate in blood virtually the whole generation of the original Bolsheviks, before they could consolidate their power.

But despite all the crimes and betrayals of the Stalinists, great masses of radical workers in Western Europe still identify them with the Soviet Union and, in turn, identify the latter with the revolution which gains attractiveness in their eyes the more that capitalism reveals its irremediable bankruptcy. Herein is the main secret of the malevolent influence of Stalinism in the European labor movement.

By far the greatest power of Stalinism derives from the illusion in the minds of the European workers that Stalinism means communism as represented by the great Russian revolution. They want the same kind of revolution, and they will not be freed from Stalinism until they are freed from the illusion that Stalinism can help them to get it. Most anti-Stalinists, especially the professionals, identify Stalinism with communism. This only serves to embellish Stalinism in the eyes of the radical workers, to reinforce their illusions, and to strengthen the position of Stalinism in their midst.

For there is one thing that the workers of Europe have very few illusions about, and that is capitalism. In this fundamental disillusionment lies the great hope for the future. Two world wars within one generation, with their sum total of forty million dead and uncounted wounded; the wholesale destruction of material culture in Europe; the crises, the unemployment, and insecurity between the wars; and the universal hunger, poverty, and misery at the end—all this has served to convince the masses of European workers in their bones that they have no further need of the social system which engendered these horrors and promises nothing better for the future.

The workers of Western Europe can see a way out only along the lines of socialism. They demonstrate their will to socialism at every opportunity, as in the revolutionary upsurge following the conclusion of hostilities, in the subsequent elections, etc. And when they think of socialism, they look to the East, not to the West. They have had victorious "democracy" brought to them twice already in the shape of guns and bombs from America and they don't want a third visitation of that blessing.

How explain the well-established fact that the workers follow the Stalinists in increasing numbers, while the Social Democratic parties are more and more pushed out of the labor movement and obliged to base themselves on a predominantly petty-bourgeois composition? It is absurd to imagine that this result is simply brought about by the terrorist activities of an army of GPU agents. No, the sweeping movement of the masses is to be explained by the fact that they think the Stalinists represent socialism more truly and more militantly than do the Social Democrats. Those who do not take due note of this phenomenon and make it the starting point of their tactical struggle may rail all they please against the Stalinists, but they will not defeat them in the European labor movement.

The illusions of the masses as to the real nature of Stalinism are continually nourished and kept alive by the Stalinist propaganda machines with their perfected technique of demagogy and mass deception. Stalinism is, first of all, a political influence in the labor movement in the capitalist countries. And it exerts this influence, primarily, not as a police force or a terrorist gang, but as a political party. The fight against Stalinism is first of all, and above all, a political fight. This political fight will never make any serious headway with the radicalized workers—and they are the ones who are decisive—unless it is clearly and unambiguously anticapitalist from beginning to end. No propaganda that bears, or even appears to bear, the slightest taint of Trumanism will get a hearing from the anticapitalist workers of Europe. That kind of "anti-Stalinism" which is currently popular in the United States is absolutely no good for export.

We have no reason to minimize the terrorist apparatus of Stalinism, unexampled in its magnitude and monstrousness in all history. It is a bloody and fearsome thing; we have paid enough in blood to know it. This terrorism must be exposed and fought. We must keep the pitiless light of publicity shining on it. But the exposure of the terrorist activities of the GPU is only one part, important to be sure, but not the most important part of the struggle against Stalinism.

Leaving out of consideration altogether the capitalist demagogues who exploit the fraudulent slogan "democracy versus totalitarianism" for their own imperialistic purposes, there are a great number of people who sincerely hate Stalinism for its violence and terror, its bloody and awful tyranny, its utter disregard for human life and human dignity. But in their revulsion against this horror—which does them credit, no doubt—they fall into the same basic error as that of the Stalinists themselves. They overestimate the power of naked force. The Stalinists think that violence can accomplish anything, and this fallacy will eventually facilitate their downfall. Many of their opponents likewise imagine that violence and terror are omnipotent, able to repeal the historical laws explained by Marx.

It is wrong to make a fetish of violence and terror, to see only the GPU and not the tens of millions of Communist and Socialist workers in Europe. It is fatally wrong to lose faith in the ability of these workers to overcome their illusions and take their destiny into their own hands. And it is criminal to proceed from these errors—as so many anti-Stalinists are doing in this country—to the dreadful and monstrous conclusion: The destruction of hateful Stalinism must be entrusted to Truman and his atomic bombs.

If Stalinism were merely a totalitarian police state in the USSR and a terrorist apparatus in the labor movement of the capitalist countries, then the struggle against the terrorists by publicity, exposure, and any other means at our disposal would be the main, if not the only, task. But the problem doesn't end there; it only begins. The real fight against Stalinism, the main fight, takes place on the political field. That is the way Trotsky explained the question and conducted his struggle. And that is why the Stalinists have always regarded Trotskyism as their most serious and consistent enemy. Trotsky's method must be the model for the revolutionary workers of the present day.

The influence of Stalinism today is stronger in France and Italy than in the countries of Eastern Europe which have experienced Russian occupation, and stronger by far than in the Soviet Union itself. To those who are prostrated before the fetish of police and gangster violence, who see the Stalinist police machine ruling supreme everywhere, over a vast domain in the East, this may appear as an astonishing, even as an absurd statement. But it is true and can be demonstrated.

Stalinism has a million members in the party in France, and controls the trade union federation with its six million members.

In Italy the number of party members is even greater. In these two countries it appears from all the evidence that Stalinism virtually dominates the proletarian sector of the population, along with a substantial section of the peasantry. From all reports, the Socialist parties in Western Europe—in France and Italy especially—steadily lose their working class support to the more radical-appearing rival. This tremendous mass influence of the Stalinists is not the result of police measures. In the main it is the product of the illusions of the masses, nourished and reinforced by the demagogy and deception of the Stalinist propaganda machine.

On the other hand, reports from Eastern Europe, where the first approaches of the victorious Red Army were greeted by revolutionary uprisings and mass acclaim, indicate that the workers have already been sadly disillusioned and the moral position of Stalinism has apparently been hopelessly shattered. The conditions are maturing there for the construction of genuine Socialist (or Communist) parties—anti-Stalinist as well as anticapitalist.

What, then, can be the real situation within the Soviet Union itself, after all the bitter, bloody years? Can the masses still *believe* in Stalinism? Are there any illusions left? The known reaction of the masses in the occupied territories should give us the answer. The very fact that the terror, instead of mitigating, grows worse from year to year, with the police apparatus swelling to ever more monstrous proportions—all this testifies not to the strength of the Stalinist regime within the country, but to its weakness, to its isolation and lack of mass support. The Stalinist regime in the USSR, isolated from the masses and ruling by terror alone, is weakest at the moment when it appears to be most secure. The strongest assaults of the Nazi military machine proved unable to bring about the downfall of the regime in the USSR from within. And that is convincing evidence, we think, that the Russian masses don't want liberation from accursed and hated Stalinism in the shape of capitalist restoration and the colonial dismemberment of the country. But one strong revolutionary demonstration from the outside can bring the whole regime, with all its apparatus of repression and terror, crashing down in ruins.

The salvation of the Soviet Union, or rather what is left of it, from the curse of Stalinism, depends in the first place on a strong revolutionary impulse from Europe or America, or some other part of the world. This impulse will come, we firmly believe, and this will change everything. This task of liberation belongs to the workers. It cannot be farmed out to their class enemies, the Anglo-American imperialist gang, in the hope that somehow something good will come from the greatest evil. To assign the task of liberating the Soviet Union and the labor movement of the West from Stalinism to Truman and his atomic bombs is to renounce faith in the future of humanity, to pass a premature death sentence on civilization.

We must go back to Marx, and reassert and be guided by his affirmation that "the emancipation of the working class is the task of the working class itself." Only on that basis can we make an effective common front against Stalinism and free the labor movement from its malign power and influence. Only on that basis can we see the future clearly and prepare for it.

In a personal letter a prominent European anti-Stalinist wrote: "I sincerely do hope that all anti-Stalinist elements of the socialist camp will be able to form a united front in the difficult days ahead."[146] We share this hope and heartily support it as a program, with only one explicit proviso: those whom we count in our socialist camp must be real socialists and not bourgeois agents masquerading as such, not ignoble stooges of Yankee imperialism, not "Truman socialists."

The revolutionary socialist movement in Germany during and following the First World War had to reconstitute itself in mortal struggle against those traitor socialists who had led the German workers into the imperialist slaughter—the "Kaiser socialists," as they were derisively called. The best hope today for the German workers—and not only for the German workers but for all the workers everywhere, all over the world—is that they will succeed by their own efforts and with their own strength in cleansing the labor movement of the influence of both the Stalin "communists" and the Truman "socialists." That is the way to victory and socialism. There is no other way.

2. The Communist Party and the Red-Baiters

The Communist Party, which served American capitalism well during the war, and in return basked in its favor, is getting into trouble again. The American Stalinists' support of the Kremlin, in the current diplomatic conflicts, is provoking retaliatory measures from the owners of America and their servitors. American Stalinism is under heavy attack along a wide front in the United States these days, and this time it is a real attack which takes on more and more the color of persecution. Red-baiting is the order of the day.

The powerhouse behind the assault on the Communist Party and its trade union positions and peripheral organizations is the National Association of Manufacturers. On the political field it is led, of course, by the Republican-Democratic coalition in Washington, as part of the propagandistic buildup to put the home front in shape for a war against the Soviet Union, which is being deliberately planned and prepared. Under this formidable leadership a broad supporting movement has been mobilized in the population generally, as well as in the labor movement. The capitalist press, the hierarchy of the Catholic Church, and the American Legion—the three most reactionary influences in American life—speak with one voice in support of the new holy crusade for "democracy against totalitarianism."

Almost the whole of the non-Stalinist trade union bureaucracy has taken its place in the campaign. The Association of Catholic Trade Unionists, a sinister, priest-ridden outfit which menaces the unions with a split along religious lines, is very active and aggressive in the pogrom against the "Commies." Drawing encouragement from the governmental campaign and the general reactionary trend in the country, the ACTU grows ever bolder and more brazen in its attempts to switch the allegiance of the progressive trade unions from Moscow to Rome. The rear of the anti-Stalinist united front is brought up by a vociferous assortment of New York Social Democrats and ex-radical intellectuals who do their best to supply the "ideology" for the frenzied campaign.

The current drive against the Stalinists is labeled "anticommunist" and every attempt is made to identify the two terms—Stalinism and communism—in the popular mind. This is the result of ignorance on the part of some and of deliberate deception on the part of others who know better, but in any case it is completely false. And that is the reason why the whole campaign, while it is undoubtedly weakening some of the organizational positions of the Stalinists and dislodging them from some strategic posts in the trade union movement, and furnishing not a few Stalinist careerists an excuse to run for cover, is actually strengthening the moral position of the Communist Party.

The ranks of the sympathetic radical workers and party

members are being solidified by the crude reactionary ballyhoo, and the support of new groups of workers is being drawn to the party which is made to appear as the persecuted revolutionary opponent of the big money sharks and their antilabor plus atomic war program. For example, the CP, according to the *Daily Worker*, raised a "defense fund" of $250,000 in less than twenty days. This important sum could properly be posted in the financial report of the party treasurer as a free donation from the associated red-baiters.

We Trotskyists, as everybody knows, are also against Stalinism and have fought it unceasingly and consistently for a very long time. But we have no place in the present "all-inclusive" united front against American Stalinism. The reason for this is that we are anticapitalist. Consequently, we can find no point of agreement with the campaign conducted by the political representatives of American capitalism in Washington, with the support of its agents in the labor movement and its lackeys in the literary and academic world. We fight Stalinism from a different standpoint.

We fight Stalinism not because it is another name for communism, but precisely because of its betrayal of communism and of the interests of the workers in the class struggle. Our exposition of the question is made from a communist point of view, and our appeal is directed not to the exploiters of labor and their various reactionary agencies of oppression and deception, but to the workers, who have a vital interest in the struggle against the capitalist exploiters as well as against perfidious Stalinism.

The problem of advanced and progressive workers is to learn how to fight Stalinism without inadvertently falling into the camp of capitalist reaction and thus hurting only themselves. For this it is necessary, first of all, for them to understand the question and to get a clear picture of the Communist Party, of what it used to be and how it came to be the hideous thing it is today.

The Communist Party of the United States originated as an honest revolutionary organization designed to serve the interests of the working class. By degrees, over a period of years, and from causes which are known and can be explained, this same party was transformed into an agency of imperialism in the labor movement—from communist to anticommunist. That is the truth of the matter, and that is what is really wrong with the

Communist Party, as we shall undertake to demonstrate. In doing so we hope to convince the militant workers that they must think and discriminate in taking their position on Stalinism and anti-Stalinism. It is a fatal error to think that rapacious American capitalism can be effectively fought under the banner of Stalinism. It is a no less fatal error for them to allow their hatred of the disruptive and treacherous methods of the Stalinists to push them into the camp of capitalist reaction.

The Communist Party of the United States is not a newcomer on the labor scene; it is already twenty-eight years old, and in that time has gone through a curious evolution. It was originally constituted by the revolutionary left-wing section of the Socialist Party. The struggle of this left wing for a revolutionary program, which they had carried on as a faction of the SP for a number of years, finally culminated in a split at the September convention in 1919. The new party quickly enlisted many of the most militant representatives of the IWW and other radical formations of the earlier day, and was in fact the legitimate successor and continuator of prewar revolutionary radicalism in the United States. The party unfurled the banner of the Russian revolution, which was the veritable banner of authentic communism; affiliated itself to the newly created Communist International founded by Lenin and Trotsky; and declared war on American capitalism.

The party from its very beginning encountered the fiercest persecution on the part of the "democratic" government at Washington. Those were the days of the notorious "Palmer raids." The members suffered wholesale arrests and imprisonments even before the new party had had an opportunity to properly constitute itself. In the fierce persecution of that period the party was driven underground and was compelled to conduct its activities illegally for several years. Under the fierce onslaught of reaction and persecution many fell by the wayside, but the main cadres of the new party stood firm, held fiercely to their revolutionary convictions, and gradually fought their way back into the open as a legal party.

Due to the inexperience of the leadership, numerous mistakes were made; but the early CP was an honest working class party, carrying on an uncompromising struggle against capitalism and defending the interests of the workers as best it could. In the early and middle twenties the party attracted to itself the best, most idealistic, and self-sacrificing of the advanced workers and soon became the recognized organizing center of American labor radicalism; while the Socialist Party fell into innocuous, senile decay and the trade union bureaucracy became more and more subservient to the capitalist exploiters and their governmental agencies.

But toward the end of the twenties, while the "prosperity" boom was still riding high, the picture began to change. This party, which began with such bright promise, whose founding members had been inspired by such honesty, courage, and idealism, eventually fell victim to the innumerable pressures of its hostile environment, as had happened with other workers' parties many times in the history of the international labor movement. Degeneration set in, and the party began to lose its revolutionary character. From an irreconcilable enemy of capitalism, the party was changed, by degrees and over a long period of time, into a treacherous and servile tool of capitalism.

This was shown most glaringly during the recent war, when the Stalinists became the worst jingoes and strikebreakers in the labor movement, and when Browder, then the official chief of the party by grace of Stalin, even went so far as to offer to shake hands with J. P. Morgan. The Communist Party became anticommunist, the most perfidious enemy of authentic communism.

That is what really happened. But the course of degeneration did not go unchallenged. The genuine communists, the Trotskyists, revolted against the degeneration and the betrayal as soon as it was first discerned; organized a determined fight against it; were expelled from the party in 1928 and organized a new movement on the old program, which is today known as the Socialist Workers Party. Thus the banner of communism, which the official Communist Party renounced, was not lost or surrendered to the class enemy. It was taken up and carried forward by the Trotskyist minority who believed then, as they believe now, that it is not the program of communism which has been discredited and refuted but only those who have deserted and betrayed it.

3. Why and How the Communist Party Degenerated

The degeneration of the Communist Party derives from the same source as the degeneration of their professional opponents, the labor fakers of the old school who are flanked by the New

York ex-radical intellectuals and "Socialist" or ex-Socialist labor skates. This source is the pressure of the capitalist-imperialist environment, which they lacked the historical foresight and the moral strength to resist. The Stalinists and the anti-Stalinists equally share an awe-stricken prostration before the seeming invincibility of American capitalism and a corresponding lack of faith in the proletarian revolution, in the power of the workers to save the world by reorganizing it on a socialist basis.

This delusion—and it is the most tragic of all delusions—is the main psychological source of all varieties of opportunism in the labor movement. It transformed onetime opponents of capitalism into its agents and servants. The opponents of Stalinism, with the exception of those who fight it from a revolutionary point of view, suffered essentially the same degeneration as did the Stalinists, from the same basic cause, and the degeneration is complete in each case, as we hope to demonstrate. This degeneration consisted in shifting their basic allegiance from one class to another.

The converted Stalinists campaign in every election, and all the year around, on their basic slogan: "Socialism is *not* the issue!" And if they have their way it will never be the "issue." The Social Democrats and the repentant ex-Communist and ex-Socialist intellectuals coyly refer to themselves nowadays as "liberals," although in truth they are not even very liberal. If they mention socialism at all it is only by way of satiric jest at those who still believe in it and still fight for it, and in sentimental recollections of the "follies" of their younger days.

As for the old-line labor fakers, if they didn't "degenerate" it is only because they have always been "labor lieutenants of the capitalist class," as De Leon called them, and didn't have to change much. But even many of them, if not the majority, began better than they ended. Not a few of them started out as trade union militants and picket captains who showed energy and courage in defending the immediate interests of the workers in struggles against individual employers. Lacking socialist consciousness and any broad and comprehensive view of the class struggle as a whole, they succumbed to the pressure of the class enemy even more easily than did the ex-Communists and ex-Socialists, but the end result is essentially the same: the transformation of working class militants into conservative bureaucrats who view the conflict of labor and capital as a struggle without a goal.

It may be maintained that we overstate the case or oversimplify it by thus seeming to identify two currents in the labor movement—the Stalinists and the anti-Stalinists—who appear to be always at each others' throats in the fiercest antagonism. But this contention can be granted only conditionally, and within very narrow limits which do not encroach upon the essence of the question.

It is not even correct to say without qualification that the two quarreling factions of traitors to the working class serve different masters. True, the immediate allegiance of the anti-Stalinists is to America's imperialist government of the Sixty Families, while the Stalinists are indubitably the direct agents of the Stalin regime in the USSR. But the Kremlin gang is itself an agency, and the most important agency, of imperialism in the world labor movement. That is its most essential role. The Stalinists hate and fear the proletarian revolution more than anything else, and their unbridled demagogy, their lies, their organized terror, their assassinations, and their organized mass murders have been employed to prop up decaying capitalism, not to overthrow it.

The Stalinists and the anti-Stalinists serve the same master—world imperialism—in different ways. Every labor bureaucracy has a contradictory nature. The Stalinist bureaucracy has its own special interests and seeks to serve them first of all, and this frequently come into conflict with the capitalist class which they serve fundamentally. The opposition of the entire American labor bureaucracy to the pending antiunion legislation in Congress is a case in point. But in the essence of the matter, in the great fundamental and irreconcilable conflict of historical interests between the workers and the imperialists, both the Stalinist bureaucracy and the other bureaucracy fight on the side of the capitalists and against the workers. The fierce struggle between them is a clique struggle, and not a principled struggle.

The anticapitalist "ideology" of the radical intellectuals and the "Socialist" labor leaders and functionaries was scarcely more than skin-deep to start with. Their transformation from fellow travelers of the proletariat into fellow travelers of the bourgeoisie was accomplished so quickly and easily and smoothly, under the first squeeze of real pressure with the approach of World War II, that it was hardly noticed by anybody. They hardly noticed it themselves.

The degeneration of the Communist Party along the same lines, however, was a far more serious matter. Here it was a question of changing the fundamental nature of a party that was genuinely revolutionary into its counterrevolutionary opposite. This took a much longer time and was unavoidably accompanied by the most violent and bloody convulsions.

Stalinism originated in the Soviet Union after the death of Lenin, when the retardation of the expected European revolution on the one hand, and the subsequent temporary stabilization of capitalism on the other, raised doubts of the revolutionary perspective. These doubts soon crystallized into a complete disbelief in the capacity of the workers in Europe and the rest of the world to overthrow capitalism. The privileged bureaucracy in the Soviet Union made this disbelief the basis of their policy. These Soviet bureaucrats felt impelled at all costs to secure their own privileges, enjoyed at the expense of the Russian masses, and decided to call that "socialism in one country." Like every other crystallized labor bureaucracy, they wanted above all to be let alone in peace and comfort regardless of what happened to the masses of the people in one country or another, or in all countries put together. A conservative program of narrow-minded nationalism, and of collaboration with the world of capitalist imperialism, was evolved by the privileged bureaucrats to express their moods and serve their special interests.

The same doubts and sentiments infected a section of the leading staffs of the Communist parties in the capitalist countries at the same time and from the same cause. The stagnation of the movement and the apparent—though only apparent—recovery and resurgence of the capitalist system from its wartime and postwar shocks and dislocations, seemed to empirical leaders to postpone the realization of the socialist program to the distant future. They mistook a temporary situation for a historical epoch. This created the conditions for the dry rot of bureaucratism to set in, even among the leading staffs and the paid party functionaries and trade union officials of the most revolutionary parties history had ever known, They began to visualize careers for themselves as functionaries of a party machine which existed for itself, that is, for them, and not for the purpose of organizing and leading a proletarian revolution.

But the transformation of the Communist parties in the capitalist countries, as well as in the Soviet Union, could not be easily or smoothly accomplished. A section of the leading staffs everywhere, supported by the most militant proletarian elements in the parties, retained the long view; they remained faithful to the revolutionary program and tradition and resolutely fought the course of degeneration. They were the first to stigmatize Stalinism, to analyze and expose its real tendency, and to declare irreconcilable war against it in the name of communism. And they have been its most consistent, most uncompromising opponents ever since.

This struggle, organized and led by Trotsky and supported by other authentic communists in every country in the world, against the degeneration of the Communist parties was a stubborn struggle, long drawn-out and irreconcilable, conducted with unexampled energy and courage. How could it have been otherwise? The fate of a revolution was at stake, and the leader of the fight was the greatest man, and the best man, of our troubled and stormy time.

Before they could succeed in substituting an essentially reformist program for the original program of proletarian revolution, and transforming the nature of the Communist parties accordingly, the Stalinist bureaucrats who had seized the apparatus of the Russian state and of the Communist parties had to resort to every kind of method alien to socialism and alien to the means required to serve the socialist end. They misrepresented everything, turned every question upside down, pictured the Left Opposition of Trotsky as counterrevolutionary and themselves as defenders of the Leninist doctrine. They slandered the Oppositionists in the press, which they had monopolized, and deprived them of the opportunity to answer. They abused the principle of party discipline, designed by Lenin to insure united action against the class enemy, and turned it into a trap for the Communist workers, a device to suppress critical opinion and free discussion within the party. They corrupted the parties by advancing subservient careerists and removing the independent-minded revolutionists from party posts. They abused the good faith of the Communist workers everywhere by confronting them with accomplished facts, and then compelling them to ratify the actions under penalty of expulsion as counterrevolutionaries and enemies of the Soviet Union.

All this did not suffice. The Opposition could not be terrorized and could not be silenced. One step followed another on the reactionary course with a fatal logic. Next came the wholesale expulsions of the leaders of the Opposition in Russia and in all the parties of the Comintern. After the struggle had raged for five years, the great majority of the original leaders of the Communist parties in almost every country, those who had founded the parties and carried them on their shoulders through their most difficult years, had been expelled. In place of the independent-minded revolutionary fighters who had created the movement in struggle, a new type of leader was installed, the type of functionary who looks to some power for instructions and does what he is told.

All this was not enough to complete the degeneration and transformation of the Communist parties. The revolutionary tradition was so strong, the Marxist logic of the Opposition so powerful, that opposition groupings kept rising anew. The parties had to be purged again and again. But the struggle did not end. The Stalinists then turned the fatal corner on the road of counterrevolutionary infamy from which there could be no turning back: the physical annihilation of the Communist Left Opposition. The Oppositionists in the Soviet Union, with Trotsky at their head, were arrested and imprisoned by the tens of thousands. When that failed to quell the Oppositionist movement, Trotsky was deported from the country in which he, side by side with Lenin, had led the greatest revolution in all history.

But the ideas of the Trotskyists were correct, and therefore could not be destroyed. The imprisonment of tens of thousands of the best Bolshevik fighters in the Soviet Union, the deportation of Trotsky from the country, and the expulsion and isolation of the incorruptible communists from the Communist parties in the capitalist countries, did not end the struggle of the Left Opposition (the Trotskyists) to correct the policy of the Comintern and turn it back on the Marxist road. They continued to fight as an expelled faction; and some of the richest Marxist literature in the entire history of the world labor movement was produced by the Opposition in that period, primarily by Trotsky himself.

In 1933, after ten years of unceasing struggle, came the great and final test, and the turning point in the tactics of the Trotskyists. The Stalinists surrendered the German working class to the Nazis without a fight—the greatest and most criminal betrayal in all history. Then it became finally clear beyond dispute that the Stalinist Comintern was corrupted to the core, and that its reformation was impossible. The Stalinists had gone over into the imperialist camp, as had the bureaucracy of the Social Democracy in 1914, only even more shamefully, more brazenly, and more criminally. The Left Opposition thereupon raised the banner of the Fourth International. The mortal struggle still goes on, no longer as faction against faction but as party against party. Since 1933 the Trotskyists have conducted their struggle on a worldwide scale as a completely independent movement, irreconcilably hostile to Stalinism as well as to capitalism. This is the most important struggle in the world, for its goal is nothing less than the socialist reorganization of the world.

4. The Crimes and Betrayals of American Stalinism

The Stalinist bureaucracy proceeded from its abandonment of revolutionary internationalism, and thereby of the most basic principle of Marxist politics, while still basing itself on an economic system created by a proletarian revolution. Beset by contradictions at every step, it gradually began to take shape as the greatest monstrosity the world has ever known.

The Stalinists raised the technique of falsifying, lying, and slandering to a degree unknown or unimagined by any precedent or contemporary political grouping based on privileges, none of whom have been strangers to these techniques. Obsessed by the mad delusion that ideas count for nothing and that physical force decides everything, they embarked on a campaign of bloody violence, mass murder, and assassination that has already taken its toll not in thousands or in tens of thousands, but in millions of human lives.

The whole generation of the original Bolsheviks were murdered in cold blood under cover of the Moscow frame-up trials. The whole of Russia was converted into a prison and a torture chamber where terror rules supreme. Many of the best leaders of the Fourth International outside Russia were assassinated by the agents of Stalin, including the leader and founder of the movement, the companion of Lenin, L. D. Trotsky.

Stalinism, through its reactionary policy executed by a murder machine, was mainly responsible for the defeat of the Spanish revolution. And this same Stalinism has acted as the gendarmerie of capitalism in suppressing by bloody violence every attempt at revolutionary uprising in those territories where its army penetrated in Europe, and by deception and demagogy in the other countries behind the Anglo-American lines.

The American Stalinists have not gone so far in violence only because they have lacked the power. But they have endorsed and defended all the crimes and betrayals of Russian and international Stalinism, and therefore fully share the guilt for them. The apologist and defender of assassins is himself an assassin.

But aside from mass violence and murder, from which the American Stalinists have been restrained only by their weakness and incapacity, they have committed enough crimes and betrayals in the United States on their own account to damn them forever in the eyes of the advanced workers. And these crimes, like the crimes of Stalinism everywhere, have not been directed against the capitalist exploiters, as many erroneously believe, but against the workers and the masses of the people. Their conspiracies have not been dedicated to the overthrow of capitalism, as stupid reactionaries allege against them, but to propping it up and striking against the genuine revolutionary movements aiming at the socialist goal. Roosevelt understood this much better than those color-blind aborigines, such as Bilbo and Rankin, and others of similar mentality in the labor movement, who see "red" whenever Stalinists are mentioned.

Roosevelt knew what he was doing when he made the war alliance with Stalin, and made no mistake in relying on him not to promote the proletarian revolution in Europe but to crush it in blood or balk it with demagogy. The suppression of Trotsky's book on Stalin during the war, by the pressure of the State Department on the publishers, was a tacit recognition of the counterrevolutionary services of Stalin. So, likewise, was the production, under quasi-governmental auspices, of the monstrous movie *Mission to Moscow,* a vulgar glorification of the Moscow frame-up trials and a defamation of their victims.[147]

The betrayals of the American Stalinists began, as betrayals of the workers always begin, with the revision, perversion, and eventual renunciation of the theory of Marxism, the only revolutionary, the only truly proletarian theory there is. Trotsky warned that the theory of "socialism in one country," first enunciated by Stalin in 1924 to justify the policy of national reformism, could only lead to social-patriotism in the capitalist countries. His warning seemed to many to be farfetched at the time, but it had a tragic verification in the United States, as everywhere else.

The new revisionist theories espoused by the American Stalinists, following the Moscow lead, ran so counter to the tradition and the socialist consciousness of the party membership that they could not be imposed on the party under conditions of free and democratic discussion, which had characterized the party in its early years. Party democracy had to be suppressed, and the Marxist dissidents who could not be silenced had to be expelled. Following the expulsion of the Left Opposition, the Trotskyists, in 1928, the right wing, led by Lovestone, who criticized the policy from another point of view, was expelled six months later. Thus the party was disrupted and converted into a bureaucratic caricature of the democratic revolutionary organization it once had been.

From the disruption of the party, the Stalinist bureaucracy, as one who says "A" must say "B," was obliged to carry disruption into the mass organizations and trade unions where dissidents and critics, including those who had been expelled from the party, also appeared. The Stalinists sought not to serve the mass organizations but to establish an iron-bound control over them, by any and every dishonorable means, in order to manipulate them at will. The Communist Party came to appear in the mass movement as an organization with special interests of its own to serve, and which served them ruthlessly and brutally against the interests of the mass movement. The Marxist axiom which says that "The Communist Party has no interests separate and apart from the interests of the working class as a whole," was turned upside down and made to read: "The working class has no interests separate and apart from the interests of the Communist Party."

The destructive weapon of expulsions and splits was carried over from the party into the mass organizations and the trade union movement. The Stalinists became hated and feared as *disrupters* who would stop at nothing to serve party aims dictated by the momentary interests, or supposed interests, of the Kremlin bureaucracy, which regulated the day-to-day policy of the American Communist Party as imperiously and automatically as a business firm directs the activities and policies of a branch office. Apart from everything else—and there is much else—the American Stalinists wrought untold damage in the trade unions and mass organizations of the American workers by their policy of ruthless disruption and suppression of workers' democracy.

The ultraradical policy of the American Communist Party, carried out from 1928 to 1933 by Moscow command, prompted the Stalinists to lead the advanced workers under their influence out of the established conservative trade unions to form separate, isolated "red" unions of their own. This insane policy, which had been so tragically refuted in life so many times in the past history of the American labor movement, was a crime against the working class, and especially against its progressive vanguard.

Following that, when Stalin began to seek a bloc with the bourgeois-democratic imperialists after Hitler came to power in Germany, the American Communist Party immediately followed suit with its infamous policy of the "People's Front." The slogan "class against class," which is the basic slogan of the workers' emancipation struggle, was discarded in favor of the treacherous formula of class-collaboration between the workers and their exploiters. The good and correct slogan of the united front of the workers was replaced by the slogan of an all-class political combination. The movement for an independent labor party, which had gained such a wide response in the progressive labor movement, was sabotaged and strangled.

The Rooseveltian Democratic Party, the other half of the bipartisan political mechanism of American capitalism, was recommended to the workers as their means of salvation in the struggle against this same capitalism. The CP bureaucrats did everything to dragoon the workers into supporting the capitalist Democratic Party, by hypocritical indirection in 1936, openly and directly in 1944.[148]

The earlier crimes of the Communist Party became swollen into betrayals, and the betrayals increased in magnitude and cynicism. After some obscene gestures at ultraradicalism, in accord with the Kremlin policy during the Soviet-Nazi pact, the American Stalinists promptly jumped onto the democratic imperialist bandwagon with the start of the Soviet-Nazi war. And after the entry of American imperialism, they became the most blatant jingoes in the American war camp. In return for Roosevelt's lend-lease to the Kremlin, the American Stalinists sold out the American workers in the most shameless and cynical fashion.

They were the loudest shouters for the no-strike pledge which shackled the workers and kept their wages frozen while prices rose during the war. In the strategic situation created by the labor shortage during the war, they viciously fought every attempt of the rank and file of the workers to use their organized strength to improve their conditions. They became militant advocates of "incentive pay" plans by which the workers could be speeded up more efficiently, while their solidarity in the shops was undermined. They became the most unabashed finks and strikebreakers in every labor dispute that flared up during the war; and they put the stool pigeon's finger on every revolutionist and every militant, howling for their arrest and prosecution.

The record of American Stalinism is indeed a record of crimes and betrayals. But here is the important point for militants to get clear in their heads: These crimes and betrayals have been directed against the interests of the American workers. It is on this ground and no other that the militant workers who are conscious of their own class interests must expose and fight them.

5. Stalinist Bureaucrats and the Other Bureaucrats

Some people, who carry their understandable and quite justified hatred of the Stalinists to the point of phobia, seem to overlook the fact that there are other evils in this world, and in the labor movement. They tend to limit their political program to the single simple formula: United front of everybody against the Stalinists. This does not state the problem correctly. And, moreover, it doesn't hurt the Stalinists. They can live and thrive on the indiscriminate campaign of "red-baiting" directed against them, and even gain a certain credit in the eyes of radical workers which they by no means deserve.

We define the Stalinists as a bureaucracy in the labor movement, with special interests of its own to serve. This bureaucracy seeks to gain, and does gain, special privileges at the expense of the masses of the workers, tenaciously holds on to these privileges and fiercely defends them, and is ready at any moment to sell out the workers to maintain them.

But the Stalinists are not the only bureaucrats in the labor movement. There are others, and in America the others are more numerous, and stronger. By the same token they constitute a far more useful instrument of the capitalists in preventing, restraining, and sabotaging the emancipation struggle of the workers. We refer, of course, to the old-line, conservative, trade union bureaucracy and its "progressive" and "Socialist," or ex-Socialist, appendages. This bureaucracy is also based on special privileges which differ from those of the American Stalinists mainly in the circumstance that their privileges are more extensive, more firmly established over a longer period of time, and more secure.

A vast horde of these privileged bureaucrats, ranging from the overfed business agents of a good many of the local unions to the high-salaried International officers, have raised themselves up on the backs of the workers. They enjoy standards of living which the workers cannot even dream of, and think and act more like businessmen than like workers. Most of them feel more at home in a conference with bosses and capitalist party politicians than in a meeting of rank-and-file workers.

The pickings of the conservative American labor bureaucracy are the richest in the world, and their consciousness is determined accordingly. When they fight it is always mainly for the defense of these privileges. Whether it is a fight to smash a rank-and-file revolt one day, by any and every dirty means of demagogy, expulsion, and brutal violence; or another day against antiunion legislation which threatens the existence of the unions and therefore their own basis of existence; or a third day against another union in a jurisdictional quarrel—their primary motivation is always the same: the defense of their pickings.

The good-standing members of this corrupt and reactionary gang are fierce Russophobes and red-baiters; and superficially they appear to be diametrical opposites of the Stalinists, whom they are attacking with exceptional energy at the present time in response to the Washington tuning fork. In reality, however, they are essentially the same type as the Stalinists. They are motivated by the same kind of privileged special interests and defend them with very much the same mentality. There are differences, of course, between them and the Stalinist bureaucrats, but the points of difference are superficial and secondary. The points of similarity are fundamental.

That is why they attack the Stalinists not for their crimes and betrayals of the workers but rather for their virtues; more correctly, what would be their virtues if the accusations were true. Leaving aside the stupid allegation that the American Stalinists are promoting and planning to organize a workers' revoltution to overthrow capitalism—a "crime" which they are not in the least guilty of—there is not much substance to the furious bluster of the reactionary red-baiters in the labor movement against the "Commies." These anti-Stalinists are guilty of the very same crimes as the Stalinists, and in every crucial test they find themselves allied with the Stalinists in the commission of these crimes against the workers. Strange as it may seem, that is what the record says, and the record does not lie.

We have already recounted the most important crimes and betrayals of which we accuse the Stalinists in the American labor movement. We cited their disruption, class collaboration, and support of capitalist political parties, leading up to the crowning infamy: support of the imperialist war. On top of that, strike-breaking activity to keep the workers in shackles during the war, and stool-pigeon collaboration with the capitalist government for the prosecution of militant and revolutionary workers. That is a "criminal record" if there ever was one. And where were the noble red-baiters while all this was going on? The anti-Stalinist labor bureaucrats were committing the very same crimes, point for point; many times in intimate collaboration with these same Stalinists with whom unbalanced Stalinophobes imagine them to be in irreconcilable conflict.

The old-line trade union bureaucracy has always sought to restrict the trade union movement to the more or less skilled trades that constitute the aristocracy of American labor. They did more to hinder than to help the organization of the great mass of the unskilled. Prior to the thirties, whenever they entered the unskilled and mass-production field, it was hardly ever to organize the unorganized, but nearly always to disrupt the organizing campaigns of rival organizations, such as the IWW and the independent unions. In this field, where the most exploited workers stood most in need of the benefits of organization, the old-line labor skates have always done ten times more union busting than union building.

The movement of the mass-production workers for unionization surged forward mightily in the thirties, and its driving impulse came from below, not from the top. The shameless and cynical fakers feared the entrance of these great masses into the organized labor movement as a possible threat to their bureaucratic stranglehold, and consequently to their privileges. The heroic rank-and-file efforts to attain effective unionization were disrupted again and again by the AFL bureaucracy. The auto workers and the rubber workers, especially, can tell a tale about that; to say nothing of the electrical workers who, in order to create their own union, had to break out of their "Class B" prison in the AFL union, where they had the right to pay dues but not to breathe or to vote. It required a split with the AFL bureaucracy before the mass-production workers could finally break through and secure for themselves the protection of organization under the banner of the CIO.

Rank-and-file militants in many a local union know from experience that every attempt to take advantage of a favorable opportunity to improve their conditions by strike action must take into account not only the bosses and the cops, but also the top officers of their own organization. There is always the danger of their interference, which does not stop at gangsterism and strikebreaking. These bureaucrats would rather bust up a local union any time than allow it to come under an honest militant leadership that might endanger their control in the International organization and the emoluments and perquisites appertaining thereto and accruing therefrom.

Approximately 40 percent of the local unions of the International Brotherhood of Teamsters, for example, at the present time are under "receivership," i.e., deprived of all their constitutional rights to elect officers, etc., for precisely these reasons. It was the attempt, by the way, to impose such a "receivership" on Minneapolis Local 544, in order to get rid of its militant leadership and line the union up for the war program, that led to the big fight and the subsequent arrest and imprisonment of eighteen of the union and SWP leaders—all Trotskyists. Tobin, the president of the Teamsters International, appealed directly to Roosevelt and directly instigated the prosecution. And he worked hand-in-glove with the Stalinists, first to put us in prison and then to prevent any union under their control from aiding our defense committee. These cynical labor skates couldn't learn anything about disruption, union busting, stool pigeoning, or violations of trade union democracy, from the Stalinists; they are past masters at all these dark and evil arts.

When it comes to class collaboration on the political field—another crime we charge against the Stalinists—it cannot be said that the Stalinists taught this scheme of class betrayal to the conservative labor bureaucrats. On the contrary, they learned it from them. The labor leaders of the old school operate in every election as procurers for the capitalist parties, urging the trade unionists to "reward their friends," who almost invariably turn out in every real showdown to be their enemies. Witness the present Congress, a large percentage of which, if not a majority, sailed into office with the "endorsement" of the labor leaders; not to mention the strikebreaking president who was recommended as labor's "special friend."

We have cited the especially abominable record of the Stalinists during the war—their support of the war, their support of the no-strike pledge, and their collaboration with the employers and governmental agencies to frame up and break up every attempt of the hard-pressed rank and file to get through it or around it. We denounced the Stalinists during the war for these real and heinous crimes against the interests of the working class. But the red-baiting anti-Stalinist labor bureaucrats, who are making so much noise today in synchronism with the governmental drive against the Stalinists, had absolutely nothing to say against these crimes committed by the Stalinists during the war. And for good reason. They were engaged in the same dirty business. They were, in fact, united with the Stalinists in the conspiracy against truth which was required to dragoon the workers into the war. They jointly put over the "no-strike pledge," and jointly fought the militant rank and file whenever they tried to assert their right to strike during the war.

And this applies to the so-called "progressive" labor leaders of the CIO as well as to their more stolid brethren of the AFL. Visualize once again the unforgettable picture, drawn by Art Preis in *The Militant,* of the convention of the United Automobile Workers in 1944. Thomas and Reuther and Addes and Leonard, the whole administration in all of its factions, were lined up solidly on the platform in fraternal unity with the Stalinists to beat down the rank-and-file revolt against the no-strike pledge.

The transitory leaders thrown to the top of the first great wave of the new unionism represented by the CIO are showing a marked inclination to imitate the AFL fakers and a tendency, like them, to grow fat, especially around the ears. They strive constantly to consolidate their positions in official machines, permanent and secure, and independent from all control, on the pattern of the AFL—and to constrict the membership in a bureaucratic straitjacket. If they have not succeeded—as they have not and will not—it is by no means owing to the lack of ambitions in this respect, but primarily to the power of resistance that resides in the rank and file of the new unions of the mass-production workers; to the alertness of these workers, and their mighty striving for democracy and for an aggressive, militant policy.

The closer you look at the dubious program of united front with the conservative and "progressive" labor bureaucrats against the Stalinist bureaucrats, the clearer it becomes that in practice, wherever the vital interests of the masses of the workers are concerned, the "united front" usually takes a different shape, with or without a formal agreement. When it comes to the fundamental conflict of interests between the classes, the burning reality which serious workers must take as their starting point, the Stalinist bureaucrats and the anti-Stalinist bureaucrats find themselves lined up on the same side, and it is not the side of the workers.

"But," say the AFL fakers, and the CIO "progressive" red-baiters, and the Association of Catholic Trade Unionists, and the ex-radical Stalinophobes—"but," they all say in chorus, "there is one crime of the Stalinists you have not mentioned, and it is the greatest crime of all which should unite all men of goodwill in opposition to them: They are the servants of a foreign power." That is true. The official leaders of the Communist Party of the United States are indubitably the hired agents of the Stalin regime in Russia; and they servilely carry out its instructions and serve its interests with every twist and turn of Kremlin policy, no matter how such conduct may contradict and injure the interests of the American working class. For that we condemn them and denounce them, and wage war against them.

But not under your leadership, Messrs. Labor Fakers and Russophobes! You are just as much the agents and servants of the capitalist government at Washington as the Stalinists are the agents and servants of the Stalin regime. What kind of a government is that, if you please? Didn't it drag the people of America into two wars of imperialist conquest under the fake slogan of "democracy," and isn't it now plotting and planning a third? Didn't it preside over the ten-year depression of the thirties with its terrible toll of broken lives and broken homes, and isn't it heading the country straight into another depression, and a still worse one? Isn't it the cynical instrument of the monopolists and profit hogs, serving their interests against the interests of the American people? Isn't it an antilabor, strikebreaking government, owned lock, stock, and barrel by the Sixty Families of monopoly capitalism?

The main enemy of the American workers is in their own country; and as far as their most basic interests are concerned, this government at Washington is also a *foreign power*. It is a far mightier, and a far more immediate threat and danger to the American working class than the government of Stalin, as the experience of the past year has amply demonstrated once again. It is not the Stalin government that is breaking strikes and threatening the rights of unions in the United States at the present time. It is the bipartisan capitalist government at Washington. That is a foreign power, workers of America, and those who serve this foreign power cannot be your allies in the struggle against Stalinism.

The united front the workers of America really need is the united front of the rank and file, who have no privileges, who serve no foreign powers, who have nothing to lose but their poverty and insecurity, and have a world to win. This united front must be directed at the capitalist system, and thereby against both of its servile agencies—the Stalinist bureaucrats and the other bureaucrats.

6. Is the Communist Party a Working Class Organization?

Stalinism, like every other force obstructing the emancipation struggle of the workers, thrives on confusion and assiduously disseminates it in the labor movement. The Stalinists also profit not a little by the confusion in the heads of some of their bitterest and most conscientious opponents. The misunderstanding of the question by these opponents arises in part from an emotional approach to the question. Hatred is permitted to obscure reason, and no good ever came from that.

Nothing is better calculated to lead the opponents of Stalinism in the United States astray than the simple description of this monstrosity as the agency of a foreign power, and in turn, the designation of this foreign power as an exploiting class, imperialistic to boot, which dominates more than one-sixth of the earth and is reaching out for the rest of it.

This conception, which would put the Communist Party in the same category as the unlamented German-American Bund, clashes with reality at every step and leads to tactics in the struggle against Stalinism which are futile and self-defeating every time. It bars a tactical approach to the masses of workers under the control and influence of the Communist Party, and thus inadvertently aids the Stalinist bureaucrats in consolidating and retaining this control and influence.

Such a theory would be absolutely fatal in Western Europe where the Stalinists dominate virtually the whole working class movement. And it certainly is of no help even in the United States. Stalinism is relatively weak here, and for numerous and weighty reasons can scarcely be expected ever to play the dominating role it plays in Europe. Nevertheless, it is a serious obstacle to the development of a genuinely revolutionary movement, and consequently to the mobilization of the masses for resolute action in the class struggle which would lead objectively to the socialist goal. For that reason we should fight it. But in order to achieve success we must fight Stalinism with a correct understanding of its nature and role.

If the Communist Party were merely a "fifth column" and terrorist gang operating in America as the agency of a foreign "imperialist" government, then the problem would be considerably simpler and easier for the working class movement. And it would be no problem at all to the government at Washington, which is indeed imperialist and has the means to cope with foreign agents and spies. This was shown in the case of the German-American Bund. Fritz Kuhn's sorry "Bund"—equipped with "storm troopers" and all—was easily isolated and could gain no serious influence in the American trade unions. The FBI and other governmental agencies had no difficulty in liquidating this fantastic Hitlerite agency when they got ready to do so. And it never once occurred to any working class tendency, faction, or party to come to the defense of the "Bund."

The same prescription does not work, however, and will not work in the case of American Stalinism. Fascism and Stalinism, although much similar in their methods and practices, have entirely different social foundations on their home grounds where they wield state power, and this applies to their foreign extensions too. The rather widespread conception that the Communist Party is a formation similar to Hitler's "fifth column," and can be treated accordingly, is profoundly false. The Stalinists make the labor movement the main base of their operations, and it is there that they must be fought, and fought, moreover, with working class means.

The analogy which can best aid our thinking on this question is provided by the experiences of the Russian Bolsheviks and the early Comintern in the struggle against the Social Democrats. The German Social Democracy betrayed the proletariat in the First World War; and following that, after they came into control of the government, they employed the police and the army to slaughter tens of thousands of workers in suppressing the proletarian revolution. Besides that, the noble Social Democrats were accountable for a substantial number of "unofficial" murders of revolutionary leaders, such as the murders of Karl Liebknecht and Rosa Luxemburg.

Despite these crimes, the Social Democrats retained a strong organization and influence in the labor movement, as do the present-day Stalinists—despite their crimes. A strong tendency arose among the revolutionary workers to regard the Social

Democratic Party as no longer a workers' organization, and to reject any kind of tactical approach to its members. This characterization proved to be one-sided, too simple, and therefore false and harmful to the further development of the workers' revolutionary movement. This attitude had to be radically changed before the young Communist Party of Germany could make any real headway in the struggle against the Social Democratic traitors.

By their program and their policies the Social Democratic parties then, as now, were petty-bourgeois and not proletarian parties. But by their tradition and composition, by the fact that they made their main base of operation the working class movement, and by the fact that the workers considered them to be workers' organizations—they had to be designated as such. More precisely, as an organized tendency within the labor movement which the revolutionary party had to combat by tactical means as well as by frontal principled struggle. The Leninist policy of the united front followed inexorably from this basic analysis. This opened the path of the revolutionary party to the Social Democratic workers.

There are many differences between Social Democracy and Stalinism, especially in the domain of methods, but in our view they are differences of degree and not of principle. The Social Democrats substituted the program of class collaboration and reform for the program of class struggle and the proletarian revolution. The Stalinists do the same thing, on a far greater scale. The Social Democrats lied and slandered, murdered and betrayed. The Stalinists do the same thing, also on a far greater scale. Both confuse, disorient, and demoralize the advanced workers and disrupt their struggle against capitalism. And they are able to do so precisely because they work inside the labor movement and demoralize it from within.

Traditional Social Democracy doesn't amount to much in the United States. Its place and its essential function is taken over by the official trade union bureaucracy. This bureaucracy also represents a tendency, although an alien tendency, within the labor movement, which also serves a foreign power—the government of the capitalists—and it is more firmly rooted, more influential, more powerful, and therefore a more formidable enemy, at the present time at least, than the Stalinists.

Our method of fighting this formidable bureaucracy in the American labor movement is and must be the method worked out by the Russian Bolsheviks to combat the Mensheviks and the Social Revolutionaries, and later taught by them to the young Communist parties of the early Comintern. We oppose the reactionary bureaucrats in principle, and the main burden of our irreconcilable struggle against them must be devoted to denunciation and exposure of their perfidious role. Subordinate to that, but inseparably connected, goes the tactical approach to the vast masses of workers under their influence and domination.

This is the Leninist tactic of the united front. We demand of the bureaucrats that they break their alliance with the capitalist political parties and follow an independent class policy on the political field. We give critical support to the bureaucrats in all cases where they find themselves obliged to lead the struggles of the workers for the improvement of their conditions or the defense of their rights. We defend the unions and the individual labor leaders against any attack or infringement from the side of the government. The workers learn more from experience than from propaganda. It is only by participating in the struggles of the workers along these lines that we will win them over to an aggressive class-struggle policy and eventually to a socialist consciousness.

On the ground that the Communist Party is not a working class organization and not a tendency in the labor movement, a contention is advanced that we can have a different attitude toward the Communist Party, or to those trade unions or other workers' organizations under its control, when they find themselves in clashes with the capitalist class or its governmental agencies. To think so requires an absurd, subjectively motivated denial of reality. Such a mistake can only lead its proponents, if they follow out the logic of their analysis, into the bourgeois camp. Unfortunately, that is precisely what has happened to the great majority of American anti-Stalinists.

Stalinism is a new phenomenon of the last quarter of a century, and is unique in many ways. But this does not change the essential fact that it is a tendency in the labor movement. It is rooted in the trade unions and wields influence over a section of the progressive workers. That is precisely the reason that it is such a great problem and such a great obstacle to the emancipation struggle of the workers. In our opinion, it is impossible to wage an effective struggle against Stalinism without proceeding from this premise. Stalinism is an *internal problem* of the labor movement which, like every other internal problem, only the workers can solve.

The gist of the matter, let us repeat, consists in the fact that the misnamed Communist Party makes its main field of activity the trade union movement; wields a certain influence there; and by a combination of demagogy, machination, bureaucratic repression, and gangster violence—aided no little by the stupidities of its opponents—has gained the controlling position in numerous unions and represents an influential force in others. And these unions, just like the unions under the control of the anti-Stalinist conservatives, by the logic of the class struggle frequently come into conflict with the employers and even with the government and find themselves involved in strikes.

Shall these strikes be supported on the general principle of class solidarity, or should support be withheld because of the circumstance that the official leaders are Stalinists? And should these leaders, in case they are arrested in the course of strike activities, be defended—also on the general principle of class solidarity against the class enemy? And should the legal rights of the Communist Party be defended against the red-baiters?

Those who say no, end the debate so far as we are concerned. By that fact they take their place in the camp of the class enemy. Those who say yes, thereby recognize implicitly the falsity of the contention that Stalinism is not a tendency in the labor movement, to be contended with as such. There is no getting around this question. It must be squarely faced and answered.

This question arose very acutely in last year's strikes of the Stalinized UE [United Electrical Workers] against Westinghouse and General Electric. And again in the long drawn-out strike of the auto workers at Allis Chalmers, which was indubitably dominated by a Stalinist leadership. And again in the recent strike of the National Maritime Union, which had been completely under Stalinist domination for years, and was still partly so. And it is sharply posed right now by the movement to pass legislation outlawing the Communist Party.

A clear understanding and recognition of the class nature of the Communist Party as a workers' organization—as a tendency in the labor movement—determines the tactical approach of the revolutionary workers to the problem. Stalinism cannot be disposed of by reliance on police measures of the bourgeois state—the very idea is ludicrous—nor by anathema and excommunication from the labor movement, when the power to enforce it is lacking. Nothing will do but an uncompromising principled fight, combined with a tactical approach which will enable the revolutionary party to win the workers away from its perfidious influence. From the revolutionary point of view, that is the heart of the problem of fighting Stalinism in a way that will lead to its elimination from the working class movement, not in fancy but in fact.

7. The Working Class Fight Against Stalinism

The preamble of the old IWW, on which a whole generation of worker-militants was raised and taught the class struggle, began with the declaration: "The working class and the employing class have nothing in common." This is certainly true as far as social interests are concerned.

The struggle between the classes never ceases and cannot cease until the workers are completely victorious. The social evils which plague the world today, and even threaten the continued existence and future development of civilization, are due fundamentally to the fact that the international proletarian revolution, the necessary precursor of world socialism, has been unduly retarded and delayed. Outlived and decadent capitalism is stretching out the period of its decline—or rather, its death agony—for too long a time. Capitalism is the root of the evil.

The overthrow of capitalism is the historic mission of the working class, and all of its daily struggles are instinctively directed to this end. When this struggle becomes conscious and properly organized and led, the downfall of capitalism and the beginning of socialism will be equally assured. Power is on the side of the workers, thanks to their numbers and their strategic social position. They cannot fail to be victorious once they get a clear view and understanding of the central requirement: that their policy be anticapitalist, and that their organizations and their activities be independent, free from capitalist influences and agencies. This is the core of what Marxism teaches us about the politics of the working class.

The foregoing considerations fully apply to the problem of Stalinism, which is one of the agencies of capitalism in the labor movement, and the fight against it. The advanced workers above all must give thought to this problem and work out their policy from an independent class standpoint. Stalinism helps the capitalists by introducing disruption, confusion, and demoralization into the labor movement, and sells its services to the capitalists in this destructive capacity. To be sure, Stalinism tries to drive a hard bargain with the imperialists. The bargaining over the terms of betrayal sets up conflicts and irritations, as at the present time in the United States, which give the false appearance of a revolutionary struggle.

This, however, does not change the basic fact that Stalinism is essentially an agency of world imperialism in the labor movement of the advanced countries, as well as in the colonial world. But for Stalinism, all of continental Europe would long since have been united in a Federation of Socialist Republics. Even today, after all that has happened, after all the harm that has been done and all the destruction that has been wrought, not a single capitalist regime would stand up for a month in continental Europe unless it was propped up and supported by Stalinism, the "loyal opposition."

It is from this point of view that the fight against Stalinism must be conducted—as an integral part of the general fight against capitalism. It should be clear that the advanced workers need a class policy for this fight as for all others, and one that is completely independent. For this fight the workers need and can expect no help from the capitalists; it is stupidly incongruous to speculate on it for a moment. The workers need rather to get rid of the agents of capitalism—and that means all of them. "Class against class" must be the guiding line for the fight against Stalinism, as for all other fights of the workers.

The current red-baiting campaign is inspired and directed by the exploiters of labor. They are more class-conscious than the workers and always try to keep their class interests in mind in elaborating any policy. Ostensibly directed against the Stalinists alone—or the "Communists" as they falsely label them, partly through ignorance and partly through the design to confuse—the witch-hunt is in reality directed against labor and the rights of labor in general. Notice how intimately it is tied up with the program of war preparation and antiunion legislation now being railroaded through Congress. That is no accident.

In part the red-baiting campaign is designed also as a diversion to distract attention from the ripening disturbances of the American social system and the mounting inequalities, injustices, and deprivations inflicted upon the mass of the people. "Don't look at the harsh realities of American life. Don't think of your real troubles. Look at Russia and the 'reds.'" To fall for this transparent fake requires a rather high degree of gullibility. For the American militants and trade unionists to join in a "united front" with the American exploiters for the prosecution of the red-baiting campaign would simply be to adopt a severely efficient method of cutting their own throats.

Some labor leaders who understand or partly understand the truth of the matter are taking part in the red-baiting campaign stemming out of Washington, in the hope of buying immunity for themselves. Besides being unprincipled, that tactic is sheer folly. The campaign is aimed at all the organizations of the workers and will strike them all with increasing violence as it gathers momentum. The appetite of the red-baiting reactionaries grows by what it feeds on. They become more aggressive with every attempt at unprincipled appeasement offered to them by one section of the labor leaders or another.

Evidence is accumulating that the rank-and-file workers in the more progressive and democratic unions are getting the pitch. They are taking a somewhat reserved, and in some places, even a hostile attitude toward the anti-red campaign, to the consternation of some short-sighted "progressive" labor fakers who thought they could easily dispose of their rivals and get themselves elected simply by raising the red scare.

In the recent election in Ford Local 600 of the UAW, the largest local union in the world, the Association of Catholic Trade Unionists, the Roman pope's foreign legion in the American labor movement, led a well-organized, boastful, and confident "anti-Moscow" campaign. They suffered a completely unexpected disaster. The Thomas-Addes slate backed by the Stalinists swept the elections by a majority of three to one. In the last convention of the CIO Electrical Workers, likewise, the red-baiting office-hunters got a brutal and well-deserved beating.

The workers in the plants apparently took a more serious view of their problem as a whole than the red-baiters counted on. They apparently linked the anti-red drive with the drive against labor in general, and decided by their votes to give a rebuke to the opportunist labor politicians and reactionaries who tried to fish in the troubled waters without bothering to present a serious program on union issues.

Unfortunately, the Stalinists profited by the confusion in these cases. That is not to be desired, for they are a real menace to the trade union movement and must be fought tooth and nail. They try to stigmatize every criticism of their wrecking activities as "red-baiting," but this dodge is playing out. There is no reason why we should take their definition and refrain from the struggle against them just because some stupid reactionaries are also fighting them, from another point of view.

The thing is to put the fight on the proper basis and conduct it from the standpoint of the interests of the working class. That means to fight the red-baiters without covering up or shielding the criminal record of the Stalinists. It means, no less, to fight the Stalinists without falling into the booby trap set by the reactionary red-baiters. This discrimination is not so difficult as it may appear. It has been done. From all indications it is being done right now with very good results in the National Maritime Union.

The Stalinist machine has controlled the NMU since it was first organized ten years ago. They have run things there, as they do in every union that falls under their control, with brutal disregard for the wishes and interests of the workers. The union was converted into a political instrument of the Communist Party, and made to serve every zigzag of policy in conformity with the interests and demands of the Kremlin. At the same time, the union apparatus was converted into a happy hunting-ground for careerists and bureaucrats. The chief qualification required to secure their places on the swollen payroll was that they be always ready to carry out any and every policy dictated by the Stalinist machine, regardless of how it might affect the interests of the workers who paid the dues.

The treacherous policies and bureaucratic brutality of the Stalinist machine in the NMU provoked more than one revolt in the ranks in the past, as has been the case in all other Stalinist-dominated unions and will always be the case in the future. But these previous revolts, inspired in the main by the justified resentment of honest workers, fell under the leadership of ignorant, reactionary, red-baiting place-hunters. They simply made good punching bags for the Stalinist demagogues in the "ideological" struggle, and couldn't even hold their own in the physical struggle which they, like so many of their breed, imagined could accomplish everything. They found out that muscle-stuff is a game that more than one side can play at, just as the Stalinists, who are addicted to the same theory, are finding out now and will find out increasingly, as the tide of revolt rises against them.

The Stalinists, following their regular procedure, manipulated the expulsion of their leading opponents. All opposition was driven underground. For a long time the CP stranglehold on the union seemed to be absolutely unshakable. But the logic of the class struggle proved to be stronger than the bureaucratic machine of Stalinism. The antiworker policy followed by the leadership of the NMU during the war went to such monstrous lengths of cynicism and betrayal that it stored up a tremendous reserve of resentment in the ranks. Finally, this brought about a split even in the Communist Party fraction which dominated the union. With that, came a split in the union apparatus and the creation of conditions for the real sentiment of the rank and file to assert itself.

The new opposition attacked the Stalinist machine not for its radicalism but for its conservatism, for its betrayal of the interests of the workers in the trade union fight against the shipowners. President Curran, who had long been a fellow traveler of the Stalinists, took the leadership of the fight; and to his credit it must be said that on the whole he has led it wisely and effectively, abstaining from stupid and reactionary red-baiting, and fighting on issues of vital concern to the seamen in their daily struggle. The rank and file of the union were only waiting for the signal, and have rallied around the anti-Stalinist leadership in what appears to be a very substantial majority. If the fight is continued along these lines, there is every reason to be confident that victory will be assured and that an important union with a great future will be cleansed of the Stalinist pestilence.

Two important lessons can be drawn from the experience of the NMU: (1) The masses are stronger than any bureaucratic apparatus, whether it is a trade union apparatus or any other kind, and demonstrate it every time they find an opening to break through and have proper leadership. (2) The workers who mistakenly follow the Stalinists are also their victims, and by the logic of the class struggle must come into conflict with the bureaucratic betrayers. Many of them can be counted upon as reserves for the future in the victorious struggle against perfidious Stalinism—provided they are approached with a worker policy, not a procapitalist one.

Stalinism can and will be defeated and cast out of the labor movement. But the workers themselves must do it.

8. The Prospects of American Stalinism

The most reactionary power and the most formidable enemy of the workers in their struggle for a better life is American imperialism. This holds true on a world scale; and it is a hundred times true as far as the direct struggle of the American workers is concerned. It is unpardonable to overlook this simple truism, and to see the main enemy in the person of the discredited, hounded and harried, and numerically weak Communist Party of the United States.

The strength and influence of the Communist Party here is in no way comparable to that of European Stalinism. There the Stalinist parties command the support of millions and are the chief prop of the decadent capitalist system, which could not maintain itself anywhere on the continent without their support. Here the role played by the CP is a minor one, and most probably will remain so.

Historical reasons in the main account for this disparity. The socialist consciousness and tradition of the European proletariat attracted them very strongly to the Russian revolution from the first. Since then, as the Soviet Union demonstrated its strength and viability, they transferred their sympathies to the Stalin regime, seeing behind its shoulders the image of the Soviet Union, and not noticing or not taking full account of the frightful degeneration wrought by this usurping bureaucracy.

Moreover, the European workers, who in their vast majority are anticapitalist, recognize American imperialism as an irreconcilable enemy of their socialist aspirations, and feel the need of alliance with a power to counterbalance it. They turn more and more to the Soviet Union since the latter demonstrated its power on the field of battle against the Nazi war machine.

In America the situation is quite different. Due to a number of historical conditions peculiar to the country, the great masses of the American workers never attained a socialist consciousness, not even to the extent of independent political action on a reformist basis, such as even conservative Britain has experienced now already for several decades. In addition to that, the American workers have shared the isolationist provincialism which dominated almost the whole population up until the most recent years. Except for a very thin stratum represented by the class-conscious vanguard, they saw Russia as a faraway country in which they had little interest; and such interest as they manifested was more hostile than friendly. Besides all that, beneath all their apparent conservatism the American workers have a not inconsiderable feeling of independence and of confidence in their own power. They see no need of the help of any "foreign power."

All these circumstances have operated up till now to restrict and limit the growth and influence of the Communist Party, which appeared in the popular mind as the most radical party. On the other side, Stalinism has perhaps been more thoroughly exposed, and subjected to more effective criticism from the revolutionary point of view in America than in any other capitalist country. The forces of genuine communism, as counterposed to Stalinism, have made more headway with the development of their independent organization and the extension of their independent influence here than elsewhere. Thus for reasons which may appear to be somewhat contradictory, Stalinism in the United States has been stunted in its growth. And, if we continue to follow a correct policy, there is good ground to believe that American Stalinism cannot hope to attain the present powerful position, and thereby the capacity for evil and betrayal, of its European counterparts.

The main strength and danger of American Stalinism lies not in its numbers and its popular influence, nor in its apparatus, its money, and its terrorist agents—although it disposes of considerable forces in all these fields and departments—but rather in its demagogical capacity to deceive, demoralize, and disorient the more radical elements who have attained a conscious anticapitalist attitude, or are awakening to it. These forces of the class-conscious vanguard are as yet not very numerous in comparison to the size of the American working class as a whole. But they are the most decisive for the future, for it is their destiny to lead the others. Once the class struggle in America is posed in its sharpest and most irreconcilable form, they alone can lead; and they will then represent the greatest power in the world.

It is primarily on this ground, in the fight for the minds and souls of the awakening militant workers of the class-conscious vanguard, that the real fight against Stalinism must take place. Here we can already record considerable success; and we confidently count on more because we are gaining right along, steadily if slowly, thanks to our correct approach to the question.

Stalinism was a much more formidable danger when we first opened up the irreconcilable fight against it in 1928, and in the ensuing decade or so, than it is today, even though its numerical forces and its apparatus were smaller then than now. At that time the Communist Party *dominated* virtually the whole radical labor movement in this country. In the first years of the depression the party drew into its train a supplementary army of radical intellectuals, disillusioned in capitalism by the crisis, who rendered them great service in propagandizing and popularizing the lie that Stalinism was true communism.

In those days also the economic progress recorded by the Soviet Union under the Five Year Plan, while capitalist world economy, including its American sector, was plunged into the greatest difficulties, gave a new attractive power to Stalinism and its myth of "socialism in one country." The critics from the Left Opposition, the Trotskyists, appeared to be refuted by events and were pushed into isolation on the sidelines. Thanks to this, the American Stalinists were able to vastly expand their propaganda mediums; to dominate the movement of the unemployed in the first years of the crisis; and then later to play a big role in the organizing of the unorganized, and to entrench themselves in various unions of the newly created CIO.

But since the late thirties, both the organizational position and the influence of American Stalinism have declined rather than advanced. The Moscow trials, which were so thoroughly exposed in the United States, dealt powerful blows to the moral position of American Stalinism and alienated a large section of its intellectualistic periphery. The great majority of the latter, now disillusioned in Stalinism, acquired a new faith in capitalism coincident with the temporary improvement of the economic conjuncture, and have since become professional red-baiters who damn and expose Stalinism on every occasion as assiduously as they once praised it and glossed over its crimes.

A smaller section of the former intellectual fellow travelers of Stalinism carried their criticism through to its logical conclusion and joined the Trotskyist movement, and have contributed fruitfully to its ideological work. So also, numerous communist workers, who had mistakenly believed that Stalinism was communism, drew the necessary conclusions from the new events and revelations and transferred their allegiance to the genuinely revolutionary and communist party, the Socialist Workers Party.

Each turn and twist of American Stalinist policy, in consonance with the zigzags of the Kremlin on the world diplomatic field, produced new defections, desertions, and splits. The signing of the Soviet-Nazi pact brought with it the desertion of a small horde of careerists and muddleheads who had mistaken Stalinism for the champion of bourgeois democracy, pure and undefiled. At the next turn the Stalinist support of the war, and their antiworker jingo policy in support of American imperialism, steadily alienated increasing numbers of honest workers who had mistaken Stalinism for communism.

The betrayals, bureaucratic abuses, gangster methods, and false policies inflicted by the Stalinists upon the unions which had fallen into their control are now beginning to bear fruit in widespread and violent revolts against the Stalinists. Increasingly numerous and militant oppositions are rising up against them from two sides: on the one side, from reactionary red-baiters who want to displace the Stalinist bureaucrats in order to take their places and appropriate their plums; on the other side, from militant workers, some of them former Stalinists, who want to throw out the Stalinist bureaucrats in order to provide the unions with a militant policy and an honest leadership.

The Communist Party has to face these increasing troubles with a leadership of very low caliber.

The sterile bureaucratic regime of the Stalinized party prohibited any normal renewal of the leadership. The seed of talent could not sprout and grow. Independent-minded revolutionists could not breathe in that poisoned atmosphere. The party has to rely for leadership mostly on old hacks who know nothing but to do what they are told and lie to order, and characterless careerists who frequently desert them for greener fields. Budenz is only the latest of this unsavory crew, but by no means the last.

The present prospects of American Stalinism are not very bright, all things considered. Only one thing could rescue them from their difficulties and give them a new lease on life. A great wave of labor radicalism is in the making in the U.S. If the Stalinists are allowed to appear as the persecuted champions of the workers, instead of the cynical betrayers they are, there is danger of the radicalization being diverted to Stalinism. Therein is the tragic error of red-baiting, especially if the progressive workers go in for it. That error must be avoided.

The American workers will turn toward communism, and they will move swiftly and massively once they start; of that there can be no doubt. Will Stalinism be able to seize upon this great movement, pervert it and demoralize it, and turn it aside from its goal? That depends on us. If we explain things correctly and work with the necessary energy, the American workers will embrace communism in its genuine form and reject the Stalinist counterfeit. In the struggle for the American working class, Stalinism will be defeated by its revolutionary nemesis—Trotskyism.

9. Workers' Revolution and Bureaucratic Degeneration

Will the American workers lose the revolution after they have won it? Will they overthrow capitalism with all its power only to fall victim to a new bureaucracy and be subjected to a new form of slavery?

The people who ask these questions—and there are many of them—have in mind the post-Lenin developments in Russia. Rashly concluding that the revolution has already been completely destroyed there—which is far from the truth—and taking the Russian experience as a universal pattern—another serious mistake—they fear that Stalinism or something like it, with its totalitarian police state, forced labor camps, and terroristic suppression of all democracy, will be the eventual outcome of the workers' victory in any case. This line of thought and speculation has led not a few people to conclude that the revolutionary cure for capitalism will turn out in the end to be worse than the disease. It is the perfect formula for passivity leading up to capitulation and renegacy.

Those who take this gloomy view of the ultimate outcome of a victorious proletarian revolution sound something like the worker who refuses to join a union and prepare a strike for higher wages because of previous bad experiences with bureaucratic sellouts and betrayals. "How do I know the leaders won't sell us out as the others did? If the strike is lost we will be worse off than we are now. How do I know the union will not fall into the hands of racketeers and be more a detriment than benefit to us?"

Those who demand guarantees as to the eventual outcome of a strike—or a revolution—ask more than we can give. Defeats and setbacks are always possible in every struggle. Naturally, as revolutionists we should look ahead and take into account the possible difficulties and dangers of the future and consider how to deal with them. But we must do this without exaggerating them and without permitting ourselves to be diverted from the task of the day. That task is the struggle against capitalism, and with that, the struggle against the reactionary labor bureaucracy. This bureaucracy is a powerful obstructive force.

It is this bureaucracy, *as it exists today,* which must first be dealt with and overthrown. Only then will we confront the possible danger of a new bureaucracy *of the future,* which no longer has any privileged section of the working class to lean on and no capitalist government to support it. In our view this problem will be much simpler and easier to cope with in the United States.

The real danger of bureaucratism with which we must concern ourselves first of all is not one that will arise on the morrow of the workers' victory. Rather, it is the burning reality of the present day, and of the whole period between now and the American workers' revolution. The breakup of the bureaucracy in the labor movement and the freeing of the working masses from its strangulating grip is the indispensable condition for the overthrow of American capitalism. Can this be done? Those who doubt it, or those who skip over the problem in favor of gloomy speculations about the dangers of bureaucratism *after the revolution,* are no good for the struggle.

In the early years of the Comintern some extremely interesting and instructive discussions took place on the trade union question between the Bolshevik leaders and some "left" Communists. The specific point at issue was posed as follows: Should Communists accept the reactionary trade unions controlled by the reformist bureaucracy as they were and work within them to overthrow the bureaucrats, as the Bolsheviks said; or should they abandon these unions to the bureaucracy, withdraw from them, and build new unions of their own, free from the presence of the bureaucrats, as the "lefts" maintained? This was also the position of the American IWW, and was one of the reasons for its failure.

The "lefts" of that time were unquestionably serious and sincere revolutionists—that is why Lenin took the trouble to debate with them at great length and with the utmost patience. They were confident that the workers could overthrow the capitalist regime and reorganize society on a socialist basis. But they seemed to be equally convinced that it was impossible to "reform" the reactionary trade unions—that is, to win over the majority, throw out the bureaucrats, and transform the unions into militant organs of the class struggle.

Lenin pointed out that the "lefts" lacked the sense of proportion. Look, he said, you are confident of being able to defeat and overthrow the power of the bourgeoisie concentrated in its state apparatus, its army, its police force, etc.; but you consider it impossible to overthrow the reactionary trade union bureaucracy, which is only one of the agencies of this bourgeois power which you expect to defeat in its entirety. This, said Lenin, shows a glaring inconsistency on your part; an overestimation of the power of the bureaucratic rabble which has seized control of the trade unions and an underestimation of the power of the masses of workers who make up the union membership.

The same inconsistency, on a thousandfold greater scale, is today manifested by not a few people who have been demoralized by Stalinism and horrified by its crimes. The same doubts and fears formerly advanced in support of the discredited theory of the "left" Communists with respect to the trade union bureaucracy under capitalism—based on the foolish belief in its invincibility—are here expressed again in connection with the broadest problems of socialism, with far more dangerous implications than when they were first revealed in the limited field of trade union tactics. These people underestimate the mass power of the workers—the motive force of every revolution—and surrender the field to a possible future bureaucracy before it has even made its appearance.

Genuine revolutionists who have confidence in the ability of the American working class to overthrow capitalism do not and cannot have the slightest doubt of the ability of the workers to dispose of the conservative bureaucracy, which serves as an agency of capitalism in the labor movement. The struggle of the rank-and-file workers against this bureaucracy is one of the surest expressions of their instinctive striving to settle accounts with capitalism and solve the problems of poverty and insecurity which haunt their lives.

As far back as 1931 Trotsky directly linked the coming radicalization of the American workers with a determined and irreconcilable fight against the trade union bureaucrats. He wrote: "With the first signs of economic recovery, the trade union movement will acutely feel the need to tear itself from the clutches of the despicable AFL bureaucracy."[149] This was written when the bureaucracy seemed to have an unshakable grip on the existing unions, which then had less than three million members, and an unlimited power to prevent the organization of the unorganized outside of their control.

There were many croakers who scoffed at Trotsky's "optimism." But within the brief space of less than a decade, the movement of the masses proved itself to be strong enough to break this bureaucratic grip and achieve the organization of the unorganized in the mass-production industries under the independent auspices of the CIO. The "new unionism" took shape in struggle against "the despicable AFL bureaucracy." This example shows how ridiculous it is to make a fetish of the power of the labor bureaucracy—or any other bureaucracy. The bureaucracy can dominate the masses only when they are passive. But the masses *in motion* can smash any bureaucracy. This is the law demonstrated in every great revolution. It will be demonstrated once again, and finally, we think, in the greatest revolution of all—the coming American revolution.

This magnificent movement of the CIO, which has wrought such a profound change in the whole labor movement and in the position and outlook of the American working class, is only the beginning. So far we have seen only the first tentative steps of the American workers on the road of radicalism and class militancy. Considering this, it does not require much imagination to foresee what a genuine, deepgoing revolutionary movement of the working masses will do to the bureaucratic barricades still standing in their path.

The American workers can and will make their revolution; and, as is quite obvious, they will smash the present trade union bureaucracy in the process. "But," say the defeatists, "what then? After the victory, after the expropriation of the capitalists and the consolidation of a workers' government and the organization of socialist production—will not then a new bureaucracy arise? What guarantee do we have that power will not be usurped by a new bureaucracy, as happened in Russia, which will oppress and enslave the workers and rule by totalitarian terror?"

Such a thought indeed opens up "a perspective of profoundest pessimism," as Trotsky once remarked, and is all the more to be condemned because it has no real justification. It can only debilitate the movement of the revolutionary workers by robbing them of their will to struggle, which must presuppose the prospect of victory and the emancipation of the workers. An aversion to the Stalinist regime in the USSR is quite justified, for it is indeed a horrible monstrosity, but the fear of its duplication here, after a victorious revolution, has no basis in reality.

There are profound differences between America and Russia, and these differences create different problems both before the revolutionary victory of the workers and afterward, when the problem of consolidating the victory comes to the fore.

Russia was the most backward of the big capitalist countries. The proletariat, although highly concentrated, was numerically weak in relation to the population as a whole. Its industrial development and technique lagged far behind. On top of all that, the victorious workers' revolution inherited from tsarism and the destruction of war and civil war a devastated, ruined, poverty-stricken country and a frightful scarcity of the most elementary necessities. The disrupted productive apparatus taken over by the revolution was incapable of turning out a volume of goods sufficient to overcome the scarcity in a short period of time.

The Russian revolution was not an end of itself and could not build "socialism" by itself, in one backward country. It was only a beginning, which required the supplementary support of a revolution in more advanced Europe and a union of the European productive apparatus and technology with the vast natural resources of Russia. The delay of the European revolution isolated the Soviet Union, and on the basis of the universal scarcity a privileged bureaucracy arose which eventually usurped power in the state and destroyed the workers' organizations—soviets, trade unions, and even the revolutionary party which had organized and led the revolution. A horrible degeneration has taken place, but for all that, the great revolution has not yet been destroyed, and its ultimate fate has not yet been decided.

Socialism can be constructed only on the basis of a highly productive economy capable of producing abundantly. Where there is scarcity, with the consequent scramble for the meagerest necessities, the fight for privileges takes place; the material basis for a privileged bureaucracy appears, as was the case in Russia. We cannot see any prospect of such a situation in richly productive America once the power of the capitalist class is broken and production is organized, under a workers' government, for use and not for profit. America is a much more advanced country than was the Russia of the tsars, and consequently the American bourgeoisie is much stronger than was its Russian counterpart. Because of that, the overthrow of the capitalist regime in the United States will be much more difficult. But for the same reason the consolidation of the workers' victory, once it has been attained, will be all the easier.

Thanks to the extraordinary development of American industrial technique, its vast resources and skilled working class, the organization of production on such a scale as to ensure plenty and thereby economic equality for all, can be assured almost immediately after the consolidation of the victory. This is the main point to keep in mind; it is the greatest assurance that neither capitalist counterrevolution nor bureaucratic degeneration can find a firm material base here. Once the American workers have made their revolution, the decisive factors of American resources and technology will provide the material basis for the broadest workers' democracy, leading to the fulfillment of the revolution in the classless socialist society. The thing is to make the revolution.

Jean van Heijenoort and Jan Frankel, 1937.

THINK IT OVER, MR. DUBINSKY

Published May 3, 1947

The following article was published in The Militant *in Cannon's occasional column, "Notebook of an Agitator."*

The rights of workers to make a living and speak their minds freely are taking quite a beating these days, and Congress is not the only scene of the crime. A rough job was done this week by Justice E. L. Hammer in New York's Supreme Court. Justice Hammer gave the business to four suspended members of Cutters Union Local 10 of the International Ladies Garment Workers Union.

The four men—Arnold Ames, Charles Nemeroff, Irving Kotler, and Emanuel Brownstein—had been suspended from Local 10 for periods of three to five years on charges of circulating defamatory literature against David Dubinsky, the highly touted president, and other officers of the garment union. Their appeal to the court was denied by the judge, who denounced them as "Communists" in a forty-page decision. Emil Schlesinger, attorney for the ILGWU, hailed the decision as a "milestone in the defense of American labor against communist deceit and treachery." Mr. Schlesinger, according to the press reports, expressed certainty that the ruling would serve as a precedent in future cases affecting "communist penetration of trade unions" and applauded "the determination of the courts to prevent totalitarian forces from using democratic institutions as a weapon in their efforts to overthrow democracy."

It seems that the leadership of the ILGWU, which has been widely advertised as the most progressive and democratic of all unions, is giving us a new definition of this famous "democracy," in cahoots with a friendly Supreme Court justice. First taking my shoes off, and saving Mr. Dubinsky's presence, I would like to make a few remarks about the matter and pass on a suggestion to Mr. Dubinsky.

I don't for a minute doubt that the four suspended cutters, who were leaders of the Stalinist-backed opposition slate in the union elections in 1944, defamed Mr. Dubinsky and probably also slandered him and other officers of the union—such procedures are in the nature of Stalinism. No one could blame the aggrieved labor leaders for objecting to it and seeking redress. The method employed in this case, however, was not a happy one.

The real authors and inspirers of the defamation and slander are the Stalin-picked bosses of the Communist Party. They escape unscathed, and have been gratuitously handed a democratic issue to exploit, which they do not deserve, while four of their deluded followers, rank-and-file men who work for a living, get the lumps. Suspension from the union in a trade that is 100 percent organized is far too severe a punishment for harsh words—or even false accusations—made in the heat of a union election struggle. And if, as is the general practice in such cases, it is followed by removal from the job and, consequently the denial to the victims of the right to make a living at their trade, it is a brutal injustice, a murderous abuse of power. The whole business makes a mockery of this same "democracy" which Mr. Dubinsky and his fellow Social Democrats seem to preach better than they practice.

The first place where the workers have to win the battle of democracy is in their own organizations. Suspension or expulsion from the union is a penalty fit for strikebreakers or violators of union discipline in struggle against the bosses. But not for dissidents and critics, Mr. Dubinsky. Such a rule reverts to the theory that "the king can do no wrong," and makes lese majesty a capital crime. That is not democratic. It is very easy to be agreeable to those who agree with us. Stalin accepts that formula, and so did Hitler in his time. But real democracy begins only when those who disagree and criticize have the right to live and breathe in the union and enjoy full rights of membership, including the right to make a living, as long as they observe the union rules and discipline in the conflicts with the employers.

It may be argued that in spite of everything, a critic gets a much better chance for his white alley[150] in the ILGWU than in any Stalinist-controlled union. That cannot be gainsaid. But in this case under discussion the leaders of the ILGWU are making serious concessions to the Stalinists by imitating the methods they have made notorious.

Of course, this is only one incident resulting from what was doubtless a great provocation, but it points in the wrong direction. It is not only wrong in principle for leaders of workers' organizations and minority groups to encourage, by example, the stultification of democracy. It is also dangerous from a practical point of view. Such actions serve to feed the general trend of reaction in the country, which is running too strong already, and they might be the first victims.

It is an ironical coincidence that the April 4 issue of the *Wage Earner,* the Detroit organ of the Association of Catholic Trade Unionists, files an editorial protest against the Stalinized District Executive Board of the United Electrical Workers of West Michigan for suspending a dissident member named L. Carlton Sanford, and then notifying Sanford's employer to exclude him from the local's bargaining unit. The *Wage Earner* goes on to say: "The UE officials responsible for this blow at a man's livelihood would do well to study the American constitution and try to understand the democracy which protects their rights so generously."

I don't think much of the ACTU and its *Wage Earner,* but in this instance they make a suggestion to the Stalinists which might profitably be accepted by the Social Democrats who denounce the Stalinists so bitterly in the name of democracy. Think it over, Mr. Dubinsky.

A LETTER TO V. R. DUNNE

May 6, 1947

The following letter to Vincent Raymond Dunne in Minneapolis has not been previously published. The text is from a copy in Cannon's files.

Dear Vincent:

I am very glad to see how energetically your campaign for mayor is being pushed and the publicity you are getting. The whole thing is not only good in itself. It is also a good example for the other locals about the necessity of digging in locally and pounding away till they create a base for themselves and become known as a factor in the community on their own account, not merely as representatives of a national party. "High politics" on a national and international scale is all very good and necessary for the elaboration of the general line, but can never be a substitute for local spadework.

Similarly, the elaboration of political positions and theoretical conclusions in theses form for the instruction of our own people is correct and necessary as a starting point. But it doesn't amount to much until it is translated into popular language and communicated to wider circles. Our best comrades have been educated in the Trotskyist movement, and because of historical circumstances have grown up in isolation from the mass movement. It is surprising how long it takes them to learn that talking to each other and explaining things to each other is useful only as a preparation for explaining things to wider masses.

This is what I am trying to exemplify in the articles I have been working on and have projected for the future. I am trying all the time to write for people who don't know about our theses and to whom things must be explained simply, without it being taken for granted that they understand everything already. Those who already understand everything don't need me to write for them.

By the way, I have just written a 2,000-word Notebook piece about your friend Tobin, with the affectionate title: "The Mad Dog of the Labor Movement."[151] I go into some detail about his character and his methods of fighting the rank and file, breaking strikes and hiring gangsters to prosecute the civil war against the brewery workers. I have already finished it, but am waiting for Farrell's return from a short trip at the end of this week so that he can check everything before it is printed.

Do you think that Minneapolis and St. Louis would want some extra copies of the paper containing this piece? It will not be printed this week, but next week, so there is time for you to let us know about this. I imagine the boys in St. Louis will find it useful if they know how to distribute it discreetly. The whole article is ostensibly based on the known historical facts about Minneapolis and the revelations about St. Louis in the April number of the Teamsters' magazine. I do not intimate anywhere that I have much other inside information.

Sylvia [Caldwell] and I are working every day now on a regular schedule of literary production. We are beginning to have some trouble with the editor of *The Militant*. He is trying to hold me down to six columns a week. Six columns a week!—that's a lazy man's stint. What the hell can a man write in six columns?

Please give my regards to Grace [Carlson] and all the others, and let me know how you are getting along, how your health is; whether Harry [DeBoer] still thinks he can play checkers; how Jake [Cooper] is doing; and other important bits of similar information about the comrades which are of such great interest to me. Also ask Henry [Schultz] if I can borrow his pass in case I want to take a cross-country trip.[152]

As ever,
Jim

A MISTAKE ON THE QUESTION OF UNITY WITH THE WP

May 6, 1947

The following remarks were made to a meeting of the SWP Political Committee after a report by Morris Lewit proposing a reconsideration of the proposal to unify with the Workers Party. Cannon's and Lewit's remarks were mimeographed for circulation to the National Committee of the SWP and then published in Internal Bulletin, *vol. IX, no. 3, May 1947, under the title "Discussion of the Present Stage of Unity Negotiations Between SWP and WP."*

I am in agreement with the remarks of Stein [Morris Lewit] and wish only to emphasize a few points. It isn't very pleasant to have to admit a mistake. It is doubly unpleasant to have to admit a mistake that helped to mislead others, especially the plenum of the National Committee. That, however, is the rather disagreeable position we find ourselves in, myself in particular.

Reviewing the whole fight from the beginning, more than seven years ago, I think we were fundamentally correct all the way through, up to and including the last party convention, in our fight against the Shachtmanites, in principle as well as in our strategy and tactics. The line was absolutely right. And none of us had the slightest idea of changing the line that we had carried through, including the line of the convention.

I consider what happened since the convention as a chain of comical errors, which I am sure we can correct without damage to our cause. First came the unexpected decision of the WP to accept the conditions laid down by the Movement [the Fourth International] for participation in the EPC [Extraordinary Party Convention—the world congress of the Fourth International]. We interpreted this action of theirs as a turn in the direction of the Movement, as a capitulation to its terms which they had previously rejected. That is the way we accepted it. That was the basis of our decision at the plenum. And when in the letter of Martin, which was sent out with the agreement of other comrades, we spoke of their capitulation, we didn't do it in a derogatory sense, but in an entirely different one.[153]

As we saw it, they had come to the turning point where they would have to go one way or the other, and at the last moment they made a turn to the Movement, accepted its conditions and thereby capitulated to it. And we decided to give them credit for that move, to give them a helping hand. That was the basis of our recommendations to the plenum, where the unity resolution was adopted.

By that we demonstrated that we are communist politicians and not gang fighters. In spite of all that had happened, all the personal animosity, all the slander, etc.—at the moment they took a political turn in the direction of the Movement we were prepared to give them a helping hand, to open the door for them to come into the party and to give them liberal terms. The second thing we demonstrated—which I am not so proud of—is that after all our experience with these people, we showed a certain naiveté. It is somewhat embarrassing to be obliged to acknowledge that, in this case at least, experience did not bring wisdom; that good nature and goodwill obscured political judgment. That is a very sticky feeling. I really didn't think that even the Shachtmanites would be stupid enough to think they could play a maneuverist double game with the EPC.

Everybody at the plenum had plenty of ground for animosities against these people, whose mistakes have often amounted to crimes against the movement. But the moment the plenum members saw—or, rather, thought they saw—that the Shachtmanites were turning toward the Movement, they were willing to have them come into the party and give them good terms. Why, we even gave them better terms than those they agreed to in their meetings with Smith [Michel Pablo]. We gave them credit in advance for carrying out their decision in good faith, and offered to expedite the unity even before the EPC, provided the discussion was finished beforehand.

We followed that up with our meetings with them and the Joint Statement on unity, in which we rounded a few corners to make it easier for them, without, however, violating the instructions of the plenum. We agreed to present their return to the party in public as a merger of the two organizations, for example, accepting their verbal declarations that they know this means their coming into the SWP, etc.

Then things began to happen. First through an inadvertence, when the Martin letter to the NC members came into their hands. Long experience has taught me that inadvertences never change a fundamental course—but they often show its real direction. The Martin letter was utilized by them to reveal what their real purposes are, and this has served a useful purpose for us.

Shachtman has made it perfectly clear, in his letter to the membership of the WP and in subsequent actions, that there was a comical misunderstanding on both sides.[154] As he represents the matter, they understood that we had changed our position; that we had sharply reversed the line of the convention, and under the pressure of the Movement had changed our whole approach to the question and accepted their formula for the unification. In other words, that it was we who had "capitulated."

Shachtman makes it clear that our interpretation of their action in sending the letter to Smith [initiating the unity negotiations] was a misunderstanding on our part, that they meant no capitulation to the Movement. When they deny heatedly, not to say hysterically, that they have "capitulated"—as though they consider it dishonorable to bow to the rules and discipline of the Movement—they only reveal that they haven't changed a bit, that they stand exactly where they were before.

The series of events which followed are known to you. At the time they were signing the Joint Agreement that they wouldn't take Weber into their party, they had Weber's article against us in their hands and were preparing to publish it in *Labor Action* and solidarize themselves with him—without even notifying us, without mentioning the matter in the joint committee.[155] That revealing incident only shows their disposition to abide by the form of an agreement while violating it in spirit and essence. This way of acting is just a little bit too clever to be clever. We will have to bear it in mind and rely more on guarantees than promises in the future.

As you know, we did not publish our plenum resolution.[156] This was done deliberately, as we explained to them, to give them an opportunity to present the new unity agreement to the public in a joint statement with us. We observed the spirit of the agreement by publishing the Joint Statement without comment. They, however, published it with an introduction attempting to justify their "unity" maneuvers in the past. By that they reopened the whole question of the past for discussion. There were two or three other incidents of the same kind. The publication of the Ruth Fischer letter, without notification or consultation, was a crass violation of all normal procedures when two parties are seriously meeting in negotiation for a unification and loyally cooperating to bring it about.

The campaign now raging in the WP against Johnson—who sincerely stands for unity—is conducted in a real Burnhamite spirit. The obvious purpose of their campaign against Johnson is to discredit those who take unity seriously and to solidify and harden their people to come into our party fighting, with the perspective of another split. That is their idea. Outside of the single thing we noted—their acceptance of the conditions of the Movement, which we took too seriously at face value—there is nothing whatever to show any change of attitude on their part, either politically or organizationally. And even that letter has since been repudiated in essence by Shachtman. In his circular letter to the WP membership he refers to their disciplinary pledge to the EPC as a "formality" and said that unless "unity is achieved," they would regard their commitment "as a mere scrap of paper."

So, in a political sense we are right back where we were at the time of the convention. We have not changed our position. They have not changed. Goldman writes an article in the latest issue of their magazine with his usual compound of misrepresentation, greasy hypocrisy, and double-talk designed to trick and trap the unwary. As for "unity" he blandly explains that by coming into the SWP they will change the character of our party. He doesn't know how wrong he is. They continue all the old denunciations of our party in the old tone. Their object, obviously, is to poison and harden their people to formally accept the conditions of discipline until they get set in the SWP. Then would follow the next stage: the fight to break up the party as we have built it, and convert it into a Shachtmanite party, a windbag's paradise, with permanent discussion, driving out the workers and diverting us from our basic task of recruiting new workers and training them for the Bolshevik struggle against capitalism.

Such is the reality from which we must proceed. I agree with Stein that we should begin a political offensive against the Shachtmanites within the formula of the unity proposal. We don't need to withdraw our unity proposal. What we need to do is interpret it and apply it in the light of the new developments. We are still willing for them to come in and accept our line. But we must explain what we mean by that, so that there can be no more misunderstandings on either side. We do not withdraw our unity resolution, but just simply slow the tempo of its application. We should forget about the goodwill offer we made to them of a quick unification to do them a favor. Take our time. The members are discussing it. Let them take their time and discuss it thoroughly. Discuss it in the press.

I personally am quite sure now that there can be no unification before the Extraordinary Party Convention. Our plenum resolution distinctly specified that their disciplinary obligation to the EPC must be "carried out in good faith." Let us wait and see what they do with the "scrap of paper" they signed. After that, if they still want unification—I personally am pretty sure they will revolt against the decisions of the Extraordinary Party Convention despite their signed pledge—we should have a special convention to decide the question. No more joint statements; from now on decisions to be made by our conventions and plenums, precisely formulated and closing the door on any double interpretations, and telling them: take it or leave it. That is the form, I think, for the further developments on the unification proposal.

We have the inestimable advantage of a homogeneous party which has been built and unified in struggle. We have a leadership united in its entirety on the fundamental questions, and in its attitude toward Shachtmanism from a political point of view. So we don't need to have any great fears about big differences of opinion. What differences of opinion we had prior to the plenum were not fundamental at all. It was the question of how best we were going to serve our program. These differences are not like those we had with Goldman and Morrow. That is why the opposition to the unity [from within the SWP] in the first place didn't impress us as a hostile opposition. Nothing more was involved than the question of whether our method or theirs was best calculated to serve the program to which we all subscribe. I don't doubt that even these tactical differences will easily be eliminated in the further course of developments—if we avoid any more unnecessary "misunderstandings" and dispense with excessive good nature in scrutinizing any more "scraps of paper" which the Shachtmanites may sign.

John G. Wright, 1945

Joseph Hansen

THE MAD DOG OF THE LABOR MOVEMENT

Published May 17, 1947

The following article was published in The Militant *in Cannon's occasional column, "Notebook of an Agitator."*

Among the whole gang of corrupt and contented labor fakers who infest the labor movement to its detriment—especially the AFL unions—and fatten on their crimes against the workers, one in particular is striving, not without success, to distinguish himself as the greatest scoundrel of them all. This is Daniel J. Tobin, the $30,000-a-year president of the International Brotherhood of Teamsters, who has already won for himself the title of the Mad Dog of the Labor Movement, and is demonstrating his right to hold it against all comers.

Tobin, a relic of the horse-and-buggy days of trade unionism, is a small-souled, grasping, selfish old reprobate who thinks the Teamsters union exists for his personal benefit. In addition to his huge salary he taps the union treasury for heavy expenses and prepaid vacation trips for himself and family, and makes the union carry his son, whom he is grooming to become his successor, on the payroll at a fancy honorarium. A rich man himself, he fawns on the bosses and the capitalist politicians, but fights the rank-and-file workers with savage fury. In all his long and malodorous career he has never yet been caught in a generous impulse or a gesture of goodwill and solidarity toward the workers who pay his exorbitant salary.

Tobin never knew anything about organizing workers and leading them in struggle to better their conditions. But he is an expert mechanic in the vile trade of breaking strikes, smashing democracy in local unions, working in cahoots with the bosses to keep rebellious workers from making a living at their trade, and spilling blood in gangster raids on the jurisdiction of other unions, and he is getting more proficient as he gets older.

Tobin disposes of a huge treasury—$14,800,000 at the last report—accumulated from the dues payments of the hardworking and underpaid members of the union, and he utilizes a large part of it to maintain what amounts to a private army of murderous thugs, recruited in part from the underworld, many of whom have criminal records. These gangsters, under Tobin's direction, usually operating under the benevolent indifference of the authorities who are "taken care of" in various ways, wage war on the rank and file of the Teamsters union, and are at present especially preoccupied with a jurisdictional war to force the brewery workers to quit the union of their choice—the Brewery Workers Union, one of the oldest industrial unions and one well-respected in the labor movement—and to compel them to pay dues into the Teamsters union, whether they desire to or not.

In this campaign, beating, maiming, incendiarism, and dynamiting are routine procedures, and murder is not excluded. Announcing a "knockdown drag-out fight" against the brewery workers, Tobin sent his private army of professional thugs into Pittsburgh. They moved in on Pittsburgh to convince the brewery workers that they should give up their own union, now affiliated with the CIO as a result of a free vote of the membership for that preference, and sign up in Tobin's union. And this "convincing" process did not take the form of ideological disquisition or logical elucidation. Tobin's mobsters relied on arguments of another kind learned in their own school, which honors Capone and Dillinger more than Plato and Aristotle.

The usual practice of pulling drivers off their trucks and beating them within an inch of their lives was tried first but did not work very well. The Pittsburgh brewery drivers, with the help of other CIO fellow unionists, proved able to defend themselves on this ground. Tobin's importees then resorted to other techniques. One of their arguments in favor of the AFL as against the CIO was the use of a little homemade gadget known as the fire bomb. These fire bombs, as one reporter described them, "were simple, devilishly destructive little devices consisting usually of a 200 watt electric light bulb, with a hole cut in one end. These were filled with high test gasoline, and the hole then plugged with surgical gauze, providing a fuse to be lighted. Tossed into the cab of a beer truck they instantly sprayed both truck and driver with flaming gasoline."

These weapons were supplemented later with high-explosive bombs, charged with dynamite, which were recklessly thrown through the windows of distributors handling the CIO beer, regardless of the possible consequences to people living in the building. Testimony before the House Labor Committee, which investigated the Pittsburgh "beer war," chalked up a score at that time of ten fire-bombings of stores, five explosive bombings, and seven trucks bombed and burned. That was over three months ago. The latest scores are not in yet. At present there is a "truce" in Pittsburgh—the publicity about his fire-bombers and dynamiters got too hot for Tobin—but he is still recklessly carrying on his "war" in other parts of the country, spending lavish sums of the union's money to fight another union.

At this time, when the reactionary offensive against the workers on all fronts calls for a labor leadership which would map out the strategy of a counteroffensive and inspire the workers for the struggle, Tobin's handpicked executive board occupies itself primarily with the war against the workers. The three principal items on the agenda of the latest meeting, as reported in the March and April issues of Tobin's official magazine, the *International Teamster*, were:

(1) Hearing of appeals from rank-and-file workers who had been suspended or expelled from various local unions, which were, of course, denied;

(2) Unanimously "approving the acts of the general president and his assistant in the brewery and other matters," and "instructing and empowering the general president to continue financial aid in these matters as long as the general president deems it advisable" and

(3) The adoption of a resolution to take rigorous action against "unauthorized" strikes, i.e., strikes which the general president does not approve, which he nearly always does not. "By unanimous action the Executive Board decided that all unions bringing about unauthorized strikes be censured and condemned and if necessary that the officers be removed."

The published proceedings of the executive board dealing with the appeals of suspended and expelled members read like the minutes of an army court-martial conducted by officers who act from the premise that the private soldier is always wrong. There is the appeal of thirteen members of Local 549, Kingsport,

Tennessee, who had been expelled for unstated reasons, probably for striking or talking out of turn. "Decision sustained and the appeals denied," in the case of ten of the appellants.

But for all that, the report shows, Tobin's board will give a worker a nickel's worth of justice if he humbles himself. Tobin, like God, grants mercy to penitent sinners—but not too much. The penalty of three other appellants was modified "in view of their expressions of repentance." Their sentence was commuted to one year of suspension with "probation for a period of two additional years." Whether these three suspended members who "repented" will be permitted to work and make a living at their trade during the suspension was not stated. Probably not.

Tobin's criminal activities in Minneapolis have been rather widely advertised. It is known that he tried to break the great strikes in 1934. He didn't succeed then, and could not prevent a strong union being built up without him and in spite of him. He then tried to get rid of the honest, fighting leaders of the union in 1941 by placing the union in "receivership." When the rank and file revolted against that, he called the federal cops through his friend President Roosevelt, and simply had the leaders thrown into prison.

At the same time, a horde of Tobin's gangsters, armed with blackjacks and baseball bats, were turned loose on the trucking districts with the open connivance of the city police, to force the truckdrivers to wear the button of Tobin's "reorganized" local. The State Labor Board, under Governor Stassen, denied the workers the right of an election to register their preference. In return for that favor, the labor-hating governor, author of the notorious Minnesota "Slave Labor Law," was introduced as the guest of honor and highly praised by Tobin at the subsequent international convention of the IBT.

Having tasted blood in Minneapolis, Tobin has been running wild ever since in his violent campaign against any sign of independence or militancy in the ranks of the International Brotherhood of Teamsters. At the present time approximately 40 percent of the local unions are under "receivership" with appointed officers and no autonomous rights. This simple fact in itself is the most devastating testimony of the extent of the rank-and-file discontent and revolt against the tyranny and treachery of this mean-spirited, vicious old man and the whole gang of well-heeled labor skates and common crooks who make up his unsavory machine.

With this tide of rank-and-file revolt rising all around him, Tobin spits hydrophobic venom in the faces of the union membership and threatens to spend their own money—the money they paid into the treasury of the International Union—to fight them and beat them down. He warns "any foolish group in any district" that they "must get this into their heads now—that if they ever get so cocky and self-important that they think they can defeat this International Union they are making the mistake of their lives. We don't want trouble and disagreement, but when it is forced on us, we will never back down if it costs every dollar in the treasury." You fight me, and I'll hire more gangsters to fight you—that is Tobin's April message to the rebel teamsters. There is no doubt about it, one can buy a lot of professional thugs with $14,800,000.

Daniel J. Tobin employs yet another murderous weapon in his war against the rank and file of the IBT. He reinforces his brutal dictatorship over the local unions of the Teamsters International by the device of first expelling dissident workers and then taking their bread and butter away from them by "taking them off the job." In the April number of the *International Teamster*, Tobin boasts about breaking up an opposition to the gangster-ridden union machine in St. Louis which culminated in a strike. "The International Union sent in a number of men," he says significantly, meaning a mob of strong-arm men whose assignment was to waylay the strikers and beat them up—"and every business agent and officer of our local unions in this city of St. Louis pledged his full and undivided help." It is known to Tobin that one of these local "business agents," in fact the boss of the whole Tobin setup in St. Louis, is a gangster with a criminal record.

According to Tobin's account, the leading rank-and-file militants in the strike—truckdrivers, not gangsters—also had the bad habit of "continuously finding fault with the union officers." Consequently, "the general president ordered that charges be preferred against them." And, of course, "several of them were expelled from the union."

Next came the deal with the bosses. Says Tobin: "The employers were notified that those men were no longer members of the union and that our union shop agreement must be observed. The employers complied with the agreement, and those individuals were laid off by the employers." By this combination of antilabor measures the strike was broken. The workers were beaten and forced into line. It was "a famous victory," and Tobin gloats over it. "In a few days," he writes, the men "begged to be allowed to go back to work." Maybe the poor devils had families to support. And maybe the families were hungry. The proudest men have been known to submit under such circumstances.

But proud men who beg through clenched teeth are dangerous animals to provoke. There are many of them in the International Brotherhood of Teamsters at the present time, and their number is steadily growing. One of these days they are going to count noses and come to the conclusion that they are strong enough, if they all act together, to put a stop to the humiliations and defeats imposed upon them by brutal violence and treacherous collusion with the bosses. That will be a bad day for the Mad Dog of the Labor Movement. The dogcatchers will catch up with him.

Laura Gray

Daniel Tobin

OUR RELATIONS WITH THE WORKERS PARTY

June 18, 1947

The following are excerpts from Cannon's report to a meeting of the New York membership of the SWP. The text is from an uncorrected and previously unpublished stenographic transcript.

My speech tonight is a report of the factual developments on this question since we last discussed it some months ago. And since it is a factual report, it is not quite clear to me how there can be two or more positions on it, unless someone disputes the facts as they have been ascertained by the Political Committee and as I will report them.

I want to take a brief time for a review of our relations with the Workers Party for the benefit of comrades who have not gone through the experience with us. [. . .]

Our convention had rejected the unity maneuver of 1945 and 1946. The Shachtmanites likewise, having carried through their maneuver and having scooped up twenty or thirty Goldmanites, also rejected the idea of unity. They represent it as though they always were for unity and always will be. But that isn't what the records shows. Under date of December 4, 1946, Shachtman wrote—and it was by some strange coincidence published the same week that the new turn in the question of unity arose—they published this pamphlet on the question of unity between the SWP and the WP in which they reviewed it at great length, to prove that we had spoiled the unity, and they came to this conclusion:

> To talk about unity between the Workers Party and the Socialist Workers Party now after all that has happened in the past two years

> in particular, would either be hollow ritualism or pious hypocrisy. Unity between these two parties, a real and sound and fruitful unity, is possible now only on the condition that an awakened and reoriented membership, aided by a reoriented international movement, imposes a radical change in the reactionary pro-Stalinist "Russian line" of the Socialist Workers Party and, correspondingly, deposes the bureaucratic regime which is responsible for keeping this millstone around the neck of the Socialist Workers Party. To talk about unity under any other circumstances is quite unreal.

That was the opinion published by the Workers Party under the signature of Shachtman in February 1947, just before the new turn. Now I am not going to argue as to the rightness or wrongness of the argument that Shachtman makes as to whether unity can be anything else than a "ritual and a pious hypocrisy." That is the worst kind of hypocrisy. I quote this only to show that whereas the convention of the Socialist Workers Party in October had said unity is out of the question, they followed it up but a few months later with a review and said also for their part unity is out of the question. Unity was off the agenda of both parties when the new situation developed which I had occasion to report to you about four months ago.

It was precipitated by the call issued by the International Executive Committee of the Fourth International for the world congress. The International Executive Committee laid down conditions for participation in this congress, which was to settle all the disputed questions and establish definitively the program and line and further procedure of our international movement. And this International Executive Committee put conditions not only to its own affiliates, but also to all unaffiliated groups [. . .] under which they also might come to the congress and participate in it. [. . .]

Now this call for the congress and these conditions put the Workers Party before a very critical situation which arose from the nature of the group. A group that is petty-bourgeois in its composition, centrist in its political tendency, moving toward the right, tied by its past to the Trotskyist movement—this movement standing in between us and the Social Democracy, was put by the congress conditions before a crisis. Acceptance of the terms of the world congress required a political turn on their part. They had been ridiculing and deriding the Fourth International. They had been traveling to the right. They had been sneering at it and rejecting all of its advice and directives. Now if they wanted to make any further pretense of connection with the world movement of Trotsky they had to make a turn and recognize the existence of that which they had previously said did not exist, and moreover recognize its authority and its power to enforce discipline upon them. Rejection of the terms of the world congress on the part of the WP would have meant to close the last door open for reconciliation with the Fourth International. [. . .]

Now, that was precisely the course that was first decided by the Workers Party: to reject the conditions of the International Executive Committee. A letter rejecting the conditions was drawn up and adopted by the Political Committee of the Workers Party. This action had already been taken when the representative of the IEC arrived in New York and met with them. As a result of their meeting with him, the Shachtmanites decided to change their decision. [. . .]

As a result of their consultation with him and his meeting with their PC and later with their plenum, the Shachtmanites decided to withdraw the letter of rejection and to write another letter accepting the conditions, although under protest. That was a second step in the new developments. We received this declaration February 10, four months ago.

We took it as a political turn of the WP taken at the last moment. That is the way that I explained it here in my report to you at the time. We took it as a political turn taken at the last moment before the definitive break would close all possibility of further discussion with the Fourth International, and we decided to give them the benefit of every doubt. [. . .] On February 15 and 16, five days later, the plenum of the Socialist Workers Party adopted its resolution. This is familiar to you. I will emphasize here only a section of it. [. . .]

The two conditions are very clear. The acceptance of the authority of the world congress and submission to its discipline had to be carried out in good faith; and second, the discussion of the disputed questions had to be completed before the unification so that we don't begin in the united organization with factional discussion, but with united work on the basis of the accepted program.

On the basis of our plenum resolution and their acceptance of it, unity negotiations began and they soon culminated in the Joint Statement for unity and in the agreement for collaboration in practical work. The sentiment of the membership in both parties, in its large majority, seemed to be favorable to the new program of unification, and an early achievement of unity was envisaged. However, as you know, this atmosphere didn't last very long. Unity encountered violent opposition in a section of the Workers Party from the extreme Burnhamite wing. It encountered the most frantic opposition from the periphery of the Workers Party, which is made up primarily of renegade intellectuals who feel that their last pretense to radicalism would be taken away if the Workers Party were to unite with the Socialist Workers Party. And they know how much a periphery they can be to us—which is nothing at all. The ink was hardly dry on the Joint Statement before the Shachtmanites began to violate it.

There was another factor in the situation. The Johnson group took the unification on face value and began an active agitation for it, and Shachtman was caught between the contradictory forces of a section of his party actually moving toward unification with the Fourth International, another section resisting and sabotaging, and he made his decision, which was more or less characteristic of him, to go with the right. And their program took the form of first signing the unity statement and then beginning systematically to violate it. [. . .]

Instead of printing the Joint Statement as it was, they printed it with a preface which gave an entirely false picture of past developments and vitiated the statement. They had signed an agreement with us that they would not take Weber into the Workers Party. They asked us why we wanted this condition that people who had left our party and had not joined them up to the time of February 10 should not be taken in. We told them the reason why. We said, we don't want anybody to leave our party and come back in the back door. We want them to come back through the front door. Weber hurled a stink bomb at our party and then ran out the back door. We want him to come back through the front door and we want to ask him a few questions, such as —Where have you been, Weber? What have you been doing? Why did you run out? A member of the National Committee of the party, he didn't even show up for the 1944 convention after he hurled a document this long at the party membership.

That is all, we said. We don't want you to take him in. And if you insist on taking him in, all right, we won't sign the Joint Statement. They agreed to do this, signed their names to it, and at the very time they were doing it they had a vicious document from Weber in their pocket, which they had already prepared for printing a few days later in *Labor Action*. [. . .]

They did the same thing with the Ruth Fischer letter. The very week when we were signing negotiations for unity, setting up a joint committee with the understanding that anything that would arise which would create friction should naturally be taken up in this joint committee of equal numbers from both sides in order to first at least try to come to an agreement, so as not to sharpen antagonisms as in the past, then they hurl that at our face.

Then, a week later, they printed an article in the *New International* in which they informed us that it was no longer possible for them to work with us even in practical respects on the question of Stalinism. We opened our eyes very wide when we read that. We knew they had big differences with us. We didn't conceal any more than they did. Let me just quote a sentence there:

> But it is no longer possible to reconcile the divergent evaluations of the Stalinist parties. If this is true, it follows that the area in which even practical agreements in the struggle against Stalinism can be made will continue to narrow as the divergence on the fundamental evaluation grows deeper. No attempt should be made to reconcile these evaluations![157]

That couldn't mean anything else to us except the threat of a new split, since we, far from changing our evaluation of the Stalinist parties, together with our co-thinkers intend to reaffirm it in the decisions of the world congress, and if they disagree with us not only on the theoretical aspect, but disagree with us on practical agreements in the class struggle, then they must contemplate another split with us. At least that is the way it impressed us.

We took note also that Johnson in the Workers Party, with whom we don't agree about the Russian question and some others—we disagree in the most fundamental way on the Russian question—has a fetish of unity. The Johnson group in the WP really wants unity with the Socialist Workers Party and the Fourth International.[158] Now, we don't agree with him in that either, because he makes a fetish of unity. He seems to think that unity is a prerequisite for the solution of the problem of developing the revolutionary party in this country, and we don't agree. But the point of importance for us here is that Johnson hailed the unity resolution enthusiastically and scraped up against the real sentiment of the Burnhamite right wing with whom Shachtman had meantime lined up. They started a lynching campaign against Johnson with a very strong Burnhamite taint in it. Johnson is pictured as a renegade and a traitor because he was putting unity and solidarity with the Fourth International above factional allegiance with Shachtman's party. But if Shachtman meant anything by this declaration he signed, Shachtman himself would have put solidarity with the Fourth International above allegiance to the faction in his own party. [. . .]

From all these things it became obvious to us who were doing nothing but merely observing at the time, that the Workers Party turn to the left—if it was such a turn—had been followed by a wide and violent swing to the right, and that this coincided with the enunciation of the Truman Doctrine.[159] And the coincidence was so pertinent that comrades all over the country wrote in to us about it and said this will affect their sentiment for unity with us, this new violent campaign leading to war with the Soviet Union, under the leadership of Truman and Marshall, and it is no accident that coincident with that they will cool off, as they did in 1939 under the stress of a similar campaign. [. . .]

After we had accepted their approach in February and said on that basis we will work toward unity, having established the political prerequisites, as we thought, we said then, now let us work together in practical affairs as much as possible. The first thing that came up was the Chicago elections. The Workers Party had a candidate on a write-in—Al Goldman. We had a candidate on a write-in—Bartell. So the joint negotiating committee said, naturally, let us combine the election campaign in Chicago—withdraw one of the candidates and get both parties behind the other. What could that mean? The Workers Party had signed an agreement that the Workers Party is going to be dissolved and the Socialist Workers Party will be the united organization. The Socialist Workers Party is the majority and they are the minority. The only practical course could be, support the Socialist Workers Party and popularize its name. What is the point of supporting the Workers Party, because it isn't going to exist very long after unity is reached. But they didn't make the joint campaign. The Workers Party said, you have it all wrong. Our theory is that the majority should submit to the minority and you should withdraw the candidate of the Socialist Workers Party in favor of the candidate of the Workers Party. Now they didn't say their principle is the majority should submit to the minority. That is one of the things they don't say but want to apply. Naturally our comrades broke off discussion and refused to even talk on such a stupid basis.

There were elections going on in Los Angeles at the same time. [. . .] What was involved in the Los Angeles elections was not rival candidates but the fact that a Negro candidate was running, I think for councilman, in a primarily Negro neighborhood on the kind of ticket they had in Toledo, I believe, and a number of other places. We had a more or less established policy in our party that where the Negro people put up a candidate of their own, who is not a Trotskyist, and may not be a radical, and we don't have the organizational basis for a Trotskyist candidate, that we don't stand aside, because we advocate the idea of Negroes in public office and we give critical support to this candidate as a matter of policy. This we were doing there.

The Shachtmanites had a member of their party running for the same office, and the two committees met to see how they could reconcile it, and they said they didn't agree with the policy of supporting this Negro candidate. Our comrades answered, it is a matter of policy with us to give critical support so you must withdraw your candidate. Majority rules. You are going to be a member of the Socialist Workers Party in a few months and you will have to carry out this policy. No. So there was no agreement in the Los Angeles election.

Then we had the Oakland elections where there was some sort of semi-labor-party movement, which was reported at length in *The Militant*. The Workers Party did not support that as they did not support a similar movement in Detroit a couple of years ago. Our party supported critically this movement as a big step toward the labor party. I believe that at the last minute the Workers Party there saw the light and changed their position and then we had a form of collaboration. [. . .]

Trade union work—about the same kind of experience. A little cooperation in the rubber industry, little or none, as far as I know, in auto, and in other fields we don't encounter the Shachtmanites to any great extent. They don't have the forces. And the net result of four months during which we were supposed to be working together is that nothing has been accomplished. And it hasn't been due to personal incompatibility. It has been due to inability to agree on fundamentals, on either policy or majority rule. [. . .]

Along came the Truman Doctrine. Do you recall that magnificent meeting we had here that night where George Clarke appeared on the platform? The Truman Doctrine, the central question of the day, the open announcement of American imperialism that they are going to conquer the world with atomic warfare—we couldn't even think of a joint meeting with the Shachtmanites on that. I don't think there was even a discussion on that.

The red-baiting campaign in Congress. No joint campaigns even discussed. Because the minute you discuss the Truman Doctrine or the red-baiting, they want the emphasis on the Soviet Union or Stalinism and we want to put it all on Truman and American imperialism. [. . .]

A protest demonstration against the Greek terror was held with great difficulty. [. . .] We had a telegram from Greece that our comrades' lives were endangered by the terror in Greece which is raging on a plane with that in Franco Spain. [We proposed to get out in the street] and denounce the Greek government. They wanted to issue slogans or a leaflet denouncing Stalinism at the same time. No, nothing doing. We are in favor of denouncing Stalinism, but not at the Greek consulate. That's where we denounce the Greek government, which is an agency of Wall Street. At the last minute, I think, they reconsidered and withdrew with a protest and so there was a joint picket line.

The last experience and the one that is really saddest is in relief work for our hungry comrades in Europe and other parts of the world. Any two parties of goodwill ought to be able to work together on that without difficulty. But we haven't been able to work with them for two years. We set up our own committee because we felt responsible to our comrades in Europe.[160] But the moment the unity agreement was signed they immediately agreed to dissolve their committee, combine their forces with ours, and turn over to us all the names of people on their lists in need of help. This went along very well for three months and they apparently felt that they had gotten acclimated there and they suddenly appeared with a demand for parity on the committees.

The local committees and the national committee should give to this small minority equal representation with the representatives of the SWP. Nothing could incense us more than that as a sign of factionalism and irresponsibility, and we brusquely told them, don't bring any more of those propositions to us. We feel responsible for these people in Europe and they are depending on us and we want to do what we can to help them. If you want to help, you're welcome to come in and help and you're entitled to representation in the committee and entitled that any friends you have in Europe be treated on the same plane as our friends, but if you want to break it up and start over again, have a factional work in the relief movement, then you better quit now, start your own committee, and we'll continue ours. That is the way the thing stands now and I don't know what will be the further development.

It is only four months since the disciplinary obligation was signed and a little more than three months since the joint statement. The International Executive Committee meeting a month or so ago began further steps in its preparation for the world congress, perhaps the most important gathering in the history of the human race. The plenum of the IEC had good representation.

England was represented, France, Italy, Spain, Belgium, Holland, Indochina, a number of other smaller countries—a really representative gathering of the leaders of the most important sections of the Fourth International already there. As far as representation is concerned, it was a conference with better representation than the founding congress of the Fourth International. Among other things they decided the conditions for representation at the world congress.

If I am not mistaken, they were unanimously adopted by all the delegates, among whom were different factions. There was the French majority, which is conciliatory toward Stalinism, opportunistic in that sense. There were the Italians who have a sectarian trend; the British majority, which is an unprincipled group which agrees with us in principles and combines with anyone against us in practice.

Now this is a very important point: How to arrange the representation in the Fourth International. Shall every country have the same number of delegates, the same votes? Manifestly impossible. Some are big parties, some are small, some are in big and important countries, others not so big. Shall it be strictly proportional? No. That is not the way things were regulated in the Comintern. The Comintern had the principle that delegations were grouped by a double criteria. One: the importance of the country from a political and economic point of view. And second:

the numerical strength of the party. Thus the USSR and Germany, France and England, Czechoslovakia and the United States, as countries of world power, were given greater consideration than other countries even though they might have bigger parties, etc. We had another thing to consider—that due to a number of circumstances, the numerical strength of the American party is bigger than that of other parties in important countries. A strictly proportional representation would give the American party four or five times as many delegates as the British, at least three times as many as the French, and would completely snow under the smaller groups in Italy, Spain, Belgium, Holland, etc. I give this as a hypothetical example, because the American delegates would have only consultative and not binding vote, since we are not members of the Fourth International because of the reactionary Voorhis Act.

Then there are factors such as countries of great importance which have small parties due to illegal conditions, etc., and it would be a manifest absurdity that a party in Switzerland could have as many delegates as a party from India or China although they might have as many or more members, due to the differences in conditions, legality, etc.

On the basis of all this a category was worked out, set out in the decisions of the IEC plenum. They put in the first category countries of great importance economically and politically.

First category: Countries of great importance (USSR, United States, China, India, Great Britain, France, Germany).

Second category: Countries of medium importance (Spain, Italy, Austria, Belgium, Holland, Greece, Canada, Mexico, Brazil, Argentina, Chile, Bolivia, Indochina).

Third category: Countries of lesser importance (Norway, Denmark, Bulgaria, Ireland, Palestine, Egypt, Cyprus, Cuba, Peru, Uruguay, Switzerland, Australia, South Africa, etc.).

And then they decided that every organization having up to 150 members would get three delegates if it belonged in the first category, two delegates if it belonged in the second, and one delegate if it belonged in the third, provided that every group, regardless of the importance of the country, would have at least one delegate. And if the countries are of greater importance, even though the membership would be smaller they would get more delegates. But that applies only to the first 150. And the same scale applies to those from 150 to 500 members. They will get an additional delegate. Then from 500 to 1,000 members, one more delegate. And from 1,000 to 1,500, one more delegate, etc. So that after you pass the 500 mark—whereas the other parties who have only 150 members can get three delegates—after you pass the 500 mark you only get one additional delegate for each additional 500.

Why was that done? The principal reason was to prevent the SWP from having too great a numerical predominance in the total consultative and decisive votes of the congress, and the proposal came from the SWP. This is the way it works out in practice: The French party with about 500 members gets three delegates to start with and then one for its additional members over 150—a total of four votes for 500 members.

The British party with about 500 members gets four. The SWP with 1,500 members gets a consultative vote of 3 for its first 150, and then it gets one additional consultative vote for its next 500—a total of six. The SWP gets six consultative votes; the French, with 500 members, four votes; and the British, with 400 members, four votes. So if you made it a strictly proportional representation, the situation would be considerably different. As it is, the French and British parties, the majority of which are both at the present time opposed to us, have eight votes for 900 members, and we have six consultative votes for 1,500 members.

As I said, we proposed this because we recognize the necessity of taking into consideration other things besides mere numerical strength and we did not want to overweigh the various votes in our favor and cause dissatisfaction. This was unanimously adopted because the manifest fairness of it appealed to all the smaller countries no matter how small their group is—if they have twenty people they get one vote. But we were shocked and somewhat surprised—but we shouldn't have been perhaps—to get a letter from Comrade Andrews [Jules Geller] in Ohio who reported to us that he had a recent conversation with the local organizer of the WP. It seems the WP had an Ohio conference at which [Nathan] Gould was the reporter for the PC.

> At this conference Gould reported that the plenum of the IEC adopted a method of apportioning delegates to the extraordinary convention on the following basis:
>
> Countries are divided into three categories; first-class nations, second-class nations, and third-class nations. A country which is classed in the first category would be given more voting power than a country in the second category, though the size of the organizations

might be the same. Gould then reported that this system, which is undemocratic, was a typical Cannonite method of rigging a convention.

On the basis of the above, it is obvious that the WP leadership is preparing in advance to declare their pledge to abide by the decisions of the extraordinary convention null and void because it was rigged, undemocratic, etc.

Now then, on May 28 the National Committee of the Shachtmanite party sends a letter to all sections of the Fourth International and to the IS which I will quote some extracts from. [. . .]

> Our committee also discussed the decision of the executive on the basis of representation to the congress. We reject this decision in its entirety. . . . It is a decision which not only has no authorization in the statutes of the International (1938) but it violates the spirit of democratic representation and true internationalism, and can only arouse repugnance if not in the sections of the countries placed in the first category then at the very least in the countries placed in the second and third.
>
> Under the concrete circumstances of the life of the International, of the actual numerical strength of its sections, and of their relations to each other, no other basis of representation can be considered just and democratic and appropriate to the needs of the movement than that of alloting delegates in strict accordance with proportional numerical strength. . . .
>
> We are addressing ourselves to all sections on this matter too with a request that they immediately take the measures necessary to achieve a reversal of the decision of the executive and the adoption of a decision which will help assure the democratic character of the congress.

What is noticeable about this last document, which is only a couple of weeks old, is not only the falsity of the objection and the complete distortion of the problem in order to cater to any dissatisfied small grouping in any part of the world on the ground that they are a "second-class" or a "third-class" category. Perhaps there is somebody in Mexico or Chile or Venezuela who is dissatisfied and whose pride has been hurt. This is an attempt to stir them up against the Yankee imperialists who are rigging the convention against them. What is noticeable is the impudent and venomous tone with which they address the International leadership and our party and try to stir up malcontents against it. What is evident is the obvious aim to discredit the world congress in advance, to cast over it before it starts the suspicion that the thing has been rigged and that the decisions are not going to be valid; a propaganda campaign for the rejection of its decisions and proceedings. It is equally obvious that these objections are absolutely disloyal, as I have pointed out to you; that is, if we accepted their proposal for proportional representation, the chief gainer would be the SWP and the losers would be especially parties like the French and the British which at the present time are in opposition to us.

When we offer categories and the IEC unanimously adopts it, it is denounced in favor of proportional representation. Suppose it had been the other way and the decision had been in favor of proportional representation? A hue and cry would have been raised that the 1,500 members of the SWP would so swamp the Mexican group and other groups that the congress would be nothing but an enlarged version of the SWP. The determination to find a basis for disagreement and discreditment in any case.

That is where the situation stands today on the factual side. And from these developments I believe it will be clear to you, as it is to us in the National Committee, that a possible early unification with the Shachtmanites before the world congress, as it was envisaged in the plenum resolution, has no realistic basis. Our only possible course in the new situation is to concentrate on the work of political clarification and demarcation, to devote all our efforts to the work in the mass movement, the recruiting of new workers, and the building up of the workers' cadres in the party, to strengthen the organizational bonds with our co-thinkers throughout the world and to work with them to smash any attempt to disrupt and discredit the world congress.

And it is equally obvious that any further consideration of the unity question with the Shachtmanites must await the terms of the congress. The terms of our plenum resolution do not in our opinion at present require any alteration. The plenum says that the obligation they undertook to submit to the congress must be carried out in good faith, and that can only be tested by the congress itself.

Some comrades here and in other parts of the country have objected to my remarks printed in the internal bulletin about an error in connection with the plenum resolution, and they maintain that the plenum resolution was correct and was not in error, that it forced the Shachtmanites to show their colors once again as a petty-bourgeois group. Now I am not confessing errors for others and I don't ask anybody else to share my view that an error was made on my part. I consider that I and some others did make an error to this extent, that the turn made by the Shachtmanites in February was taken too much at face value and that sufficient allowance was not made for a zigzag in the other direction. [. . .]

Others in the ranks maintained that it was wrong to consider the question of unity under any circumstances and that we should now flatly reject it. So, you may say, there are three points of view. One: that everything that was done was done exactly right. There is a strong group in the leadership that maintains that—I believe a majority around the country. Second: a smaller group, including myself, which thinks that not sufficient allowance was made for the petty-bourgeois centrist nature of this group and that their turn to the left was not taken with the necessary reserves and cautions and anticipation of another zigzag to the right. And then there is a third, that says we shouldn't have had anything to do with it in the first place. But all these differences, taken together, are not serious, no ground for quarrels, because they all proceed from the same fundamental premise: the strengthening of our party, its program, and its organizational position. [. . .]

NOTES

1. The final twelve of the eighteen Minneapolis case defendants were released from prison on January 24, 1945. They had entered prison with sixteen-month terms on December 31, 1943, and were released early for good behavior. Eleven had served their time at Sandstone penitentiary in upstate Minnesota: James P. Cannon, Jake Cooper, Oscar Coover, Sr., Farrell Dobbs, Vincent Dunne, Max Geldman, Albert Goldman, Emil Hansen, Carlos Hudson, Felix Morrow, and Carl Skoglund. Grace Carlson was incarcerated at Alderson, West Virginia. Six of the eighteen had been sentenced to one year and were released in October 1944: Harry DeBoer, Clarence Hamel, and Edward Palmquist, who were imprisoned at Sandstone, and Carl Kuehn, Alfred Russell, and Oscar Shoenfeld, who served their sentences at Danbury, Connecticut.

2. Grace Carlson was nicknamed "the Senator" from a United States senatorial campaign she waged in Minnesota on the SWP ticket in 1940.

3. Natalia Sedova began to develop political differences with the Trotskyist movement in 1942. She established close political ties with a number of critics of the leadership of the SWP and the Fourth International, including Grandizo Munis, Alfred and Marguerite Rosmer, and Jack and Sara Weber. Toward the end of World War II she became critical of the stress the SWP and the Fourth International gave to the slogan for defense of the Soviet Union, counterposing the need to warn of the Stalinist threat to the European and colonial revolutions. From 1944 on she became more and more sympathetic to the positions of Max Shachtman's Workers Party. In 1951, she broke publicly with the Fourth International, declaring that capitalism had been restored in the Soviet Union.

4. The Eleventh Convention of the American Trotskyist movement (the sixth for the SWP), held November 16-20, 1944, in New York, adopted a resolution on "The European Revolution and the Tasks of the Revolutionary Party," which contained the following statement: "Throughout the period when the Nazi military machine threatened the destruction of the Soviet Union, we pushed to the fore the slogan: *Unconditional Defense of the Soviet Union Against Imperialist Attack.* Today the fight for the defense of the Soviet Union against the military forces of Nazi Germany has essentially been won. . . . The present reality is the beginning of the European revolution, the military occupation of the continent by the Anglo-American and Red Army troops, and the conspiracy of the imperialists and the Kremlin bureaucracy to strangle the revolution. We therefore push to the fore and emphasize today *that section* of our

program embodied in the slogan: *Defense of the European Revolution Against All Its Enemies*" (*Fourth International,* December 1944, p. 367, emphasis in original).

5. From December 1942 the editorial page of *The Militant* featured a photograph of Trotsky accompanied by the quotation: "To defend the USSR as the main fortress of the world proletariat, against all assaults of world imperialism and of internal counter-revolution, is the most important duty of every class-conscious worker." In the March 31, 1945, issue it was replaced by another Trotsky quotation: "Only the world revolution can save the USSR for socialism. But the world revolution carries with it the inescapable blotting out of the Kremlin oligarchy."

6. The *International Bulletin,* vol. III, no. 1, February 1945, contained two letters to the Secretariat of the Fourth International from the Spanish Group in Mexico of the Fourth International dated June and September 1944, and a letter from Natalia Sedova to the SWP on the Russian question. The Spanish emigrés in Mexico criticized *The Militant's* position of defense of the Soviet Union and declared that the definition of the Soviet Union as a workers' state "is more and more static and false." Natalia Sedova, in her letter dated September 23, 1944, wrote: "I do *not* propose that we take off the slogan 'defense of the USSR' but I find that it must be pushed back to the second or third rank." She added her opinion that "The military defense of the USSR in the present world situation has become transformed into the problem of struggle against Stalinism."

7. The proposal to postpone the November 1944 SWP convention was made by Oscar Shoenfeld and Alfred Russell in "A Statement on the Internal Situation" (undated), written after their release from prison on October 20, 1944 (published in *Internal Bulletin,* vol. VI, no. 12, December 1944). Shoenfeld and Russell were supporters of the Goldman-Morrow faction. Goldman and Morrow themselves had given their approval for the convention in correspondence from prison at the end of July.

8. Jack Weber, who used the pseudonym "A. Roland," and Sara Weber were personal friends of Natalia Sedova. On the eve of the 1944 SWP convention he submitted a document, "We Arrive at a Line," announcing that he had differences with the party on the Russian question. He argued there: "The Allies need Stalin to help drown the proletarian revolution in blood, or at least to strangle it. This problem is paramount, so long as Stalin remains in power. The Allies, far from attacking the Soviet Union in that case, will do everything they can to uphold Stalin's rule, leaving it to him to bring about, under their economic pressure, the slow restoration of capitalism in Russia" (*Internal Bulletin,* vol. VI, no. 12, December 1944).

9. See Cannon's *Letters from Prison,* pp. 201-14.

10. The American Trotskyists, then organized in the Workers Party of the United States, voted in March 1936 to join the Socialist Party as a left-wing faction. The Trotskyists were expelled from the SP during the summer of 1937 and founded the Socialist Workers Party at a convention

in Chicago, December 31, 1937–January 3, 1938.

11. Three Moscow show trials were staged by Stalin between 1936 and 1938. Virtually all the surviving members of Lenin's Central Committee were arrested and forced to falsely confess to crimes such as economic sabotage, spying for imperialist powers, organizing anti-Soviet terrorist activities, and seeking to restore capitalism. Most were executed. Trotsky and his son, Leon Sedov, were the chief defendants, in absentia. Burnham contended that the Stalinist purges were representative of the true spirit of Marxist communism.

12. The Fifteenth Anniversary Plenum of the SWP National Committee was held in New York, October 29–November 1, 1943. For Cannon's reply to Goldman's criticisms of the majority's organizational methods, see his speech on "The Problem of Party Leadership" in *The Socialist Workers Party in World War II,* pp. 350-88.

13. The Transitional Program, whose formal title is "The Death Agony of Capitalism and the Tasks of the Fourth International," was written by Trotsky in 1938. It is included in the Pathfinder Press book *The Transitional Program for Socialist Revolution* by Leon Trotsky.

14. The internal bulletin Cannon refers to here contains Natalia Sedova's letter on the Russian question of September 23, 1944 (see note 6 above), and an undated letter from Martin (Cannon) written from Sandstone which criticizes "Natalia's letter." The Martin letter was written between September 26 and October 1, 1944 (it appears on pages 175-81 of *Letters from Prison*). It does not refer to Natalia's September 23 letter, which reaffirmed the need to defend the USSR against imperialism. It is actually a comment on an earlier, unpublished letter from Natalia Sedova to the SWP leadership dated August 16, 1944. A copy of this letter in Cannon's papers includes the following statement: "You seem to be hypnotized by the slogan of the 'defense of the USSR' and in the meantime profound changes, political as well as moral-psychological, have taken place in its social structure. In his articles, especially the last ones, L. D. wrote of the USSR as a *degenerating* workers' state and in view of this outlined two possible paths of further social evolution of the first workers' state: revolutionary and reactionary. The last four years have shown us that the reactionary landslide has assumed monstrous proportions within the USSR" (emphasis in original).

15. See *Letters from Prison,* pp. 260-74.

16. Carlo Tresca was assassinated on a New York street corner on January 11, 1943. The gunmen who killed him were never apprehended, but it was widely believed that they were either Italian gangsters acting on behalf of Mussolini or agents of Stalin's GPU. The police refused to make a serious investigation because of the unpopular views of the victim. Some 1,200 people attended a Tresca memorial meeting in New York on January 11, 1945, the second anniversary of his death, to honor his memory and to protest the inaction of the police.

17. Lenin's *One Step Forward, Two Steps Back,* though written at the

beginning of 1904, was first published in English thirty-seven years later, in a British edition put out by Lawrence and Wishart in 1941. Because of wartime conditions it reached the United States after a further delay.

18. Almost from the time of its founding in 1929, the Communist League of America (CLA), the original Trotskyist organization in the United States, was torn by differences between Cannon on one side and Max Shachtman and Martin Abern on the other. Many of the issues were organizational with no clear political content. Shachtman accused Cannon of organizational inefficiency and conservatism and viewed Cannon's search for contacts in the labor movement as nonpolitical and opportunist. Cannon opposed many of Shachtman's organizational proposals as beyond the means of the group and hence irresponsible. He regarded Shachtman as tied to a petty-bourgeois layer in the New York section of the CLA that was incapable of finding its way to real workers and that tried to substitute literary propaganda activity for a genuine communist perspective. The organization came to the point of split in 1933, when Trotsky intervened through a series of letters to effect an organizational compromise until the differences should take on a more political form. Two of these letters are contained in *Writings of Leon Trotsky (1932-33)* ("The Situation in the American League," March 7, 1933, and "More on the American Dispute," April 17, 1933). Cannon and Shachtman dissolved their respective factions at this time and worked together until 1939 when Shachtman came out in support of Burnham's revisions of Marxism.

19. The British Trotskyist movement splintered in 1933, just a year after its founding, and was not unified until 1944. Cannon went to England in 1938, prior to the founding conference of the Fourth International, as a representative of the International Secretariat with the object of promoting a fusion of the four then-existing Trotskyist groups. He succeeded in uniting three of these to form the Revolutionary Socialist League (these were the Revolutionary Socialist Party; the Marxist Group, led by C. L. R. James; and the Militant Group). The RSL was represented at the founding conference of the FI and was recognized as the British section. A fourth group, the Workers International League, led by Ralph Lee and Jock Haston, refused to join the unified movement and boycotted the founding congress of the FI. Under pressure from the world movement, the RSL and WIL fused in 1944 to form the Revolutionary Communist Party.

20. This speech was given on the eve of the defeat of Nazi Germany by the Allied powers. The Berlin garrison abandoned defense of Hitler's capital on May 2 and Germany's formal surrender was signed at Supreme Allied Headquarters in Reims, France, on May 7, 1945.

21. The founding conference of the United Nations opened at the San Francisco Opera House on April 25, 1945. It concluded with the signing of the UN Charter on June 26. The UN was conceived at the Teheran meetings in 1944 between Stalin, Churchill, and Roosevelt as a

replacement for the defunct League of Nations. Its form, which was initially a congress of the victors of World War II, excluded the defeated Axis powers and most of the colonial and semicolonial nations.

22. The Nazi occupation forces withdrew from Greece in September 1944, under pressure from the Greek partisan movement and under the threat of being cut off by a Soviet advance in the Balkans. The Stalinist-led ELAS (National Popular Liberation Army), in accord with Stalin's policy of ceding Greece to the British sphere of influence, welcomed British troops into the country in October, even though the ELAS had 50,000 troops under arms and was the only serious contender for governmental power. On December 3, 1944, Greek monarchist troops fired on a mass ELAS demonstration in Athens, provoking a month-long battle between the city's working class and the British and monarchist armies. The ELAS agreed to disarm in February in exchange for a truce agreement that promised it legality. This agreement was soon violated and civil war broke out in 1946.

23. The government had fought a long battle to try to break the militant United Auto Workers Local 365 at the giant Brewster Aeronautical plant in Long Island, New York. In 1944 it sought to frame up the local's president, Thomas De Lorenzo, on charges of falsifying civil service forms. In April 1945 Washington officials asked that the charges against De Lorenzo be dropped so that he could be drafted into the army, despite the fact that at the age of thirty-six he was two years over the usual exemption age for defense-plant workers. De Lorenzo appealed but lost and was drafted later that year.

24. "On the Party Press" by Martin (Cannon) appeared in the *Party Builder,* vol. 1, no. 4, February 1945. This material can be found in Cannon's *Letters from Prison,* pp. 260-74.

25. At the May 1945 plenum of the SWP National Committee the Goldman-Morrow minority raised the first of a series of organizational proposals leading toward a call for unification with Max Shachtman's Workers Party. Under the point on trade union work, Goldman put forward a motion stating in part: "On the trade union field the Workers Party has a program basically identical with ours. . . . The party should formally propose to the Workers Party the formation of a bloc between the members of both parties working together in the same union, for the purpose of building left-wing organizations on the trade union field." This proposal was opposed in the majority report, given by Morris Lewit. After the discussion, including Cannon's remarks, Goldman's motion was defeated by a vote of 22 to 3.

26. The Provisional Committee for Non-Partisan Labor Defense was established early in 1934 when the Stalinist-controlled International Labor Defense withdrew its support from imprisoned Anthony Bellussi because of his Trotskyist views. Bellussi, a coal miner in Wilkes-Barre, Pennsylvania, had emigrated to the United States from Italy in 1924 to escape persecution by the fascists. He was arrested on June 17, 1933, and

imprisoned for ten months, threatened with deportation to Italy. The Non-Partisan Labor Defense promoted an appeal in Bellussi's behalf signed by Carlo Tresca, Roger Baldwin, A. J. Muste, Cannon, Max Eastman, and Sidney Hook. It succeeded in winning his right to emigrate to a country of his choice and raised the money for him to go to South America in May 1934. The committee also defended emigré communists and socialists threatened with deportation to Nazi Germany.

27. Homer Martin, elected the president of the United Auto Workers union in 1936, soon became embroiled in a struggle for control of the union with the Stalinists. Jay Lovestone was one of Martin's advisers. The Trotskyists favored democratic control of the union by the ranks. To prevent the capture of the union by the bureaucratic Stalinist apparatus they temporarily blocked with Lovestone and Martin.

28. Traditionally, the only criterion for membership in a trade union is that a worker be employed in the industry or craft organized by that union. Dual unionism occurs when a group of workers or a political party tries to split the recognized mass trade union in an industry and establish a rival union based on political differences with the established union leadership.

29. See "More on the American Dispute" in *Writings 1932-33,* pp. 203-5.

30. In January 1939 the United Auto Workers split into two factions, one led by Homer Martin, which called a convention in Detroit, and one led by Walter Reuther and the Stalinists, which called a convention in Cleveland. Burnham, who was acting national secretary of the SWP while Cannon was working in France for the Fourth International, proposed to support the Martin forces even though they wanted to take the UAW out of the CIO and into the more conservative AFL. His policy was rejected by the party's auto fraction, which advocated support to the CIO gathering in Cleveland.

31. In June 1944, four SWP members in New York, Abe Stein, Sylvia Rainer, Helen Russel, and Ruth Winkler, organized a private political discussion meeting with members of the Workers Party to exchange views on the Russian question. When this came to the attention of the SWP city leadership a Control Commission investigation was ordered. Helen Russel told the commission that she wanted a discussion group in which "there is no need to have as the paramount aim winning advantages for one party or another." The four were censured for establishing relations with an opponent organization that were not regulated by the party. Goldman and Morrow made an issue of the censure, protesting the lack of democracy in the SWP. For Cannon's comments on the issues involved, see his *Letters from Prison,* pp. 186-200.

32. In the second week of July, 1945, some 150,000 railroad workers, coal miners, and civil service workers went on strike in Ibadan, Nigeria, demanding a raise in the minimum wage from US$.50 a day to US$.60. The British colonial government arrested ten leaders of the Nigerian Trades Union Congress and banned two African newspapers, the *West*

African Pilot and the *Daily Comet.* Nnamdi Azikiwe, the editor and publisher of the newspapers, was threatened with deportation. Cannon's telegram of protest reprinted here was answered by the British embassy in Washington, D.C., on August 24, which justified the suppression of the two newspapers on the ground that they were "misrepresenting the facts concerning this strike." On January 9, 1946, the Trades Union Congress of Nigeria wrote to the SWP, saying: "Your spontaneous support and collaboration during these hectic days were very inspiring and were of immense value to the cause of the workers."

33. At the April 1940 convention of the SWP a resolution was adopted outlining the conditions under which the unity of the party could be preserved and the Burnham-Shachtman faction remain within it. This document, entitled "Supplementary Resolution on the Organization Question," appears on page 240 of Cannon's *The Struggle for a Proletarian Party* (Pathfinder Press, 1972). The resolution stipulated: "The decisions of the party convention must be accepted by all under the rules of democratic centralism. Strict discipline in action is to be required of all party members." It added: "No measures are to be taken against any party member because of the views expressed in the party discussion. Nobody is obliged to renounce his opinion. There is no prohibition of factions. The minority is to be given representation in the leading party committees and assured full opportunity to participate in all phases of party work." The Shachtman faction voted against the resolution, and at a subsequent meeting of the Political Committee declared it would not abide by its conditions. The Shachtmanites then proceeded to set up the Workers Party.

34. "A Petty-Bourgeois Opposition in the Socialist Workers Party," December 15, 1939, *In Defense of Marxism* (Pathfinder Press, 1973), p. 43.

35. When Burnham, Shachtman, and Abern split from the SWP they appropriated the party's theoretical magazine, *New International,* which had been registered with the post office in their names as trustees for the SWP. The party began publication of a new magazine, *Fourth International,* to replace the one that had been stolen. This last quotation from Trotsky is taken from his article "Petty-Bourgeois Moralists and the Proletarian Party," April 23, 1940, *In Defense of Marxism,* p. 169.

36. Following the outbreak of war in Europe the Fourth International held an emergency conference in New York, May 19-26, 1940. The conference adopted a resolution on the internal fight in the SWP which stated in part: "The Emergency Conference of the Fourth International endorses the action of the American section of the Fourth International in suspending all those who violated the decisions of its April convention. The Conference suggests to the N.C. of the S.W.P. that it set a definite time limit of one month after publication of the Conference decisions within which the suspended members must signify their acceptance of the convention decisions under penalty of unconditional expulsion from the party" (*The Struggle for a Proletarian Party,* p. 252).

37. "An Open Letter to Comrade Burnham," January 7, 1940, *In Defense of Marxism,* p. 94.

38. The "Three Theses on the European Revolution and the Political Tasks" were written in October 1941 by the leaders of the "Committee Abroad of the International Communists of Germany" (AK of the IKD). The theses were published in the SWP's *International Bulletin,* vol. II, no. 3, September 1942. They argued in essence that German fascism represented a qualitatively new and more repressive form of capitalism based on forced labor and that the German occupation regimes in Europe had thoroughly destroyed the parties and organizations of all classes. In this situation the main task for socialists was to form a multiclass "national liberation" movement that would fight to achieve a "democratic revolution" that would stop short of socialism. The SWP supported working class resistance movements against the Nazis but rejected joining resistance movements led by the bourgeoisie. It characterized the "Three Theses" as falling into a bourgeois nationalist deviation and reviving the idea of the revolution by stages. Beginning in 1944 the authors of the theses began publishing articles in Shachtman's *New International.*

39. On China, the SWP and the Fourth International urged support to Chiang Kai-shek against the Japanese imperialists as a just struggle by a semicolonial nation for independence. Shachtman agreed with this position while in the SWP, but later argued that a colonial independence movement under bourgeois leadership could only serve one or the other of the two big imperialist camps while World War II continued. On the basis of this same argument the WP refused support to struggles against British imperialism in India when these were led by the bourgeois Indian National Congress.

40. Shachtman wrote an account of the November 1944 SWP convention in his *New International* under the title "From the Bureaucratic Jungle."

41. "The Organizational Principles Upon Which the Party Was Founded," in *The Struggle for a Proletarian Party,* p. 230.

42. "The Organizational Conclusions of the Present Discussion," in *The Struggle for a Proletarian Party,* p. 237.

43. Leon Trotsky, *The Third International After Lenin* (Pathfinder Press, 1970), p. 157.

44. The "Call for the Formation of a Faction to Support the P.C. Minority Resolution on Unity with the Workers Party" issued by Oscar Williams (Shoenfeld), Felix Morrow, and Albert Goldman in mid-July, 1945, stated that the formation of a faction was not motivated primarily by their desire to promote the unification: "Important as this question is, however, we would not under other circumstances necessarily form a faction to fight for it. In a normal, healthy atmosphere it is possible to avoid having a faction even where there are differences on important questions. . . . The conduct of Comrade Cannon at the July 12th meeting

of the Political Committee, when the resolution on the Workers Party question was first introduced, shows the real nature of Cannon and his immediate followers when confronted by the necessity to discuss an important issue. He proceeded to question the minority P.C. members concerning their relations with W.P. leaders. When asked what was the purpose of the question, he stated: 'We want to know what party you are working for.' To this he added the charge that Comrade Goldman 'is a stooge for Shachtman.' Thus, at the very outset he has created an atmosphere making impossible a calm and objective discussion of the question. This typifies what can be called Bolshevism-a-la-Cannon."

45. As World War II drew to a close, the wartime alliance between Moscow and Washington came under strain. Stalin still envisaged a lengthy period of peaceful and friendly relations with world imperialism, based on the spheres-of-influence pacts at Yalta and Potsdam. But he sought to free the hands of foreign Communist parties to act more effectively as pressure groups in support of the interests of the Soviet government. The American Communist Party, in accord with Stalin's policy of support to Roosevelt, had dissolved itself in May 1944, its members reconstituting themselves as the Communist Political Association, "a nonpartisan association of Americans." At the beginning of 1945, Stalin met with French Stalinist leader Jacques Duclos. In April 1945, Duclos published in the French journal *Cahiers du Communisme* an attack on the "revisionism" of the American CP and its national chairman, Earl Browder, who had headed the party since 1930. This was reprinted in the New York *Daily Worker* on May 24. The CPA called a special convention at the end of July, where Browder was summarily removed from the leadership and replaced by William Z. Foster, amidst confessions by the whole party leadership that they had been "duped" and "misled" by Browder. This convention reestablished the CP. Browder was expelled from the party in February 1946 for "social imperialism."

46. In Germany in 1923 the French occupation of the Ruhr sparked a mass protest movement against the Versailles Treaty that had ended World War I by ceding German territorial rights to the Western Allies. The Communist Party planned an uprising for October, but canceled it at the last minute. For Trotsky, this signaled the loss of a unique revolutionary opportunity. He blamed not only the German party but principally the Comintern, led at that time by Stalin and Zinoviev.

47. Cannon is referring to union support for the SWP defendants in the Minneapolis case.

48. Browder's offer to "clasp the hand" of banker J. P. Morgan, Jr., if Morgan would join the "antifascist alliance" headed by Roosevelt, was made in a speech at Bridgeport, Connecticut, published in the January 1944 issue of *The Communist,* the CPA's theoretical magazine.

49. Following the Stalin-Hitler pact in 1939, Browder was tried on trumped-up charges of unlawful use of his passport and sentenced to four years in prison. He entered the federal penitentiary at Atlanta, Georgia,

in March 1941. After the German invasion of the Soviet Union in June 1941 the CP became prowar and in May 1942 Browder was released after Roosevelt commuted his sentence.

50. Foster's program was embodied in a resolution of the National Board of the CPA published in the June 4, 1945, *Daily Worker*. It stated in part: "It is imperative that the American people resolutely support every effort of the Truman administration to carry forward Roosevelt's program for victory, peace, democracy and 60 million jobs." And that workers should "continue uninterrupted war production and uphold labor's no-strike pledge for the duration."

51. Benjamin J. Davis, a prominent Black leader of the CP, was elected to the New York City Council on the CP ticket in 1943. Shortly before his term expired in 1945 he made a deal with the New York Democratic Party, known commonly as Tammany Hall, to receive the Democratic nomination. Davis registered as a Democrat and was presented at a Democratic Party rally by party officials. The Democrats withdrew the nomination before the election, and Davis was reelected on the Communist Party ticket.

52. On October 18, 1938, Trotsky made a recorded speech in English hailing the founding conference of the Fourth International and the tenth anniversary of American Trotskyism. It was first played at a New York mass meeting on October 28. The text can be found in *Writings 1938-39,* pp. 85-87.

53. Roosevelt proclaimed the "Four Freedoms" as a goal of American foreign policy in an address to Congress, January 6, 1941. They were: freedom of speech and expression, freedom of worship, freedom from want, and freedom from fear.

54. *The Militant*'s staff cartoonist was Laura Gray (1909-1958), the paper's regular cartoonist from 1944 until her death.

55. On August 22, 1945, Max Shachtman wrote to Cannon on behalf of the Workers Party to relay a statement on the possible unification of the two organizations adopted by the National Committee of the WP. This statement, along with a reply by Cannon dated August 27, 1945, was published in the September 1945 issue of *Fourth International.* Cannon's August 27 letter is omitted from this book because he summarizes it fully in this speech to the New York membership.

56. The undergroundists split from the Communist Party of America in January 1922 in protest over the organization the previous month of the legal Workers Party as a CP affiliate. They held that the nature of communist organizing required a secret conspiratorial organization and that a legal party would have to water down its program to the point of reformism. Based on the immigrant worker federations, primarily among Latvians and Russians, the undergroundists took with them between 2,000 and 4,000 of the CP's then 10,000 members.

57. The Trotskyist Left Opposition was expelled from the Soviet CP in 1927; Cannon, Shachtman, and Abern were expelled from the CPUSA at

the end of 1928. The perspective of the Trotskyists was to act as an expelled faction of Communist parties and seek to reform the Comintern and the Soviet CP. When the German CP failed to effectively oppose the rise of Hitler in 1933 Trotsky declared the Comintern bankrupt and unreformable and issued the call for the formation of the Fourth International.

58. Frederick Engels to August Bebel, October 28, 1882, Marx and Engels *Selected Correspondence* (Moscow: Foreign Languages Publishing House, undated), p. 427.

59. Engels to Bebel, June 20, 1873, in ibid., p. 345.

60. Loc. cit.

61. Marx's *Critique of the Gotha Program* written in 1875 was directed at the unity program presented to the socialist congress held at Gotha, Germany, May 22-27, 1875. This congress unified the Social Democratic Workers Party, led by August Bebel and Wilhelm Liebknecht, which followed Marx and Engels, and the General German Workers Union headed by followers of the late Ferdinand Lassalle. The new organization that issued from the congress was called the Socialist Workers Party of Germany.

62. The Anglo-Russian Trade Union Unity Committee was formed by Soviet and British trade union officials in May 1925. The British members of this committee used the prestige of their association with the Soviet Union to help break the near-revolutionary general strike in Britain in May 1926. Trotsky condemned the placing of Soviet government diplomatic interests above the need to support the general strike, and demanded a public break with the Anglo-Russian Committee by the Soviet trade unions. The Chinese revolution of 1925-27 went down to defeat as a result of the Comintern policy of support to the bourgeois-nationalist party, the Kuomintang, of Chiang Kai-shek. Chiang turned on his Communist allies in April 1927 and staged a massacre in the industrial city of Shanghai which became a signal for reactionary forces throughout China to attack the workers' movement. Trotsky opposed the subordination of the workers' and peasants' movement to the Chinese bourgeoisie.

63. Cannon is referring to Trotsky's December 1932 document, "The International Left Opposition, Its Tasks and Methods," which was directed to the international preconference of the ILO held in Paris February 4-8, 1933. In the section on the Bordigists, Trotsky wrote: "Within the framework of a mass party it would be possible to live together with the Bordigists—under the condition of firm discipline in action. But within the framework of a faction it is completely impermissible, especially after the entire experience we have gone through, to support the fiction of unity with an alien group which remains ideologically rigid and isolated in a sectarian manner" (*Writings 1932-33*, p. 59).

64. The Molinierists were a group in the French section led by

Raymond Molinier and Pierre Frank. They were expelled from the section in 1935 for setting up their own newspaper, *La Commune.* A reunification in 1936 led quickly to another split. Reunification negotiations continued for several years, but they were not concluded until 1944. See Trotsky's *The Crisis of the French Section (1935-36)* (Pathfinder Press, 1977).

65. In a letter to Farrell Dobbs, January 10, 1940, Trotsky wrote: "In the case of Molinier as in the case of some American comrades (Field, Weisbord and some others), I was for a more patient attitude. In several cases I succeeded, in several others it was a failure. But I don't regret at all my more patient attitude towards some doubtful figures in our movement. In any case, my 'defense' of them was never a bloc at the expense of principles" (*In Defense of Marxism*, p. 97).

66. "Declaration of the Editorial Board of *Iskra*," September 1900, in Lenin's *Collected Works* (Moscow: Progress Publishers, 1972), vol. 4, p. 354.

67. On July 20, 1945, an antifascist rally of 17,000 persons was held at the Olympic auditorium in Los Angeles to counter a profascist meeting at the nearby Shrine auditorium the same night. The profascist meeting, which heard an address by Gerald L. K. Smith, drew 5,000 people. The meeting at the Olympic was called by a united-front committee dominated by the Communist Party, with considerable union support. The SWP supported this rally and had been instrumental in pressuring the CP into organizing it. The Shachtmanites counterposed to the July 20 rally a series of tiny "united front" picketlines in front of auditoriums where Smith was speaking. Restricted to only non-Stalinist socialist participation and without any support from the labor movement, the largest of these picket lines, on June 25, drew only 150 people.

68. June 13, 1932, in *Writings 1932*, p. 112.

69. The SWP's Black work director in 1939-40 was C. L. R. James, who used the pseudonym Johnson. Cannon's figures here for Black membership in 1939 are undoubtedly too small, although his point is correct that there were at that time very few Black members of the SWP.

70. On August 28 Natalia Sedova had written to Usick (John G. Wright) expressing her support for Goldman's proposals of common activities with the Workers Party. Her letter said in part: "A thousand times more important [than the WP's position on the defense of the Soviet Union] at the present time is unification, rather than the existence of two *independent* groups who *in the fundamentals* march under the one and the same banner. The program of the minority [the WP] is known to the majority from the former's literature; there is no necessity to discuss it. . . . At the present moment . . . our party ought to take the road of the unity of the two parties." She added: "Incomprehensible to me, dear friend, is the persistence with which you put aside the danger of bureaucratism in our ranks. The danger is possible; it is in the air; to be *conscious* of the possibility of such a danger in and of itself already means to forestall it and it consequently signifies the possibility of avoiding it."

71. On September 10, Natalia Sedova replied to Cannon as follows: "Assuredly I wanted my letter to Usick of August 28 (like all the preceding letters) to be read first of all by you as well as other members of the party, *the majority and minority* alike, who are interested in the question, without of course their being published or becoming known through any other channels to the group with which unity negotiations are being conducted but not yet consummated." The August 28 letter was read to the PC on October 2. There was unanimous agreement that the letter be mimeographed for the SWP NC. Goldman then introduced a motion that the letter be sent to all the branches of the SWP and read to the membership. This was carried 3 for, none against, with 8 abstentions (the PC majority as a whole abstained to indicate they disagreed with the wisdom of the proposal but would not put themselves in the position of "suppressing" the letter). In a letter to Grace Carlson of November 19, 1945, Natalia Sedova wrote: "I am rather upset about the fact that my letter has been published and distributed at the party cells. I would never have dared to speak to them through such a letter. This letter absolutely did not deserve to play such a role." She cited the internal publication by Cannon and the majority of her letter without her permission as an example "in a small way [of] what I mean by bureaucratism."

72. With Japan's surrender to the Allies, the Japanese occupation regime in formerly French Indochina collapsed. A spontaneous popular revolution swept Vietnam on August 19 and led to the proclamation of an independent Vietnam with Ho Chi Minh as president. The new government, a coalition between the Vietnamese Communist Party and various capitalist parties, pledged to uphold the Potsdam agreements and welcomed British troops to Saigon at the beginning of September. The British, however, with some American support, attacked the independence forces in Saigon and restored power in the south to the French colonial regime.

73. The Atlantic Charter was a declaration issued by Roosevelt and Churchill on August 14, 1941, following a meeting on the USS *Augusta* in the North Atlantic. It stated that the U.S. and Britain "seek no aggrandizement, territorial or other," that "they respect the right of all people to choose the form of government under which they will live," and called for "the abandonment of the use of force" in disputes between nations.

74. On September 15, Shachtman sent a second letter to the SWP leadership proposing steps toward unity of the two parties. In this letter Shachtman stated the readiness of the WP to accept discipline as a minority of the SWP and promised a period of "intensive common activity" after unification and not a new faction fight. As specific steps toward fusion, he suggested the publication of a joint discussion bulletin, common activity at the branch level, followed by the appointment of a joint National Committee to be confirmed in a joint convention. The SWP PC discussed this letter at its meeting of September 21. The majority proposed two steps: the calling of an NC plenum for October 6-7 to discuss

a reply to the WP letter, and the scheduling of a meeting between WP leaders and a subcommittee of the SWP PC. This subcommittee had been set up August 27 and consisted of Cannon, Bert Cochran, and Morris Lewit. The committee met with Shachtman, E. R. McKinney, and Ernest Erber at the end of September and reported back to the PC on October 2. At that time Cannon stated that the WP had definitely agreed to accept the status of a disciplined minority, but that they had asked for their own internal bulletin. A second meeting was to be held before the plenum. The majority report to the plenum was made by Morris Lewit. He presented a resolution drafted by the subcommittee—himself, Cannon, and Cochran. This resolution specified three decisions: "a. To endorse the letter and actions of the Political Committee in response to the letter from the WP [referring to Cannon's letter of August 27, 1945. See note 55]; b. To authorize the Political Committee to prepare and carry through a thorough discussion and clarification of the theoretical, political and organizational issues in dispute, and fix the position of the party precisely on every point in preparation for the consideration and action of the next party convention; c. To reject any united front for propaganda. The SWP must continue to conduct its propagandistic activities in its own name and under its own banner and utilize these activities to aid direct recruitment of new members into the SWP. At the same time, the plenum authorizes the Political Committee to invite the WP to collaborate with our party in practical actions in those cases where, in the judgment of the Political Committee, such collaboration would be advantageous in serving practical ends without blurring or compromising political lines."

75. The Second National Active Workers Conference of the Workers Party was held in Detroit, August 18-19, 1945.

76. Technically, all that regroupment means in Marxist terminology is the breaking down of existing organizational lines in response to changing political positions. It can include fusions as well as alliances of a more temporary character. What Shachtman seems to mean is a regroupment between the WP and the Goldman-Morrow faction in which the latter would quit the SWP and join the Shachtmanites.

77. Max Shachtman, "The Character and Perspectives of the Party Today," *Active Workers Conference Bulletin*, no. VI, July 30, 1945.

78. Peace negotiations between the new Bolshevik government of Russia and German imperialism were begun at the Ukrainian town of Brest-Litovsk in December 1917. Trotsky headed the Bolshevik delegation. He broke off negotiations on February 10, in accord with a Central Committee decision to protest the harshness of the German terms. The Bolshevik leadership was divided on how to meet a possible German offensive. Lenin proposed immediate capitulation and the signing of the peace terms that had been offered. Trotsky proposed a surrender to the terms, but only after the Germans had taken definite military action that showed to the world that the Soviet representatives signed under duress. Bukharin and a majority of the Central Committee proposed to fight a

revolutionary war against Germany. When the Germans launched their offensive on February 18, support began to shift to Lenin, and Trotsky on February 21 abstained in order to give Lenin a majority over the so-called left Communists led by Bukharin. With this majority the Treaty of Brest-Litovsk was signed on March 3, 1918. The "left Communists" refused to accept their defeat and began publication of a daily newspaper, *Kommunist*, in Petrograd from March 5 to March 19, 1918. During those two weeks, the CC majority debated with the unauthorized paper in the pages of party organs such as *Pravda*. *Kommunist* ceased publication by decision of the Petrograd city party conference held on March 20, 1918. Throughout the Brest-Litovsk events extensive debate, much of it public, took place in the Soviet party and press, but with this exception it was the elected majority that decided in all cases the format and scope of publication of minority views.

79. The ICL plenum Cannon attended was held in Paris, October 14-16, 1934. It was this gathering that approved the entry of the French section into the French Socialist Party.

80. Cannon's description of Trotsky's relations with the German SAP is not fully accurate. Trotsky did not abandon attempts to fuse with the SAP when they were driven into exile but only after an experience with them in the movement for the Fourth International. At a conference of left socialist and communist organizations held in Paris in August 1933, the SAP, the Dutch OSP, and Sneevliet's Revolutionary Socialist Party (RSP) joined with the Trotskyist International Left Opposition in issuing "The Declaration of Four," which called for the formation of a Fourth International. Trotsky at that time proposed fusion of the German section of the ICL and the SAP, as well as the fusion of the RSP and OSP in Holland. When Cannon met with Trotsky in the fall of 1934, the SAP was moving rapidly away from the ICL and broke openly with the movement for the Fourth International in February 1935.

81. Beginning in the spring of 1935, Cannon and Shachtman, then the leaders of a common faction within the Workers Party of the United States, proposed an orientation toward the Socialist Party of Norman Thomas. This was opposed by the WP majority, composed of a bloc of A. J. Muste, Martin Abern, and Hugo Oehler. (Goldman had split from the Trotskyists in 1934 and had already joined the SP as an individual.) The Cannon-Shachtman group won a majority in the WP at the June 1935 plenum of the NC, but did not propose to enter the SP at that time because the SP was then dominated by a hard-core right-wing leadership centered in New York. Oehler and Abern charged that Cannon had already decided on fusing with the SP and was carrying on secret negotiations with the SP leadership. In fact, it was only after the split with Oehler at the end of October 1935, and the walkout of the SP right-wing leadership in December, that the Cannon leadership, in full agreement with the majority of the ranks, began negotiations with the SP left wing, the so-called Militant caucus. The entry tactic was approved by

the March 1936 convention of the WP after which the Trotskyists joined the SP as individuals. The entry lasted until the summer of 1937, when the Trotskyists were expelled.

82. The twenty-one conditions were adopted by the Second World Congress of the Comintern (July-August 1920) to prevent the affiliation of centrist parties that had not fully broken from reformism. They were drafted by Lenin (see his *Collected Works*, vol. 31, pp. 206-12).

83. See Cannon's *Letters from Prison*, pp. 201-14.

84. In the early morning hours of May 24, 1940, a large band of men armed with machine guns broke into Trotsky's house in Coyoacán, a suburb of Mexico City. Led by the Stalinist artist David Alfaro Siqueiros, they machine-gunned Trotsky's bedroom. Trotsky and Natalia Sedova escaped death by taking refuge in an alcove of the darkened room. One of Trotsky's guards, Robert Sheldon Harte of New York, was kidnapped by the Stalinists and murdered.

85. The Great French Revolution broke out in 1789 when the third estate, representing the commons or bourgeoisie, broke with the nobility and clergy and set up a National Assembly in defiance of the feudal monarchy. The monarchy was abolished in 1792 and King Louis XVI was executed on January 21, 1793. The revolution moved sharply to the right with the arrest of Robespierre, the principal leader of the radical Jacobins, on 9 Thermidor (July 27), 1794. (The revolutionary government had adopted its own calendar, renaming the months of the year.) The corrupt Directory ruled from the overthrow of Robespierre until it was itself toppled in a military coup by Napoleon Bonaparte on 18 Brumaire (November 9), 1799. Napoleon eventually had himself crowned emperor of France. In 1814, after the military defeat of Napoleon in the European wars, the old monarchy—the house of Bourbon—was restored under King Louis XVIII. The monarchy did not restore feudalism, however, but ruled over a bourgeois state.

86. After the signing of the Stalin-Hitler pact in September 1939 and the Soviet-German partition of Poland, Moscow demanded territorial concessions from Finland. When these were refused, the Soviet Union bombed Helsinki on November 30, 1939, and sent an invasion force against the Finnish Mannerheim Line. After a series of initial defeats at the hands of the Finnish army, the Russians staged a massive assault that broke through the defenses. An armistice on Russian terms was signed on March 13, 1940.

87. The "Theses on the American Revolution" were completed in October 1946 and appear later in this volume.

88. On November 16, while Cannon was in Chicago, the minority announced at a class given by Goldman that it was sponsoring a party the following night with the aim of initiating "fraternization" between members of the SWP and the WP. On November 21 Mike Bartell, the Chicago local organizer, in a letter to Morris Lewit filed charges against Lydia Beidel ("Bennett"), a minority member of the National Committee,

for her role in this affair. Bartell wrote: "Comrade Lydia Bennett, in the name of the faction, sent a mailing to a long list of nonparty people inviting them to attend" and that she "also sent a letter to the Chicago branch of the Workers Party inviting all of its members to attend and participate in the social." At the December 4 PC meeting, Cannon made a motion calling for a Control Commission investigation of the Chicago event and of a similar social given by the minority in New York. In a December 18 letter to the PC from F. Simington, secretary of the minority in Chicago, the minority declared: "The minority faction in Chicago wishes to state that it takes joint responsibility for the actions of Comrade Bennett in this matter; it arranged and conducted the social for the purpose of breaking down the estrangement between the membership of the two parties; this is in line with our fervent desire to see unity between the two parties effected." Bennett and Bartell appeared before a Control Commission subcommittee in Chicago on January 4, 1946, where written depositions were taken. The CC's findings, dated January 24, characterized Bennett's action as a "violation of basic party loyalty." The matter was referred to an NC plenum, held in May 1946.

89. After the creation of the Workers Party of the United States in December 1934 by the fusion of the AWP and CLA, the Allentown branch was dominated by supporters of A. J. Muste. A secret Stalinist nucleus developed among these former AWP members, led by Arnold Johnson. On the eve of the March 1936 WP convention, Johnson and two others announced in the *Daily Worker* that they had joined the Communist Party. In *The History of American Trotskyism* Cannon mentioned the role played by Sam Gordon, who had come from the CLA, in battling Johnson in Allentown, but omitted to mention that Ramuglia, a former Musteite, had sided with the party majority in Allentown against the Johnson group. For Cannon's account, see *The History of American Trotskyism*, pp. 228-31.

90. Dave Jeffries and Leo Lyons of New York resigned from the Goldman-Morrow faction in a letter dated December 16, 1945. There they stated that their reason was that the faction "is no longer organized principally on the basis of the struggle for this unity [with the WP]. . . . It has been transformed from a faction for unity into a faction for split." While the faction had formally declared that it would not walk out of the SWP, they said that "Comrade Goldman explained how this contradiction was to be resolved—the faction was going to be expelled, and if it was not expelled for what it was planning to do in the immediate future, it would go further—to the point of writing for and distributing *Labor Action.*"

91. See note 70 above.

92. In the November 6, 1945, New York City mayoralty race, Farrell Dobbs, the SWP candidate, received 4,267 votes compared to 869 for Max Shachtman, the WP candidate.

93. In January 1942 Grandizo Munis wrote a criticism of the SWP's conduct in the Minneapolis trial. The gist of his objections was that

Cannon and Goldman had failed to advocate revolutionary violence against the bourgeois state as an avowed aim of the socialist movement. Cannon wrote a lengthy reply in May 1942. Both are available in an expanded edition of *Socialism on Trial,* the transcript of Cannon's testimony in the Minneapolis case (Pathfinder Press, 1973).

94. See note 74 above.

95. On March 6, 1946, sixty French police with machine guns and drawn pistols surrounded a Paris meeting hall and arrested twenty-eight Trotskyists. The meeting was the first postwar world gathering of the Fourth International. Those arrested included delegates and observers from France, the United States, Belgium, Britain, Holland, Ireland, Switzerland, Greece, and refugees from Spain. The French government, at that time headed by Félix Gouin, who had replaced de Gaulle in January 1946, was a coalition regime in which seventeen out of the twenty-three ministerial posts were held by representatives of the Socialist and Communist parties. The Trotskyists were held overnight, concluded their conference in the French prison, and were released. To protect the delegates from further reprisals it was decided at the time to refer to the conference simply as a meeting on international questions sponsored by the French Trotskyist organization, the Parti Communiste Internationaliste. The world gathering, referred to as an international preconference preparatory to a world congress, was reported in the Trotskyist press as having taken place in Belgium at the beginning of April. The PCI mounted an effective protest against the arrests, including a meeting of 1,000 persons in Paris on March 12. The government responded in mid-March by lifting the postwar ban on the PCI's newspaper, *La Vérité.*

96. On February 25, 1946, a Black woman in Columbia, Tennessee, was struck by a white radio repairman during an argument. When her son came to her aid the two were arrested and charged with assaulting a white man. Racist lynch mobs then gathered and staged an armed attack on the Black community of Columbia. White police and state troopers sided with the mobs. On the pretext that some of the Black families had armed themselves for self-defense, the police invaded the Black part of town, firing indiscriminately and looting homes and stores. More than 100 Blacks were arrested. Two Black men were shot by police in the city jail; they were denied admission to the white city hospital and died en route to a segregated hospital forty-three miles away. Nationwide protests secured the release of the imprisoned Blacks on March 8.

97. At the April 9, 1946, meeting of the SWP PC, Felix Morrow protested the majority's handling of discussion materials from the minority in the internal bulletin and in *Fourth International* magazine. As regards the magazine, Morrow had written a letter criticizing the tactics of the European sections of the Fourth International on July 10, 1945. This was published in the internal bulletin. The majority agreed to later publication in the *FI* when a reply from the European Secretariat (ES) of the Fourth International had been received. This reply was

written in January 1946 and the two items were published together in the March 1946 *FI.* Morrow protested the delay. At the PC meeting Morrow ("Angel") made two motions: (1) that he be permitted to immediately publish a reply to the January ES letter in the pages of the *FI,* and (2) that the SWP minority be given joint editorship of the party's internal bulletin. Cannon ("Walter") made two countermotions: (1) that a decision on publication of Morrow's new letter be deferred until a reply to it was received from the European Secretariat; and (2) that the minority be given one representative on the SWP's Secretariat, the subcommittee of the PC in charge of day-to-day organizational work of the party, including publication of the internal bulletin. Following the discussion, Cannon's motions were carried 9 to 1, with Morrow voting against.

98. This second round in the debate over European perspectives was published in the July 1946 *FI,* where Morrow's letter appeared along with a reply by Michel Pablo.

99. Morrow's objection on the internal bulletin concerned the handling of his criticism of party policy in the recent General Motors strike, where critical support had been offered to the Walter Reuther wing of the UAW leadership on its tactics in the fight. At the December 18, 1945, meeting of the PC, Morrow had made a motion accusing the SWP majority and *The Militant* of holding "a definite line of support of Reuther without any criticism." Morrow submitted this motion to the internal bulletin, where it was published in the March 1946 issue, vol. VIII, no. 4. His objection was to the majority's decision to include with his motion a one-paragraph rebuttal by Morris Lewit taken from the minutes of the December 18 PC discussion. Lewit said that an editorial in the December 15, 1945, *Militant* criticized by Morrow "was no endorsement of Reuther. It tried to indicate a division within the [UAW] leadership which is genuine, has been existing for a long time. And a revolutionist who doesn't know how to take advantage of a division in the bureaucracy doesn't know the first thing about trade union activity. . . ."

100. The May 19-22, 1946, NC plenum had a seven-point agenda. Morrow, representing the minority, was given extended time to present counterreports under four of the points (international report, unity with the WP, SWP internal situation, and the discussion over the slogans relating to wage and price controls). The plenum opened with a majority international report by George Breitman. In Morrow's counterreport, later published in *Internal Bulletin,* vol. VIII, no. 8, July 1946, he stated for the first time that "all the reasons we gave for defending the Soviet Union have disappeared." He declared that he had changed his position on the "Three Theses" (see note 38 above) and now supported the idea of all-inclusive, multiclass "national liberation movements" in Europe. When this concept, which had been rejected by the majority of the SWP and the Fourth International, had first been raised by exiled German Trotskyists in 1941, it had been aimed at the Nazi occupations. Morrow now proposed to support such movements in the postwar period, aimed principally at

the Soviet occupation of Eastern Europe, but also at the Allied troops in Western Europe. He argued that the entire Fourth International had missed what revolutionary opportunities there were during the war by failing to join such resistance movements, and that the Fourth International as a whole exaggerated postwar revolutionary possibilities. Another major issue he raised concerned the May 5 constitutional referendum in France, where he, in support of a faction of the French section of the Fourth International, had urged a vote in favor of the new bourgeois constitution on the grounds that it had been drafted by a constituent assembly with a CP-SP majority.

101. At the April 23, 1946, meeting of the PC, Morrow announced that his faction intended to submit a resolution to the plenum challenging the legitimacy and authority of the March international conference of the Fourth International. He reported that his faction's representative at the conference had cast a consultative vote against all the resolutions that had come before the gathering. Morrow told the PC: "The resolution will center on . . . the absolute illegitimacy of what we consider a coup, of suddenly attempting to transform an international preconference into a world congress or conference" (from the PC minutes). The resolution was never submitted to the plenum. The majority at the plenum adopted a resolution in support of the international conference and endorsing the new leadership elected there.

102. This statement was made by Morrow at the April 23 meeting of the PC and is taken from the minutes. Morrow said he had been informed by his faction's representative at the international conference that an attempt had been made to expel the German section from the Fourth International. The German group he referred to were the authors of the "Three Theses" document (see note 38 above). This was a small group of exiles in New York whose leaders worked closely with Shachtman's WP. This group, the Committee Abroad of the International Communists of Germany (AK of the IKD), boycotted the world conference and announced that they would not accept its decisions. They were not expelled, but were criticized in a public resolution charging them with substituting a "national-democratic program" for the perspective of socialist revolution (*Fourth International*, June 1946). The minority of the French section, led by Albert Demazières and Yvan Craipeau, supported the positions of the Goldman-Morrow faction, as did the majority of the British RCP, led by Jock Haston.

103. Cannon is wrong on the year. The international meeting that established the International Left Opposition was held in Paris in April 1930.

104. The name International Communist League was not adopted until 1933, when Hitler's victory over a demoralized Communist Party convinced Trotsky that it was necessary to break definitively with the Comintern and launch a course toward the building of a new International. The 1930 conference adopted the name International Left Opposition.

105. Filed with the SWP's PC minutes for the spring of 1946 is a set of galley proofs of the article "The Eruption of Bureaucratic Imperialism" by Daniel Logan (Jean van Heijenoort), typeset for *Fourth International.* Before the *FI* went to press, the article appeared in the March 1946 issue of Shachtman's *New International.*

106. Trotsky wrote a number of articles at the end of 1932 and the beginning of 1933 on the capitulations of the petty-bourgeois leaders of the German section. The quotation Cannon has in mind would appear to come from Trotsky's letter to the German leadership of December 28, 1932, where he wrote: "But what the German Opposition needs is a leadership which is made up of workers who are firm in their convictions and which is not subject to the changing mood of eternal political nomads" ("The Crisis in the German Section," *Writings 1932-33,* p. 43).

107. In its May 1946 issue, *Fourth International* began publication of "A Documentary History of the Fourth International," starting with letters written by Trotsky shortly after his exile from the Soviet Union at the beginning of 1929. The letter to Souvarine of April 25, 1929, and the letter on "Groupings in the Communist Opposition" of March 31, 1929, can be found in *Writings 1929.* For more on the Anglo-Russian Committee and the Chinese revolution of 1925-27, see note 62 above.

108. In two articles criticizing the European Secretariat of the Fourth International, written in July 1945 and February 1946, and published respectively in the March and July 1946 issues of *Fourth International,* Morrow proposed that the Trotskyists of Europe join the mass Social Democratic parties in order to reach the workers under their influence.

109. The chairman of the May 20 session of the plenum was Arne Swabeck; the chairman the previous day was Carl Skoglund.

110. See "To the Memory of the Old Man," *The Socialist Workers Party in World War II,* pp. 54-65.

111. The French constitutional referendum was held on May 5, 1946. On April 28, Morrow, Logan (Jean van Heijenoort), and Charles Millner sent a telegram to their co-thinkers in the minority of the French Parti Communiste Internationaliste urging a public statement of the minority's stand in favor of a "yes" vote on the constitution. Unknown to them at the time, the minority, led by Albert Demazière and Yvan Craipeau, had gained a majority at an April 20 meeting of the PCI Political Bureau, defeating the previous majority led by Marcel Bleibtreu and Pierre Frank. The new relationship of forces was sustained by a slim margin at a meeting of the Central Committee on April 23, and the PCI officially endorsed the bourgeois constitution in the May 5 referendum. Its position was condemned by the SWP's May plenum and by a meeting of the IEC of the Fourth International later in the summer. The Bleibtreu-Frank group regained the majority in 1947 and in 1948 Craipeau quit the organization and Demazière was expelled.

112. The Control Commission completed its report on May 16 for submission to the plenum (see note 88). This report sustained three

charges against the Goldman-Morrow minority: (1) that they had violated the section of the party constitution stipulating that political relations with nonmembers must be conducted under the direction of the party; (2) that the "Goldman-Morrow faction conducted its activities in direct collusion with the leadership of the Workers Party"; and (3) that "the plan of operations was to provoke expulsion through a series of flagrant violations of discipline." The CC cited specific violations of discipline. These included the fact that Goldman and Morrow began discussion on the unity question with the WP leaders before submitting such a proposal to the SWP. Documents of the October 1945 plenum of the SWP were handed over to the WP for publication before being distributed to the members of the SWP. Joint public meetings of the minority and the WP were conducted in Chicago and New York in the guise of socials and classes. The minority lent its support and attendance to public meetings and rallies of the WP while not attending similar meetings sponsored by the SWP. Morrow attended a plenum of the NC of the WP without informing the SWP leadership. The members of the minority had withdrawn their financial support from the SWP. And documents submitted to the PC of the SWP for discussion were simultaneously handed over to the WP. The minority split among themselves on the eve of the plenum. On May 10, Morrow and most of its New York supporters issued a statement entitled "We Remain in the Party," announcing their readiness in the future to abide by discipline. Goldman, Lydia Beidel, and most of the Chicago minority refused to sign this declaration. In a statement to the plenum, Goldman and Beidel denounced the "police psychology of the leaders of the majority." At the same time, they said: "The bill of particulars listing the various acts of the minority which are designated as 'disloyal' is approximately correct. We have never concealed or tried to conceal that we were fraternizing with the WP comrades."

113. The Committee Abroad of the IKD, while agreeing politically with the WP and with many of the positions of the minority, opposed the split. On December 5, 1945, it sent a letter to the SWP leadership that said in part: "From the beginning the minority intended to carry through a split, if its maneuver of 'unity' aimed exclusively against the leadership ran up against difficulties." This letter was published in the SWP *Internal Bulletin,* vol. VIII, no. 4, March 1946.

114. Cannon is paraphrasing here two letters from Max Shachtman to Albert Goldman dated November 3, 1945, and January 10, 1946. These letters, which included detailed descriptions of planning sessions on the minority's tactics with leaders of the WP, were published in *Bulletin of the Workers Party,* vol. I, no. 6, March 8, 1946. They were reprinted in the SWP *Internal Bulletin,* vol. VIII, no. 6, May 1946. Shachtman repeatedly warned Goldman against trying to provoke his own expulsion from the SWP. In the November 3 letter he wrote: "Well, I am not against a ruse in politics. But in this case, it seems to be unnecessary. What is more, it will

impress *everybody* with its artificiality. The 'wise' ones will say: That was cooked up; it was just a pretext; why did they need it?" (Emphasis in original.) In the January 10 letter Shachtman wrote: "What, however, if Cannon is possessed of normal shrewdness and says: 'Your joint statement [with the WP, a project Goldman was then considering] is only one of a series of provocations. I do not intend to accommodate you in your tactics. There will be no suspension or expulsion—at most a censure. Now, comrades, just what is the next in your series of irresponsible provocations?' In my opinion, that is the greater likelihood. What does the minority do then? It has to 'figure out' some additional steps which will drive Cannon to decisive organizational measures against it. It then becomes clear not only to the entire SWP and to the entire WP and to the entire International, but also to all the radical sympathizers that the course followed by the minority was one of a series of provocations; that it did not have the courage of its convictions . . . and that it sought to place the responsibility for its own political step on the shoulders of Cannon."

115. Morrow had put forward the slogan for use in the fight against inflation of "Wage increases without price increases." The majority rejected this on the basis of the arguments advanced by Trotsky in the Transitional Program where he held that price controls could not be effectively enforced under a capitalist government. The majority counterposed the slogan of the "Sliding scale of hours and wages," i.e., the automatic raising of wages to keep pace with inflation, combined with a shortening of the workweek to eliminate unemployment.

116. Following Cannon's report, Goldman told the plenum that his wing of the faction intended to immediately leave the SWP and join the Workers Party. He submitted his letter of resignation on May 28 and together with ten of his supporters went over to the Shachtman organization. Morrow remained in the SWP.

117. For Cannon's discussion of the personal grouping in the SWP led by Martin Abern, see his *The Struggle for a Proletarian Party,* pp. 35-49.

118. In response to the world depression, the British government in 1932 abandoned its previous policy of free trade and adopted tariff barriers against foreign competitors. At a conference at Ottawa, Canada, the same year it established the Empire Preference System, which exempted from tariff duties countries of the British Commonwealth.

119. The Lend-Lease Act was passed by Congress in March 1941. It authorized the delivery of immense quantities of war materiel to Britain (and later to the Soviet Union). Congress and the president rejected the idea of a cash loan because Britain had already defaulted on its payment of debts incurred to American creditors from World War I. The British government opposed an outright gift as an affront to its pride. This led to the fictitious formula that the munitions and equipment shipped by the U.S. government were being "leased" by the British and would be returned or paid for at the end of the war.

120. The term "Sixty Families" was popularized by the book *America's*

Sixty Families (1937) by Ferdinand Lundberg. In this work Lundberg showed that the basic core of the American ruling class consisted of sixty immensely wealthy families, the most famous of which are the Morgans, Rockefellers, and Du Ponts.

121. In his "Report on the World Economic Crisis and the New Tasks of the Communist International," delivered to the Third World Congress of the Comintern on June 23, 1921, Trotsky said: "The second source of the revolutionary struggle is in the severe spasms of the entire economic organism of the United States: an unprecedented boom, elicited by the European war, and next—a cruel crisis engendered by the drawn-out consequences of this war. The revolutionary movement of the American proletariat can under these conditions acquire the same tempo, unequaled in history, as the economic development of the United States in recent years" (*The First Five Years of the Communist International* [New York: Monad Press, 1972], vol. 1, p. 223).

122. In a letter written in May 1929 and published under the title "Tasks of the American Opposition," Trotsky wrote: "The work to be achieved by the American Opposition has international historic significance, for in the final analysis all the problems of our planet will be decided upon American soil. There is much in favor of the idea that from the standpoint of revolutionary succession, Europe and the East stand ahead of the United States. But a course of events is possible which may alter this sequence in favor of the proletariat of the United States" (*Writings 1929*, p. 131).

123. Transcripts of these discussions, in which Cannon participated, can be found in the Trotsky collection *The Transitional Program for Socialist Revolution* (Pathfinder Press, 1977).

124. *The Living Thoughts of Karl Marx* (Philadelphia: David McKay, 1939) is now out of print, but Trotsky's introductory essay is available in pamphlet form under the author's original title, *Marxism in Our Time* (Pathfinder Press, 1970).

125. The SWP was recognized as the American section of the Fourth International at the International's founding congress in 1938. In October 1940, the U.S. Congress passed the Voorhis Act, which required registration with the government and the turning over of membership lists and names of financial contributors for any group affiliated to a foreign government or to an international political organization. Rather than comply with these provisions, which would subject the party's members and sympathizers to government harassment, a special convention of the SWP in December 1940 voted to disaffiliate from the Fourth International. Cannon's reasons for this decision are explained in "The Voorhis Act and the Fourth International," in *The Socialist Workers Party in World War II*, p. 130.

126. Blasco was the pseudonym of Pietro Tresso. His fate has never been fully verified. In his notes to the collection of Trotsky's writings entitled *Le Mouvement Communiste en France (1919-1939)* (Paris:

Editions de Minuit, 1967), Pierre Broué gives this account: "Condemned in 1943 to ten years at forced labor by a Vichy tribunal, Blasco disappeared under circumstances that have still not been completely clarified. But apparently it was because the leaders of the FTP, who had helped him, along with others, to escape from the prison at Puy, discovered that he was a Trotskyist leader" (p. 631). The FTP was the Francs-Tireurs et Partisans Francais (the Sharpshooters and Partisans of France), the Stalinist-led resistance movement.

127. The mass murder of Greek Trotskyists by the Stalinists mentioned by Cannon took place in Athens and in Salonika in December 1944. The Trotskyists, then split into three organizations, had opposed the position of the Stalinists, which was to welcome British troops into Greece in October 1944 (see note 22 above). When the British turned on the Stalinists in December, the Stalinists sought to prevent the exposure of their false line from leading to a growth of Trotskyism by rounding up and shooting as many Trotskyists as possible under cover of the month-long battle of Athens—in which the Trotskyists fought alongside the Stalinist-led organizations against the British and monarchist forces. In Athens, thirty-one Trotskyists were murdered by the Stalinists, including two members of the Central Committee of one of the Trotskyist groups, Demosthenes Bouzoukis and Nicos Aravantinos. In Salonika, which was far from the scene of the fighting, 230 revolutionists were shot without trial by the Stalinists. Most of these victims were either Trotskyists or members of the left-centrist Archio-Marxist organization.

128. The "Palmer Red Raids" took place early in January 1920 at the order of Attorney General A. Mitchell Palmer, under the Democratic administration of Woodrow Wilson. The raids were organized by Palmer's special assistant, J. Edgar Hoover, who came to national prominence through them and later came to head the FBI. The repression and the officially induced hysteria against "reds" continued until the Republican administration of Warren G. Harding took office in 1921, when it slowed down and gradually tapered off.

129. Morrow's position on the economic conjuncture in the United States was presented in a document of November 9, 1946, entitled "Against the Political Committee's 'Theses on the American Revolution' and 'Tasks of the SWP in the Present Political Situation.'" This was written too late to appear in the internal bulletin, but was mimeographed by the party national office and distributed at the convention. There Morrow wrote: "The temporary inflation of the price-structure due to wartime shortages is coming to an end. Far from inflation being inevitable under declining capitalism, including the United Sates, as the Political Committee's resolution on wages and prices asserted, it was a temporary phenomenon in a victor country whose productive machinery remained not only unimpaired but expanding. A *short-term* effect of the decline in prices will be a slowing up of production, consequently of employment, in many fields, during the period of the adjustment of the

price-structure. One can safely hazard the prediction that this period will last no more than a year. The *long-term* effect of the decline in prices will be to expand both the home market and export trade for a period of years. . . . By confusing the *short-term* period of price-adjustment with the eventual development of a new economic crisis on the scale of the 1930s, and leaving out entirely the long-term effect of lower prices in facilitating the home market and export in an interim period of at least several years, the Political Committee conjures up an immediate crisis." (Emphasis in original.)

130. This quotation is from a June 16, 1939, letter from Trotsky, evidently addressed to Cannon, a copy of which was found in Cannon's archives. The text appears in *Writings 1938-39*, p. 349, under the title "For a Courageous Reorientation."

131. Cannon evidently has in mind here several of Trotsky's comments on the future of American Marxism made in 1937 and 1938. See in particular, "For a Revolutionary Publishing House," November 29, 1937, and "Discussions with Trotsky: I—International Conference," March 20, 1938, in *Writings 1937-38*.

132. While Cannon seems to be referring here as above to Morrow's document directed at the "American Theses," his reference to the "Three Theses" (see note 38) suggests that he also has in mind another document submitted by the Morrow faction to the convention: "'The National Question' in Europe, A Critique by the Minority of the SWP's Stand on the National Question and Democratic Demands" (November 10, 1946). In this resolution the Morrow faction came out in full support of the positions advocated by the group of emigré German Trotskyists who wrote the "Three Theses" document in 1941. Here the Morrowites advocated national liberation struggles in Europe directed at both the Allied occupation forces and at "Soviet imperialism." This document called for "defense of the interests of the nation by the proletariat," arguing that this would have an objectively socialist thrust because the bourgeoisie no longer consistently defended national self-determination. The document gave as examples where this policy should be applied, Germany, Poland, Greece, Palestine, and Korea.

133. In his document against the "American Theses," Morrow criticized the section of the theses that stated: ". . . the Bolshevik party, headed by Lenin and Trotsky, bounded forward from a tiny minority, just emerging from underground isolation in February to the conquest of power in October—a period of nine months." The gist of his criticism was that while at the beginning of 1917 the Bolsheviks had been reduced to a relatively small organization, before World War I they had considerable mass influence in the Russian working class. He claimed that the most favorable opportunities for the growth of the Fourth International had been during the Second World War; that these supposed opportunities had been missed by the FI's refusal to seek the leadership of the bourgeois-democratic "national liberation movements" in Europe; and that "World

War II provided far more favorable objective conditions for the revolutionary vanguard than are likely to occur for a long time."

134. Spain entered a long prerevolutionary period in April 1931, when the monarchist and clerical parties were defeated in municipal elections by the liberals and the workers' parties, forcing the abdication of the king. Disappointed in their expectations of immediate concessions from the new government, the Spanish workers began a strike wave in July and August. This was the first of a series of class struggles that culminated in the revolution and civil war of 1936-39. In France, the election of a Popular Front government led to a massive strike wave in June and July 1936 involving as many as seven million workers.

135. The Russian revolution of 1905 began with a peaceful march on the tsar's Winter Palace on January 23 that was fired on by tsarist troops. Trotsky was then a member of the revolutionary Social Democracy but did not adhere either to the Bolshevik or Menshevik faction. He returned from exile in Europe to St. Petersburg, the center of revolutionary activity, in the spring of 1905. In October a general strike swept St. Petersburg, in the course of which the workers spontaneously formed a mass revolutionary representative body, the Soviet of Workers' Deputies. The Bolsheviks were initially hostile to the Soviet because it was not directly led by the party, though in the course of the revolution they came to support it. Trotsky almost immediately became the leading figure of the St. Petersburg Soviet, and was elected its chairman at the end of November.

136. The POUM (Partido Obrero de Unificación Marxista—Workers Party of Marxist Unification), a Spanish centrist organization led in part by former Trotskyists, called for a vote for the class-collaborationist Popular Front ticket in the February 1936 Spanish elections. The Spanish Popular Front, which stood on a program of defending capitalist property relations, was composed of the Socialist and Communist parties and the parties of the liberal bourgeoisie. In September 1936, the POUM joined the regional capitalist government in Catalonia, leading Trotsky to break all political relations with its leaders.

137. In his article "The Treachery of the POUM," January 23, 1936, Trotsky wrote: "A few months ago in Madrid, Juan Andrade's book was published, *The Reformist Bureaucracy and the Labor Movement*. . . . Juan Andrade forwarded his book to me twice, each time with glowing dedications, in which he calls me his 'leader and teacher.' This fact, which under different conditions would have only made me happy, compels me at present to announce all the more decisively in public that I never taught anybody *political betrayal*. And Andrade's conduct is nothing else than betrayal of the proletariat for the sake of an *alliance with the bourgeoisie*" (*The Spanish Revolution, 1931-39*, p. 209, emphasis in original).

138. The POUM had been formed in 1935 by a fusion, which Trotsky opposed, between the Spanish Left Opposition and the Workers and

Peasants Bloc of Catalonia, a right-centrist organization led by Joaquín Maurín.

139. Cannon is referring here to the novelist James T. Farrell, who was a close sympathizer of the SWP in the late 1930s and early 1940s. Farrell became involved on the side of Goldman and Morrow in a controversy they began in 1944 over two articles in *Fourth International* magazine, "How the Trotskyists Went to Jail," by Joseph Hansen, and "A Defamer of Marxism," by Harry Frankel. Hansen's article was a description of the trip to Minneapolis by SWP leaders to serve their sentences in the Minneapolis labor case; Frankel's article was a polemic against Max Shachtman's introduction to a WP edition of Trotsky's *The New Course.* In a July 30, 1944, letter to the editors of *Fourth International* Farrell accused Hansen of "adulation of leadership" and "bathos," and said Frankel had launched an "unfair, unprincipled, utterly unjust attack" on Shachtman. The SWP Political Committee, at Cannon's suggestion, published Farrell's letter in an internal bulletin rather than in the *FI,* although Farrell was not a member of the party. Cannon's reason was that since Farrell's views paralleled those of a minority within the SWP, a public answer to him would be taken as an attack on the SWP minority (Goldman and Morrow) and would prejudice the discussion. Cannon wrote three letters on this question while in prison. The first, which while disagreeing sharply with Farrell, took a relatively conciliatory tone, appears in his *Letters From Prison,* pp. 141-45. The other two letters, of a much sharper character, were printed in the *Internal Bulletin,* vol. VII, no. 2, April 1945, as part of a selection entitled "Notes on the Party Discussion," signed Martin. When Cannon edited his *Letters From Prison* for publication in 1968, he decided not to include them.

140. See note 52.

141. After the Vietnamese Communist Party had welcomed the British troops in Saigon in September 1945, the imperialists had used this toehold to import French troops and drive the VCP's coalition government out of South Vietnam. An uneasy truce prevailed throughout most of 1946 between the French colonial regime in the South and the coalition government headed by Ho Chi Minh in the North. In March 1946 the VCP signed an agreement with France which recognized the Democratic Republic of Vietnam in the North as a semiautonomous part of the French Union, but this agreement authorized the landing of French troops in Hanoi. Using this beachhead, the French military ordered a massive bombardment of Haiphong harbor in November 1946 in which 6,000 people were killed. In response to this act of imperialist brutality the French Trotskyists sought to organize a mass protest rally in Paris on December 6. They approached the Socialist and Communist parties for their endorsement, but both of these parties were then in the government and voted in favor of the military expedition against Vietnam. The only organization to offer support to the demonstration called by the Trotskyists was the Algerian People's Party. The protest rally was to be

held in a Paris auditorium. Several thousand Algerian, Indochinese, and French workers came to the auditorium, where they were met by hundreds of police who refused to allow them to enter. The rally was banned by the government of Socialist Premier Léon Blum. About 1,000 people broke through the police cordon to hold an impromptu open air meeting where Trotskyist leaders and representatives of the Algerian organization spoke. After the speeches, a march was staged. At that point the police attacked the crowd, injuring seventeen persons and jailing a large number overnight.

142. The question of unification between the SWP and the WP, which had seemed closed at the November 1946 SWP convention, was reopened by new developments at the beginning of 1947. First was a trip to the United States at the end of January by Michel Pablo, who had been elected secretary of the International Secretariat reconstituted at the March 1946 precongress of the Fourth International. Preparations were under way for the Second World Congress, planned for the fall of 1947 and ultimately held in April-May 1948. As the first formal postwar congress, the agenda would include recognition of sections and sympathizing groups. The IS proposed to accept as participants in the congress all organizations calling themselves Trotskyist that would pledge to abide by the congress decisions on both organizational and political questions. Shachtman had decided to appeal to the world congress for reinstatement of the WP in the International. In addition, a faction within the WP led by C. L. R. James ("Johnson") strongly favored unity with the SWP. Through Pablo's intervention the WP leadership agreed to the conditions for unity with the SWP that they had rejected the previous year, in particular giving up their demand for a special internal bulletin of their faction within the SWP. On February 1 the SWP Political Committee called a plenum of the National Committee to discuss this new turn. This letter by Cannon was to inform the committee members of the developments before the plenum began.

143. The grouping led by C. L. R. James in the WP did not agree either with the WP majority or with the SWP on the class character of the Soviet State, though its views were closer to those of the WP. The WP held that the Soviet Union was an example of "bureaucratic collectivism," a new and different form of exploitative society headed by a managerial ruling class. The Johnsonites held that the USSR was essentially similar to the existing capitalist countries but with a higher degree of state ownership, which they designated as "state capitalism." The SWP maintained that the USSR was a bureaucratically deformed workers' state in which the preservation of nationalized property and a planned economy constituted progressive achievements that should be defended against imperialist attack despite the retrograde character of the bureaucratic caste.

144. The term "extraordinary party convention" used here refers to the forthcoming world congress of the Fourth International. Since neither the SWP nor the WP were members of the Fourth International, the

disciplinary obligation meant in effect that the WP made a moral pledge before the membership of the world Trotskyist movement to accept the discipline of the SWP if the unification was completed.

145. Ruth Fischer, who had been a leader of the German Communist Party in the 1920s and who served briefly on the International Secretariat of the Trotskyist movement in 1935, was in exile in the United States after World War II. At the beginning of 1947 she appeared before the House Committee on Un-American Activities, where she testified against her brother, Gerhart Eisler, an agent of Stalin's GPU. *The Militant* ran an editorial in its February 15, 1947, issue dissociating the SWP from Fischer. This editorial labeled Fischer as an "informer" and as "a tool of American imperialism," characterizations that Cannon here withdraws. This incident became an issue in the relations between the SWP and the WP. On March 10, Fischer wrote a letter to Cannon, protesting the editorial in *The Militant* and pointing out that Trotsky had proposed that he testify before the Dies Committee, the predecessor of the HCUA. This letter was published in the March 24 issue of *Labor Action,* the same issue that carried the "Joint Statement on Unification." This article by Cannon, which was run in the editorial column of *The Militant,* was his first comment on the issues Fischer raised. Fischer's letter to Cannon was published in the following issue, April 5, along with the first installment of Cannon's pamphlet *American Stalinism and Anti-Stalinism,* which was written in part as a reply to Fischer and the Shachtmanites.

146. The letter to Cannon was from Ruth Fischer.

147. The film *Mission to Moscow,* starring Walter Huston and Ann Harding, was released by Warner Brothers in 1943. It was based on the 1941 book of the same title by Joseph E. Davies, who had been U.S. ambassador to the Soviet Union from 1936 to 1938. The film was a piece of pro-Stalinist propaganda, prettifying the Stalin regime as part of the wartime alliance between Moscow and Washington. In particular it endorsed the Moscow trials and the regime's execution of the Old Bolsheviks.

148. In the 1936 presidential elections the CP ran Earl Browder. But his campaign was waged in support of the Democratic candidate, Roosevelt, against Roosevelt's Republican rival, Alfred Landon. Browder's campaign slogan was "Defeat Landon at all costs." In the 1940 elections, which took place during the period of the Stalin-Hitler pact, when Moscow was on bad terms with Washington, Browder ran a more or less independent campaign for president. In 1944, however, the CP openly endorsed Roosevelt.

149. From "Germany, the Key to the International Situation," in *The Struggle Against Fascism in Germany* (Pathfinder Press, 1971), pp. 118-19.

150. The best playing marbles are made of white alabaster, known as "alleys" for short.

151. The article appears later in this volume.

152. In his contribution to *James P. Cannon As We Knew Him* (Pathfinder Press, 1976), Harry DeBoer describes a checkers tournament organized by the Trotskyist prisoners in Sandstone penitentiary in which he was the winner. Henry Schultz worked on the railroad, which entitled him to a pass for free rail travel.

153. The letter from Martin (Cannon) to the National Committee of February 8, 1947 ("A New Turn on the Question of Unity"), referred to the WP's acceptance of the conditions for unification proposed by the SWP and the Fourth International as a "capitulation." When the WP leadership received a copy of this letter they made a major issue of it, insisting that it was the SWP that had given in to their terms and that the fusion would be a step in the direction of an all-inclusive party. This was accompanied by a series of sharp polemics against the SWP in *Labor Action* that indicated that the WP had had second thoughts about going through with the unification.

154. On March 8, 1947, Shachtman wrote a sixteen-page letter to the members of the WP to explain the impending unification. He stated that the WP had not changed its position on any question, including the character of the revolutionary party. He said that the unity would be placed in question if the SWP carried out its proposal to put on the agenda at the forthcoming world congress a condemnation of the 1940 split by the WP. And he qualified the agreement the WP had signed to publicly defend the positions adopted by the forthcoming world congress: "We made it perfectly clear to Smith [Pablo] that this commitment would be considered valid and operative by us *only* if unity was achieved between the WP and the SWP, and that failing such unity we would not have the slightest hesitation in regarding the commitment as a mere scrap of paper without any binding value upon our party." (Emphasis in original.) This document was later published in the SWP's *Internal Bulletin,* vol. IX, no. 2, May 1947.

155. The provision in the "Joint Statement on Unification" that neither side would admit into its ranks members of the other party who applied for membership after the agreement was signed had in mind specifically the case of Jack Weber. Weber had dropped out of the SWP after the 1944 convention without notifying the leadership that he was doing so. He had distributed a document filled with hostile criticisms outside the 1946 SWP convention, although he had not joined the Workers Party. In the March 17, 1947, issue of *Labor Action* a long letter by Weber was published criticizing *The Militant*'s February 15 editorial on Ruth Fischer (see note 145). Weber argued that the Stalinists had ceased to be a working class tendency in any sense and that "The politics of Cannonism serves not to unmask but to abet both Stalinism and the GPU apparatus."

156. See "Resolution on Unification with the Workers Party" (February 16, 1947) earlier in this volume.

157. Max Shachtman, "The Nature of the Stalinist Parties," *New International,* March 1947.

158. The grouping in the WP led by C. L. R. James held its own national conference on July 5-6, 1947, and voted to leave the WP and join the SWP.

159. The Truman Doctrine was announced in a presidential speech of March 12, 1947. It marked the official beginning of the cold war. Truman asked Congress for $400 million in military aid to prop up the dictatorial governments of Greece and Turkey, threatened with overthrow by insurgent mass movements. Truman declared that American military might would be used throughout the world to "support free peoples who are resisting attempted subjugation by armed minorities or by outside pressure."

160. The American Committee for European Workers Relief was established in April 1946. Its executive secretary was Rose Karsner. The committee raised thousands of dollars to send food and clothing to European revolutionists and Fourth Internationalists, many of whom had been imprisoned by the Nazis during World War II.

GLOSSARY

Abern, Martin (1898-1949)—A founding member of American CP and later of Trotskyist movement. Member of first NC of CLA. Split from SWP in 1940 and became leader of Shachtman's WP.

Addes, George P. (1910-)—Secretary-treasurer of UAW (1936-47). With R.J. Thomas and Richard Leonard led postwar opposition to Walter Reuther in UAW, supported by Stalinists. Defeated at 1947 UAW convention, left union movement.

Allard, Gerry—Early member of CLA. Edited newspaper of Progressive Miners Union, formed in Gillespie, Illinois, in 1932 in left-wing split from United Mine Workers. Elected to NC of WPUS in 1934. Entered SP with Trotskyists in 1936 but remained there when they were expelled.

American Workers Party (AWP)—Formed in December 1933 by Conference for Progressive Labor Action led by A. J. Muste. Fused with CLA in December 1934 to form WPUS.

Andrade Rodríguez, Juan (1897-)—Founding member of Spanish Communist Party in 1920. Expelled for Trotskyism in 1927. Broke with Trotskyism in 1935 to become a founder of POUM.

Andrews, Joseph—Pseudonym of Jules Geller.

Angel—Pseudonym of Felix Morrow.

AWP—See American Workers Party.

Balabanov, Angelica (1878-1965)—Russian-Italian leader of pre-World War I Italian SP. Joined Russian Bolsheviks in 1917 and became Comintern secretary in 1919. Expelled from CPSU in 1924; returned to Social Democracy.

Baldwin, Roger (1884-)—A founder of American Civil Liberties Union and its executive director until 1950. Collaborated with Cannon on civil liberties work in 1920s when Cannon headed CP's International Labor Defense. Supported defendants in Minneapolis case.

Barr—Pseudonym of Farrell Dobbs.

Bartell, Mike—Pseudonym of Milton Zaslow.

Bebel, August (1840-1913)—Cofounder with Wilhelm Liebknecht of German Social Democracy in 1869. Collaborator of Marx and Engels. Leader of First and Second Internationals. Moved toward centrist positions in later years.

Beidel, Lydia (d. 1974)—Joined CLA in 1933. Went with Goldman into SP in 1934. Rejoined Trotskyists in SP in 1936. Elected to SWP NC in 1941. Business manager of *The Militant* (1941-42). A leader of Chicago branch, she supported Goldman-Morrow faction and resigned from SWP in May 1946 with Goldman to join Shachtman's WP.

Bennett—Pseudonym of Lydia Beidel.

Bernstein, Eduard (1850-1932)—Prominent German Social Democrat; friend and literary executor of Frederick Engels. Became principal theoretician of class-collaborationist revisionism in German Social Democracy after Engels's death.

Bilbo, Theodore G. (1877-1947)—White-supremacist Democratic U.S. senator from Mississippi (1935-47).

Black Legion—White racist organization centered in Detroit. Formed in mid-1930s, with close ties to Ku Klux Klan.

Bolsheviks—Majority faction formed in RSDLP at Second Congress in 1903. Led by Lenin. Became separate party in 1912. Organized October revolution of 1917 that established first workers' state. Changed name to Communist Party in 1918.

Bordiga, Amadeo (1889-1970)—Founding leader of Italian CP. Expelled in 1929 for "Trotskyism." Founded ultraleft group, which adhered to Left Opposition but broke with Trotsky in 1932.

Brandler, Heinrich (1881-1967)—A leader of German CP in early 1920s. Made a scapegoat by Comintern for failure of German revolution of 1923. Expelled in 1929. With August Thalheimer founded Communist Party Opposition (KPO) in 1930, supporting Bukharin right wing in Soviet CP. Brandlerites continued as independent grouping until World War II.

Breitman, George (1916-)—Joined WPUS in 1935. Member of SWP NC from 1939. Editor of *The Militant* (1941-43 and 1949-54). Attended March 1946 international preconference in Paris as an observer. Editor of books by Trotsky and Malcolm X.

Browder, Earl (1891-1973)—Joined American SP in 1907. Edited weekly *Workers World* with Cannon in Kansas City in 1919. In CP, a supporter of William Z. Foster in factional disputes of 1920s. Elected CP general secretary in 1930 on Stalin's directive after expulsion of Trotskyists and Lovestoneites. Deposed by Stalin in 1945 and expelled from CP in 1946.

Budenz, Louis (1891-1972)—Leader of AWP. Participated briefly in WPUS after fusion with CLA, then joined Stalinists. Became editor of *Daily Worker*. In 1945 quit CP to rejoin Catholic Church. Became a religious anticommunist crusader.

Burch, Arthur (1897-)—Joined Trotskyist faction in SP in 1936. Member of SWP NC in 1940s and 1950s. Branch organizer in Detroit and Newark. Later withdrew from politics.

Burnham, James (1905-)—Professor of philosophy at New York University. Member of AWP National Committee. Elected to NC of WPUS in 1934. Renounced defense of Soviet Union after Stalin-Hitler pact in August 1939 and with Max Shachtman split from SWP in April 1940. Broke with Shachtman in May, moving to far right. At present an editor of William Buckley's *National Review*.

Caldwell, Sylvia—Pseudonym of Sylvia Callen.

Callen, Sylvia (1913-)—Joined Young People's Socialist League in Chicago in 1937. Joined SWP in spring of 1938, moved to New York and in December became Cannon's secretary in SWP national office (1938-47). Withdrew from politics.

Carlson, Grace (1906-)—Joined WPUS in 1936. Member of SWP NC from 1941. Convicted and imprisoned in Minneapolis case. Ran for vice-president on first SWP presidential ticket in 1948. Resigned from SWP in June 1952 to return to Catholic Church.

Carter, Joseph—Founding member of CLA. Elected to NC of SWP in 1938. Split from SWP with Shachtman and Burnham and became a leader of WP.

Chester, Bob (1912-1975)—Joined Trotskyist faction in SP in 1936. Branch organizer in New York and San Francisco. Elected to SWP NC in 1950. Was active member of Painters' union in San Francisco and well known as educator and speaker.

Chiang Kai-shek (1887-1975)—Headed Chinese bourgeois Kuomintang (Nationalist Party) from 1925. Crushed second Chinese revolution in 1927. Headed central government of China (1928-49). Ruled splinter regime in Taiwan after CCP conquest of mainland.

Civil Rights Defense Committee (CRDC)—Organization that rallied public support for defendants in Minneapolis case. Its officers were James T. Farrell, chairman; John Dos Passos, vice-chairman; and George Novack, secretary.

CLA—See Communist League of America (Opposition).

Clarke, George (1913-1964)—Joined CLA in 1929. Elected to NC of WPUS in 1934. A merchant seaman in 1940s. Campaign manager of SWP's 1948 presidential campaign. Later edited *Fourth International* and was SWP representative in Europe. Left SWP in 1953 with Bert Cochran. Killed in automobile accident.

Cochran, Bert (1917-)—Joined CLA in 1934. Elected to SWP NC in 1938. Union organizer for Mechanics Educational Society in Toledo, Ohio. Later a staff member of UAW. Left SWP in 1953. Author of biographies of Adlai Stevenson and Harry Truman. Became a resident at Columbia University's Institute on Communist Affairs.

Communist International (Comintern)—Founded by Lenin and Trotsky in 1919 as instrument of world revolution. Transformed into agency of Soviet diplomacy by Stalin in late 1920s. Dissolved in April 1943 as good-will gesture to Stalin's democratic imperialist allies in World War II. (Also known as Third International.)

Communist League of America (Opposition) (CLA)—Founded in Chicago in May 1929 by Trotskyists expelled from CP in October 1928. CLA fused with AWP in December 1934 to form WPUS.

Coolidge, David—Pseudonym of E. R. McKinney.

Cooper, Jake (1916-)—Joined Minneapolis Teamsters Local 544 in 1936. One of eighteen members of SWP and of Minneapolis Teamsters jailed in 1944 in wartime "sedition" trial.

Craipeau, Yvan (1912-)—Joined French LO in 1929. A leader of French section of FI during World War II. Led minority in Parti Communiste Internationaliste after war, sympathetic to positions of Goldman and Morrow. Won majority in 1946 and became general secretary. Quit Trotskyist movement in 1948 to join various centrist groups.

Curran, Joseph (1906-)—President of National Maritime Union (NMU). Worked closely with CP in 1930s and during war. Broke with Stalinists in postwar period, eventually moving sharply to the right.

Curtiss, Charles (1908-)—Early member of CLA in New York and Los Angeles. Elected to NC of WPUS in 1936. Worked with Trotsky in Mexico (1938-39) as representative of IS of FI to Mexican section. In army in World War II. Left SWP in 1951 and joined SP.

Daily Worker—Newspaper of CP, founded in 1924. Name changed to *Daily World* in 1968.

DeBoer, Harry (1907-)—A leader of Minneapolis Teamsters union from 1934. One of eighteen defendants convicted in Minneapolis trial.

De Leon, Daniel (1852-1914)—Joined Socialist Labor Party in 1890 and became its principal leader until his death.

Dobbs, Farrell (1907-)—Leader of Minneapolis truck drivers' strikes of 1934. Joined CLA in March 1934 and elected to NC of WPUS in December. Became SWP national labor secretary in 1939. One of eighteen political prisoners in Minneapolis case. SWP national secretary (1953-72). Four-time presidential candidate of SWP (1948-60). Has written a four-volume history of role of Trotskyists in Minneapolis Teamsters' movement.

Dubinsky, David (1892-)—Social Democratic president of International Ladies' Garment Workers Union (1932-66).

Dunne, Vincent Raymond (1890-1970)—Member of Western Federation of Miners. Founding member of IWW (1905) and of CP (1919). Founding member of CLA and member of its first NC. A central leader of 1934 Minneapolis strikes. One of eighteen convicted in Minneapolis trial. An active leader of SWP until his death.

Eastman, Max (1883-1969)—Editor of *The Masses* before World War I. Supporter of CP in early 1920s and of Left Opposition from 1923. Translated several of Trotsky's books. Rejected dialectical materialism. Repudiated socialism at end of 1930s and became anticommunist.

ECCI—Executive Committee of the Communist International.

Eisler, Gerhart (1897-1968)—Joined Austrian CP in 1918. Comintern and GPU agent from 1926. In China in 1929, helped to purge Chinese Trotskyists from CCP. In exile in U.S. (1933-38 and 1941-49). Arrested as Soviet spy in 1946. Escaped to Eastern Europe in 1949. Became a leader of East German government and at his death headed State Broadcasting Commission.

Engels, Frederick (1820-1895)—Lifelong collaborator of Karl Marx and co-founder of modern scientific socialism. A leader of First and Second Internationals. Editor of Marx's posthumous works, including second and third volumes of *Capital.*

Farrell, James T. (1904-)—American novelist and literary critic, best known for his *Studs Lonigan* trilogy in 1930s. Became sympathetic to Trotskyist movement in 1936. Member of Trotsky Defense Committee and national chairman of CRDC, defense committee in Minneapolis case. Broke relations with SWP in 1945. Supported WP until 1948 when he became sympathizer of SP.

Field, B. J.—Member of CLA in New York. Expelled in 1932 for violating branch discipline. Readmitted at request of Trotsky. Expelled again in 1934 for violating party discipline in New York hotel workers' strike. Founded League for Revolutionary Workers Party, which survived into war years.

Fischer, Ruth (1895-1961)—Founding member of Austrian CP in 1918. Became a leader of German CP after 1919. Member of ECCI (1924-26). Expelled from German CP as Zinoviev supporter in 1927. Founder, with Maslow and Urbahns, of Leninbund, which collaborated with Left Opposition until 1930. Broke with Leninbund. Joined Trotskyists in mid-1930s, serving on IS of ICL (1934-36). Withdrew from Trotskyist movement by 1938. After World War II lived in exile in New York.

Foster, William Z. (1881-1961)—Main organizer of unsuccessful 1919 steel strike. Joined CP in 1921. Led a joint faction with Cannon in CP, but sided with Stalin and approved Cannon's expulsion in 1928. Became party chairman after purge of Browder in 1945.

Fourth International (FI)—The World Party of Socialist Revolution, founded by Leon Trotsky in 1938.

Fourth International magazine—Name given to SWP's theoretical magazine beginning with May 1940 issue after Shachtman had appropriated mailing rights for *New International,* party's magazine from 1934. *Fourth International* changed name to *International Socialist Review* in 1956.

Frank, E.R.—Pseudonym of Bert Cochran.

Frankel, Jan—A Czech Oppositionist from 1927. He became a member of Trotsky's secretariat and guard in Turkey, Norway, and Mexico. Moved to New York in 1937. Left Trotskyist movement at end of World War II.

Frankensteen, Richard T. (1907-)—Elected UAW vice-president in 1937. Ran for mayor of Detroit in 1945 nonpartisan election, where he was supported by SWP. Won highest vote in mayoralty primary but defeated in election. Supported Thomas-Addes-Leonard opposition to Reuther; defeated at 1947 UAW convention. Left union movement and became a corporate executive.

Gabe—Pseudonym of Michel Pablo.

Gabriel—Pseudonym of Michel Pablo.

Gates—Pseudonym of Albert Glotzer.

Geller, Jules (1913-)—Joined Trotskyist movement in mid-1930s. Elected to NC of SWP in 1939. Branch organizer in Akron, Ohio, in mid-1940s. Left SWP in 1953 with Bert Cochran. At present, director of Monthly Review Press.

Germain, Ernest—Pseudonym of Ernest Mandel.

German-American Bund—Organized in 1936 out of previous Friends of New Germany. Its uniformed members campaigned in support of Hitler and against communism, labor unions, and Jews. Headed by Fritz Kuhn.

Giotopoulos, Demetrios—A leader of Greek Archio-Marxists, which were affiliated to ILO in early 1930s. Greek representative on IS in Paris. Archio-Marxists broke from Trotskyism and affiliated to London Bureau in 1934. Known in ILO under name "Witte."

Glotzer, Albert (1908-)—Member of Cannon faction in CP. Founding member of CLA and member of its first NC. Split from SWP with Shachtman in 1940 and became a leader of WP.

Goldman, Albert (1897-1960)—Member of CP in late 1920s. Joined CLA in 1933. Left in 1934 to join SP. Rejoined Trotskyists when they entered SP in 1936. Elected to SWP NC in 1938. Served as Trotsky's U.S. attorney. Was chief defense counsel as well as defendant in 1941 Minneapolis trial. Formed faction with Felix Morrow in 1943. Left SWP in May 1946 to join Shachtman's WP. Left WP in 1948 to rejoin SP. Renounced Marxism and supported U.S. government in Korean War.

Gordon, Sam (1910-)—Joined CLA in 1929. Elected to NC of WPUS in 1934. Worked with leadership of FI in New York during war. Attended March 1946 international preconference in Paris as observer. Was SWP representative in Europe in postwar years. Has lived in England since 1952.

Gould, Nathan (1913-)—Joined CLA in 1932. Elected to SWP NC in 1938. Led Trotskyist youth organizations, Spartacus Youth League and YPSL (Fourth Internationalists). Split from SWP with Shachtman and became a leader of WP.

GPU—Stalin's secret police. Also known at various times as NKVD, MVD, and KGB. Was used in worldwide intelligence and assassination operations on behalf of Stalinist bureaucracy.

Grant, Ted—British Trotskyist. Split from Militant Group in 1937 to become a founder of WIL. A leader of RCP from its formation in 1944. Expelled from Trotskyist movement by Gerry Healy in 1950. Formed small group which affiliated to IS in 1957, during period of split in FI (1954-63). Participated briefly in reunification of FI in 1963, then founded unaffiliated Militant Group, active today in British Labor Party.

Green, William (1873-1952)—President of AFL (1924-52).

Haston, Jock—British Trotskyist leader. Member of Militant Group. Split in 1937 to form WIL. Became main leader of RCP formed in 1944 by fusion of WIL and RSL. Broke with Trotskyism in 1949.

Haywood, William D. (1869-1928)—Leader of Western Federation of Miners. A founder of Industrial Workers of the World (1905). Tried on charge of murdering former governor of Idaho in 1907, but mass defense movement led to acquittal. Arrested for opposing World War I in 1917. While on appeal, went into exile in Soviet Union in 1921.

Healy, Gerry (1915-)—Joined Militant Group in Britain in 1937. Split later that year with Ralph Lee, Jock Haston, and Ted Grant to form WIL. After WIL fused with FI section in 1944, Healy led pro-SWP opposition in new RCP. Became central leader of British Trotskyism after 1949. Broke with FI in 1963 and led ultraleft sect now called Workers Revolutionary Party.

Hillman, Sidney (1887-1946)—President of Amalgamated Clothing Workers (1915-46). Vice-president of CIO. Roosevelt's chief labor lieutenant during World War II.

Hook, Sidney (1902-)—Student of John Dewey at Columbia University. Close to CP in early 1930s. Was a leader of AWP but did not take part in WPUS after 1934 fusion. Became right-wing Social Democrat. Supported cold war and polemicized against Marxism, particularly in field of philosophy.

Hoover, J. Edgar (1895-1972)—Special assistant to Attorney General A. Mitchell Palmer (1919-21), directing Palmer Raids. Director of FBI (1924-72). After World War II a leader of anticommunist witch-hunt.

Industrial Workers of the World (IWW)—Founded in Chicago in 1905. Revolutionary anticapitalist industrial union. Initial leaders included William "Big Bill" Haywood, Vincent St. John, Eugene V. Debs, and Daniel De Leon. Led important strikes before World War I. Rejected political action or work in AFL unions. Went into decline after formation of CP in 1919.

International Communist League (ICL)—Name of world Trotskyist movement, 1933-36. Succeeded by Movement for Fourth International in 1936, and Fourth International in 1938.

International Left Opposition (ILO)—First world Trotskyist organization, formed in 1930. Changed name to ICL in 1933.

International Secretariat (IS)—Day-to-day administrative body of Fourth International, elected by International Executive Committee. IS functioned in New York during World War II. New IS elected by world preconference of FI held in Paris in March 1946.

Isaacs, Harold R. (1910-)—Worked closely with Chinese CP as a journalist in China in early 1930s. Broke with them in 1934 and became a Trotskyist. Best known as author of *Tragedy of the Chinese Revolution* (1938). Joined American Trotskyist movement on his return to U.S. in 1936. Left SWP during war. Later repudiated Marxism. Now a professor at MIT.

Iskra (The Spark)—First all-Russian illegal Marxist newspaper, founded in 1900 by Lenin, Martov, Plekhanov, Potresov, Zasulich, and Axelrod. In 1903 Mensheviks gained a majority on its editorial board and it continued as organ of Menshevik faction of RSDLP.

James, C. L. R. (1901-)—West Indian author. A leader of Militant Group and then of Marxist Group in Britain in 1937-38. Moved to U.S. in 1938 and became a leader of SWP under name J. R. Johnson. Member of IEC of FI (1938-40). Went with Shachtman in 1940 split. Rejoined SWP with a group of his followers in October 1947. Split again in 1951.

Johnson, J. R.—Pseudonym of C. L. R. James.

Joyce, Sam—Supporter of Goldman in San Francisco branch of SWP. Left party in May 1946.

Kamenev, Lev. B. (1883-1936)—Joined RSDLP in 1901. A leader of Lenin's Bolsheviks. With Zinoviev opposed October 1917 Bolshevik insurrection. After Lenin's death, a member of ruling triumvirate with Zinoviev and Stalin. With Zinoviev formed United Opposition with Trotsky (1926-27). Expelled from party in December 1927. Defendant in 1936 Moscow trial. "Confessed" and was executed.

Karsner, Rose (1889-1968)—Member of pre-World War I SP left wing. Founding member of CP. Cannon's companion from 1924. A founder and leader of American Trotskyist movement from 1928 until her death.

Keller, W.—Pseudonym of Jan Frankel.

Kerensky, Alexander (1882-1970)—Prime minister of bourgeois Provisional Government established by February 1917 Russian revolution. Overthrown by Bolsheviks in October 1917.

Konikow, Antoinette (1869-1946)—Joined Russian Marxist movement in 1886. Attended founding congress of Second International (1889). Emigrated to Boston (1893). Member of the Socialist Labor Party. Founding member of SP in 1901. A leader of SP left wing and a founder of CP in 1919. Physician and advocate of birth control. Expelled from CP for Trotskyism shortly before Cannon in 1928. Made honorary member of NC at founding convention of SWP in 1938.

Kovalesky, Theodore—Buffalo steelworker and radical journalist. Joined Shachtman's WP in 1941. Came over to SWP in 1943. After World War II wrote a column for *The Militant* called "Diary of a Steel Worker." Split from SWP in 1959 with Sam Marcy to form Workers World Party.

Krivitsky, Walter (1889-1941)—Chief of Soviet military intelligence in Western Europe in mid-1930s. Defected in December 1937, revealing information to U.S. government. Died in Washington under mysterious circumstances.

Labor Action—Newspaper of Shachtman's WP after split from SWP in April 1940. Not to be confused with SP left-wing newspaper of same name edited by Cannon in San Francisco (1936-37).

Landau, Kurt (d. 1937)—Austrian Left Oppositionist. Headed German United Left Opposition when it was formed in 1930. Split from Left Opposition in 1931. Assassinated by Stalinists in Spain during civil war.

Lassalle, Ferdinand (1825-1864)—German socialist. Founder of General Union of German Workers in 1863. After his death this group fused with Marx's followers to form Social Democratic Party.

Lenin, Vladimir Ilyich (1870-1924)—Leader of Bolshevik faction in RSDLP. Central leader of Russian October revolution in 1917 and first head of Soviet government. Co-founder with Trotsky of Communist International. Most outstanding theoretical and practical leader of twentieth century Communist movement.

Leonard, Richard T. (1902-)—Held various posts in UAW leadership from 1937. Joined with George Addes and R. J. Thomas in opposition to Walter Reuther in 1946-47. Defeated at 1947 UAW convention. Joined CIO national staff (1948-72).

Lesoil, Léon (1892-1942)—A founder of Belgian CP and a member of its Central Committee. Joined Left Opposition in 1927. Elected to IEC of FI in 1938. Arrested by Gestapo in June 1941. Died in a concentration camp.

Lewit, Morris (1903-)—Joined CLA in 1930. Became member of NC of WPUS in 1934. Under name Morris Stein served as acting national secretary of SWP while eighteen Minneapolis defendants were in prison. In postwar period was national organizational secretary. Withdrew from political activity in early 1960s.

Li Fu-jen—Frequent contributor to world Trotskyist press in 1930s and 1940s on Chinese and Asian politics.

Liebknecht, Karl (1871-1919)—A leader of left wing of German Social Democracy. Imprisoned during World War I for his antimilitarist stand. Founder, with Rosa Luxemburg, of Spartakusbund, predecessor of German CP. Participated in Berlin uprising in 1919. Arrested with Rosa Luxemburg and shot by agents of Social Democratic government.

Logan—Pseudonym of Jean van Heijenoort.

London Bureau—Officially, International Bureau of Revolutionary Socialist Parties. Established in 1935 from committee set up in 1932. Loose federation of centrist parties opposed to Second and Third Internationals but unwilling to join in founding of Fourth International. Included among its adherents SAP (Socialist Workers Party) of Germany, Independent Labour Party of Great Britain, Spanish POUM (Workers Party of Marxist Unification), French PSOP (Workers and Peasants Socialist Party), and in U.S., Independent Labor League (Lovestoneites).

Lore, Ludwig (1875-1942)—Member of German Social Democratic Party before turn of century. Emigrated to U.S. in 1903. Leader of German Socialist Federation. Founding member of American CP in 1919. Supported Left Opposition in 1924; expelled in 1925. Later a leader of AWP, elected to NC of WPUS in December 1934 after fusion with Trotskyists. Quit in 1936, moving to right. Became prowar journalist for *New York Post.*

Lovestone, Jay (1898-)—Leader of a faction of American CP in 1920s. Expelled in 1929. Founded Communist Party (Opposition), renamed Independent Labor League. Disbanded in 1940s. Later became chief adviser on foreign policy to AFL-CIO President George Meany and a supporter of cold war.

Luce, Henry R. (1898-1967)—Headed magazine publishing empire. Cofounder of *Time* magazine (1923) and later its editor. Founded *Fortune* (1930), *Life* (1936), and *Sports Illustrated* (1954).

Lundeberg, Harry (1901-1957)—Head of Sailors' Union of the Pacific from mid-1930s and of Seafarers International Union, AFL, from its chartering in 1938. Leader of "antipolitical" syndicalist tendency in labor movement in opposition to Stalinists and progovernment forces. Supported government in World War II but maintained more militant union policy than Stalinists. Became a right-wing Republican in 1950s.

Luxemburg, Rosa (1870-1919)—Leader of left wing of Polish and German Social Democratic parties. Jailed in 1915 for opposition to war, she helped found Spartakusbund, which later became German CP. Took part in Spartacus uprising in Berlin in 1919. Arrested and murdered with complicity of Social Democratic government.

McKinney, Ernest Rice (1886-)—Contributing editor of *The Messenger,* published in Harlem in 1920s by A. Philip Randolph. Elected to NC of WPUS in 1934. On staff of Steel Workers Organizing Committee in 1936. Split from SWP with Shachtman and became secretary of WP. At present a staff member of A. Philip Randolph Educational Fund.

MacLeod, Hildegarde (1892-1969)—Joined CLA in 1934 as member-at-large in Wichita, Kansas. Spent part of each year in Chicago branch until 1948 when she moved to Chicago. Married Arne Swabeck in early 1950s and moved to Los Angeles. In 1960s became leader with Swabeck of pro-Maoist tendency in SWP. Left SWP in 1967.

Mandel, Ernest (1923-)—Joined Belgian section of FI under German occupation at beginning of World War II. Elected to Central Committee in July 1941, at age of eighteen. Active in underground during World War II. Elected to IS at international preconference in 1946. A central political and theoretical leader of FI. Went with Pablo in split of 1953-54. A leader of United Secretariat after reunification of 1963. Author of many books on Marxist economic theory.

Mangan, Sherry (1904-1961)—American writer and journalist. Joined Trotskyist movement in 1934. Active in France during German occupation until expelled by Pétain regime. Served on European Secretariat during last years of war and then on IS. Went with Pablo in split of 1953-54 in FI.

Marshall, George C. (1880-1959)—U.S. army chief of staff (1939-45). Special ambassador to China (1946-47). Became Secretary of State early in 1947. Author of European Recovery Program (Marshall Plan), proposed in June 1947. Secretary of Defense (1950-51).

Martin—Pseudonym of James P. Cannon.

Martin, Homer (1902-1968)—President of UAW (1936-39). Led small group of UAW locals in break from CIO to rejoin AFL in 1939. Left labor movement, later becoming antilabor attorney for an employers' organization.

Martov, Julius (1873-1923)—A close associate of Lenin in leadership of RSDLP from 1890s. Broke with Lenin at Second Congress in 1903 to become leader of Mensheviks. Opposed October revolution in 1917. Emigrated to Germany in 1920.

Marx, Karl (1818-1883)—Founder, with Frederick Engels, of modern scientific socialism. Co-author of *Communist Manifesto* (1848) and author of *Capital.* Leader of International Workingmen's Association (First International).

Maslow, Arkadi (1891-1941)—German Communist. Expelled from German CP in 1926. Supporter of Zinoviev in Russian CP. Formed Leninbund with Ruth Fischer and Hugo Urbahns in 1928. Close associate of Ruth Fischer throughout 1930s. With her, joined movement for FI but left before founding congress in 1938.

Mensheviks—Minority faction at Second Congress of RSDLP (1903). After 1912 became separate party. Supported bourgeois Provisional Government created by February 1917 revolution and opposed Bolshevik seizure of power in October 1917. Remained part of reformist Second International.

The Militant—Newspaper of American Trotskyists starting with their expulsion from CP. First issue appeared in November 1928. In December 1934, name changed to *New Militant* as result of fusion with AWP. Ceased publication in June 1936 when Trotskyists entered SP. In August 1937, after expulsion of Trotskyists from SP, *Socialist Appeal,* an internal SP paper, became public paper of Trotskyists. Name changed to *The Militant* in February 1941.

Mill, M.—A member of the Jewish Group in French section of ILO. Chosen by Russian Opposition as its member of Administrative Secretariat of ILO in 1930, largely because of his knowledge of Russian language. Removed from this post in 1932 because of his personal intrigues. Became a Stalinist agent. Also known under name J. Obin.

Millner, Charles (1911-)—Pseudonym of Louis Rigaudias. A leader of French Trotskyist youth organization during mid-1930s, under name Louis Rigal. In exile in U.S. during World War II. Supported Morrow wing of Goldman-Morrow faction. Left FI in late 1940s.

Minor, Robert (1884-1952—Syndicated newspaper cartoonist. Joined SP in 1907. Became an anarchist in 1912. Highly critical of Russian revolution, but changed mind and joined CP in 1920. Chief lieutenant of Lovestone, and then of Browder. Remained in party when they were expelled.

Molinier, Raymond (1904-)—A co-founder of French Trotskyist movement with whom Trotsky collaborated until 1935, when his group was expelled for violating discipline by publishing its own newspaper, *La Commune.* Attempts at reunification were made several times in following years but proved unsuccessful until 1944.

Morrison—Pseudonym of Albert Goldman

Morrow, Felix (1906-)—Joined CP in 1931. Joined CLA in 1933. Elected to NC of SWP in 1938. Editor of *Socialist Appeal* and *The Militant* from Shachtman split in 1940 to early 1942. Editor of *Fourth International* (1942-43). Formed faction with Albert Goldman in 1943. One of eighteen prisoners in Minneapolis case. Expelled at November 1946 SWP convention for unauthorized collaboration with Shachtman's WP. Did not join WP. Moved to right in 1950s, supporting Korean War.

Munis, Grandizo—A leader of Spanish Trotskyists during civil war (1936-39). Escapted to Mexico several months after Franco's victory. Defended ultraleft and sectarian positions that led to break with Fourth International in 1947. Imprisoned in Spain for a period in 1950s. In 1960s in exile in France.

Murray, Philip (1886-1952)—Vice-president of United Mine Workers under John L. Lewis (1920-42). Succeeded Lewis as president of CIO in 1940. First president of United Steel Workers of America (1942-52).

Muste, A. J. (1885-1967)—Protestant minister and pacifist. Founded Conference for Progressive Labor Action (1929), which in 1933 organized AWP. Fused with CLA in December 1934 to form WPUS. Broke with Marxism in summer of 1936 to return to church. In 1960s played leading role in movement against Vietnam War.

Naville, Pierre (1904-)—Joined French CP in 1925 and became co-editor of its magazine, *Clarté*. Expelled in 1928 for Trotskyism. A founder of *La Vérité* and of French Trotskyist movement. Member of IS. Quit movement at start of World War II. At present a leader of Unified Socialist Party (PSU).

New International—Theoretical magazine of American Trotskyists, starting July 1934. Ceased publication during entry into SP (summer 1936 to end of 1937). In April 1940 Shachtman and Burnham appropriated magazine on legal technicality that they were trustees for SWP of its mailing rights. SWP then published *Fourth International* (1940-56), which in 1956 changed name to *International Socialist Review*.

New Leader—Social Democratic journal published in New York.

Nin, Andrés (1892-1937)—A founder of Spanish CP and secretary of Red International of Labor Unions (Profintern). Supported Left Opposition and was expelled from CP in 1927. Participated in formation of ILO. Broke with Trotsky in 1935 to merge Spanish section of ICL with Workers and Peasants Bloc of Joaquín Maurín to form POUM. Supported Popular Front slate in 1936 elections and accepted post in Catalan regional government. Arrested by Stalinists in Barcelona in June 1937 and murdered.

Novack, George (1905-)—Joined CLA in 1933. Secretary of American Committee for the Defense of Leon Trotsky, formed early in 1937, which was instrumental in bringing together Dewey Commission of Inquiry into the Moscow Trials. After indictments in Minneapolis case in 1941, was secretary of CRDC, which organized legal defense. Elected to SWP NC in 1941. Well-known socialist scholar and author of many books on Marxist philosophy and history.

Oehler, Hugo—CP trade unionist in Kansas City in 1920s. Joined CLA in 1930. Elected to NC in 1931. Opposed entry into SP and was expelled from WPUS in October 1935. Founded Revolutionary Workers League, which survived into 1950s.

Pablo, Michel—Greek Trotskyist and central leader of FI after World War II. Elected to European Secretariat established by underground conference in France in February 1944. Elected secretary of IS reestablished by international preconference, March 1946. Led IS in split in FI in 1953-54 with International Committee (supported by SWP). Participated in reunification of FI in 1963 but split from world Trotskyist movement in 1965. Later led Revolutionary Marxist Alliance (AMR), then joined French Unified Socialist Party (PSU). Author of books under his original name, Michel Raptis.

Paz, Maurice (1896-)—French lawyer. Early leader of Left Opposition, associated with magazine *Contre le Courant* (Against the Stream). Broke with Left Opposition in 1929 and went over to French SP.

Pouliopoulos, Pantelis (1900-1943)—Translator of Marx's *Capital* into Greek. Delegate of Greek CP to Fifth Congress of Comintern (1924) and elected head of party in 1925. Expelled in 1927 as Trotskyist. Thereafter headed Greek Trotskyist organization. Went underground following Metaxas coup in

1936. Arrested in 1939. Shot as hostage by Italian occupiers.

POUM (Workers Party of Marxist Unification)—Formed in September 1935 by fusion of Spanish Left Opposition, led by Andrés Nin and Juan Andrade, with the Workers and Peasants Bloc headed by Joaquín Maurín. Signed election manifesto of Popular Front coalition in February 1936. Accepted posts in regional Catalan government in September 1936. Outlawed in June 1937. Continues as small group of Spanish exiles, mainly in France.

Preis, Art (1911-1964)—Joined AWP in 1933. A leader of 1934 Toledo Auto-Lite strike. Elected to SWP NC in 1940. Labor editor of *The Militant* from 1940s until his death.

Proletarian Party—Originated as Michigan State organization of SP. Expelled for left-wing views in May 1919. Led by Dennis E. Batt and John Keracher. Briefly adhered to CP, but split away in 1920 to form Proletarian Party, based in Michigan. A small sect committed to socialist educational propaganda and abstaining from practical action.

Ramuglia, Anthony—A leader of Musteite Conference for Progressive Labor Action and of AWP. Elected to NC of WPUS in 1934. President of National Unemployed Leagues in mid-1930s.

Rankin, John (1882-1960)—Right-wing, racist member of U.S. House of Representatives from Mississippi (1921-53).

Rein, Marc—Son of Russian Menshevik leader Rafail Abramovich. Correspondent in Spain during civil war for a Swedish Social Democratic newspaper. Kidnapped by Stalinists and disappeared.

Reuther, Walter (1907-1970)—A leader of Detroit autoworkers in mid-1930s. Became director of UAW General Motors department in 1939, and president of UAW in 1946. Succeeded Philip Murray as president of CIO in 1952. Helped engineer merger of AFL and CIO in 1955, but withdrew UAW from federation in 1968.

Revolutionary Communist Party (RCP) (England)—British section of FI, formed in 1944 by fusion of RSL and WIL. Dissolved in 1949 when its members entered Labour Party.

Revolutionary Socialist League (RSL) (England)—British section of FI, formed in 1938. Merged with WIL in 1944 to become RCP.

Roland, A.—Pseudonym of Jack Weber.

Roosevelt, Franklin Delano (1882-1945)—Thirty-second president of the United States (1933-45). Died in April 1945, and was succeeded by Vice President Harry Truman.

Rosmer, Alfred (1877-1964)—Revolutionary syndicalist before World War I. Joined Communist movement and was elected to ECCI in 1920. A leader of French CP until expelled as Oppositionist in 1924. A leader of ILO and member of its IS until November 1930, when he withdrew over differences with Trotsky. Renewed his personal friendship with Trotsky in 1936 but did not join FI.

RSDLP (Russian Social Democratic Labor Party)—Forerunner of CPSU. First Congress in 1898. Split at Second Congress (1903) into Bolshevik and Menshevik wings. Reunited briefly in 1906; split definitively in 1912. Changed name to Russian Communist Party (Bolsheviks) in 1918.

Schultz, Henry (1902-1969)—Joined CLA in Minneapolis in early 1930s. Participated in 1934 strikes. Organizer for electrical workers, and, after 1941, a railroad worker. Elected to SWP NC in 1940. Left SWP in mid-1960s.

Second International—Founded in 1889 as loose association of Social Democratic and labor parties. Included revolutionists and reformists. Strongest section was German Social Democracy.

In 1914 most sections supported their own capitalist governments in World War I and International collapsed. Revived in 1919 as reformist opponent of Third (Communist) International founded same year.

Sedova, Natalia I. (1882-1962)—Born in Ukraine. Became a radical in late 1890s. Joined *Iskra* group in Switzerland. Met Trotsky in 1902 and lived with him from then until his death in 1940s. Their two sons, Leon and Sergei, were murdered by Stalinists in 1930s. Active in revolutions of 1905 and 1917. After founding of Soviet republic worked for several years in Commissariat of Education. After Trotsky's death, lived in Mexico until 1961. Died while on visit to France. She began to develop differences with FI in 1941 and severed her ties with it in 1951.

Shachtman, Max (1903-1972)—Member of Central Executive Committee of American CP. Expelled with Cannon and Abern in 1928 for Trotskyism. A central leader of Trotskyist movement until April 1940 when he, Abern, and Burnham split from SWP to form WP. In 1958 dissolved his organization into SP.

Shoenfeld, Oscar (1916-)—Joined SWP in New York. Active in Minneapolis SWP in late 1930s. Convicted in 1941 Minneapolis trial. Elected to SWP NC in 1941. Resigned from party in April 1946 to join Shachtman's WP. Left WP in 1948, renouncing Marxism.

Short—Pseudonym of Morris Lewit.

Simmons, William—Pseudonym of Arne Swabeck.

Skoglund, Carl (1884-1961)—Emigrated to U.S. from Sweden in 1911. Joined SP in 1914 and became a leader of its Scandinavian Federation. Founding member of CP in 1919. Expelled for Trotskyism in 1928. Member of first NC of CLA. President of Minneapolis Teamster Local 544 (1938-40). Member of IEC of FI (1938-40). One of eighteen political prisoners in Minneapolis case. Remained a leader of SWP until his death.

Sloan—Pseudonym of George Breitman.

Smith—Pseudonym of Michel Pablo.

Sneevliet, Henricus (1883-1942)—Joined Dutch Social Democratic Party in 1902. Emigrated to Java where he founded Indonesian CP. Elected to ECCI in 1920 and was Comintern representative in China (1921-23). Became Oppositionist in 1924 and broke with CP in 1927. Formed Revolutionary Socialist Party in Holland in 1929, which joined ICL in 1933. Broke with Trotskyist movement in 1938. Executed by Nazis.

Social Democrats—Name used by most Marxian socialists affiliated to Second International from its founding in 1889. Synonymous with revolutionary socialism until outbreak of World War I. After Russian revolution and founding of Comintern, became a term signifying procapitalist reformism.

Socialist Labor Party (SLP)—Formed in 1877 when American followers of Ferdinand Lassalle took control of earlier Working Men's Party. Came under leadership of Daniel De Leon in 1890, who headed SLP until his death in 1914. Deteriorated into sect after founding of Debsian SP in 1901.

Socialist Party (SP)—Founded in 1901 by Eugene V. Debs. Became mass movement in decade prior to World War I. Left wing supported Russian revolution of 1917 and split from SP in 1919 to form Communist Party, taking two-thirds of membership. Trotskyists joined SP as left-wing faction in spring 1936; expelled in summer 1937. SP declined to small sect by beginning of World War II. Split in 1972 into Social Democrats, USA, and Democratic Socialist Organizing Committee.

Socialist Workers Party (SWP)—Trotskyist party founded in Chicago, December 31, 1937–January 3, 1938, by expelled members of SP.

Socialist Workers Party of Germany—SAP (from its German initials) formed in October 1931 by left-wing expelled members of German Social

Democratic Party. In 1933 agreed to work with Left Opposition in forming Fourth International but soon changed its line and remained affiliated to London Bureau.

Social Revolutionaries (SRs)—Russian populist party. Along with Mensheviks, dominated soviets (workers' councils) from February 1917 revolution to September. Right wing of SRs led by Kerensky. Left wing joined Bolsheviks in Soviet government, but soon moved into opposition, organized terroristic attacks on Bolsheviks, and were suppressed.

Solow, Herbert (1903-1964)—Radical American intellectual and labor journalist in 1930s. Supported CP until 1933, then became sympathizer of CLA. Participated as a journalist in 1934 Minneapolis strikes. Joined WPUS in 1934; quit in 1935. Supported Dewey Commission of Inquiry into the Moscow Trials. Renounced Marxism at beginning of World War II. An editor of *Fortune* magazine.

Souvarine, Boris (1895-)—Joined left wing of Social Democracy in France during World War I. Founding member of French CP in 1920. A member of ECCI (1921-24). Expelled in 1924 for supporting Trotsky. Broke with Trotsky in 1929, later renouncing Leninism. His name became synonymous with Stalinophobic pessimism and defeatism.

Spanish Group in Mexico of the Fourth International—Formed in Mexico City in 1941 by exiles from Franco Spain. Its main leader was Grandizo Munis.

Stein, Morris—Pseudonym of Morris Lewit.

Stuart, J. E. B.—Pseudonym of Sam Gordon.

Swabeck, Arne (1890-)—A founder of American CP, and of CLA. Member of CLA's first NC. Visited Trotsky in Turkey in 1933. A central leader of CLA and WPUS in New York in 1930s. Active in Chicago from 1937 until early 1950s, then in Los Angeles. Became a Maoist and split from SWP in 1967.

Third International—See Communist International.

Thomas, Norman (1884-1968)—Leader of SP from late 1920s. Six-time presidential candidate on SP ticket (1928-48).

Thomas, R. J. (1900-1967)—Elected UAW vice-president in 1937. A leader of anti-Reuther bloc after World War II, with George Addes and Richard T. Leonard. Defeated in 1947 UAW elections and went on CIO staff. Retired in 1964.

Tobin, Daniel J. (1875-1955)—President of International Brotherhood of Teamsters (1907-52). Also chairman of Democratic Party's National Labor Committee. Asked Roosevelt's aid in prosecution of Minneapolis Trotskyists and SWP national leadership.

Trade Union Educational League (TUEL)—Formed by William Z. Foster in November 1920, prior to his joining the CP. Originally an antipolitical, syndicalist organization, and pro-AFL. When Foster was recruited to CP in Moscow in 1921, TUEL became CP union organization. Name changed in 1929 to Trade Union Unity League; dissolved in 1935.

Tran Duc Thao—Vietnamese scholar and Stalinist philosopher. Active in support of Vietnamese independence in Paris after World War II. Left a career at the Sorbonne in 1951 to return to fight for Vietnam's independence.

Treint, Albert (1889-1971)—Joined French SP in 1912. A founder of French CP in 1920. Elected to ECCI in 1924. Supporter of Zinoviev, expelled from French CP in 1928. Member of Left Opposition (1931-32). Joined French SP in 1934 and in 1937 founded a small syndicalist group.

Tresca, Carlo (1878-1943)—Well-known Italian-American anarchist, labor leader, and journalist. A leader of IWW before World War I, close associate of Sacco and Vanzetti, and editor of

New York Italian anarchist newspaper *Il Martello* (The Hammer). Assassinated in New York by unknown persons. Believed to have been killed at order either of Mussolini or Stalin.

Trotsky, Leon (1879-1940)—Joined revolutionary socialist movement in 1898 in Ukraine. Collaborated with Lenin on *Iskra* in London (1902-03). Leader of St. Petersburg Soviet in 1905 Russian revolution. Joined Bolshevik party in 1917. Chief organizer of October insurrection. First commissar of foreign affairs of Soviet government. Headed Soviet Red Army (1918-25) in civil war. Formed Left Opposition in 1923 to implement agreement with Lenin to fight rising Stalinist bureaucracy. Expelled from CPSU in 1927. Exiled to Turkey in 1929. In 1933 called for formation of a new communist International. Founded Fourth International in 1938. Assassinated in Mexico in August 1940 by a Stalinist agent.

Truman, Harry (1884-1972)—Democratic vice-president under Roosevelt; succeeded to the presidency on Roosevelt's death in April 1945. Ordered atom bombing of Hiroshima and Nagasaki. In spring 1947 announced Truman Doctrine of "containing" communism, implemented through Marshall Plan (June 1947) to rebuild and rearm Europe.

Urbahns, Hugo (1890-1947)—Joined German Social Democrats before World War I, and German CP in 1920. Expelled in 1926. Helped to found Leninbund in 1928; supported Left Opposition until 1930. Emigrated to Sweden after 1933.

Usick—Nickname of John G. Wright.

van Heijenoort, Jean (1912-)—Early French Trotskyist. Was Trotsky's secretary in Turkey, France, Norway, and Mexico, between 1932 and 1939. During World War II was part of FI leadership in New York. Supported Goldman and Morrow in dispute with SWP majority in 1945-46. Left FI in 1946. Became a professor of philosophy.

La Vérité (The Truth)—Newspaper of French Trotskyists (1929-36). Renamed *La Lutte Ouvrière* (1936-39) after fusion of two Trotskyist organizations created Parti Ouvrière Internationaliste (POI). Was revived as *La Vérité* in August 1940 under Vichy regime as first antifascist newspaper to appear in underground. Became organ of Parti Communiste Internationaliste (PCI), formed at new fusion conference in 1944.

Walter—Pseudonym of James P. Cannon.

Warde, William F.—Pseudonym of George Novack.

Weber, Jack (1896-)—Joined CLA in 1930. Elected to NC of WPUS in 1934. Supporter of Abern in early 1930s. Broke with him over entry into SP in 1936. Close friend of Natalia Sedova. Left SWP in 1944, moving close to Shachtman's WP, but not joining it.

Weiss, Murry (1915-)—Joined CLA in 1932. Elected to SWP NC at 1939 convention. Leader of Los Angeles branch of SWP. Editor of *The Militant* (1954-56) and of *International Socialist Review* (1959-63). Left SWP in mid-1960s.

Well, Roman (1901-1962)—Pseudonym under which Ruvelis Leiba Sobolevicius worked in Trotskyist movement in Germany. He and his brother, who used the name Senin, were Latvians. Both brothers deserted to Stalinism at end of 1932 and may have been agents provocateurs. Well, under name Robert Soblen, was tried as Soviet spy in U.S. in early 1960s. Fled to Israel; was refused entry, and committed suicide in London.

White—Pseudonym of Bert Cochran.

Widick, B. J. (1910-)—Joined CLA in early 1930s. Elected to NC of WPUS in 1936. Active in trade union movement in Akron, Ohio. Became SWP national labor secretary in 1938. Split from SWP with Shachtman and became a leader of WP. Later a labor journalist, college professor, and author.

Williams, Oscar—Pseudonym of Oscar Shoenfeld.

Wood, Art—Pseudonym of Arthur Burch.

Workers International League (WIL) (England)—Formed in 1937 by Ralph Lee, Jock Haston, Ted Grant, and Gerry Healy in split from Militant Group. Boycotted founding conference of FI. Joined FI in 1944 through fusion with British section, the RSL, forming RCP.

Workers Party (WP)—Organization formed by Max Shachtman in April 1940 in split from SWP. Changed name to Independent Socialist League in 1949. In 1958 dissolved into SP.

Workers Party of the United States (WPUS)—Formed in December 1934 by fusion of Trotskyist CLA and A. J. Muste's American Workers Party. Dissolved in spring 1936 when Trotskyists joined SP as left-wing faction.

Wright, John G. (1902-1956)—Political name of Joseph Vanzler. Joined CLA in 1933. Elected to SWP NC in 1939. A translator of Trotsky's works and contributor to Trotskyist press on Soviet affairs and theoretical questions. Remained on SWP writing staff in New York until his death.

Young People's Socialist League (YPSL; also: **Yipsels)**—Youth organization of SP. Majority of YPSL won over by Trotskyists during entry into SP (1936-37) and became youth organization of SWP under name YPSL (Fourth Internationalists). Majority of this group went with Shachtman and became youth organization of WP. During World War II, YPSL was reconstituted by SP.

Zaslow, Milton—Under name Mike Bartell, a member of SWP in Los Angeles before World War II. Left SWP with Shachtman in 1940 and became a leader of Los Angeles branch of WP. In 1941 brought a group of WP members over to SWP. Elected to SWP NC in 1944. Branch organizer in Chicago and New York. Left party in 1953 with Bert Cochran.

Zinoviev, Gregory (1883-1936)—Member of RSDLP from 1901. Supported Lenin in split with Mensheviks in 1903. After Lenin's death (1924) blocked with Stalin and Kamenev to exclude Trotsky from leadership. Joined Trotsky in United Opposition to Stalin (1926-27). Capitulated to Stalin in 1927. Defendant in 1936 Moscow trial. Executed.

INDEX

Entries from the glossary included in this index are identified by the letter *g* after the page number. Entries from the notes are identified by the letter *n*.